CW01667680

A & G Murray and the Cotton Mills of Ancoats

I Miller
C Wild

With contributions by
S Little
R McNeil
K Moth

Illustrations by
A Stewardson, M Rowland, C Wild
A Parsons, and C Healey

13
LANCASTER IMPRINTS
2007

Published by
Oxford Archaeology North
Storey Institute
Meeting House Lane
Lancaster
LA1 1TF
(*Phone:* 01524-541000, *Fax:* 01524-848606)

Distributed by
Oxbow Books
Park End Place
Oxford
OX1 1HN
(*Phone:* 01865-241249, *Fax:* 01865-794449)

Printed by
The Alden Group, Oxford, UK

© Oxford Archaeology North 2007

ISBN 978-0-904220-46-9
ISSN 1343-5205

Series Editor
Rachel Newman
Indexer
Sue Vaughan
Design, layout and formatting
Marie Rowland

Front Cover: New Mill from the corner of Jersey Street and Bengal Street in 2006
Rear Cover: Engraving of A & G Murray's Mill published in 1909, showing the junction of Jersey Street with Murray Street

LANCASTER IMPRINTS

Lancaster Imprints is the publication series of Oxford Archaeology North. The series covers work on major excavations and surveys of all periods undertaken by the organisation and associated bodies.

Contents

List of Illustrations

Figures

Plates

Tables

Contributors

Ian Miller
Oxford Archaeology North, Storey Institute, Meeting House Lane, Lancaster LA1 1TF

Chris Wild
Oxford Archaeology North, Storey Institute, Meeting House Lane, Lancaster LA1 1TF

Steve Little
26 Alvaston Avenue, Heaton Moor, Stockport SK4 4EW

Robina McNeil
University of Manchester Field Archaeology Centre, Architecture Building, Oxford Road, Manchester, M13 9PL

Ken Moth
Building Design Partnership, Sunlight House, PO Box 85, Quay Street, Manchester M60 3JA

Sponsors

Abbreviations

ABPT	Ancoats Buildings Preservation Trust
AUVC	Ancoats Urban Village Company
BCSA	British Constructional Steelwork Association
BDP	Building Design Partnership
CBA	Council for British Archaeology
EH	English Heritage
FCSDA	Fine Cotton Spinners' and Doublers' Association
GMAU	Greater Manchester Archaeological Unit
MRIAS	Manchester Region Industrial Archaeology Society
NMR	National Monuments Record
OA North	Oxford Archaeology North
OS	Ordnance Survey
PRO	National Archives
RCHME	Royal Commission on Historic Monuments of England (now part of English Heritage)
RSJ	Rolled steel joist
SM	Scheduled Monument
SMR	Sites and Monuments Record

Summary

In 2003, Oxford Archaeology North commenced a large-scale programme of archaeological study at A & G Murray's Mill in Manchester (SJ 8508 9865), on behalf of the Ancoats Buildings Preservation Trust. The study formed an important element of a major scheme of repairs to the mill complex, which has been given Listed Buildings status (Grades II and II*) in recognition of its immense historic significance, not least for incorporating the only surviving eighteenth-century steam-powered cotton mill in Manchester. The project was financed by the Heritage Lottery Fund in conjunction with the North West Regional Development Agency, and was intended to secure the long-term future of the mill buildings, and avert their impending loss through structural failure and neglect.

The mill complex was established by Adam and George Murray in 1798, and was one of the first in the world to have been designed to house steam-powered spinning mules. Within eight years, the Murrays had quadrupled the size of their premises to comprise four multi-storey factories arranged in a quadrangle around a central courtyard, which contained a private canal basin that connected with the Rochdale Canal. When completed in 1806, it was the largest complex of cotton-spinning mills in Manchester, housing an unprecedented number of spindles and providing employment for more than 1000 operatives. The Murrays concentrated on the production of finely spun cotton, rapidly gaining a reputation for producing the finest yarn available, and supplying national and international markets.

The Murrays chose to establish their factory on a green field site in the Ancoats area of Manchester, situated on the north-eastern fringe of the town. A former rural district, Ancoats was subsumed by the expansion of Manchester from the mid-1770s, as land was sold off in individual plots to entrepreneurial builders, who developed the land rapidly. The creation of an inland network of waterways across north-west England, which centred on Manchester, accelerated this process of urbanisation. In particular, the opening of the Ashton under Lyne Canal and the Rochdale Canal through Ancoats, in 1796 and 1804 respectively, was an important catalyst to the development of the area, not least for providing the local transportation infrastructure demanded by the new industries. This was coupled with the successful application of steam engines to power machinery, signalling the origins of the steam-powered textile mill.

Within a few decades, Ancoats had been transformed from a rural backwater to a densely populated mixed industrial and residential area that was in itself larger than many towns in the surrounding region, yet it was unplanned and largely devoid of amenities and public buildings. It was also widely acknowledged as the manufacturing heart of Manchester, which itself was emerging as a global centre of the cotton industry. In many respects Ancoats represented a new type of townscape, comprising a dense concentration of steam-powered mills and associated factories that were interspersed with tracts of low-cost housing, intended for occupation by the burgeoning population. This manifestation of the urban factory system based on the application of steam power was to characterise numerous northern towns, if not the entire region, into the twentieth century.

A & G Murray remained in production for more than 150 years, spanning the entire era of the steam-powered textile factory, and the mill complex has survived into a post-industrial age as a monumental reminder of the crucial role played by the cotton-spinning industry to the expansion of Manchester. The mill is one of a small group of former textile factories in the area, representing a mere handful of those that once dominated the townscape.

The buildings experienced severe neglect by the late 1990s, however, raising the possibility that they would collapse and ultimately have to be demolished, a fate experienced by many former industrial buildings in Ancoats. The complete loss of A & G Murray's Mill was averted in 1997, when the Ancoats Buildings Preservation Trust became involved with the site and obtained full funding from the Heritage Lottery Fund and the North West Development Agency for the permanent repair of the structure and fabric of the buildings.

The project allowed for a comprehensive archaeological investigation of the site, presenting an invaluable opportunity to carry out a detailed survey of an eighteenth-century cotton mill. The scope of archaeological works included research, analysis, survey, and targeted excavation of the mill complex, and was designed to inform decisions regarding the repair, management, and long-term sustainability of the buildings. It was also intended that the work would be published in order to disseminate the results obtained from one of the most detailed archaeological surveys of a steam-powered textile mill ever undertaken. This has been coupled with the presentation of the results obtained from archaeological excavations carried out on other early textile mills in Ancoats to provide a context in which to view the rise and progress of A & G Murray, and their contribution to one of the nation's most important industries.

Foreword

Ancoats and its mills hold a special place in the history of global industrialisation and therefore in Britain's industrial heritage. Over a period of 50 years from the late eighteenth century, a rural environment on the outskirts of Manchester was transformed into one of the most densely developed industrial landscapes in the world. Its multi-storey steam-driven cotton mills, which had been hailed as a marvel of the late Georgian era and featured on the itineraries of European visitors to England, had become a magnet for workers whose housing and living conditions were to be condemned by social commentators a generation later. This book, by its careful examination of the surviving physical evidence of Ancoats mills and their environment, puts flesh on the bones of that transformation.

The factory-based textile industry played a pivotal role in the economic, social, and industrial development of England from the late eighteenth century, and the resultant steam-powered mills became dominant features of urban landscapes in the northern counties for more than two centuries. The loss of a significant proportion of textile mills through disuse, neglect, and demolition, frequently without any form of permanent record, can be linked to the decline of the industry in the twentieth century. This resulted in an often dramatic change to the landscapes of numerous mill towns, reflecting the conflicting requirements and expectations of a post-industrial age. More recently, however, perceptions of the nature of the historic environment as a whole have changed, mirroring a growing and widespread interest in industrial heritage. This is highlighted by the inscription of the Derwent Valley, New Lanark, and Saltaire textile areas as World Heritage Sites in 2001. Against this background, it may be anticipated that many surviving mills and associated buildings are now recognised as valuable assets that convey the unique character of industrial landscapes, particularly in the north of England, and contribute to regional distinctiveness.

Manchester is arguably the archetypal city of the Industrial Revolution, noted for its outstanding combination of industrial heritage and Victorian architecture expressed in the magnificent warehouses of the central commercial district. This is encircled by the manufacturing districts, the most notable of which is Ancoats. Widely acknowledged as the world's first industrial suburb based on steam power, Ancoats contained an extraordinary concentration of multi-storey textile mills, interspersed with tracts of workers' housing, and a network of canals. By the end of the eighteenth century, some of the earliest cotton-spinning sites designed for steam-powered spinning mules had been built there, representing one of the most important advances in the textile industry.

A & G Murray's Mill is a rare survivor from that period, even more remarkable for the retention of its original layout. Despite the perilous physical state of the buildings by the 1990s, and their inclusion in English Heritage's Buildings at Risk Register, the site has been rescued from complete loss by a substantial grant-funded programme of repair that has secured its long-term future. Crucially, this has been coupled with major regeneration initiatives in Ancoats, which have reversed the failing commercial and social infrastructure of the area.

This volume arose from the archaeological study that accompanied the repair work to A & G Murray's Mill. It has been designed to synthesise other important archaeological work in Ancoats, which has formed an important element of regeneration initiatives. It is hoped that, through this publication, the study of the Murray's Mill will provide a reference tool for future researchers studying the early development of the steam-powered textile mill and Ancoats as an industrial suburb. The detailed recording of Ancoats' standing buildings, coupled to the excavation of buried remains, has cogently demonstrated the potential wealth of new information on the industrial heritage that can be gained from these sources. But by doing so it has also exposed the lamentable lack of such work elsewhere, partly caused by the paucity of the resource of available skilled recorders. This paucity must be remedied by targeted education and training before too much more of the industrial archaeological resource is lost across the country.

This book, by helping a wider audience appreciate the immense archaeological and historical significance of A & G Murray's Mill and by placing these monumental buildings more securely in their regional and national context, is an important addition to the literature on our industrial heritage.

Sir Neil Cossons

(Chairman, English Heritage)

Acknowledgements

This book arises from a detailed programme of conservation-led archaeological study at A & G Murray's Mill, and would not have been possible without the support and enthusiasm of many people. The project was financed through to publication by the Heritage Lottery Fund and the North West Development Agency as part of the programme of major repairs to the mill complex, and their support is gratefully acknowledged. The funding was administered by the Ancoats Buildings Preservation Trust (ABPT), who provided considerable support, guidance, and encouragement throughout the project. In particular, Kate Dickson and Chris Campbell are thanked for their invaluable input. Further thanks are due to Robina McNeil and Norman Redhead, of the Greater Manchester Archaeological Unit, for their guidance, support, and enthusiasm. Special mention is made of Mike Williams of English Heritage, who led the *Greater Manchester Textile Mill Survey* during the 1980s, and commented upon the present text. Andrew Davison of English Heritage is also thanked for supporting the project, and for his comments on the draft publication text.

The archaeological research required the efforts of numerous people. Daniel Elsworth undertook a study of the available material within the Boulton and Watt Archive in Birmingham, which kindly gave permission to reproduce several original drawings. The staff of the John Rylands University Library of Manchester, the Greater Manchester Record Office, the Lancashire Record Office, Bolton Archives, and the Manchester Central Library are all thanked for facilitating access to primary material. Special mention is made of the staff at the Local Studies Unit within Manchester Central Library, who generously allowed the reproduction of several photographs for publication. These were drawn from a significant collection of historic photographs, which constitute an important record of many aspects of Manchester and the surrounding areas. Staff within Manchester City Council, and especially David Hilton, are thanked for kindly allowing access to Building Control Plans. In addition, Oxford Archaeology North (OA North) is grateful to David Hodgson of Dorothea Restoration, to Bernard Champness and Mike Redfern of the Manchester Region Industrial Archaeology Society (MRIAS), to Sam Roberts, and to Jonathan Schofield, who all provided valuable information on aspects of the site. Other original research and support was provided by Mark Watson, who is gratefully acknowledged. Thanks are also expressed to Caroline Jones at the British Waterways Archive in Gloucester, and to Nicola Samuel, archivist at the David Owen Waterways Archive.

The collation of data from the various stages of fieldwork similarly required the hard work and dedication of many individuals. OA North is grateful to Casey Construction Ltd, and particularly to Jed Cohen, for support and assistance during the survey and excavation of A & G Murray's Mill, and to Wates Construction Ltd for their considerable support and enthusiasm during the archaeological watching brief that was maintained throughout the programme of repairs. Thanks are also due to Ken Moth, Steve Blundell, Alan Davies, and Jonathan Davis of Building Design Partnership (BDP), for their considerable help and information, and to Jonathan Williams of Gardiner Theobald Management Services for logistical support. Special mention is made of Dr Ron Fitzgerald of Structural Perspectives, who provided invaluable technical advice, and Ian Gibson of the Lancashire County Museum Service, for sharing his specialist knowledge of textile machinery, and for undertaking some analysis of yarn samples recovered from the mill complex. Thanks are also expressed to John R Hornsby of the Lancashire County Museum Service for his assistance with identifying textile-machinery components. The series of surveys and excavations at A & G Murray's Mill by OA North was directed by Chris Wild and Ian Miller, supervised by Chris Healey and Karl Taylor, and variously assisted by Austin Ainsworth, Richard Jackson, Lisa Keys, Andrew Lane, and Jon Onraet. The archaeological watching brief during the repairs to the complex was maintained by Chris Wild and Ian Miller. Shortly after the completion of the repair works, the project was nominated as a finalist in the Association of Industrial Archaeology Award for the best adaptive, innovative reuse of any historic or industrial building, as part of the British Archaeology Awards for 2006.

The archaeological excavations at Salvins' Factory, New Islington Mill, and Waller's Mill were facilitated and funded by the New Islington Client Group, which comprises English Partnerships, Urban Splash, and Manchester City Council, who are gratefully acknowledged. Thanks are also due to Stephen Coultard of Martin Stockley Associates, and Stuart Newby, Gary Robinson, and Terry Driffield, of Volker Stevin Ltd, for considerable logistical support and encouragement during the fieldwork, and for providing aerial photographs of the development. These excavations were directed for OA North by Sean McPhillips, who was assisted by Jason Clarke, Chris Healey, Lisa Keys, Dave McNicol, Sophie Pullar, and Chris Ridings. Elsewhere in

Ancoats, OA North carried out archaeological excavations of workers' housing at Bengal Street and Jersey Street on behalf of Nikal Investments. These excavations were directed by Chris Wild and Sean McPhillips, who were assisted by Alex Beben, Ged Callaghan, and Pascal Eloy, and palaeo-environmental analysis was undertaken by Elizabeth Huckerby and Sandra Bonsall.

Gratitude is expressed to English Heritage for allowing the reproduction of aerial photography and images of the Murray's Mill taken during the *Greater Manchester Textile Mill Survey*. Crown copyright material is reproduced by permission of English Heritage acting under licence from the Controller of Her Majesty's Stationery Office.

Compilation and editing of the various texts was undertaken by Ian Miller, who received invaluable support and advice from Terry Wyke and Professor Michael Rose, who are gratefully acknowledged. The final draft was edited by Rachel Newman. Illustrations provided by individual authors have been manipulated by OA North, particularly by Anne Stewardson, Marie Rowland, Chris Wild, Adam Parsons, and Chris Healey. The design and layout of this volume was by Marie Rowland. Line art drawings were completed by Adam Parsons and Pip Haworth, and photography of the artefacts was carried out by Andrew Bates of OA North.

Considerable effort has been made to acknowledge the copyright relating to illustrative material, and to ensure permission for reproduction has been obtained. Any omission is regretted, and information regarding copyright in any such cases is welcomed.

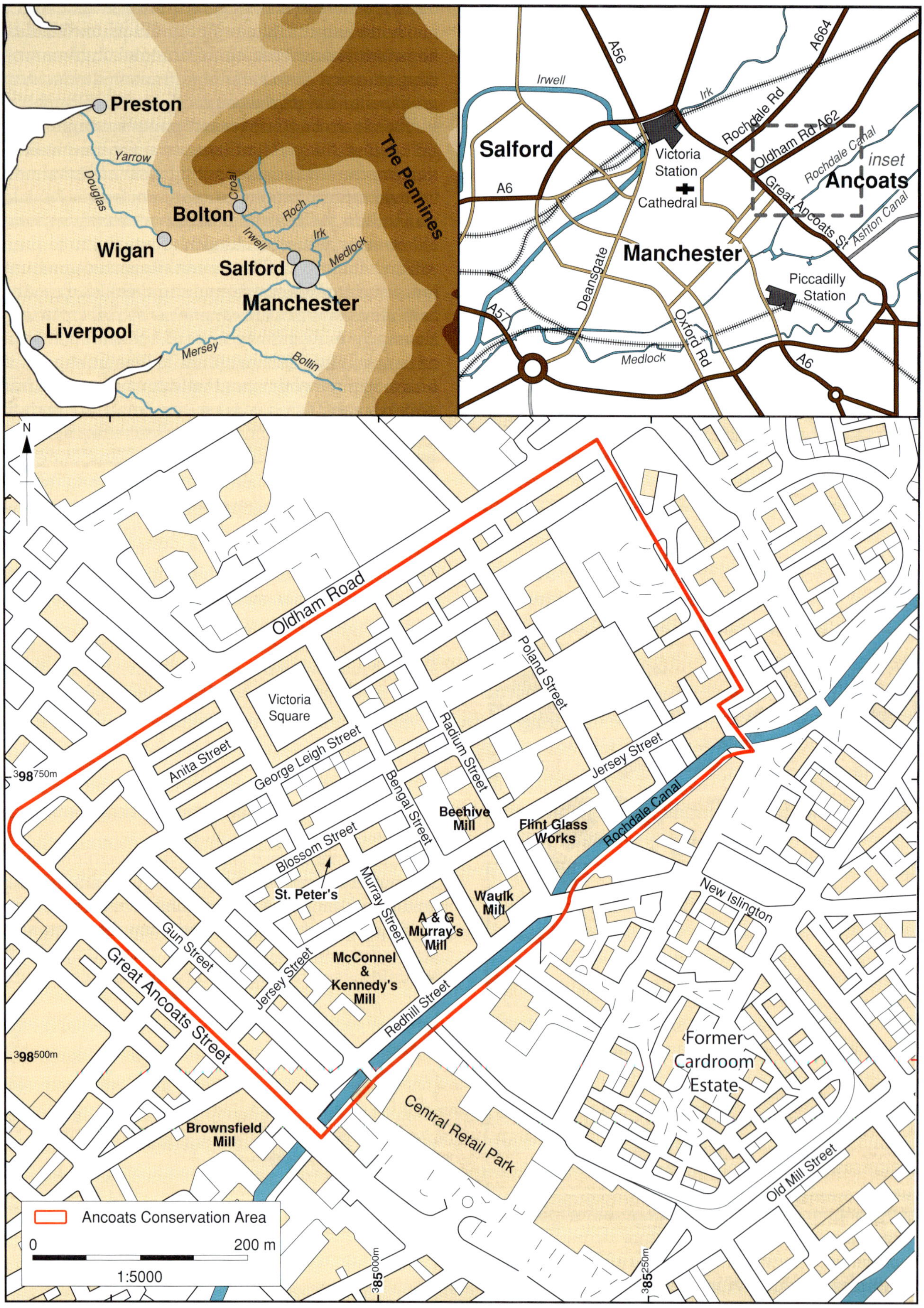

Figure 1: Location of Ancoats, based on the Ordnance Survey mapping of 1990

1

INTRODUCTION

This volume documents and celebrates one of the most important surviving steam-powered textile factories in Britain, if not the world: the cotton-spinning mill of A & G Murray. This was established in the Ancoats area of Manchester by two young Scottish entrepreneurs, Adam and George Murray, in the final years of the eighteenth century, and expanded rapidly to become one of the largest cotton-spinning sites in the country. Specialising in the production of the finest cotton yarn available, the mill supplied national and international markets, and formed the manufacturing heart of Manchester's rise as a global centre of the textile industry in the nineteenth century. The extant buildings incorporate the oldest-surviving steam-powered mill in Manchester, and form part of an impressive group of cotton factories that flank the Ancoats section of the Rochdale Canal (Pl 1), cumulatively providing a spectacular illustration of urban industrial architecture from the period.

Ancoats is widely recognised as the archetypal industrial suburb (*eg* Little 2002, 31), where a plethora of steam-powered textile mills, associated factories and workshops, a network of local canals, and tracts of workers' housing were built at an incredible rate during the late eighteenth and early nineteenth

Plate 1: Aerial view, taken in 2001, of A & G Murray's Mill and the adjacent cotton-spinning complex of McConnel & Co, overlooking the Rochdale Canal (© English Heritage. NMR)

centuries. The net result was a new type of industrial townscape, dominated by steam-powered cotton mills, which contrasted starkly with the rural 'factory colonies' associated with the Arkwright-type water-powered mills of the 1770s and 1780s (Aspin 2003). The scale and pace of development, moreover, was a defining feature of Ancoats, and one that distinguished the area from the expansion of factory-based industry in other towns. The boom in textile production acted as a catalyst for the development of other industries, which cumulatively ensured the importance of Ancoats as a manufacturing centre for more than a century. In particular, the growth of the textile industry demanded the rapid development of technological expertise, especially in machine-making, which led to Manchester becoming a world centre of engineering by the end of the nineteenth century (Hartwell 2001, 15). Some of the leading engineering firms of the period, including Peel, Williams & Co, and Fairbairn and Lillie, were established in Ancoats and derived most of their initial business from textile manufacturers (*Ch 3, p 28*). Other industries in Ancoats, including the production of glass, furniture, hat-blocks, brewing, and printing, were all important to the local economy from the mid-nineteenth century, as testified by some of the buildings in the area (Pl 2). The historical significance of all these trades, however, has tended to be eclipsed by the textile and engineering industries, whose factories dominated the skyline.

Throughout the nineteenth century, the mills in Ancoats attracted visitors from across Europe, who marvelled at their size and density, and the advanced technology that was applied to the manufacture of cotton (*Ch 5, p 79*). Against this background, it is perhaps remarkable that few serious studies of the mills in Ancoats have ever been undertaken, although they are frequently cited as examples. A notable exception is the *Greater Manchester Textile Mill Survey*, which was undertaken as a joint project between the former Royal Commission on the Historical Monuments of England (RCHME) and the Greater Manchester Archaeological Unit (GMAU) during the 1980s (Williams with Farnie 1992). During this survey, the former cotton-spinning mill of Adam and George Murray was selected for detailed recording, the results of which have provided a firm basis for the present survey.

Plate 2: Former beer-retailer's and latterly a printer's premises on Gun Street, prior to renovation

The Setting

A & G Murray's Mill occupies a prominent position adjacent to the Rochdale Canal in Ancoats (SJ 8508 9865), which lies a short distance to the north-east of Manchester city centre. This section of the canal corridor forms one of the foci for Manchester's nomination for inscription as a World Heritage Site, reflecting the immense significance of the surviving mills, and the development of Ancoats as the world's first industrial suburb based on steam power (Falconer 2002).

Topographically, the Manchester conurbation as a region is within an undulating lowland basin, which contains the heavily meandering river Mersey within a broad flood plain (Countryside Commission 1998, 125). It is bounded by the Pennine uplands to the east and to the north (Fig 1), and is open to prevailing winds from the west and the south, which provide the climatic conditions ideal for cotton spinning: high annual rainfall with high humidity. The largest tributary of the Mersey is the river Irwell, a navigable watercourse that divides Manchester from the neighbouring city of Salford, situated to the west (Fig 1). The centre of Manchester lies between two tributaries of the river Irwell, the Irk to the north and the Medlock to the south. The topography of Ancoats, however, reflects the shallow valley of Shooters Brook, a rivulet that flows south-westwards from Newton Heath, through Ancoats and into the river Medlock (*Ch 3, p 27*). Shooters Brook was culverted during the early nineteenth century, and the topography of the valley has since been masked considerably by urban expansion.

The geology of the area comprises Carboniferous sedimentary material and a series of Permo-Triassic rocks, consisting mainly of New Red Sandstone. The overlying drift incorporates Pleistocene boulder clays of glacial origin, and sands, gravels, and clays of fluviatile and lacustrine origin (Hall *et al* 1995, 8).

Regeneration Initiatives

Manufacturing industries characterised Ancoats through the late nineteenth and early twentieth centuries, although high land prices coupled with a lack of space available for expansion led some of the larger firms to relocate their businesses elsewhere. The changing fortunes of Ancoats at this time have reflected in it becoming a centre for ice-cream making and organ building, associated with the Italian immigrants that settled in the area (Little 2002, 33). The demise of the area's manufacturing base, which accompanied the collapse of the British textile industry during the second half of the twentieth century, and the resultant depopulation, caused the local commercial and social infrastructure to fail. These circumstances led to the rapid decay, neglect, and dereliction of Ancoats, although the architectural legacy of the industrial era remained in the surviving buildings. This factor was capitalised upon during the final years of the twentieth century, which proved to be a period of renaissance for Ancoats, providing a focus for regeneration initiatives.

Ancoats has a history of hosting initiatives that have facilitated the improvement of local economic and social conditions, and encouraged the physical regeneration of the area. A prime example is Victoria Square, a five-storey housing block with an inner courtyard that was built in 1897 as a vast slum replacement (Hartwell 2001, 287). It originally comprised 235 two-room and 48 single-room flats and, together with a similar block at Granville Place on Pollard Street in Ancoats (Pl 3), represented the first municipal housing in Manchester (Little 2002, 32). The 'model' housing on Sanitary Street (re-named subsequently as Anita Street), which was also in local authority ownership but comprised two-storey terraces, was built as part of the same initiative.

Plate 3: Municipal housing (now demolished) at Granville Place, Ancoats, 1898 (reproduced courtesy of Manchester Archives and Local Studies)

More recently, a major programme of regeneration was activated during the 1970s, when the demand for council housing prompted the City Council to replace decaying buildings between the Rochdale and Ashton Canals with some 200 new houses. This development was called the Cardroom Estate in recognition of the area's rich history of textile-manufacture (Fig 1), although it rapidly earned a reputation for high tenant turnover and poor-quality open spaces, which contributed to growing levels of neglect and vandalism. This was compounded by problems of physical isolation, caused by its distance from major routes of communication, and exacerbated by the construction of the Central Retail Park during the 1980s on the eastern side of Great Ancoats Street, which formed a barrier between the estate and the city centre.

Plate 4: The Daily Express building on Great Ancoats Street, designed by Sir Owen Williams (1939)

The closure in 1989 of the Express Printers, in their striking all-glass fronted building on Great Ancoats Street (Pl 4), perhaps marked a turning point in the area's fortunes, as the impact of low investment and increasing unemployment became acknowledged at the highest levels. During the same year, the part of Ancoats between the Rochdale Canal and Oldham Road, and Great Ancoats Street to Poland Street, was designated a Conservation Area and 13 buildings were listed, seven of which (including A & G Murray's Mill) are Grade II or Grade II*. This statutory designation afforded some protection to the historic industrial townscape, although, it also stifled regeneration by private sector initiatives due to cost implications.

Plate 5: St Peter's on Blossom Street, during restoration

The first modern organisation created specifically to target the socio-economic problems in Ancoats was Eastside Regeneration, which was established in the early 1990s as a charitable trust to manage funding obtained from the Single Regeneration Budget (SRB) to address problems of education and rising crime. It was transferred to Manchester City Council, and operated for six years. During this period, Eastside Regeneration acted as a catalyst for the creation of other regeneration agencies, notably the Ancoats Buildings Preservation Trust (ABPT) and the Ancoats Urban Village Company. The former was established in 1995 to repair and refurbish historic buildings in Ancoats for which no commercial developer could find an economically viable and sympathetic solution. The Trust was facilitated by English Heritage's Conservation Area partnership scheme, which was also developed during the late 1990s. Using funding provided by this scheme, ABPT was able to undertake the first phase of the restoration of St Peter's in Ancoats, with a view to providing community facilities or a venue for an exhibition centre or museum (Pl 5).

The Ancoats Urban Village Company (AUVC) was established in 1996, initially as a charitable trust, with a remit to provide direction and focus for the regeneration of the Ancoats Conservation Area, which was then designated as the Ancoats Urban Village. AUVC was charged with securing the appropriate development of new buildings to complement the conversion of existing structures, with the aim of building the critical mass of population to support new businesses. The goals of the regeneration agencies were assisted by the North West Regional Development Agency which, in 2002, implemented a Compulsory Order Scheme to halt speculative property purchase

Plate 6: Aerial view of the New Islington Millennium Community during construction in 2006, showing the Central Retail Park (building block to the left) and A & G Murray's Mill (in the background) during structural repair work (reproduced courtesy of Volker Stevin Ltd)

in the area, allowing reputable developers to devise appropriate mixed-use schemes.

Initiatives in the Ancoats Urban Village have maintained the unique identity of Ancoats provided by the surviving historic buildings, many of which are being refurbished for sustainable future use in addition to new development. Examples include Waulk Mill on Bengal Street and the warehouse of the Percival, Vickers & Co Ltd flint glass works on Jersey Street, which have both been converted for office space (*Ch 3, p 29*). The development of Royal Mills involved the conversion of McConnel & Kennedy's former cotton-spinning mill into apartments, shops, offices, and leisure outlets. New housing and business premises, from small workshops to office suites, will continue to be developed within the Ancoats Urban Village until it reaches its target residential population of 15,000 in around 2010. These are to be coupled with new public spaces, overlooked by shops, cafes, bars, and restaurants, whilst community facilities, galleries, and museums are destined to form part of the regenerated neighbourhood.

In 2000, the Government accepted the proposed 'New Islington Millennium Community' project, a £250 million redevelopment of a 12.5 ha site between the Rochdale and Ashton Canals in Ancoats, incorporating the former Cardroom Estate. This was the third Millennium Community project to be implemented in England, and involved partnerships creating sustainable development built to the highest level of architectural design and environmental standards, mixing homes, shops, work spaces, and community facilities (Pl 6). This major programme of regeneration complemented the Ancoats Urban Village initiative, and cumulatively reinvigorated Ancoats as a community. It also provided an invaluable opportunity to study the buried remains of historically significant buildings that had been cleared without record after the 1960s, making an important contribution to the growing body of archaeological data for Ancoats. In particular, the archaeological study of examples from the first wave of textile factories has allowed a better understanding of the early industrial development of Ancoats (*Ch 4*), and has provided a context for viewing the next generation of mills, including those of Adam and George Murray, which still dominate the modern streetscape.

The Major Repair Project

As with many former industrial buildings in Ancoats, A & G Murray's Mill fell into economic decline during the second half of the twentieth century, which resulted in poor maintenance compounding problems of structural failure, leading to their inclusion on English Heritage's Buildings at Risk Register (English Heritage 2005). In order to save these immensely significant mills from further degeneration, and ultimately their collapse,

Plate 7: View across A & G Murray's Mill at the beginning of the archaeological survey in 2003

ABPT submitted an application to the Heritage Lottery Fund for their permanent repair (Pl 7). This application was accepted and, in conjunction with the North West Regional Development Agency, full funding was obtained. In the first instance, a Conservation Plan for the site was commissioned in 2001, which outlined several aspects of the Murrays' complex, including its physical construction, significance (both regional and national), and its potential for development and study (Donald Insall Associates and Structural Perspectives 2002). There were, however, still elements of the site that needed to be considered in more detail and, in some cases, a record completed in order to satisfy listed building and planning consent requirements. Consequently, a programme of further archaeological survey was devised by the Greater Manchester County Archaeologist, which allowed for a comprehensive physical examination of the mill complex, coupled with additional research, and some targeted excavation. This element of the project was undertaken by Oxford Archaeology North (OA North) between October 2003 and July 2006. The design of the permanent repair and strengthening of the mill was prepared by Building Design Partnership (BDP), and carried out between May 2005 and July 2006 by the construction contractor Wates.

Archaeological Recording and Fieldwork

The documentary research interrogated archival material held by numerous organisations. In particular, documents held by the Greater Manchester Sites and Monuments Record, the Archives and Local Studies Unit within Manchester Central Library, the Boulton and Watt Archive at Birmingham City Archives, and the Museum of Science and Industry in Manchester all yielded significant information. The results obtained from this research provided a framework for the comprehensive survey of the site, coupled with targeted excavation that was designed to clarify details of the site's development which were not clear from archive sources.

The intention of the building survey was to produce a complete record of the mill complex that illustrated the form and developmental sequence of the component structures. The majority of the survey was carried out by means of hand-annotation of existing architect's plans, elevations, and cross-sections. This typically involved reproducing copies of these plans at appropriate scales and adding any detail that was missing or was of archaeological significance. In some circumstances it was necessary to carry out additional instrument survey. In particular, reflected ceiling plans (plans showing ceiling detail viewed from above, rather than below) were generated for all floors, which proved valuable for understanding the sequence of power-transmission arrangements within the mill. The archaeological record was completed during a watching brief that was maintained throughout the structural repairs to the mill (*Ch 7*).

The Organisation of the Volume

The collation of this volume has called upon the wide-ranging experience of a group of people, each having considerable knowledge of Manchester, the textile industry and its buildings, and the development and regeneration of Ancoats. *Chapter 2* examines the history of Manchester and its role in the evolution of the English cotton industry, and summarises the key innovations to the cotton-spinning industry that were essential for the urbanisation of the factory system. *Chapters 3* and *4* chronicle the initial development of Ancoats as the archetypal industrial suburb and the heart of Manchester's manufacturing capacity, based on steam power. These chapters also summarise the results obtained from recent archaeological studies of other textile factories and associated workers' dwellings in Ancoats, focusing upon the first wave of water-powered mills. A & G Murray's Mill is the focus of *Chapter 5*, which provides a detailed chronological narrative of the mill complex drawn from documentary sources, coupled with an overview of working life and conditions for the mill operatives. *Chapter 6* examines the fabric of the surviving buildings, and from this interprets the structural development of the mill. This represents the culmination of one of the most detailed archaeological surveys of a textile mill ever undertaken, whilst *Chapter 7* describes the challenges of repairing and strengthening the mill for sustainable future use. The final chapter explores the historical context of A & G Murray's Mill, the family's contribution to the steam-powered factory system, and to the emergence of a new type of industrial townscape.

The Archive

The programme of archaeological recording and research of the mill complex generated a large body of data, which has been combined into a single archive that is to be housed at the Museum of Science and Industry in Manchester. It consists of *pro-forma* record sheets and indices, photographs, and drawings on drafting film and in digital format. The majority of the finds from the project were derived from secondary and tertiary contexts, but nevertheless proved to be of some value in interpreting the site (*Appendix* 2). These are to be retained for possible display in a specially designed area within the refurbished mill complex, although full finds' catalogues are available in the archive.

2

THE GROWTH OF MANCHESTER AND ITS TEXTILE INDUSTRY

Steve Little

Manchester's Origins as a Textile Centre

Manchester lay at the heart of the textile industry of north-west England, and it was here that most of the significant technological developments of the late eighteenth and early nineteenth centuries took place. The development of cotton-spinning machinery was pivotal to the dramatic expansion of the industry from the small workshop to the huge multi-storey mills that came to dominate Manchester's skyline by the early nineteenth century. Major advances in power provision were also crucial to the successful implementation of the factory-based system, which required new mechanisms to generate the substantial capital necessary for the new mills. Manchester grew from a small settlement in the fifteenth century to a thriving market town with a specialised trade in textiles by the seventeenth century, and had become a centre of the global cotton trade by the mid-nineteenth century (Farnie 1979).

The Medieval Manor and Parish

At the time of the Norman Conquest, Manchester was little more than a small village in the Hundred of Salford, which consisted of some 350 square miles, including the sparsely populated basin of the river Irwell and its tributaries (Frangopulo 1962, 14). In the late eleventh century, Roger of Poitou was granted most of the land between the Ribble and Mersey and divided much of it into several fiefdoms, the largest being the land holding centred on Manchester. By the thirteenth century the Grelley family had established a manor house at the confluence of the rivers Irwell and Irk, and the medieval town grew up around it (Tupling 1962, 116).

An urban element to Manchester had emerged by the thirteenth century, as a weekly market was held every Saturday. In 1227, Henry III granted Robert Grelley the right to hold an annual fair, which provided him with part of his annual income, and its status as a borough was granted in 1301 (Frangopulo 1962, 19). Both actions encouraged the development of a cash economy, an important consideration for barons in the relatively impoverished north of England (Higham 2004, 177-8). The Grelleys also gained income from a corn mill on the river Irk, which was accompanied by a woollen fulling mill before 1282 (Harland 1861, 315), testifying that some of the inhabitants of the manor were weavers of woollen cloth.

During the fifteenth century, the nascent linen industry was taking root in the townships on the south side of Manchester, using flax imported from Ireland via the port of Chester. During the same period, economic links were developing between the townships on the south and east of Manchester and along the Pennine edge, from which goods were increasingly exported eastwards by packhorse (Higham 2004, 196-7). The market of Manchester lay at the centre of this fledgling textile trade.

Manufacturing and Trading Woollen and Linen Cloth, 1500 – 1700

By 1539, John Leland was able to describe Manchester as the 'finest and busiest town in the whole of Lancashire, with the best buildings and the greatest population' (Chandler 1993, 263), at a time when the textile industries in south Lancashire were beginning to flourish. Woollen cloths made from fleeces were being produced on the Pennine slopes to the north and east of Manchester, and coarse linens were being woven from locally grown flax and hemp on the plain to the west (Winterbotham 1998, 22). Manchester received woollen cloth produced in the towns and hamlets of the surrounding district for the finishing processes and, most importantly, developed its role as a market centre for textiles (Willan 1980). The regional importance of this marketing role expanded to the extent that the cloth market in London at Blackwell Hall had a separate department for Lancashire goods, called the Manchester Hall, by the end of the sixteenth century (Hartwell 2001, 7).

In the sixteenth century, Walloons fleeing the Low Countries and Huguenots escaping persecution in France sought refuge in England. They brought their looms and their weaving trade, and specialised in making complicated threads and tapes. They settled initially in the south, in Canterbury and London, but soon transferred their trade to the Manchester area, a

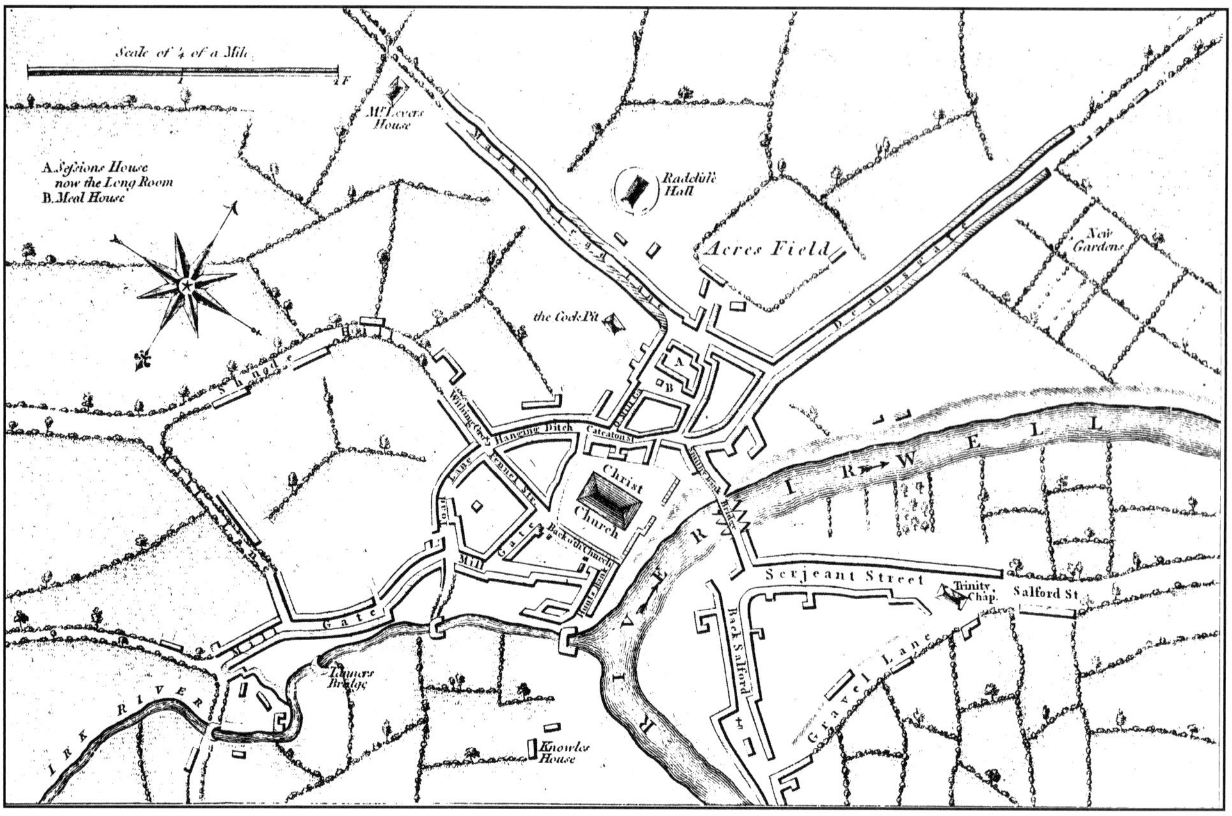

Plate 8: Plan of Manchester and Salford c *1650 (reproduced from Casson and Berry's map, 1746)*

move presumably stimulated by the lack of regulation and guilds (Wadsworth and Mann 1931, 102). This work force, using complicated and expensive Dutch looms, gave to the town a skilled and industrialised work force, and perhaps unwittingly helped to establish an industrial discipline needed with the turn to factory production.

By this time, the weaving of pure woollens in south Lancashire had started to decline in favour of mixed fabrics classed as small wares and fustians, whilst the market for linen remained buoyant. Linen yarn formed the warp for both fabrics, and whilst worsted was usually selected for the weft in small wares, cotton became frequently used in fustians; the earliest known reference to cotton in the region dates to 1601, when it was mentioned in the will of George Arnould, a Bolton fustian weaver (*op cit*, 15). A separate market for the sale of small wares was held in Manchester from the early seventeenth century, whilst fustians were being exported regularly to western and southern Europe by 1620. These were produced in a network of towns with Manchester at their hub, and the town became the principal commercial centre for the region and its specialised production of small wares and fustians. This created the roots of the later Manchester cotton industry, which owed much to 'the entrepreneurial spirit' of weavers who were prepared to combine the new fibre with linen to produce fustian (Winterbotham 1998, 40).

During this period, the centre of the town was focused on the church, and extended a short distance along Deansgate and Market Street (Pl 8). The flourishing business community was dominated by a few wealthy merchant manufacturers and fustian-dealing families, notably the Chethams, the Booths, the Wrigleys, and the Byroms. They increasingly controlled the domestic textile industry, the so-called 'putting-out' system, by which most cloth was produced (Kidd 1996, 17). In 1619, George and Humphrey Chetham described themselves as partners in the trade of buying and selling fustians and other wares, with a considerable trade in raw cotton (Wadsworth and Mann 1931, 29-36). By 1700, the manufacture of linen cloth was being superseded by fustian; probate evidence has indicated that the manufacture of fustians accounted for 30 % of textile occupations in Manchester by the mid-eighteenth century (Stobart 1998, 7).

Eighteenth-Century Growth and Technological Innovation

Manchester emerged as the premier market centre for textiles, and particularly cottons, during the eighteenth century, having superseded markets in towns such as Bolton (Aikin 1795, 263). Indeed, as early as the 1790s, Manchester's thriving export market was beginning to displace London as a centre of overseas trade in

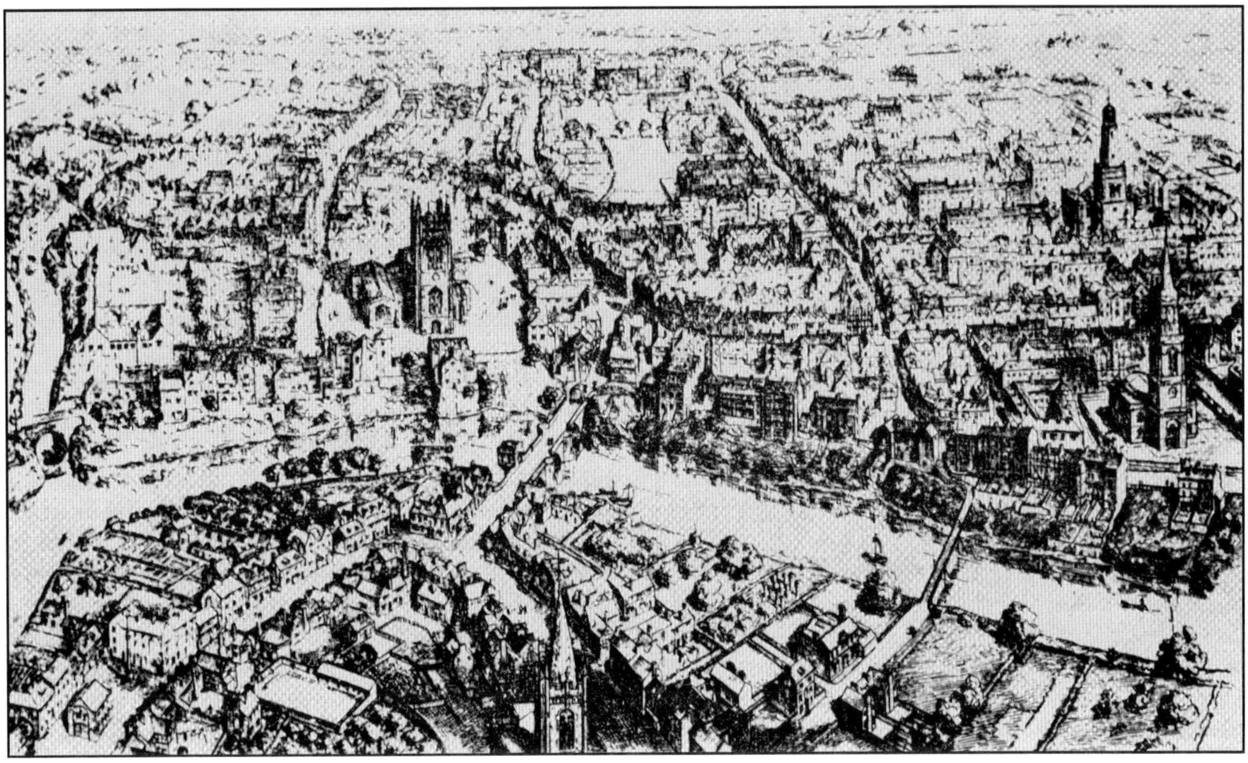

Plate 9: An engraving of Manchester and Salford in c *1761 (reproduced from* The British Architect *1893)*

cotton cloth (Edwards 1967, 176), reflecting great improvements to the transport network across the North West. Consequently, Manchester 'attracted a dynamic and increasingly cosmopolitan merchant community eager to exploit the town's proximity to the new centres of production' (Kidd 1996, 29).

The greatest indication of the town's growing prosperity was its physical expansion. The 1775 edition of Casson and Berry's *Plan of Manchester and Salford* included a summarised account of the trade of the town, which stated that within 30 years Manchester had 'become almost twice as large as it was before, so fast have its inhabitants and their riches increased...'. This can be illustrated by comparing the town's limits as depicted in *c* 1650 (Pl 8) with Yates' map of 1786 (Fig 2). A good impression of the extent of settlement is also provided by an engraving of the town in *c* 1761, which was published, and probably drawn using contemporary accounts, in 1893 (Pl 9).

Manchester's expansion and its eventual domination of the region's textile trades is not easily explained, as it resulted from several interlocking circumstances. One of the overriding factors, however, was perhaps the aggressive marketing of Manchester as a mercantile centre, represented for instance by the creation of an Exchange for this purpose in 1729 by the Lord of the Manor, Oswald Mosley (Collinge 1962, 176; Pl 10). Another important factor was the lack of regulation, and the absence of guilds, which proved to be a significant advantage to the Manchester entrepreneur. James Ogden, a native of the town, was clear that this openness was the root of Manchester's prosperity:

Plate 10: The first Exchange in Manchester, erected in 1729 (extracted from Casson and Berry's map, 1755)

> ...perhaps nothing has more contributed to the improvements in trade here, than the free admission of workmen in every branch, whereby the trade has been kept open to strangers of every description, who contribute to its improvement by their ingenuity; for Manchester being only a market town, governed by Constables, is not subject to such regulation as are made in corporations, to favour freemen in exclusion of strangers: and, indeed nothing could be more fatal to its trading interests, if it should be incorporated, and have representatives in Parliament (Ogden 1783).

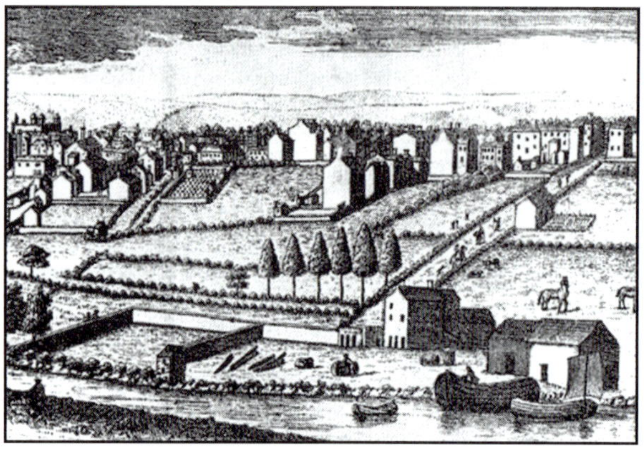

Plate 11: Manchester's first quay, established on the Mersey Irwell Navigation in 1735 by Edward Byrom (extracted from Casson and Berry's map, 1746)

Joseph Aston similarly concluded that the absence of a corporate governing body had 'induced strangers to add their stock of property, industry, and talent, to the growing prosperity [raising] the town and trade of Manchester to its present consequence on the national scale' (Aston 1816, 31).

Transport

An effective transport network was also an important part of Manchester's economy and, during the eighteenth century, the town's merchants were looking for efficient and reliable ways to move goods, especially to London. Goods bound for the capital at this time were transported by wagon and packhorse to Chester, and forwarded by ship (Vale 2004, 53). As Manchester expanded as the premier textile distribution centre, the local road system became increasingly important for goods and passengers (Timmins 2004, 70). Lancashire, however, was notorious for its poor roads, which would have required considerable investment to sustain an expansion in the volume of goods to be carried. The situation was improved with the introduction of turnpike roads after 1725, and there was great activity in road improvement throughout the region from the 1760s as traffic increased (Chaloner 1962, 131). Road transportation continued to be of importance to Manchester's industry well into the nineteenth century; one third of bulk goods such as coal was carried by road as late as 1836, and the textile firm McConnel & Kennedy certainly made more use of the road than of the canal (Freeman 1980).

More important, however, were the new communication routes based upon improved waterways (Fig 2). Of great importance was the opening of the Mersey Irwell Navigation in 1734, which formed an efficient link to the expanding port of Liverpool, and enabled sea-going vessels to sail up the Irwell into Manchester (Nevell 2004, 31). Wharfage facilities for boats of up to 50 tons were provided by a quay established in 1735 by Edward Byrom, a wealthy fustian dealer (Pl 11). The quay was

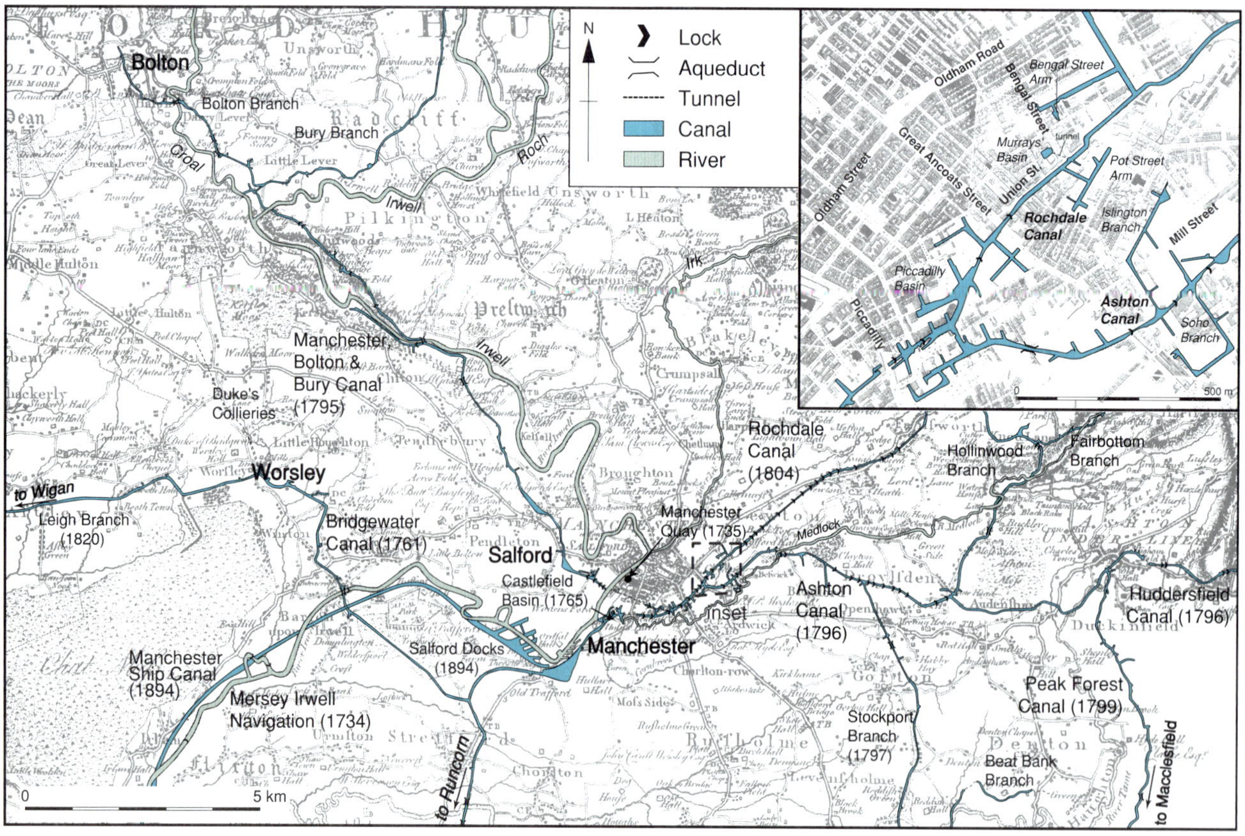

Figure 2: The network of navigable rivers and canals in Manchester and the surrounding region superimposed on Yates' map of 1786, with inset showing the canal network in Ancoats superimposed on Bancks and Co's map of 1832

built at the bottom of what in that year became Quay Street, strategically located to carry much of the town's trade, with a river frontage of 136 yards (George and Brumhead 2002, 22).

This important trading route was augmented by the Bridgewater Canal, the first true industrial canal (Little 2005), which was opened between Worsley and Stretford in 1761, from where coal was carted to Manchester until the basin at Castlefield was completed in 1765 (Hadfield 1994, 65). It had been created to allow the Duke of Bridgewater to transport coal in bulk from his mines at Worsley to the expanding markets at Manchester and Salford. While destined mainly for the domestic market, the price of coal in Manchester was halved by the opening of the canal (Ogden 1783, 7), helping to guarantee a supply of cheap fuel for industrial purposes. In 1772, the canal was extended across north Cheshire to join with the Trent and Mersey Canal at Preston Brook, representing the beginnings of an integrated system of inland waterways and a link between Manchester and the Midlands. Most importantly, however, was the extension to join the Mersey at Runcorn in 1776. This new link to Liverpool via the river Mersey halved the transport cost of raw cotton to Manchester (Kidd 1996, 32). Moreover, although not the original intention of the canal, it became an important means of bringing food into the town, helping to increase Manchester's importance as a centre of distribution and maintaining its growing population (Scola 1992).

Other waterways established during the late eighteenth century radiated from Manchester, and effectively turned the town into an inland port, with its wharves, docks, warehouses, and canal-side buildings (Fig 2). These included the Manchester, Bolton and Bury Canal, authorised in 1791, and the Ashton under Lyne Canal, authorised in 1792 and opened through Ancoats in 1796 (Hadfield and Biddle 1970, 295-6). The latter was intended to serve the coal-producing area to the north-east of Manchester, but also provided a trade route from Manchester to the textile mills of Ashton under Lyne. Of particular significance was the Rochdale Canal, which was authorised in 1794 and opened in 1804 to provide the first trans-Pennine route and a link to ports on the East Coast (*op cit*, 269-74). Both the Rochdale and Ashton Canals developed numerous short branch canals, designed to serve newly established industries in urban areas, and especially Ancoats. This network of canal arms developed into the arteries for the new steam-powered mills, and became a characteristic feature of Ancoats (*Ch 3, p 27*).

People, the Entrepreneur, and Wealth

The growing prosperity of Manchester during the second half of the eighteenth century made it an attractive place for business, one consequence of which was the rapid expansion of the town's population (Table 1). Vigier (1970, 15) pointed out that, prior to industrialisation, over three-fifths of the English population lived in the southern counties, but from 1750 the centre of gravity shifted to the North West and, by 1801, almost one half of the English population lived in that region. He also noted that the rate of population growth in Manchester during this period was unprecedented, and was far higher than most other comparable towns.

This increase in population was a result of migration to the town rather than of a significantly increased birth-rate, although better supplies of food and improved medical services were also contributory factors (Chaloner 1962, 134). The place of origin of the migrants is not well documented, although many would have travelled from Ireland, Scotland, and Wales, as well as from the countryside surrounding Manchester. In broad terms, these were the people, with some local exceptions, who populated the factories, became entrepreneurs, and brought vigour, experience, and ideas to the town.

Year	Manchester	Birmingham	Sheffield	Year	Manchester	Birmingham	Sheffield
1642	*c* 3200	*c* 5400	*c* 2500	**1831**	182,016	146,986	91,692
1717	*c* 8000	*c* 17,000	*c* 7600	**1841**	235,507	182,922	111,000
1757	19,839	*c* 29,000	*c* 20,000	**1851**	303,382	232,638	135,310
1773	22,481	*c* 40,000	*c* 24,000	**1861**	338,722	296,076	185,172
1788	42,821	*c* 52,500	*c* 34,000	**1871**	351,189	343,787	239,946
1801	75,281	73,670	45,755	**1881**	341,414	400,774	284,408
1811	89,068	85,753	53,231	**1891**	----	478,113	325,547
1821	126,066	106,722	65,375	**1901**	347,495	522,204	409,071

Table 1: Population of Manchester and comparable towns, 1642-1901. Figures for Manchester from 1801 are based on census returns for the 1838 Borough, and earlier figures are given by Aston (1816) for the Manchester Township

One well-known example of a successful migrant in the eighteenth century was Robert Owen, who came to Manchester in 1787 to gain experience as a draper, went into the manufacture of textile machinery, became a manager of a cotton mill, and then set up his own company with three sleeping partners (Owen 1857). He suggested that his experience in the cloth trade as a draper enabled him to improve on spinning techniques. Owen also claimed that it was he who persuaded the Manchester cotton spinners to use the long staple Sea Island cotton, which proved beneficial to the fine spinners and had a profound effect on cotton growing in the 'New World' (*Appendix 1*). Commercial success enabled him to make a judicious marriage to the daughter of David Dale of Lanark, which took him away from Manchester and to a new life as both a factory owner and utopian socialist, all by the time he was 28!

Whilst exceptional, Owen's experience was not unique, and happened during a period when the French Wars encouraged enterprise and investment. Interest rates on the whole were low and there was, at least in the textile industry, a fair amount of time allowed on the payment of bills (Lee 1972, 106). This economic climate was an important factor in the development of Manchester's manufacturing base, and provided an attractive prospect for entrepreneurs seeking opportunities.

Supplying an Increased Demand for Cotton

The eighteenth century saw a quickening of the British economy, which resulted in a widespread desire for consumer goods, because of the wider base of wealth ownership in England and the Scottish lowlands, rather than conspicuous spending by a wealthy few. This development can be seen in the growth of numerous towns, such as the creation of Edinburgh New Town. The increase in demand was itself a stimulus to finding new methods of production and, indeed, new industries. One strand of this demand was for clothing, from outer garments to dresses and underwear, whilst the type of fabric used to make these clothes was dictated by fashion, price, and utility (Lemire 1997, 3). One of the consequences was an increase in the demand for cottons; lighter cottons had been fashionable for dresses in Europe since the Middle Ages, and in England by the late seventeenth century, when the East India Company supplied the national market for calicos and muslins from India. Archive sources, including inventories and theft records, indicate that there was an increase in the wearing of cotton even amongst the working class by the end of the eighteenth century (Lemire 1991, 102). This appears to have reflected the relative fall in the price of cotton, and the rising prices of wools and linens that were being bought up to clothe the armed forces engaged in the war with the American Colonies and the Napoleonic Wars. Cotton goods were also easier to wash and maintain. One minor

Plate 12: Hargreaves' spinning jenny, from an engraving by T E Nicholson (reproduced from Baines 1835)

result was complaints that there was no distinction in dress between the well-to-do and their servants (Ribeiro 2002, 82).

This increase in demand for cotton during the eighteenth century could not be satisfied either by the import of expensive Indian cloth or by domestic production methods. Consequently, there were several experiments and inventions that were aimed at increasing the production of cloth. A key stage, and one that was itself a stimulus to further experimentation, was the introduction of John Kay's flying shuttle, known initially as the 'fly shuttle', which was first patented in 1733. It was perfected in 1753, by which time its use in Lancashire and Yorkshire was widespread (Wadsworth and Mann 1931, 467). This device not only increased the speed at which a weaver could work, but also the width of cloth being woven, so that the staple cloth became wider.

In areas where the flying shuttle was in general use it took three to four spinners to keep up the supply of yarn to one weaver, where the ratio before had been roughly one to one. This created a bottleneck in the spinning sector, which led to experiments in ways of improving the process, the traditional method being on a wheel with just one spindle, frequently undertaken in the home as a secondary occupation. This problem was addressed during the second half of the eighteenth century, when two successful spinning machines were introduced: the 'spinning jenny', reputed to have been invented by James Hargreaves in *c* 1764; and Richard Arkwright's 'water-frame', patented in 1769. Both machines represented an incredible increase in the production of spun yarn; by the 1780s, machines with 80–100 spindles had been produced (Tann 1970, 5). Most significantly, water-frames needed more power than could be provided within domestic premises, and their efficient use necessitated the first steps towards factory-based production.

James Hargreaves is widely credited with introducing the spinning jenny, which he originally equipped with eight spindles, but soon increased to 16. He patented the machine in 1770, by which time it was already in widespread use (Murphy 1911, 41). Guest (1823, 12-6), however, argued forcefully that Thomas Highs of Leigh had actually invented the machine several years previously, and that Hargreaves had merely improved upon the design; the truth is unlikely ever to be resolved. The spinning jenny was a simple wooden machine that, in essence, comprised several spinning-wheel mechanisms bolted together and turned on their side to be powered by a large wheel (Pl 12). The operator could spin several threads at once by turning a single wheel, although it required a fairly skilled hand to use, especially in the correct handling of the moving carriage. A significant disadvantage of the jenny was that it could spin a roving into yarn, but was not capable of being applied to the preparation of the roving itself. Nevertheless, on account of the simplicity of their operation and their low cost, spinning jennies were still in use at the beginning of the nineteenth century.

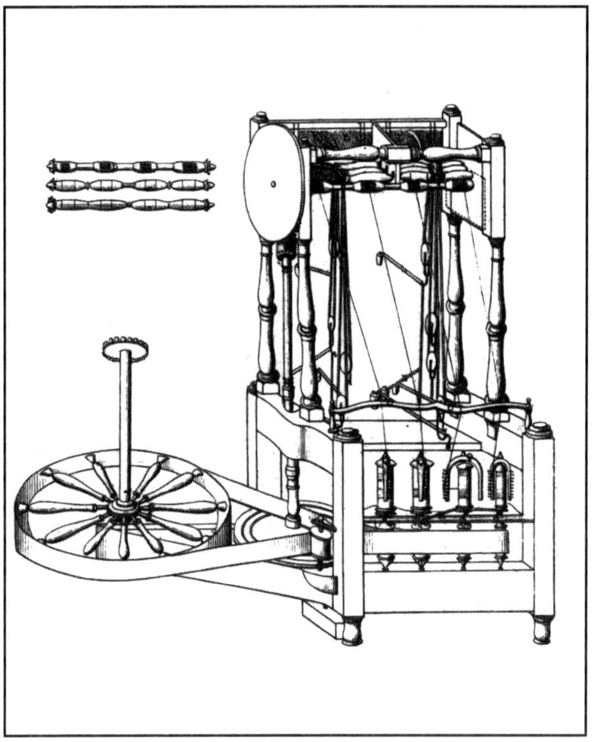

Plate 13: Arkwright's water-frame (reproduced from Baines 1835)

Like the jenny, Richard Arkwright's water-frame was intended to spin cotton roving into yarn but, crucially, could also produce a roving from the carded cotton (Baines 1835, 157). Arkwright's patent for the water-frame relied on a spindle and flyer, known since the days of Leonardo da Vinci, and a series of rollers, each one revolving slightly faster than the one before (Pl 13). This latter component drew the thread out to a fairly precise, albeit coarse, yarn, whilst the flyer put in the necessary twist. The skilled hand of the spinner was supplanted by a minder to oversee the operation of the machine. Hostility to Arkwright arose from the established hand spinners, who viewed his invention as a threat to their livelihoods. Arkwright thus chose to relocate from Preston to Nottingham and set up a business providing yarn for the knitting industry. In partnership with a hosiery manufacturer named Jedediah Strutt, he established a small factory with a number of spinning machines driven by horse power (Cossons 1975, 249). In 1771, Arkwright moved to Cromford in Derbyshire, and established a much larger factory that harnessed the power of the river Derwent to turn the machinery. This venture proved to be an enormous success and, by 1780, there were between 15 and 20 water-frame 'factories' being operated by Arkwright and his partners, or by proprietors acting under licence (Edwards 1967, 4).

Plate 14: John Kennedy's spinning mule (reproduced from McConnel 1913)

Arkwright's success as an early factory master lay in his ability to apply power to almost all processes of yarn production under one roof, enabling the term 'factory' (derived from 'manufactory') to be used to describe his enterprise without any qualification being required. These factories were usually large-scale and erected by a fast-flowing river, which sometimes equated to a site remote from the market and the other benefits of a town, thus requiring the construction of a whole community of buildings in addition to the actual mills. This created the 'factory colony' typical of the late eighteenth century, such as Samuel Greg's Quarry Bank Mill that was established in 1784 at Styal, in Cheshire. The 'factory colony' was not a feature of Manchester's townscape, although an exception was the works developed by David Holt. Known as Holt Town, this industrial colony was established in 1785 on the river Medlock at Beswick Bridge in Ancoats and, by 1792, comprised a three-storey building that contained two spinning frames 'with room for several more' (*Manchester Mercury*, 8 February 1785), together with several workers' cottages and a mansion.

A limitation of the water-frame was that the yarn produced was strong but coarse, and tended to be used as the warp rather than the weft; it was not able to produce yarn fine enough for lighter cloths. That and the fact that the development of the water-frame was dependent on good water sites led the urban spinner, especially those in Manchester, to look for other ways to solve the production problems. The answer was found in the introduction of the spinning mule. It is difficult to over-estimate the importance of the mule: it dominated Lancashire's cotton-spinning industry until well into the twentieth century (Catling 1986, 181). The initial adoption of the mule was encouraged by the fact that it was hand powered and, unlike Arkwright's water-frame, was not restricted by patents. The first mention of a mule in a Manchester context appears to be in the *Manchester Mercury* in 1786, when an advertisement on 21 March offered mules for sale.

The spinning mule was known originally as the 'Hall'i'th' Wood Wheel', after the place where it was invented by Samuel Crompton in 1779 (Kennedy 1819, 127). This machine combined elements of the water-frame and the jenny: it had the draw rollers of the former and the moving carriage of the latter. The roving was placed on the back of the machine (the stock), and was then drawn out by a set of rollers, each one running slightly faster than the one behind it. The spindles were set at the extreme end of the moving carriage, and revolved with the movement of the carriage. The cotton strand was drawn out of the rollers and, because of the angle at which the spindles were set, the strand fell off the end, giving it a twist. At the end of the carriage run, a wire (the fuller) dropped lightly on the strands of cotton and altered the direction in which they lay and, as the carriage ran back towards the stock, yarn built up on the spindle.

According to John Kennedy (1831a, 321), Crompton's first spinning machine had 30 or 40 spindles but was a fairly crude affair. The draw rollers were made of wood and, in order to increase the friction in drawing out the yarn, he covered the rollers in various materials, including sheepskin. Crompton was not involved in any further development of his invention and, because the machine was never patented, its use spread and others were able to improve the design (Catling 1986, 42). A notable improvement was that introduced in 1790 by a former apprentice of Arkwright's, a 'Mr Wright', who devised a double mule, *ie* a mule with spindles on each side of the central head stock, and fitted with 400 spindles (Kennedy 1831a, 339). Further improvements were implemented by John Kennedy, who modified the external drive arrangement and, notably, created a dual speed machine with two sets of two toothed cogs (Pl 14). William Fairbairn considered this innovation to be a major improvement:

> Mr Kennedy rendered great service to the new system of mule spinning by the introduction of a new motion called double speed, which gave to the thread any amount of twist that might be required for the number of the counts or quality of the yarn that had to be spun. This improvement of Mr Kennedy gave greatly increased facilities to the spinning of fine yarn and very soon enabled those engaged in that peculiar manufacture to raise their numbers from 40s and 50s up to 150s and 200s (Fairbairn 1861, 4).

The 'counts' that Fairbairn referred to were essentially a measurement of the fineness of the cotton yarn being spun: the higher the count, the finer the thread (*Appendix 1*). It was the spinning of the finest thread that came to typify the cotton industry in Manchester, where firms such as Kennedy's produced the highest counts in the world until the mid-nineteenth century (Williams with Farnie 1992, 20).

Buildings for Spinning

Jenny and Mule Shops

The establishment of workshops for jennies, mules, and carding machines during the late eighteenth century occurred in parallel with the development of the water-frame factory colonies, and the evidence available indicates that there were great numbers of jenny and mule shops in Manchester and the surrounding area. One newspaper advertisement offered for rent 'three rooms, 17 yards by 14, very convenient, for spinning jennies or mules...situated near Newton Lane' (*Manchester Mercury*, 11 September 1792), and another offered a factory for sale at Shude Hill, containing ten spinning jennies, with 64-84 spindles, and an 18 in (0.46 m) carding engine (*Manchester Mercury*, 10 June 1794). Comments and advertisements in contemporary newspapers and entries in trade directories suggest a growing specialism between 'soft' spinning in workshops associated with the jenny, and the production of 'hard' spinning for the warp associated with the water-frame. Editions of the *Manchester Mercury* published during the 1790s also provide numerous examples of factories built speculatively for sale in the town (*eg Manchester Mercury*, 6 July 1790), although most of these new 'factories' were probably less well-ordered. This was highlighted by Guest, who noted that many new spinning machines were 'erected in garrets or lofts, and many a dilapidated barn and cowshed was patched up in the walls, repaired in roof, and provided with windows, to serve as lodging house for the new muslin wheel' (Guest 1823, 12). Similarly, 'a late eighteenth-century "mill" or "factory" was almost any old building used for the cotton manufacture...probably relatively few buildings before 1815 were built specifically for the cotton trade' (Edwards 1967, 186). Some of the buildings that were being erected conformed to the more traditional form associated with domestic workshops, multi-storied

Plate 15: Attic workshop in Manchester (reproduced from The Builder *1862)*

(usually three), with garret workshop preferably on an east/west axis to get the north light, with long windows to catch as much light as possible (Pl 15). The mechanical spinners certainly took advantage of these buildings. The use was not restricted, as implied by an advertisement in the *Manchester Mercury* on 24 July 1784 that offered a 'house for sale could be used for warehouse or workshop'. Similarly, as the eighteenth century drew to a close, the use of the term 'factory' was used increasingly in such advertisements:

> that new erected factory in Garret Lane. Let or sell (*Manchester Mercury*, 6 July 1790);
>
> warehouse or Cotton Factory, new erected top of Deansgate (*Manchester Mercury*, 1 November 1791);
>
> to be sold, warehouse/factory 18 by 11 yards, six storeys, German Street (*Manchester Mercury*, 10 June 1794).

The size of these buildings became a more pressing consideration once multiple machines could be operated by a single spinner, and a separate power source was applied, which in the first instance could be one man supplying power for two or three machines. Those built as a traditional domestic workshop required further adaptation, such as a set of three houses at 51-3 Tib Street (Pl 16), which appear to have been made into a common shop at second-floor level with a 'taking-in' door and gantry beam having been set into the gable end, implying a significant scale of production (English Heritage 2001, 17). Removal of the access to the workshop from the accommodation below, so that access was external, would have made the space more secure. The next stage in the process of adapting any such building was the conversion of the living space to house either a machine, or a horse-wheel in the case where a horse was to supply the external power source.

Plate 16: Early nineteenth-century workshops on Tib Street

Adapting buildings to suit a particular purpose was probably quite common. A tobacco manufacturer on Hanging Ditch who, in 1798, intended to convert a domestic property into industrial premises and install a Boulton and Watt steam engine provides a good example (BWA 3147/3/485). Where there is an indication of size, there is also a noticeable increase being offered in contemporary advertisements, until the massive purpose-built mills associated with steam-powered spinning appear toward the end of the century. It was in the larger premises that the system of 'room-and-power' letting emerged, which became a route followed by many new entrants into the spinning industry.

The Beginnings of the Factory-Based Textile Industry

Entry into the Textile Industry

There were several routes by which an entrepreneur could enter Manchester's cotton-spinning sector, and a picture emerges of the relative ease in which it could be achieved, although success was not guaranteed. Boom periods could lead to high profits and potentially the ownership of a large mill; such buildings increasingly represented the manufacturing sector of the town during the late eighteenth century.

Entry into the cotton-spinning sector was made easier by an expanding cotton market, low interest rates, and the relatively long periods (usually six months) which manufacturers had to pay for raw materials. The latter factor meant that there were times when the spinners could sell their yarn before they had to pay for the raw material. The downside of this long credit period was that the spinner had to wait to be paid, which often created an instability that worked to the disadvantage of the small producer. One of the advantages that the early firms had over those setting up at a later date, however, was that there were large profits to be made during the closing years of the eighteenth and the early part of the nineteenth centuries. British yarn was superior to that being spun on the Continent and, despite the blockades of the Napoleonic Wars, much sought after. The war itself was profitable to the industry in that the army generated a demand for linens and woollens, which became scarce and expensive, and thus pushed up the demand for the cheaper cottons at home. Another stimulus for cotton producers was the development of an export market, more volatile than the home market because of problems such as those imposed by war conditions, but nevertheless profitable for those that could exploit its potential. Cotton cloth surpassed silk as an export commodity in 1767, linens in 1783, and that of woollen cloth in 1803 (Farnie 1979, 9). For fine spinners, such as A & G Murray and McConnel &

Kennedy, further areas to exploit were made available as the dictates of taste among the well-to-do created a fashion for British-manufactured lighter cotton calicos and muslins. Leaders of 'taste', such as Beau Brummell at Bath, demanded that clothing should be crisp and more importantly clean, a demand made manageable by the use of cottons, a material easier to clean and maintain than more traditional materials. The development of the spinning mule from the late 1780s made the production of fine yarn possible, increased the volume of production, and brought the price down, which helped in turn to stimulate demand.

Whilst entry into the business appears to have been relatively easy, the bankruptcy rate indicates that there was a high risk. In 1793, for instance, there were 38 bankruptcies in the textile sector notified in the *Manchester Mercury*, four of which were identified as cotton spinners. An even worse year for the cotton spinners was 1795, when seven firms were notified as bankrupt among 37 textile failures. This high turnover of firms was corroborated by George Lee, who thought that, by 1815, 'there is but one out of five [Manchester cotton mills] remaining in the hands of the original proprietors; the others have changed hands once or oftener out of the 62 factories…generally from the ruin of the proprietor' (quoted in Edwards 1967, 22). Nevertheless, the number of textile firms increased, and Bancks' trade directory for 1800 lists just over 160 spinners of various types, although the vast majority (150) are entered specifically as 'cotton spinners'.

Money and the New Entrant

For those who had little or no money, the first obstacle to establishing a new business was the raising of capital, especially for machinery, which John Kennedy suggested to be the greatest cost; during the final years of the eighteenth century, McConnel & Kennedy was selling mules for 5s per spindle, and carding engines for between £8 and £13 (Lee 1972, 105). Indeed, those engaged in machine-making, such as Adam Murray, John Kennedy, Henry Houldsworth, and Robert Owen, had a distinct advantage in setting up their own cotton-spinning concerns, as they were able to invest the capital that would have been needed to purchase new machines in other kinds of development. Conversely, little capital appears to have been needed to enter the machine-making business; Robert Owen started his industrial career by entering into partnership with John Jones, a machine-maker, with £100 of capital borrowed from his brother (Owen 1857, 30). When this partnership was dissolved, Owen received from Jones three spinning mules and other machinery as his part of the capital. In 1790 he rented from a builder named Woodruff a newly erected building, 'or factory as such places were then beginning to be called', situated on Ancoats Lane, and 'commenced business for myself in a small part of one of the large rooms in this large building'. Owen claims he used his three mules to spin rovings bought from McConnel and Kennedy, who at that time were unable to spin yarn commercially. Owen bought the rovings for 12s a pound, and sold the finished yarn to a Mr Mitchell for 22s a pound, resulting in £6 profit a week (*op cit*, 33-4). He also sub-let out the rest of the large building he was renting, which paid for his part of the rent.

In 1795, when attempting to establish the Chorlton Twist Mill Company, Robert Owen obtained the finance required from 'sleeping partners'. This was not an unusual situation, as testified by numerous adverts in the *Manchester Mercury* offering the loans of money by people looking to invest: an advert on 14 January 1794, for instance, offered up to £10,000 'on security of field land or inheritance only'. There is rarely any detail as to who was offering the money, but on at least two occasions London dealers are named: on 27 August 1790, Rose & Co of London offered advancements on goods, and on 4 December 1792 Daniel Gosset of London offered a similar service. Available finance was sometimes short during temporary slumps, but for much of the period money appears to have been chasing schemes.

Banks appear to have played little part in the raising of fixed capital. In fact, the first formal bank in Manchester, Byrom, Sedgwick, Allen and Place, was not established until after 1770. The major role of the banks appears to have been in the provision of working capital, funding the gaps between the selling of wares and the settling of accounts. Most of the monetary transactions that took place between various sections of the textile trade were via the use of bills, and the banks played an increasingly important part in this process as dealers in these bills: 'The ubiquity of the Bill of Exchange in everyday payments made every businessman a banker of sorts and, for those who became full bankers, a ready-made network of credit existed which gave to Lancashire banking its distinctive character' (Pressnell 1956, 19). This working capital went to pay wages and other items of day-to-day expenditure. The banks were not the only supply of such funding, and Edwards (1967, 216-7) gives several examples of people acting as bankers who would never have called themselves that.

The Established Entrepreneur

There were essentially two types of new entrant into the cotton-spinning industry: those already established in some form of business, having money or position, and those coming into the trade with little or no money. An examination of those that acquired a Boulton and Watt engine during the last decade of the eighteenth century reveals several in the former category. The first spinner in Manchester to invest in such an engine was Peter Drinkwater in 1789

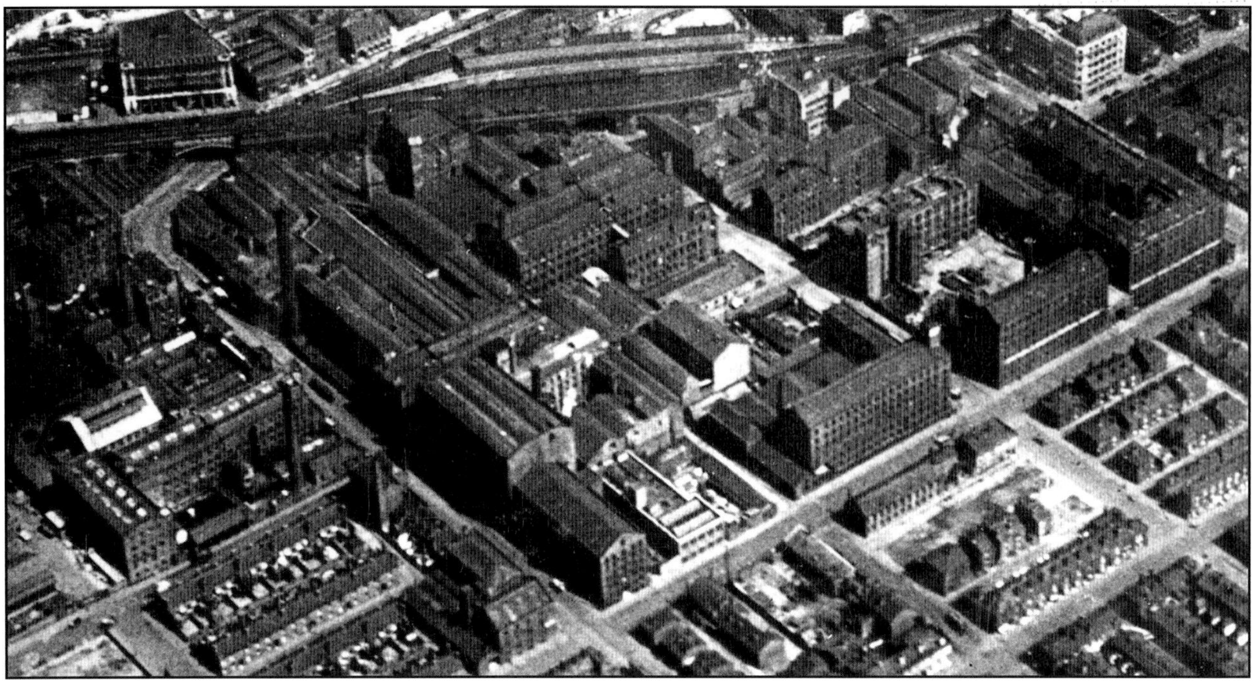

Plate 17: An aerial view of the steam-powered cotton mills between Cambridge Street and Oxford Road in 1927 (reproduced courtesy of Manchester Archives and Local Studies)

(Chaloner 1954). He had established himself as a textile merchant in Manchester by 1781 (Raffald 1781, 21), and the following year diversified into cotton spinning when he saw the profits others had been making in the industry, and purchased a water-powered cotton mill in the centre of Northwich, Cheshire (Fitton 1989, 149). He was evidently a man of considerable practical ability and knowledge, with a reputation for innovation (Butt 1971, 169), and it would seem that he recognised at an early date the huge potential of applying steam power to textile-manufacturing. Acting upon this, he became the first to establish a textile mill in Manchester that was to be specifically steam-powered, and therefore fully independent of the site requirements of a water-power system. This mill, which was erected in Piccadilly in 1789, incorporated a number of innovative design features, although the steam engine was initially intended to drive the preparatory machinery only and spinning was undertaken manually (OA North 2005a). Robert Owen had been the manager of Drinkwater's Piccadilly Mill since 1792, where he had been responsible for the day-to-day management of the factory, in addition to making the textile machines, and this undoubtedly gave him considerable experience in the running of a mill (Owen 1857, 28).

Samuel Marsland was another merchant who entered the cotton-spinning trade in the late eighteenth century, when he established a mill on Cambridge Street in 1795. This was designed as a mirror of the Chorlton Twist Mill, which had been built by Robert Owen on the adjacent plot earlier in the same year, with the intention that the two mills could share a single engine (Clark 1978, 208). These mills represented the origins of what was to become a significant concentration of steam-powered mills, which developed on a scale comparable to those in Ancoats but without the benefits of a local canal network (Pl 17).

A slightly different route into the textile trade was taken by Thomas Bound, a builder, who had made enough money from speculative building to be described as a 'gentleman' in Scholes' *Manchester and Salford Directory* of 1794. By the early nineteenth century, he was the proprietor of the William Seedhouse Mill on Leigh Street, Ancoats, providing an example of how the capital from one trade was transferred to another. This was noted by Robert Owen when writing of the late eighteenth century: 'cotton spinning was so profitable that it began to engage the attention of many parties with capital' (Owen 1857, 33-4).

Costs of a Factory

In 1785, the cost of building a 52 x 31ft (15.85 x 9.45 m) five-storey mill in brick and slate, exclusive of any machinery, was estimated to be £495. Some 12 years later, a report prepared by the three leading fire insurance companies concluded that the cost of a new mill with over 1000 spindles for water-frame spinning was £3000 (Aspin 2003, 475)), whilst the firm of McConnel & Kennedy spent £6074 2s 7d on their new steam-powered mill on Union Street during 1797-8 (Lee 1972, 101), although this was a 'state-of-the-art' factory. The greatest cost was probably in the machinery; at this time, McConnel was selling spinning mules with 180 spindles and stretching frames with 90 spindles for about £57 each, and carding engines for £27. The price of the steam-power plant varied according to the size required but, for an average-size mill, James McConnel suggested to George Hannay of Bangor in 1797 that it would cost about £800 for an 8-10 hp steam engine and associated mill work (Lee 1972, 20).

'Room-and-Power' Mills

An important stage before establishing an independent factory was the option of working in partnership and sharing rented premises. In particular, 'room-and-power' mills offered floor space for rent with powered line-shafting. Part of the mill may have been occupied by the owner, which spread their costs for establishing a new factory. Such a room-and-power mill was that owned by 'Mr Lane' on Union Street in Ancoats (*Ch 5, p 63*), Royal Exchange insurance records providing evidence of his tenants. In 1797, for instance, Robert Schofield, cotton carder and spinner, Edward Dean, cotton carder and spinner, Jonathan Pollard, cotton spinner, and Peter and Anthony McCandish & Co, cotton spinners, are mentioned (Royal Exchange 7253/158128, 7253/158142). All of these firms soon expanded beyond Lane's factory and some, such as Jonathan Pollard, achieved considerable success and built large mill complexes of their own in Ancoats (Pl 18).

The number of firms that took advantage of the room-and-power system is unknown, although evidence from rate books has shown that there were up to 30 mills in Manchester containing more than one firm in *c* 1815 (Lloyd-Jones and Le Roux 1980, 77). Indeed, it is probable that the majority of Manchester's cotton firms were accommodated in room-and-power mills before 1820, despite the expensive rates that were charged (Lloyd-Jones and Lewis 1988, 33). Two notable room-and-power mills that were built in Ancoats during the 1820s were Beehive Mill and Brownsfield Mill (Pl 19). Both of these large multi-storey factories incorporated several advanced construction details, some of which may have permitted the higher floor loadings that would have been an advantage in a room-and-power mill (Williams with Farnie 1992, 62).

Plate 19: Brownsfield Mill, a 'room-and-power' factory built adjacent to the Rochdale Canal in c *1825*

Plate 18: Jonathan Pollard's Mill and James Kennedy's Mill on Great Ancoats Street, adjacent to the Ashton Canal, from an engraving by Thomas Slack in c *1815*

The Impact of Steam Power

Problems of Power

The provision of sufficient power was a prerequisite for the successful application of the new spinning machines of the late eighteenth century. The great increase in the number of spindles to each machine meant that it became difficult, if not impossible, for the spinner to supply the power whilst performing the delicate operations needed to spin fine yarn. Similarly, the successful development of the spinning mule, even whilst it was mainly hand-operated, was hampered by a shortage of power. The problem was evident to the spinners, who foresaw the consequence of not being able to by-pass this bottleneck: 'Had it not been for this new accession of [steam] power and scientific mechanism, the cotton trade would have been stunted in its growth and compared with its present state must have become an object only of minor importance in a national point of view' (Kennedy 1819, 117). Numerous solutions to this problem were experimented with before the steam engine predominated.

Initial solutions focused upon human and animal power, which provided a useful and successful bridge between the unmechanised workshop and the full-scale powered factory. Robert Owen, for instance, used a bulky man to power the three machines he was using (Owen 1857, 33-4), whilst some manufacturers harnessed oxen and horses. This is reflected in numerous adverts in the *Manchester Mercury*, which described horse gearings available on the market (*eg* 29 January 1788; 10 February 1793). Indeed, the spinning frames in Richard Arkwright's first factory in Nottingham were driven by horse power, and that used by John Travis on Deansgate before 1782 (and possibly the first use of Arkwright's water-frame in Manchester) was worked by a horse from a yard at the rear of the building (Aspin 2003, 160). An unusual application was the use of wind power. A windmill stood on the edge of St. Peter's Field (what is today Windmill Street), which was used to grind logwood for the textile dyeing industry. This windmill was offered for sale in the *Manchester Mercury* on 7 April 1795, the advert suggesting that it could be used for grinding corn or driving textile machinery. These modes of operation all proved to be too expensive, however, and incapable of supplying the power demanded by the larger textile mills (Hills 1989, 42).

Water Power

The successful application of a waterwheel to turn spinning machinery had been achieved in Arkwright's factory at Cromford, Derbyshire, in 1771. The waterwheel technology of the eighteenth century, however, was better adapted to relatively small rivers and streams flowing swiftly, and appropriate sites were often to be found in relatively narrow valleys in the countryside. By the nineteenth century, Cheesden Brook to the north of Rochdale, for instance, had mills set one above another at a distance of only about 50 m apart (Ashmore 1969, 41-2). The major watercourses in Manchester, though, were broad and sluggish, resulting in a serious lack of appropriate sites for water-powered factories. Nevertheless, a rapid survey of Arkwright-type mills in Britain, undertaken by the lobbyist Patrick Colquhoun in 1788, recorded four such factories in Manchester and Salford (Chapman 1981), and there is considerable evidence for several others. Colquhoun completed his survey as part of his efforts to persuade Parliament to restrict the import of cheap cotton goods by the East India Company, although he seems to have only noted the larger mills, and his list is considered to be incomplete (Aspin 2003, 4).

The largest cotton factory in Manchester noted by Colquhoun was that established by Richard Arkwright on Shude Hill in 1780-2, described as the first purpose-built cotton-spinning mill in the town (Williams with Farnie 1992, 50). The other mills recorded in Colquhoun's census included Thackeray and Whitehead's Garratt Mill on the river Medlock (Fig 3), and Bank Mill, which was built in 1782 on the river Irwell immediately below the Crescent at Salford. Bank Mill was 'entirely consumed' by fire in 1813, which caused estimated damage of £30,000 (*Manchester Mercury*, 31 October 1813), although vestiges of a weir and water chamber still survive (Pl 20). Similarly, a weir on a bend of the river Irk close to its confluence with the river Irwell is the remnant of a mill at Dangerous Corner, Long Millgate. This was established in 1783, when William Edge added a three-storey factory to a corn mill and installed a 'good breast bucket wheel', which drove 15 carding engines and 'complete machinery for 1500 spindles' to spin twist (Aspin 2003, 159-60).

Plate 20: The remains of Bank Mill on the river Irwell, viewed from Salford Crescent

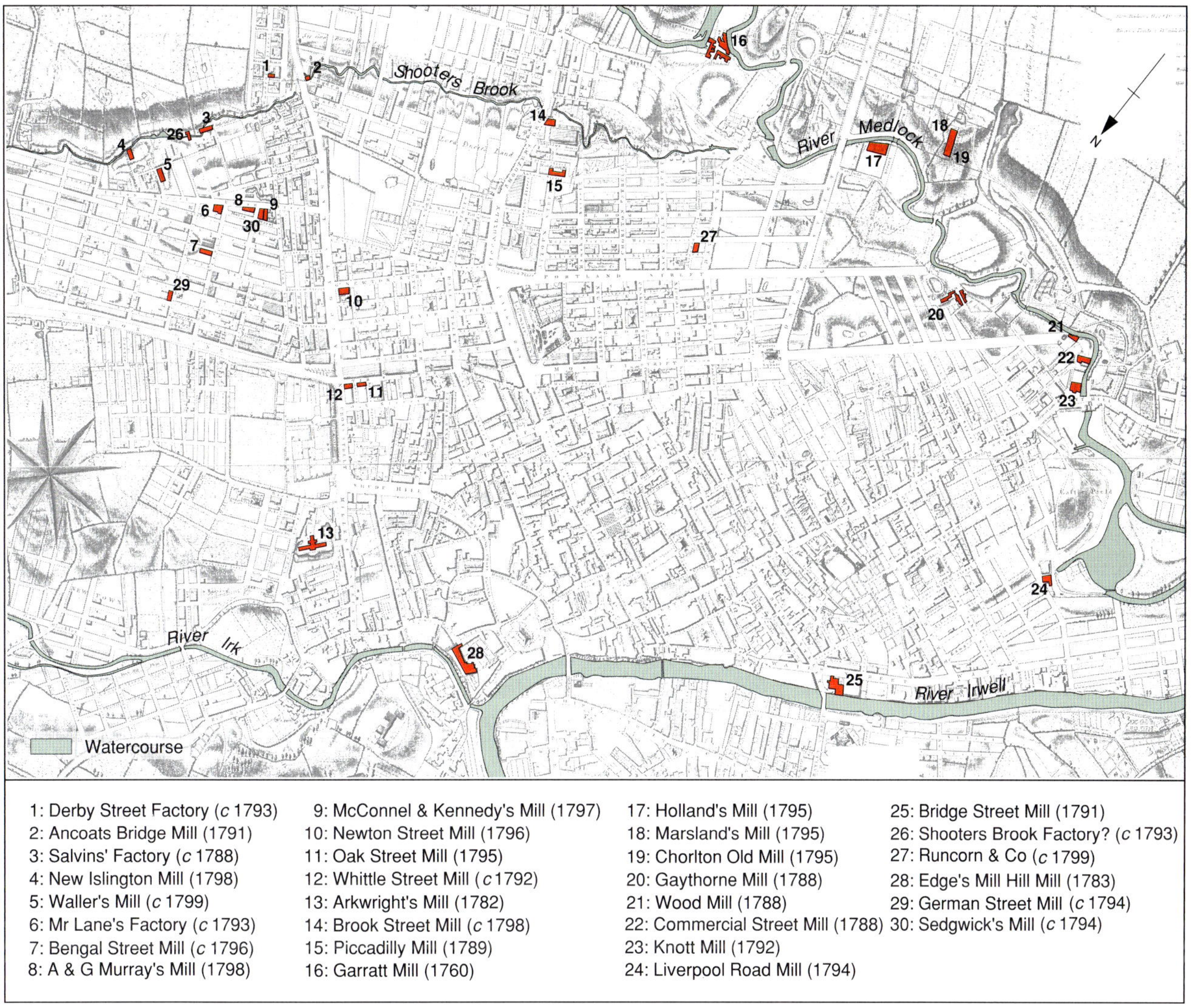

Figure 3: Distribution of late eighteenth-century mills in Manchester, superimposed upon Laurent's map of 1793

Steam Power

Given the limitations of water power in the context of Manchester, it is unsurprising that the basis of the town's industrialisation during the late eighteenth and early nineteenth centuries was steam power. Indeed, as Baines noted, 'without the steam engine Manchester and Glasgow would not have approached to their present greatness' (1835, 227). The emergence of steam as a viable source of power stemmed from an invention patented by Thomas Savery in 1698. This was designed as an apparatus for pumping water 'by the impellent force of fire', and comprised a pair of vessels into which steam was admitted alternately (Farey 1827, 99). By condensing the steam in each vessel in turn, a partial vacuum was created so that atmospheric pressure forced water into first one and then the other. The first genuine steam engine, however, may be attributed to Thomas Newcomen, who erected an engine for pumping water at Dudley Castle in Staffordshire in 1712 (Buchanan and Watkins 1976, 8-10). Newcomen's engine was the 'atmospheric' type, in which the condensation of steam created a partial vacuum in a cylinder, so that the pressure of the atmosphere forced the piston down. The application of Newcomen's engine to turn a crank and flywheel was achieved in *c* 1780, and the following ten years saw such engines being introduced into textile mills; James Watt's son noted one driving the machinery of a calenderer on Water Street in Manchester in 1791, but 'did not think much of the machine' (Farey 1827, 658).

The earliest application of steam power in Manchester's textile industry, however, relied upon a pumping engine that was used to furnish a waterwheel with a constant and regular supply of water. Perhaps the best-known of these was the improved Savery engine that was developed by Joshua Wrigley, a Manchester-based engineer described by a contemporary as a 'common pump-maker' (Aikin 1795, 174). There is evidence for several types of engine that were made by Wrigley, but his improved Savery Engine that was designed 'to impel the machinery of some of the earliest manufactories and cotton mills' in Lancashire came in for specific praise (Farey 1827, 122). The Darbys of Coalbrookdale, Shropshire, had used a pumping engine to turn the water-powered bellows in their blast furnace during the 1740s (Tann 1970, 75), and Richard Arkwright is thought to have applied this technology to his mill at Wirksworth, Derbyshire, in *c* 1780, representing its earliest use in the textile industry (Menuge 2001, 52). This system represented an important stage in the transition from water-powered mills to those driven entirely by steam, and it seems that significant technological advances were made in Manchester. There were over 100 steam engines known to have been at work within a mile of the town centre in the last two decades of the eighteenth century, and Wrigley is likely to have been responsible for a proportion of these. He was certainly responsible for supplying two small engines to the firm of Thackeray and Whitehead at Garratt Mill in 1784, and during a visit to Manchester in March 1791, James Watt junior reported to his father that Wrigley had 'orders for 13 engines for this town and neighbourhood, all of them intended for working cotton machinery of one kind or other' (Musson and Robinson 1969, 403).

The most important advances in steam-engine design were introduced by James Watt who, in partnership with Matthew Boulton, transformed the machinery from a 'rough but robust piece of hardware ... into an efficient product of skilled engineering' (Buchanan and Watkins 1976, 14). Watt's major contributions to the field were the separate condenser, patented in 1769, which negated the massive heat loss incurred by successively heating and cooling the steam cylinder, and the development of his double-acting engine in 1783 that increased the power output. The application of Watt's engine to the cotton-spinning machines, however, awaited his introduction of parallel motion (patented in 1784), and the centrifugal governor of 1787. These innovations allowed the smooth and even delivery of power essential for successful spinning.

Boulton and Watt rapidly became recognised as the makers of the best rotative engine on the market (*op cit*, 152), although the adoption of their patent engine to the cotton industry was slow, especially in Manchester. Some of the reasons for this may well have been that the Boulton and Watt engine was regarded as expensive to buy, slow to be supplied, and after a time the premiums that had to be paid on the patents became irksome. The overriding factor in Manchester, however, was perhaps the competition from local engine builders. In particular, many of the engines active in Manchester during the 1790s were produced by the Salford-based firm of Bateman and Sherratt, which built single-cylinder atmospheric models (Pl 21) and a twin-cylinder version that was fitted with a separate condenser (*Ch 4, p 42*), thereby infringing Watt's patent. In 1796, Boulton and Watt took legal action against the pirating of their design, after which Bateman and Sherratt ceased building engines with separate condensers (Dickinson and Jenkins 1989, 320. Another firm was Francis Thompson of Derby, who supplied rotary engines to the large family firm of Houldsworth for their cotton mill on Lever Street in Manchester, and James Kennedy's Mill on Ancoats Lane in 1793 (Hills 1970, 148).

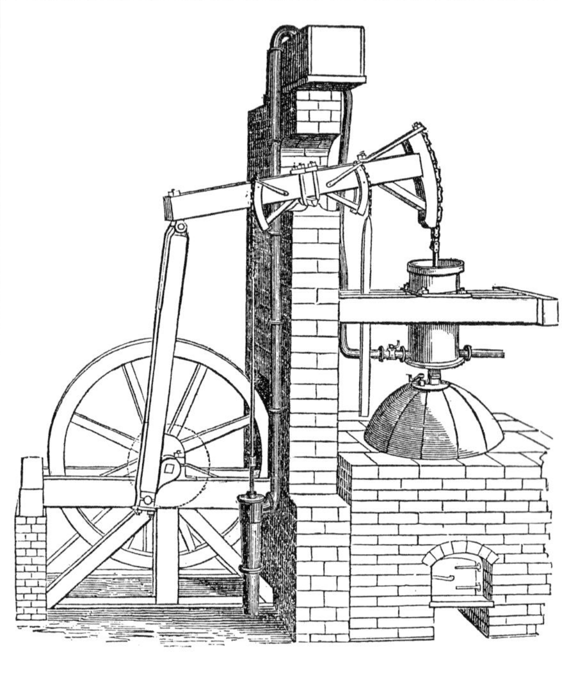

Plate 21: The self-acting atmospheric rotative engine of the type built by Bateman and Sherratt (reproduced from Farey 1827)

The success of Boulton and Watt in breaking into the supply of engines to the Manchester manufacturers came when Peter Drinkwater purchased an 8 hp machine for his Piccadilly Mill in 1789 (Ashmore 1969, 52). Although it was almost 20 years after Boulton and Watt's first patent, their engine was taken up with alacrity; by 1799, some 44 Boulton and Watt engines had been purchased by Manchester manufacturers, one or two of these being replacements for earlier engines. Indeed, a search of the Boulton and Watt engine book, which lists all those that bought engines from the company, is like a roll call of the Manchester spinners. Whilst the expiry of their patent in 1800 cleared the way for improvements to the steam engine by other firms, Boulton and Watt retained a large share of the market for several decades (Buchanan and Watkins 1976, 23). They also diversified into supplying gas lighting, heating, and fire-fighting systems to textile mills.

Conclusion

Manchester was not the birthplace of the Industrial Revolution, but where this process attained its 'age of majority'. The town's rise to the centre of the global cotton industry had been preceded by centuries of more gradual development in other parts of the country, when Manchester's textile trade was not even large on a national scale. Between 1780 and 1800, Manchester and other towns in the wider region, such as Stockport, Blackburn, and Preston, experienced an unprecedented growth of industrial activity, based on the coming together of steam-powered factories and urbanism. The individual mills in these towns were not necessarily any larger than their contemporaries in the rural 'factory colonies', but were in greater numbers with easy access to ancillary infrastructure and an expanding work force. The urbanisation of the factory system created a new type of industrial townscape, in which Manchester may be seen as the archetypal example (McNeil 2002, 42-3). The dense concentration of steam-powered mills, many served by a network of canals that penetrated throughout the town, and a plethora of smaller factories/ workshops and warehouses, had given Manchester a distinctive industrial townscape during the early nineteenth century, laying its claim to be the first true industrial city.

The basis of this new phase of industrial history was cotton, which led 'a host of private entrepreneurs into revolution' (Hobsbawm 1962, 56). As the mercantile and distribution centre for cotton goods, it is unsurprising that by the late eighteenth century Manchester was attracting from across the nation entrepreneurs keen to invest in the manufacturing side of the industry, eager to take advantage of the technological development of machinery and its application to a new type of factory. The opportunities presented were probably the driving factors for the wealth of entrepreneurial and engineering talent that was attracted to the town, including the Murray brothers, James McConnel and John Kennedy, and William Fairbairn.

Figure 4: Extract of Laurent's Map of Manchester and Salford, *published in 1793, showing the boundary of Ancoats*

3

ANCOATS: THE DEVELOPMENT OF A NEW INDUSTRIAL TOWNSCAPE

Ian Miller

Introduction

From the late eighteenth century, Ancoats expanded rapidly to become one of the most intensely developed industrial townscapes in the world, and the manufacturing heart of Manchester: 'Ancoats is to Manchester what Manchester is to London' (*Manchester Chronicle* 1849). The manufacturing prowess of the area was derived primarily from a large number of closely packed steam-powered textile mills, which were the manifestation of the urbanised factory system. These huge multi-storey factories were a marvel of the late Georgian era, acting not only as a magnet for a burgeoning workforce of immigrants from the districts surrounding Manchester and beyond, but also featured on the itineraries of visitors to England from Europe (*Ch 5, pp 79-80*). The mills were served by a network of local canals, which proved to be an important catalyst in attracting large-scale industry to Ancoats, and contributed a distinctive element to the townscape. Industries ancillary to the textile trades were also established, providing for a diverse local economy that became one of the hallmarks of the area. Another key feature of this new industrial townscape was the large tracts of terraced housing, which were intended solely for the occupation of the urban working class (Roberts 1993, 15).

Ancoats covers an area of some 404 acres (163 ha) on the north-eastern fringe of Manchester city centre. It seemingly had no precise boundaries until 1792, when an administrative infrastructure created by the new Police Commissioners partitioned the town into 14 divisions, of which Ancoats was District 1, or New Cross Ward (Kidd and Wyke 1993, 3). The boundaries were designated as Newton Lane (Oldham Road) and the river Medlock to the north and south respectively, with Ancoats Lane (Great Ancoats Street) marking the western limit (Fig 4). The irregular eastern boundary with the adjacent township of Newton Heath was followed roughly by Butler Lane, which was little more than a farm track until the nineteenth century.

Plate 22: Ancoats Hall in the late eighteenth century (reproduced from Aikin 1795)

Origins

The origin of the name Ancoats is uncertain, although it is likely to have derived from the Old English *ana cots*, which may be translated as 'lonely cottage' (Cooper 2002, 13). It was an area of open land throughout the medieval period, considered by Swindells (1908, 19-26) to have been 'an almost idyllic rural backwater', and was recorded in a survey of 1320 as having formed one of eight hamlets within the township of Manchester (Harland 1861). It is likely that settlement comprised a few cottages and farmhouses along Ancoats Lane, Newton Lane, and Butler Lane, although the most notable building in the area by the end of the medieval period was undoubtedly the timber-framed Ancoats Hall (Pl 22), which overlooked the river Medlock (Fig 4). It is uncertain when the hall was built, although it is thought to have been sold by the De la Warr family to Sir Edward Trafford during the reign of Henry VIII (1509-47), and then passed to the Byroms of Clayton (Darbyshire 1887, 118). In 1596, the Byroms sold the hall to Oswald Mosley, the then Lord of the Manor, the Mosleys then holding it as one of their family seats until the early nineteenth century.

The rural character of Ancoats during the mid-eighteenth century is captured in an engraving of

Newton Lane, dated to 1734 (Swindells 1906, 20-1), which shows the only buildings to have comprised an alehouse and a detached cottage (Pl 23). Newton Lane is depicted as a broad and busy road, although Middleton considered it to have been 'an ill-kept and muddy lane' until improvements in 1772, which laid the foundations for a 'noble thoroughfare' (Middleton 1920, 6). It is perhaps no coincidence that the process of the rapid transformation of Ancoats to an urban environment began within the next three years.

Plate 23: View along Newton Lane (now Oldham Road) from its junction with Ancoats Lane in 1734

Development and Early Growth

In 1775, members of the Cheshire gentry, George and Henry Legh of High Legh, sold land between Newton Lane and Ancoats Lane to Thomas Bound, representing an initial stage in the urbanisation of the area (Swindells 1908, 203). Early trade directories for Manchester list Thomas Bound as a 'bricklayer' (*eg* Raffald 1781, 12), although in this instance he is perhaps more appropriately described as a property developer, as some of the land he purchased was passed to others to develop. Property speculation typified the process of development in Ancoats, the land often being subject to a 'perpetual' rent with a covenant to build. This encouraged middlemen to build promptly, or sell the land on with a doubled chief rent for others to develop (Roberts 1993, 15-6). Residential development evidently occurred fairly rapidly, and new dwellings built along Newton Lane and Ancoats Lane were advertised for sale in the *Manchester Mercury* by the early 1780s (Pl 24).

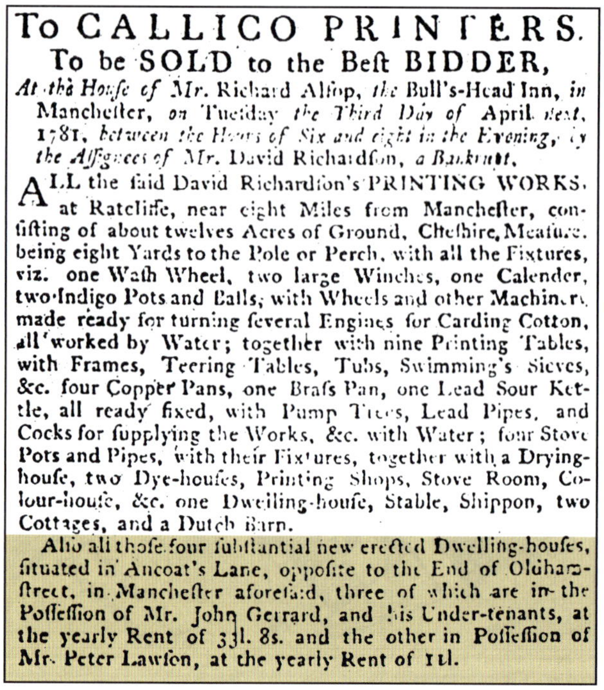

To CALLICO PRINTERS.

To be SOLD to the Beſt BIDDER,

At the House of Mr. Richard Alſop, *the* Bull's-Head Inn, *in* Mancheſter, *on* Tueſday *the Third Day of* April *next*, 1781, *between the Hours of Six and eight in the Evening, by the Aſſignees of* Mr. David Richardſon, *a Bankrupt*.

ALL the ſaid David Richardſon's PRINTING WORKS, at Ratcliffe, near eight Miles from Mancheſter, conſiſting of about twelves Acres of Ground, Cheſhire Meaſure, being eight Yards to the Pole or Perch, with all the Fixtures, viz. one Waſh Wheel, two large Winches, one Calender, two Indigo Pots and Balls, with Wheels and other Machinery made ready for turning ſeveral Engines for Carding Cotton, all worked by Water; together with nine Printing Tables, with Frames, Teering Tables, Tubs, Swimming's Sieves, &c. four Copper Pans, one Braſs Pan, one Lead Sour Kettle, all ready fixed, with Pump Trees, Lead Pipes, and Cocks for ſupplying the Works, &c. with Water; four Stove Pots and Pipes, with their Fixtures, together with a Drying-houſe, two Dye-houſes, Printing Shops, Stove Room, Colour-houſe, &c. one Dwelling-houſe, Stable, Shippon, two Cottages, and a Dutch Barn.

Alſo all thoſe four ſubſtantial new erected Dwelling-houſes, ſituated in Ancoat's Lane, oppoſite to the End of Oldham-ſtreet, in Mancheſter aforeſaid, three of which are in the Poſſeſſion of Mr. John Gerrard, and his Under-tenants, at the yearly Rent of 33l. 8s. and the other in Poſſeſſion of Mr. Peter Lawſon, at the yearly Rent of 11l.

Plate 24: Advertisement for the auction of workers' housing in the Manchester Mercury, *13 March 1781*

The sale of the Legh Estate prompted the Trustees of the Manchester Grammar School to sell part of the school's endowment in 1786, which included plots of land along Ancoats Lane to the south of Shooters Brook. The extent of development by the early 1790s is depicted on the earliest detailed maps of the area, namely those published by Charles Laurent in 1793 and William Green in 1794, which show that Ancoats Lane and Newton Lane formed an initial focus for development (Fig 4). As with other parts of Manchester that had been developed during the 1770s, such as the Aytoun Estate and the Lever Estate to the west of Ancoats, the sale of land involved surveying and laying out streets in a grid-iron pattern (Chalklin 1974, 90-5). In contrast to these other areas of Manchester, however, covenants attached to the sale of land in Ancoats typically lacked clauses regulating nuisances, suggesting that mixed industrial and residential development was anticipated (Roberts 1993, 16). Moreover, the regular arrangement of streets provides a false impression of considered town planning, whereas development was actually controlled by landowners and speculators rather than a regulatory body, and the layout reflected the pattern of sales and convenience of plot division.

Early Manufacturing

Notwithstanding Robert Waldegrave's illicit press in a cottage on Newton Lane that was seized in 1588 for printing Puritan tracts (Swindells 1908, 194-7), one of the earliest manufactories in Ancoats was David Holt's water-powered cotton factory at Beswick Bridge on the river Medlock. Established in 1785, it expanded into the industrial colony of Holt Town during the early 1790s (Aspin 2003). The site of this mill is marked on the first county map to show Ancoats, William Yates' survey of Lancashire, published in 1786 (Fig 5). The other two water-powered factories shown by Yates to have been on the Medlock included Garratt Mill, which was built in 1760 as a silk mill and converted to cotton spinning in 1783 (*ibid*), and James and William Meredith's pin and paper mill that lay close to Ancoats Hall. The lack of other suitable sites on the river led new manufacturers in Ancoats to Shooters Brook, a tributary of the Medlock, as a source of power to drive their waterwheels.

Once a 'meandering clear stream teeming with fish and home to numerous wild fowl', Shooters Brook rises in Newton Heath and flows south-westwards through Miles Platting and Ancoats to join the Medlock near Charles Street (Ashworth 1987, 22). The modern course of Shooters Brook cannot be followed from the surface, as it flows almost entirely through deeply buried culverts, although during the late eighteenth century its sinuous course provided a focus for several water-powered textile mills and other small manufactories, including an iron works and a pottery (Fig 6). Salvins' Factory is perhaps the best known of these mills (*Ch 4, p 34*), although others had been built by the 1790s, including Shooters Brook Mill and Ancoats Lane Mill (Aspin 2003, 160). In broad terms, however, there was little that could be considered remarkable about these mills, and they were probably considerably smaller than other water-powered factories in the wider region, perhaps explaining their omission from Colquhoun's survey of mills in 1788 (*Ch 2, p 20*). What is remarkable, however, is that mill owners exploited this small rivulet, which probably reflects the favourable commercial influence of Manchester and its expanding role as the centre of the region's cotton industry. Unsurprisingly, however, Shooters Brook failed to provide a regular and constant source of power for these water-driven mills, leading their occupants to experiment in earnest with steam power (*Ch 2, pp 21-2*).

Figure 5: Water-powered mills on the Medlock shown on Yates' map of Lancashire (1786)

The Expansion of Textile-Manufacturing

The application of steam power to the process of cotton spinning, facilitated by changes in industrial technology and fuelled by the national demand for cotton, resulted in the phenomenal growth of Ancoats during the early nineteenth century. The introduction of the canal system, and specifically the Ashton and Rochdale Canals, proved to be an important catalyst for the expansion of Ancoats, encouraging ribbon development of industrial works along their banks, and particularly of multi-storey cotton mills. The canals offered significant benefits of transportation, not least bulk deliveries of coal, but also provided a ready supply of water vital to the operation of the steam engines that powered the industrial supremacy of Manchester. Crucially, numerous short canal arms or branches extended into Ancoats, encouraging industrial development away from the main lines of the canals. These incorporated many wharves for the distribution of coal and timber, and provided a readily available supply of water that could serve the new steam-powered mills. This factor dispensed with the requirement for large reservoirs or riverside sites demanded by other factories of the period, and allowed the new mills to be built closely together, which became a key characteristic of Ancoats.

Despite not being completed through Ancoats until 1804, some eight years after the Ashton Canal was opened, it was the Rochdale Canal that provided an initial focus for the development of the steam-powered mills. This new breed of factory outstripped the region's water-powered mills in terms of size and output. Amongst the first were those built by McConnel & Kennedy and A & G Murray on the northern side of the Rochdale Canal during the late 1790s (*Ch 5, p 64*), although these developed rapidly into mill complexes of an exceptional scale for their date. The development of textile mills along the Ancoats corridor of the Ashton Canal formed a second wave of mills, and an important group of factories, including the impressive Brunswick Mill, flanked the canal by the 1840s (*Ch 8, p 153*).

Other Industries

Whilst the multi-storey cotton mill dominated the early nineteenth-century streetscape in Ancoats, ancillary trades were of equal importance to the local economy. Scholes' trade directory for 1794, for example, lists no less than 49 weavers on Newton Lane, many presumably operating hand looms in domestic workshops, whilst references to bleaching

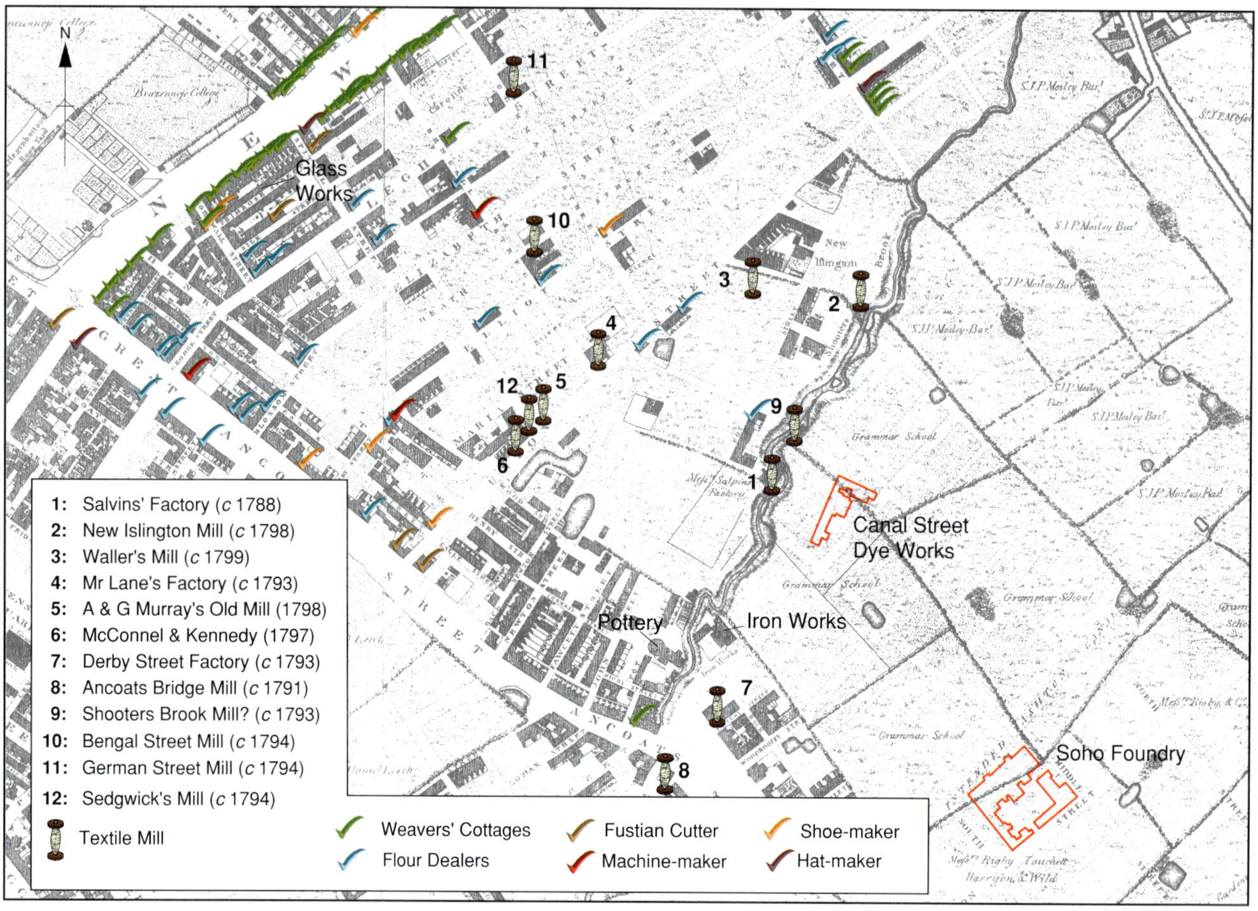

Figure 6: Extract from William Green's Map of Manchester and Salford, *published in 1794, showing the position of the eighteenth-century textile mills, and the indicative location of other trades*

crofts appear in eighteenth-century editions of the *Manchester Mercury*. An advertisement on 21 March 1786, for instance, offered a reward for information concerning the theft of 'half a piece of velveret, dyed black, but not dried' from a croft in Ancoats belonging to John and James Entwistle. By the 1790s, the Entwistles had established a large dye works on the banks of the river Medlock. The layout of their site reflected the industrialisation of textile finishing during this period, with a switch from open-air bleaching crofts to enclosed works that contained several long one- or two-storey buildings (Nevell *et al* 2003, 92-3). The adoption of this layout is also exemplified by the early nineteenth-century Canal Street dye works (Fig 6) which, notably, was built alongside a branch of the Ashton Canal, representing a departure from the usual requirement for a riverside location (Ashmore 1969, 58-60).

Another important industry that developed as a direct result of the textile trade was engineering, and Manchester played a leading role in the development of machine-tool production and precision engineering (*op cit*, 83). It is perhaps no coincidence that some of the largest cotton-spinning firms in Ancoats, including A & G Murray, commenced business as machine-makers (*Ch 5, p 62*). The largest dedicated engineering firm, however, was Peel, Williams & Co, which was established during the late eighteenth century, and purchased the Soho Foundry, situated alongside the Ashton Canal on Pollard Street in *c* 1810 (Pl 25). Components for steam engines and boilers featured amongst the range of goods that the firm produced, but it eventually specialised in the manufacture of gear wheels (Musson 1960, 8-12). Another influential nineteenth-century engineer in Ancoats was William Fairbairn, who set up business with James Lillie and '...hired a miserable shed for about twelve shillings a week' (Pole 1877, 112). After an initial and highly successful contract with A & G Murray in 1817 (*Ch 5, p 77*), Fairbairn supplied all of the line shafting to McConnel & Kennedy's Sedgwick Mill (*Ch 4, p 53*). Shortly after completing this contract, Fairbairn moved to new premises on Canal Street in Ancoats, where his business expanded greatly to become one of the leading engineering concerns in the country (Smiles 1876).

An early example of industrial diversification in Ancoats is provided by Imison and King's 'glass house' on Newton Lane, which was established in 1785 'for the manufacturing of all sorts of glasswares'

Plate 25: The Soho Foundry of Peel, Williams & Co from an engraving by Thomas Slack (1814), indicating the range of goods manufactured and the close relationship with the canal

(*Manchester Mercury*, 1 September 1785). Whilst this works was short-lived, it nevertheless represented the first of what was to become by the late nineteenth century the densest concentration of glass works in Manchester. The most important of these included the works of Molineaux Webb & Co and Percival, Vickers & Co (Pl 26), which initially manufactured a range of high-quality tableware vessels for national and international markets (Miller 2007). These firms also pioneered the adoption of press-moulding techniques of production in the region, which were pivotal to Manchester becoming a national centre for this imitation of cut glass. Despite its former regional significance, however, the only surviving building that had been connected with this industry in Ancoats is the warehouse and office block for the Percival, Vickers & Co Ltd works on Jersey Street (Pl 27).

Plate 27: Refurbished warehouse and office block for the Percival, Vickers & Co Ltd glass works on Jersey Street

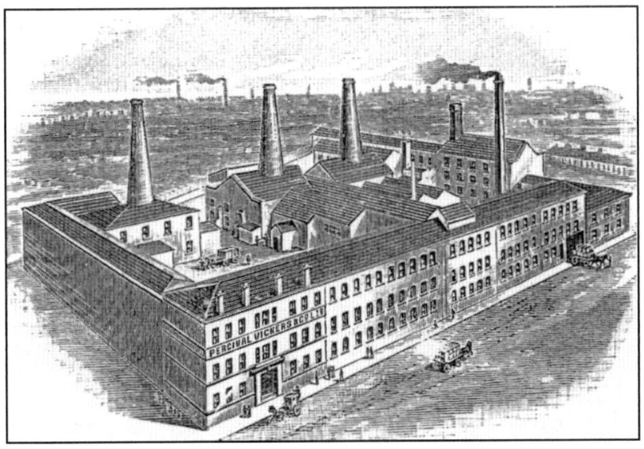

Plate 26: Engraving of the Percival, Vickers & Co Ltd glass works on Jersey Street (reproduced from the Pottery Gazette and Glass Trade Review *1903)*

A plethora of service industries was also established, not least of which included the building trades that encompassed brick-making, glazing, joining, plumbing, and a lime works near Ancoats Hall that produced the essential ingredient of mortar for the new buildings. Horses provided the main means of local transport, and required the availability of tradesmen such as farriers, blacksmiths, and coach-makers. Two coal mines were situated on the northern fringe of Ancoats, including the large Bradford Colliery. There were also numerous small workshops, many being involved in the making of shoes, hats, textile machinery, and furniture (*eg* Scholes 1794). This diverse manufacturing base helped to ensure that Ancoats remained an important industrial area when the influence of cotton spinning waned during the second half of the nineteenth century.

Housing the New Working Class

Trade directories for the late eighteenth century list several 'gentlemen' living in Ancoats (*eg* Scholes 1794), and there were some attempts at the provision of housing for the more affluent classes, although these appear to have been short-lived (Kidd and Wyke 1993, 8); an example is provided by the Crescent in Ancoats, where George Murray had resided briefly before purchasing Ancoats Hall (*Ch 5, p 74*). During the nineteenth century, however, pressures of rapidly increasing population in the town in general, and especially in Ancoats, led to a growth of the housing stock; in 1815, the Ancoats rating district contained not only the greatest concentration of cotton factories in Manchester, but also the largest number of households (Lloyd-Jones and Lewis 1988, 37). The earliest workers' houses were erected around the new factories with little legislative control, culminating in the creation of a residential district intended for occupation solely by the urban working class (Roberts 1993, 15). In contrast to the 'factory colonies' of the eighteenth century, very few dwellings were the property of factory owners, who only provided accommodation for a small number of key employees.

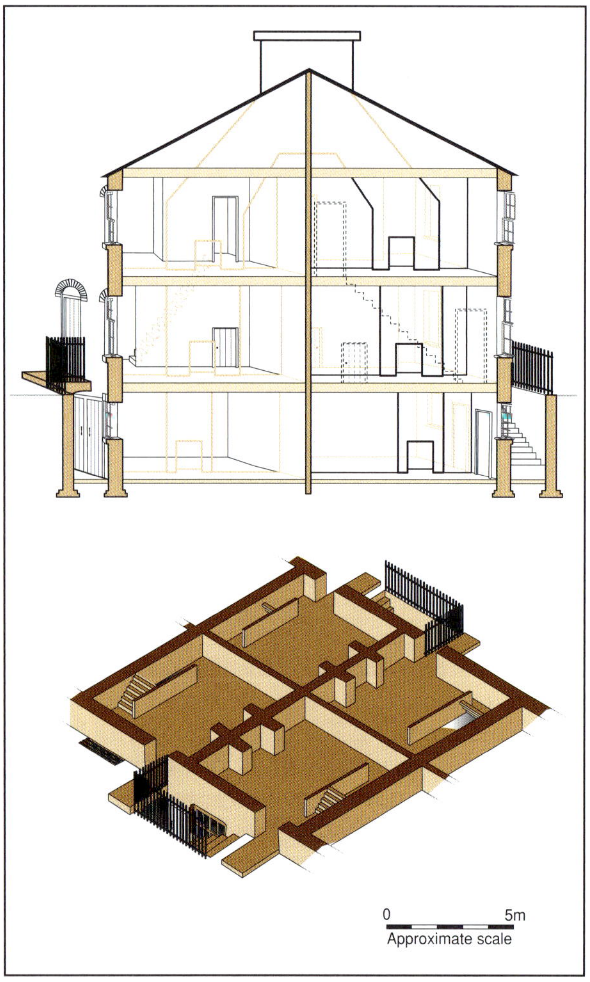

Figure 7: Section through typical back-to-back housing

Plate 28: Court dwellings on Back Boslam Street, Ancoats, 1902 (reproduced courtesy of Manchester Archives and Local Studies)

The standard pattern of speculative building in Ancoats during the early nineteenth century was to sub-divide properties into long blocks, measuring some 250 ft (76 m) long by 60-90 ft (18-27 m) wide (Lloyd-Jones and Lewis 1993, 33). Additional access to the interior was provided by the construction of courts and alleys, and rows of houses were built back-to-back so that as many as four houses could be built within the width of a block. This type of housing shared a party wall to the rear, and therefore had no back yard (Fig 7). The open spaces available were filled with extra houses, creating the narrow courtyards and alleyways that epitomised the mid-nineteenth-century residential areas (Pl 28). These houses had a characteristic layout; one door, together with any windows in the front wall, provided the only means of ventilation (Pl 29). The size of back-to-backs appears to have varied slightly; those built on Portugal Street in 1791, for instance, measured 14½ x 11 ft (4.42 x 3.35 m), with early nineteenth-century dwellings on Silk Street containing rooms 14¾ x 14 ft (4.60 x 4.27 m), and a terraced row of mid-nineteenth-century one-up one-downs on Back Mill Street had 12 ft-square (3.66 m^2) rooms (Gausden 1988). Whilst most of the housing stock in Ancoats probably comprised two-storey dwellings, some had additional storeys that could be used for workshop space; census returns and parish records identify numerous domestic textile workers operating

Plate 29: Workers' dwelling on Southern Street in Manchester (reproduced form the Illustrated London News *1862). The atypical starkness of the room reflects the poverty caused by the Cotton Famine during the early 1860s*

from attic workshops in Ancoats during the early nineteenth century (*eg* MLSU M9/40/2/79).

Between 1807 and 1815, the rateable value of housing in the area rose rapidly, with a corresponding increase in rents. This was one of the factors in the increased occupation of cellars during the early nineteenth century (Pl 30). These were usually let separately, so that several families shared the same house, and represented the worst of the housing stock (Lloyd-Jones and Lewis 1993, 34).

A survey by the Manchester Board of Health in 1831, motivated by the fear of cholera, showed that 55.4% of houses in Ancoats were without private plumbing, 15.1% were in need of major repair, and 56.1% of all streets in the district were not cleaned and contained heaps of refuse and worse (*ibid*). This situation in Ancoats was noted by Frederick Engels in 1844, who considered that 'no more injurious and demoralising method of housing the workers has yet been discovered' (Engels 1973, 89). A major step forward in housing improvement was provided by the Manchester Police Act of 1844, whereby all new houses were to be furnished with a privy, and all existing houses were to have one installed. A striking effect of this Act was that it effectively outlawed

Plate 30: Access to a cellar dwelling in Manchester (reproduced from The Builder *1862)*

the building of back-to-back houses, and none were built in Manchester after this date (Roberts 1993, 22), although nationally new back-to-back building was not prohibited until 1909 (Read 1979, 51).

The Community

A correspondent for *The Times* in 1819 considered that Ancoats had been 'created by the success of the cotton trade, and swarms with inhabitants, who all share its vicissitudes. It is occupied chiefly by spinners, weavers, and Irish of the lowest description, and may be called the St Giles' of Manchester' (*The Times*, 24 August 1819). The implication that people of Irish extraction formed a significant element of the local community is corroborated by other contemporary documents. In 1833, for instance, Samuel Moore, the owner of a cotton-spinning factory on Mill Street in Ancoats, stated to a Parliamentary Commission that a large proportion of the children he employed were of Irish extraction, who lived in 'miserable abodes of the most loathsome kind' (PP (HC) 1834 [167] XX, AI), whilst the 1851 census returns show that nearly half of the men in Ancoats were born in Ireland (MLSU 107/2225). Indeed, by the 1850s, Irish migrants formed not only the greatest proportion of the population in Ancoats, but also the largest group of Irish in Manchester (Rushton 1977, 166). Conversely, the social composition of the population in Ancoats during its late eighteenth-century development is not clear, although it was evidently not an homogeneous community. A few of the migrants to Ancoats were the entrepreneurs eager to exploit business opportunities, such as the Murray brothers (*Ch 5*), although the majority almost certainly comprised migrants seeking employment in the new factories. Many are likely to have originated from rural districts surrounding Manchester, probably with experience of the cottage-based textile industry; parish records testify that numerous hand-loom weavers were labouring in domestic workshops in Ancoats prior to the introduction of power looms in the 1820s.

It is perhaps worth noting that, in the early factories, neither employers nor employees had experience of organising or working in large-scale undertakings. The employers had no industry-based regulations that could be consulted, and had to find their own ways of running factories. The dependence of groups of workers performing one operation upon other groups engaged in another process meant that work had to be done to time, which demanded factory discipline. This is likely to have been an alien concept to the first generation of factory workers, many of who were accustomed to the domestic system where they set their own hours of labour. The net result was a new social dimension to production with a shift from task to time discipline, the effects of which were one of the greatest changes wrought by the Industrial Revolution. One consequence of this 'social revolution' was that attendance in factories during the late eighteenth century was irregular, and some firms experienced an annual turnover of labour of 100% (Holland 1976, 158). In the context of Ancoats, this reflects the abundance of work that was available (Collier 1964, 15-6).

The family economy, especially when men's work was not available, was often dependent on children finding work. Women also provided essential income to the family, but they were paid less and therefore it was in the interest of the factory owners to employ them, although they were also to be found working in family businesses, where they existed. One of the other strategies for family survival was either to become lodgers, or to take in lodgers; it has been estimated that about a tenth of Ancoats' couples took in lodgers, who were just as likely to be male as female (Rushton 1993, 41). This flexible use of housing, linked to frequent moves, was an essential part of the economy of the poor, and a common part of living in Ancoats.

In some respects, Ancoats was a town in itself by the mid-nineteenth century, with a population far larger than towns such as Burnley, Bury, Blackburn, Rochdale, or Wigan (Kidd and Wyke 1993, 4). With this in mind, it is remarkable that Ancoats lacked amenities such as a town hall, hotels, a railway station, and a market or retail area, and the only public buildings comprised a few churches and a dispensary. The Ancoats Dispensary, founded in 1828, was twinned with the mainly middle-class suburb of Ardwick to create a dispensary district, and was encouraged to form its own dispensary committee, a charity funded by subscription (Pickstone 1985, 53).

Given the size of the population, it is also perhaps remarkable that the first religious building in Ancoats was not erected until 1821, when a Methodist chapel was established. Some ten years later, the Anglicans built St Andrews, and the Catholics established the large St Patrick's on Livesey Street in 1832 (Kidd and Wyke 1993, 9-10).

The Established Suburb

By 1851, Ancoats had been almost completely developed, forming a dense concentration of industrial and domestic buildings that housed 53,737 people (MLSU 107/2225), or some 18% of Manchester's population, yet there were no parks or trees, no salubrious squares, and, apart from Great Ancoats Street and Oldham Road, no broad thoroughfares. It was, however, the accepted centre of industry, and the principal manufacturing suburb to Manchester. In many respects, it represented the archetypal urban industrial area that provided a model for the nineteenth-century development of the factory system in other towns across the region, such as Oldham, Bury, Bolton, and Preston. As the manufacturing capacity of these other towns increased during the second half of the nineteenth century, however, the relative significance of Ancoats as a new type of industrial townscape waned.

4

THE DEVELOPMENT OF ANCOATS: ARCHAEOLOGICAL CASE STUDIES

Ian Miller, Chris Wild, and Steve Little

Introduction

The huge steam-powered mills of A & G Murray and McConnel & Kennedy provide the archetypal industrial image of Ancoats, and represent the successful application of double-acting steam engines to the processes of cotton spinning, which proved to be the real revolution in yarn production. These mills manifest the zenith of factory-construction at the beginning of the nineteenth century, and together form the core of an impressive group of surviving steam-powered Georgian cotton mills (GMAU 1990, 14). In contrast, there are no above-ground remains of the small group of mills that were established from the 1780s, which represented the first wave of textile factories in Manchester, including several that were established in Ancoats (*Ch 3, pp 26-7*; Fig 6). Aspects of the firms that occupied these mills may be gleaned from archive sources, and analysis of historical maps allows the chronological development of the buildings to be broadly established, although details of individual structures other than their outline shape are rarely provided. An examination of the physical remains through archaeological investigation is often the only means of elucidating the internal layout of individual buildings, which in turn can inform a detailed understanding of their function and chronology.

Opportunities to study the buried remains of eighteenth-century mills in Ancoats, together with other former buildings, have arisen through programmes of archaeological investigations undertaken in association with the regeneration

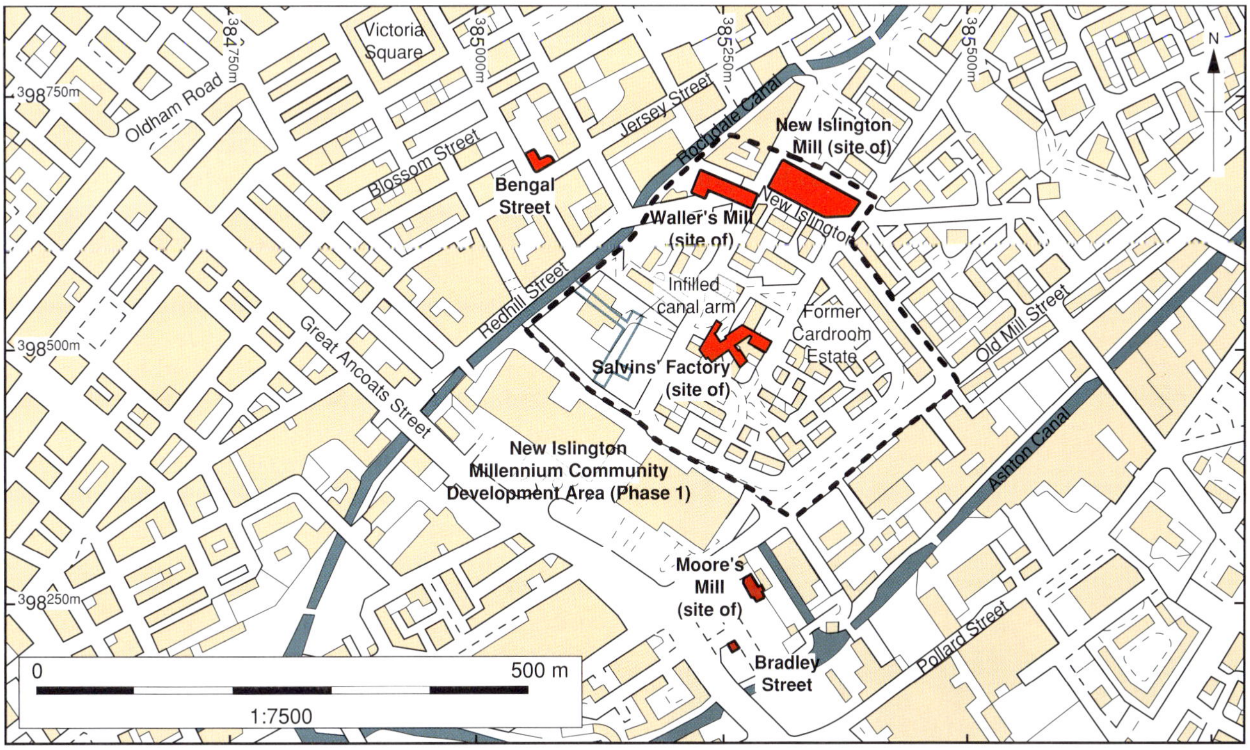

Figure 8: Location map showing the sites of Salvins' Factory, New Islington Mill, and Waller's Mill superimposed upon Ordnance Survey mapping of 1990

redevelopment of the area in the twenty-first century. In particular, a large area in the heart of Ancoats became the subject of a major regeneration programme with the inception of the New Islington Millennium Community Project in 2000, which involved the redevelopment of a 12.5 ha site between the Rochdale and Ashton canals (*Ch 1, p 5*). This development necessitated substantial earth-moving works and ground remediation, which was preceded by a programme of archaeological study that targeted a range of sites considered to be of potential interest, including Salvins' Factory, New Islington Mill, Waller's Mill, and an infilled canal arm (Fig 8). Initial archaeological evaluation of these sites revealed that extensive buried remains survived *in situ*, leading to more detailed archaeological excavation by OA North in 2004-5.

The redevelopment of McConnel & Kennedy's large mill complex into residential apartments was similarly accompanied by an archaeological investigation in 2003-6. This comprised a watching brief carried out by Steve Little, who monitored the stripping-out of the mills and earth-moving works in the courtyard area, to allow for a detailed record of the site to be generated (Little 2007).

Archaeological work elsewhere in Ancoats, again in advance of redevelopment, has allowed the remains of other former buildings to be examined in detail, including some of the earliest workers' housing in the area. The excavation of a block of housing, for instance, situated on the corner of Bengal Street and Jersey Street, and another block on Bradley Street (Fig 8), allowed details of construction and modifications to be elucidated for several types of dwellings.

The Early Textile Mills in Ancoats: Salvins' Factory

Salvins' Factory (centred at SJ 8526 9852) was established in the late 1780s, and was expanded in several episodes during the first half of the nineteenth century. It was completely remodelled after 1850 following the cessation of cotton spinning at the factory, facilitating its adaptation for reuse (Kennedy 1849). The surviving buildings were demolished during the 1970s to allow for the development of the Cardroom Estate, but buried remains of the former mill were identified during an archaeological evaluation. This led to a programme of more detailed excavation that examined an overall area equivalent to approximately 768 m^2 (OA North 2005b). The evidence produced by this fieldwork has been divided into five broad phases of activity, which are coupled with a summary of the available documentary material.

The Salvins

The Salvin family had owned estates in County Durham since the fifteenth century. Their association with the factory-based textile industry may be traced to 1785, when Anthony Salvin settled in Manchester, presumably attracted to the town by its reputation as a mercantile centre, and established a large fustian business in partnership with his two brothers, George and Henry (Aspin 2003, 39-40). Initially, they rented space for manufacturing at Hull Mill near Delph, situated some six miles to the east of Oldham, and occupied a warehouse and workshop on Fetter Lane, on the south-eastern fringe of Manchester (Fig 9); an insurance document, dated December 1785, refers to George Salvin having 'utensils, stock and goods' insured to the value of £600 at the latter premises (*ibid*). It seems that the Salvins also occupied a 'house, warehouse and a two-stalled stable' on Shude Hill, although their intention to quit these premises was notified in the *Manchester Mercury* on 1 August 1786.

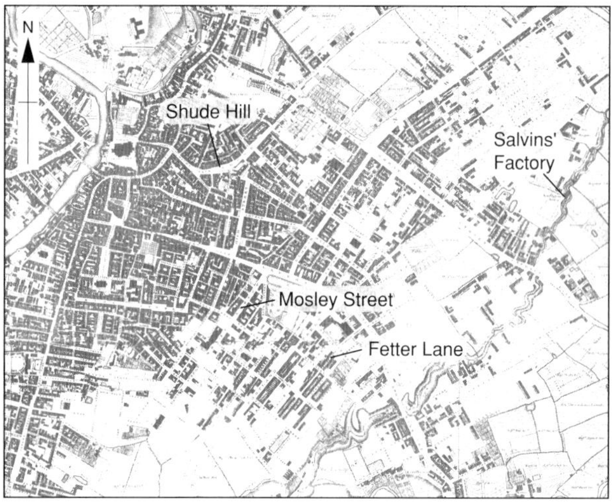

Figure 9: Extract from Green's map of 1794, showing the spatial distribution of Salvins' premises in Manchester

By the late 1780s, they had relocated the mercantile side of their business to Mosley Street, where the firm of A G & H Salvin is listed in trade directories as 'fustian manufacturers' (Holme 1788, 26; Raffald 1788, 75). This was a principal street in a 30-acre development by the Mosley family, who conveyed six acres to developers in 1788 under a covenant to spend £1000 'in building' (Chalklin 1974, 138). Once these buildings had been completed, it seems that the Salvins were amongst the first occupants of Mosley Street, which was described subsequently as being 'without exception, the most elegant street in Manchester' (Butterworth 1823, 258). An Ancoats address was given for their manufacturing premises at this date in an advertisement, which offered for sale at 'Messrs Salvins cotton factory…a good new horse wheel'. The horse wheel was 18 ft (5.49 m) in diameter, and was complete with a shaft, drums, and cog wheels, suitable for 'turning six carding engines' (*Manchester Mercury*, 29 January 1788). The same advert also sought several fustian weavers to work in the factory, and whilst the looms will have all been hand-powered, this nevertheless represents an early example in Manchester of the break from the cottage-based weaving industry, and the origination of the urban weaving factories that were to dominate the trade from the 1820s (Jewkes 1930). The exact address of the factory is not given, although John McConnel (1913, 28) considered it to have been on Shooters Brook.

Phase 1, Manufacturing with Water Power (*c* 1788 - *c* 1791)

The earliest maps of the area, namely those by Laurent (1793) and Green (1794), depict Salvins' Factory as a single rectangular block measuring some 72 x 36 ft (22 x 11 m). These maps clearly show that the north-eastern end of the mill straddled Shooters Brook, implying that it was water-powered. Excavation revealed few physical remains that could be firmly ascribed to the original construction of the mill, other than the vestiges of the north-eastern and south-western external walls (Fig 10). The uppermost surface of the northern wall (***108***) was exposed at a depth of 3.7 m below the modern ground surface, and comprised mould-thrown bricks bonded with speckled yellow lime mortar, typical of late eighteenth-century construction. The remains of this wall, however, were fragmentary, as it had been largely destroyed during later nineteenth-century remodelling. The remains of the wall (***115***) that had formed the original south-western end of the mill were more extensive. This wall measured 0.5 m wide and survived to a height of 13 courses, forming part of a semi-basement (Pl 31). The width

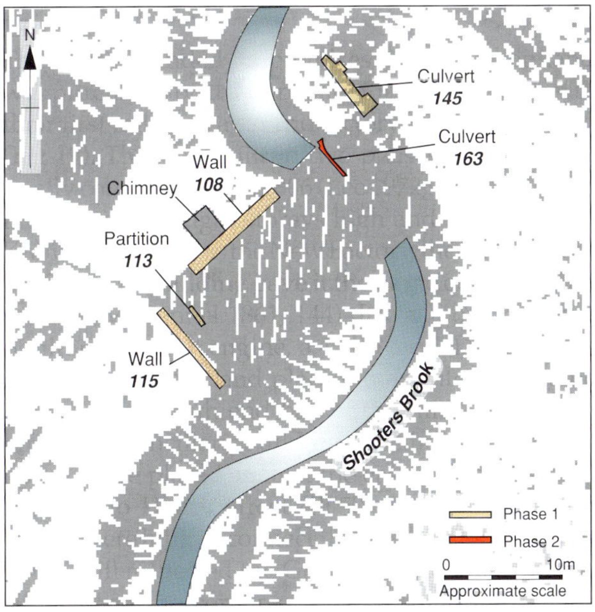

Figure 10: The excavated remains of Salvins' Factory (Phases 1 and 2), superimposed on Green's map of 1794

*Plate 31: Remnants of the wall (**115**) forming the original south-western end of Salvins' Factory*

of wall ***115*** was indicative of it having been intended for load-bearing purposes, typical of mill buildings prior to the introduction of internal structural framing in the later nineteenth century (Freeman 1891). In general terms, although the wall had been laid in an English Garden Wall bond, the lower courses had been constructed in a haphazard manner, incorporating stretcher, header, and soldier courses, failing to create the strongest structure possible.

Surviving internal features were limited to elements of internal flooring and the vestiges of a single wall (***113***), aligned parallel to the south-western end of the building. This was clearly a partition, forming a narrow passage, some 1.2 m wide, which may have been part of the common access to all floors within the mill; there was no evidence for an external stair tower. The flooring comprised mould-thrown bricks, laid in a random pattern on a thin layer of ash that formed an interface with the underlying drift geology (Pl 32).

Tentative evidence for the use of water-power within the mill was provided by a section of brick-lined culvert (***145***), situated to the north of the original building, and some 5 m below the modern ground surface. The culvert was 2.3 m wide, with an arched capping, and lay parallel to the course of Shooters Brook, but on its eastern side (Fig 10). The culvert widened to 3 m on its approach to the mill, although this expanded section only survived for a short distance as it had been largely destroyed by subsequent development. Nevertheless, it clearly represented an element of a water-management system.

It is probable that the Salvins managed their factory as a 'room-and-power' mill, renting floor space to other businesses, although the archive sources do not provide details of any firms that may have rented space in the mill until the arrival of Benjamin and William Sandford in *c* 1791 (Lee 1972, 11). Having been engaged previously as 'lapboard manufacturers' on Shude Hill, with a growing business interest in fustian warehousing (Holme 1788, 75), the Sandford brothers were joined in partnership by James McConnel and

Plate 32: Remnants of original flooring exposed in the south-western part of the mill

John Kennedy in 1791 (Kennedy 1849, 17). It seems that the Sandfords put up the majority of the capital for the new venture, whilst McConnel and Kennedy contributed some spinning mules and their expertise in textile machine-making. According to Fairbairn (1861, 3-4), the firm 'was for many years almost the sole makers ' of Crompton's spinning mule, although it was evidently with some difficulty that success in business was achieved (McConnel 1861). Nevertheless, after a short period in premises on Stable Street (Tib Street), the partners relocated to Salvins' Factory, where they rented space to build textile machinery and spin fine cotton yarn (McConnel 1913, 9). The new tenants occupied all of the factory space except for a portion retained by the Salvins for their own use (Kennedy 1849, 17). The day-to-day running of the business was managed by McConnel and Kennedy, whilst the Sandfords concentrated upon their warehousing interests (Lee 1972, 11). Shortly after their tenancy commenced, the Salvins decided to return to their native County Durham, where, in 1792, they established a 'factory colony' at Castle Eden, comprising a cotton mill, bleaching grounds, and nine double-fronted cottages for the workers (Aspin 2003, 40).

Phase 2, Steam-Powered Pumping Engine (*c* 1791 - 1796)

Shooters Brook evidently provided irregular or insufficient power for a waterwheel, and a steam-powered pumping engine was soon employed to provide a constant supply of water. Hills (1970, 141), quoting correspondence within the Boulton and Watt Archive, considered this to have been installed in 1791, and described it as 'an engine upon the Saverian plan which was to have been equal to the power of about 20 horses'. It was using this engine that, in 1793, John Kennedy is reputed to have first applied steam power to one of his spinning mules (Kennedy 1831a, 340). The engine is thought to have been installed by Joshua Wrigley, and was intended to serve a 12 ft-diameter (3.66 m) waterwheel by providing a regular and constant supply of water (Tann 1970, 73); engines of this type were not capable of working textile machinery directly, and were intended purely as a means of gaining maximum use of a waterwheel.

The available cartographic evidence, albeit limited, suggests that the installation of the steam-pumping engine had little impact on the footprint of the mill layout, implying that the engine and its associated boiler were housed inside the mill, which would have necessitated some internal remodelling. A chimney would also have been required, amongst the first of its kind in Ancoats, and this may be represented by the small projection against the north-western elevation of the mill shown on Green's map of 1794 (Fig 10). The only surviving physical evidence for this remodelling, however, was provided by modifications to the water-management features. The arched roof of culvert ***145*** was evidently rebuilt, with a corresponding reduction in the depth of the culvert to 0.90 m, perhaps in an attempt to increase the rate of water flow. Another culvert (***163***) was constructed some 4 m to the west, which took a route into the north-eastern end of the mill (Fig 10). This culvert was bonded to a substantial retaining wall, the position of which corresponded to the eastern bank of Shooters Brook as shown on Green's map of 1794. No physical remains of the engine or its associated waterwheel, however, were exposed during the excavation.

On 2 March 1795, the prosperous partnership between the Sandfords, McConnel, and Kennedy was terminated. The latter moved into rented premises on Derby Street, near Shooters Brook bridge (*Ch 3, Fig 6*), whilst Benjamin and William Sandford continued to occupy Salvins' Factory (McConnel 1861, 139). It is possible that the Sandfords rented out space in the mill at this time, as Scholes' trade directory for 1797 list Thomas Hope and Peter Walter as 'twist manufacturers' at Shooters Brook. Despite the Salvins having left the area in 1792, George Salvin insured the factory for £1200 in December 1798 (Royal Exchange 7253/164597), with additional insurance for £800 to cover a steam engine and mill shafting. During this period, they purchased spinning machinery for their factory in Castle Eden from John Kennedy, although this business relationship was terminated in October 1801 when McConnel & Kennedy ceased to build textile machines for anyone but themselves (McConnel 1913, 38-9). The Salvins' mill in Castle Eden was destroyed by fire in 1804, by which time Anthony Salvin had been called up for active service with the army, and was never to resume his interests in the textile industry (Aspin 2003, 41).

Phase 3, Double-Acting Steam Engine (1796 - 1828)

In February 1796, Benjamin and William Sandford enquired as to the cost of replacing their steam-pumping engine with a 25 hp Boulton and Watt beam engine (Tann 1970, 73). The export market for cotton goods was expanding rapidly during this time (*Ch 5, p 65*), which, combined with the improvements to spinning machinery, is likely to have been a stimulus for the Sandfords to increase production. Nevertheless, the replacement of their Wrigley engine within only a few years of its installation suggests that it was very inefficient or unreliable; correspondence within the Boulton and Watt Archive mentions that Salvins' 20 hp pumping engine was barely capable of producing half of its rated power (Tann 1970, 73). Its replacement required another episode of remodelling, with the construction of a new engine house and its associated steam-raising plant.

Engine and Boiler House

The updated power plant was seemingly housed in a new building measuring some 14 x 6 m, which was attached to the north-west elevation of the mill, enclosing the postulated location of the original chimney (Fig 11). Excavation revealed that the basement of this building contained an internal partition (***160***), which probably separated the engine from its associated boilers. Few physical remains of this power plant survived, although a displaced ashlar block to the south-west of the partition suggested that the engine may have been placed within that part of the building. The ashlar block measured 1.3 x 1 x 1 m, and incorporated two metal rods that protruded from its upper surface, implying that it had been a foundation block for the steam engine. The water required by the engine for condensing purposes is likely to have been supplied from Shooters Brook via an east/west-aligned culvert (***157***), which had been cut into the natural clay beneath the floor of the boiler room.

The area to the north-east of partition ***160*** contained large amounts of ash and clinker, adding weight to the interpretation of this part of the building as the boiler room. There were no surviving remains of the boiler housing to provide an idea of its size or shape, although the long boiler, a precursor to the wagon-type (Pl 33), was frequently installed with Boulton and Watt engines of this period (Dickinson and Jenkins 1989, 234-5). These comprised closed

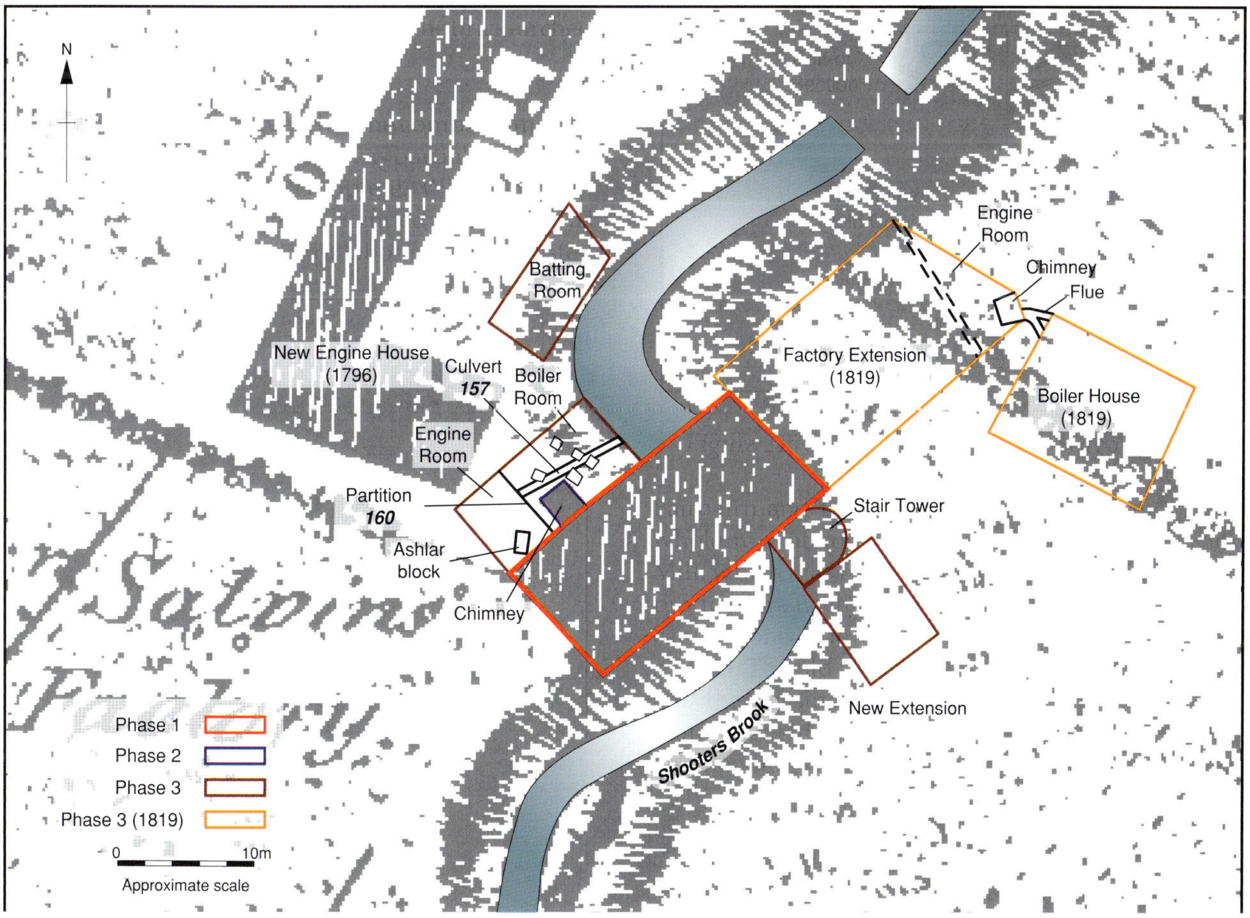

Figure 11: Expansion of Salvins' Factory (1796-1828), superimposed on Green's map of 1794, with detail shown on the Plans of All the Cotton-Spinning Mills Within the Township of Manchester *of c 1822*

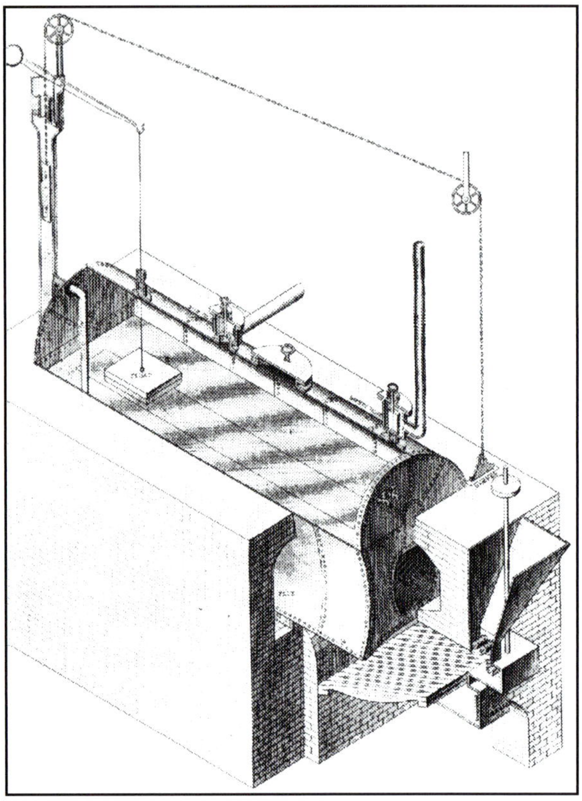

Plate 33: Wagon-type boiler (reproduced from Bourne 1872)

tanks of water set in brickwork formed into flues, which led smoke from a fire underneath and around the sides of the boiler before passing to the chimney. These boilers could only withstand a few pounds per square inch of steam pressure, and explosions were by no means uncommon.

No external walls of the boiler room were encountered during the excavation, although ten stone columns were identified as structural elements. The columns measured 1.5 m², and survived to a height of 3 m above the vestiges of the flagstone floor, providing an indication of the headroom in the boiler room (Pl 34). The columns were positioned between 2 m and 3.4 m apart, each comprising at least 30 courses of roughly coursed stone blocks, with no visible bonding material. The overlying floor, which was represented by the remnants of a flagged surface, was supported by the stone columns, in contrast to the cast-iron columns that characterised the mills of a later date.

Plate 34: The stone columns in the boiler room of 1796, with the vestiges of the overlying flagstones

The Workforce

In *c* 1809, B & W Sandford's factory was valued at £2161 (Daniels 1915a, 626), suggesting, when compared with other valuations, that it was larger than most in the area. Similarly, in 1816 the firm was accredited with employing 178 people (PP (HC) 1816 III, 367), implying that it was an above-average sized concern; during 1815, the median size of a labour force in cotton factories has been calculated at 54 employees (Lloyd-Jones and Le Roux 1980, 74). According to the evidence given by William Sandford to the Parliamentary Inquiry of 1816, his workforce of 178 included eight children under the age of ten (employed as piecers), and 32 between the ages of 10 and 18. All worked 13 hours a day, exclusive of an hour for dinner, which had been the terms of employment for 'about 18 years' (PP (HC) 1816 III, 367). Women comprised 47% of the workforce at this date, and were engaged exclusively in batting the raw cotton, and reeling the spun yarn (Pl 35). They worked 'part in a detached building, part at their own dwelling houses' (*ibid*). The 'detached building' probably housed the preparatory processes, and was almost certainly the three-storey 'batting room' shown on the *Plans of All the Cotton-Spinning Mills Within the Township of Manchester* of *c* 1822 (Fig 11), whilst reeling may have been undertaken

Plate 35: The cotton-reeling process (reproduced from Tomlinson 1861)

in the workers' dwellings. This suggests that the Sandfords combined elements of the traditional 'domestic system' of textile production with the new factory-based working practices, and also reflects that the women's payment was on piece rate. Indeed, apart from 16 people who were employed in the card room and were paid a weekly wage, all the workers were on piece rates. At this time, the firm was engaged in the spinning of fine yarn, producing counts between 90 and 140.

Further Expansion

Further expansion of the factory was undertaken in 1819 (PP (HC) 1834 [167] XX, A1), when the original block was effectively doubled in size, with an extension to the north-east (Fig 11). This new building is shown on the plan of *c* 1822, which indicates it to have been of six and a half storeys, with a full-height stair tower, a new internal engine house and chimney at the north end, and a detached single-storey boiler house to the south-east. The plan of *c* 1822 also shows that a smaller factory block had been built in the south-eastern part of the site. This is described on the plan as being of six storeys, of which three were of fireproof construction, hinting that the building may have been used for warehousing.

Excavation of this part of the site revealed that all of the new buildings had basements, and whilst the engine room had been largely destroyed, the boiler room contained the remains of several brick piers, representing the fragmentary elements of the boiler housings. The remains of a flue system were also exposed within the building, which comprised two narrow flues, each 0.25 m wide, that had undoubtedly connected the boilers to the chimney (Pl 36).

In 1821, B & W Sandford is entered in a trade directory as 'cotton spinners and merchants' (Pigot and Dean

Plate 36: Excavated remains of the flues in the boiler house of 1819

Plate 37: Sandford Street in 1897, showing the late nineteenth-century building on the site of Salvins' Factory (reproduced courtesy of Manchester Archives and Local Studies)

1821, 140). Shortly afterwards, however, Benjamin Sandford went into partnership with another cotton spinner, and the firm of Sandford & Green is listed as cotton spinners on Sandford Street in trade directories throughout most of the decade (*eg* Pigot and Dean 1825). Sandford Street appears to have been formalised in the early 1820s, and is shown on Thornton's map of 1824. It ran down the shallow valley side of Shooters Brook (Pl 37), and provided a link to Canal Street. Excavation revealed the pavement associated with Sandford Street, which comprised Yorkstone flags overlying a thin layer of coarse gravel.

Phase 4, Final Expansion (1828 – *c* 1840)

Documentary evidence indicates that the site was expanded further in 1828, shortly before Green left the partnership and was replaced by Richard Sandford (PP (HC) 1834 [167] XX, A1). Whilst excavation yielded little surviving physical evidence for this expansion, the size of the workforce was seemingly increased accordingly, as the evidence given by B & R Sandford to the Parliamentary Commission in 1833 states that the firm employed a total of 365 operatives in the preparation and spinning departments, and 17 engineers and mechanics (*ibid*). It is also stated that the firm was spinning yarn counts between 140 and 210, somewhat finer than the yarn they were spinning in 1816. This implies that they had kept apace with technological developments and invested in new spinning mules, perhaps to secure a share of the lucrative market for fine yarn demanded

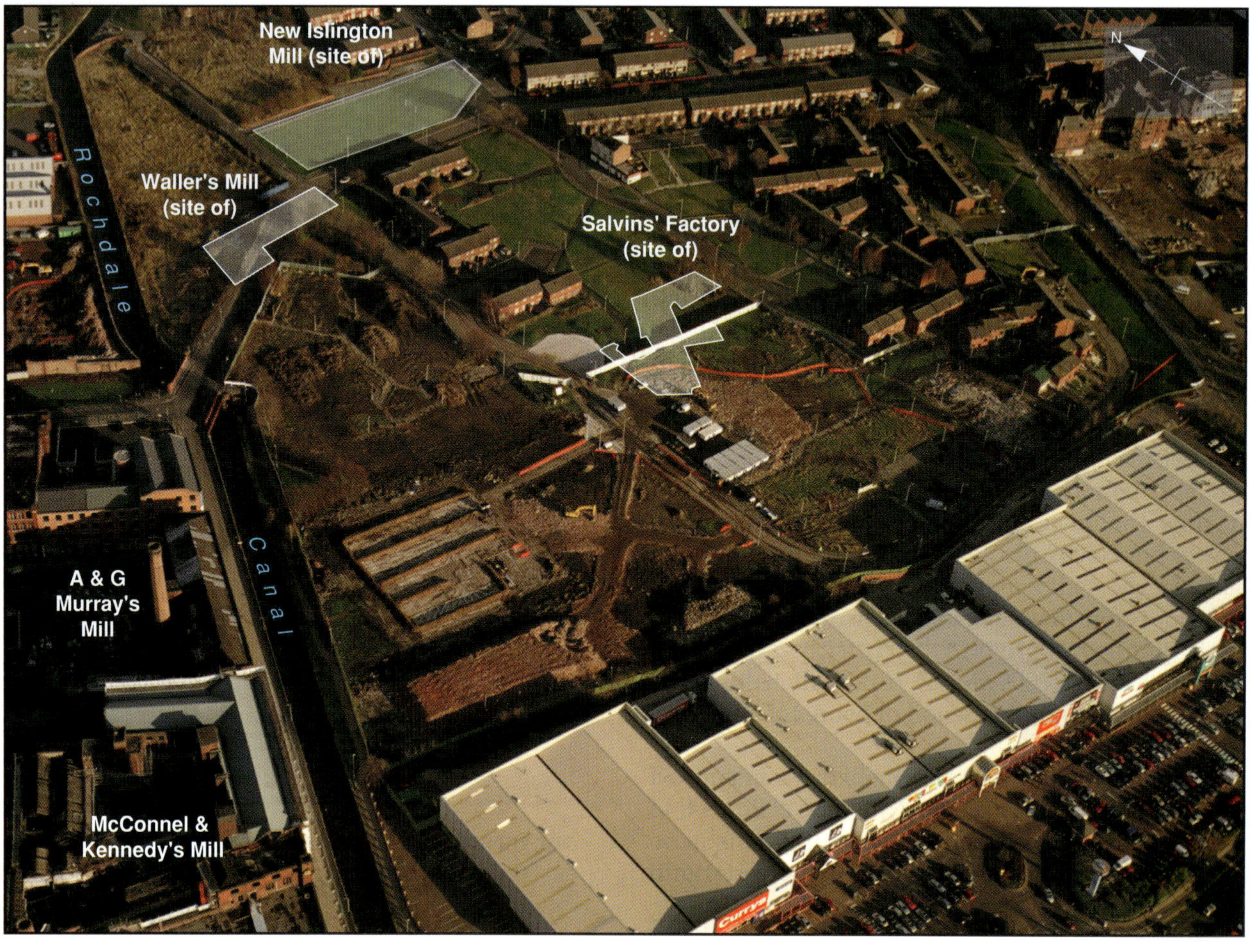

Figure 12: Position of New Islington Mill, Salvins' Factory and Waller's Mill, superimposed on an aerial view of the New Islington Millennium Community development in 2003 (reproduced courtesy of Volker Stevin Ltd)

by the expanding lace and hosiery industry in the Nottingham area (*Ch 5, p 79*).

The Sandfords are not listed in Pigot and Slater's trade directory for 1841, nor subsequently, suggesting that the factory had closed by that date. By the late 1840s, the buildings were being used temporarily as 'a cholera hospital' (Kennedy 1849, 17), and are similarly marked on Adshead's map of 1851 as a 'fever ward'.

Phase 5 (Post-Cotton Spinning)

During the second half of the nineteenth century, the mill was converted for use jointly by a coach and carriage builder and a soda-water machinery manufacturer, which necessitated a complete rebuilding of the original structure. This is evident from the detail shown on a photograph of Sandford Street in 1897 (Pl 37), which clearly depicts a building that embodies the architecture of the late ninteenth-century on the site of Salvins' Factory. This was also confirmed by excavation evidence. New walls were erected, together with concrete floors, and a cobbled yard that comprised granite setts typical of mid- to late nineteenth-century construction.

The Early Textile Mills in Ancoats: New Islington Mill

The site of New Islington Mill (SJ 8533 9866) lies some 160 m to the north-east of Salvins' Factory (Fig 12). This part of Ancoats is marked as New Islington on the earliest maps of the area (*eg* Green 1794), although the origins of the name are unclear. It seems to have been applied originally to a group of buildings at the north-eastern end of Union Street, some of which may have been artisans' workshop dwellings, although firm evidence is lacking.

New Islington Mill underwent numerous changes of ownership and remodelling episodes from its inception during the late eighteenth century until the 1970s, when it was demolished and, after landscaping, formed a recreational area. For most of its life, the mill was used for textile-manufacturing purposes, representing a rare example of longevity for an Ancoats' mill that did not have a canal-side location. In 2005, it was the first site to be developed for housing as part of the New Islington Millennium

Plate 38: Structural remains of New Islington Mill exposed immediately below the topsoil in an evaluation trench

Community Project, although construction work was preceded by archaeological investigation. The excavation of six evaluation trenches across the footprint of the mill revealed that considerable structural remains survived immediately beneath the modern ground surface in the south-eastern part of the site (Pl 38), leading to a programme of more detailed excavation. In total, an area equivalent to some 400 m^2 was excavated, exposing the remains of several phases of steam-power plant, together with their associated flues and chimney, and a complex arrangement of water-management features (OA North 2005b). Excavation did not continue below the level that was to be disturbed by redevelopment, and elements of the earliest mill's fabric were therefore not exposed. The evidence produced from the archaeological fieldwork, coupled with the available documentary material, has been divided into six broad phases of activity.

Phase 1, Water-Powered Mill (1780s - *c* 1799)

The origins of New Islington Mill are unclear, and whilst it is absent from Green's map of 1794, there is some evidence to suggest that it originated as a water-powered concern that was in operation by the late 1780s (Nevell 2003, 43). The archaeological investigation concluded that the main mill building measured some 30 m long with an internal width of 15.25 m. Excavation yielded scant physical evidence

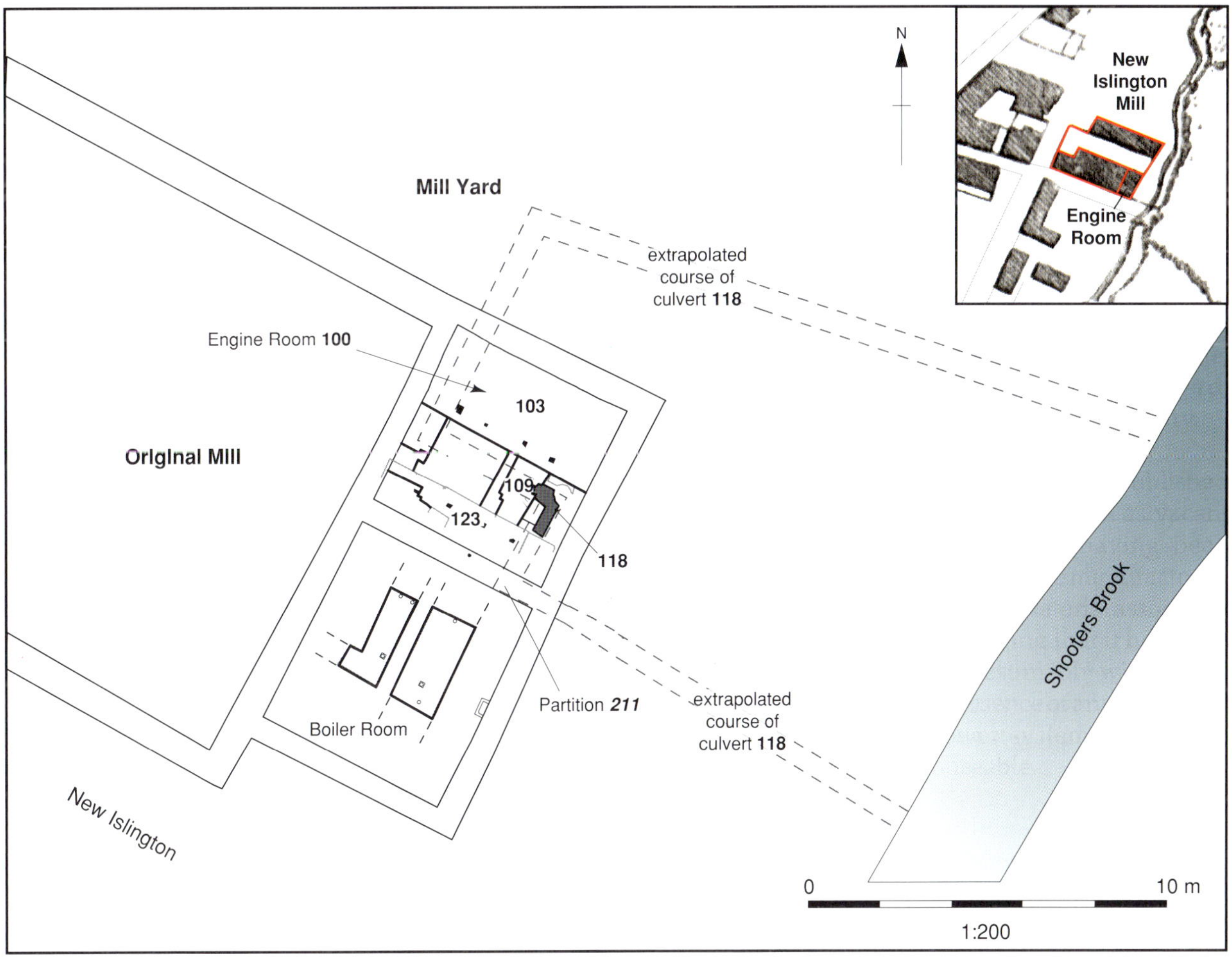

Figure 13: The excavated remains of engine room ***100*** *at New Islington Mill, with inset showing its position superimposed on Bancks and Thornton's map of 1800*

for the putative waterwheel, which in part reflected the decision not to excavate the lowest levels of the site. Nevertheless, a brick-lined culvert (***118***), identified within the south-western part of the mill, clearly represented an element of an early water-management system (Fig 13). This passed beneath a part of the mill that was converted subsequently to house a steam engine (engine room ***100***, Phase 2), continuing south-eastwards in the direction of Shooters Brook.

Phase 2, Jesse Hirst's 'Room-and-Power Mill' (*c* 1799 - 1815)

The first documented occupant of New Islington Mill was Jesse Hirst, who, in 1799, insured the factory for £200, together with a steam engine and associated millwright works for £120 and £80 respectively (Royal Exchange 7253/169411). Jesse Hirst is entered in Scholes' Trade Directory for 1794 as a 'timber merchant' based at 37 Pot Street, but is listed subsequently as a muslin and twist manufacturer (*eg* Dean and Dean 1804, 89). A separate insurance document, also dated 1799, concerns Sarah Stopford, who had machinery within New Islington Mill insured to the value of £200 (Royal Exchange 7253/159180), implying that she rented floor space within the factory.

None of the available archive sources for the mill provide any details of the engine, although excavation has revealed that it was almost certainly a beam engine. The low insurance premium Hirst paid on the steam engine implies that it was not a Boulton and Watt model, which were considerably more expensive than those supplied, for instance, by the local firm of Bateman and Sherratt. This firm gained a reputation as talented engineers during the late eighteenth century, becoming the chief rivals to Boulton and Watt in the supply of steam engines to manufacturers during this period, having built at least 38 steam engines for use in Lancashire factories by 1800 (Musson and Robinson 1969, 423).

Bateman and Sherratt

James Bateman commenced business as an ironmonger in *c* 1770 as the partner of Walter Wilson, an ironmonger on Deansgate in Manchester (Musson and Robinson 1959, 425). An advertisement in the *Manchester Mercury* on 1 January 1782, however, announced that Bateman had established an iron foundry in Salford, and was manufacturing a considerable range of cast-iron goods. He evidently achieved considerable success, becoming 'the most important iron-founding and general engineering concern in Manchester and Salford in the later eighteenth century' (Musson and Robinson 1960, 226). During the late 1780s he formed a partnership with William Sherratt, and in 1791 they built a new foundry on Hardman Street, Salford. Aikin

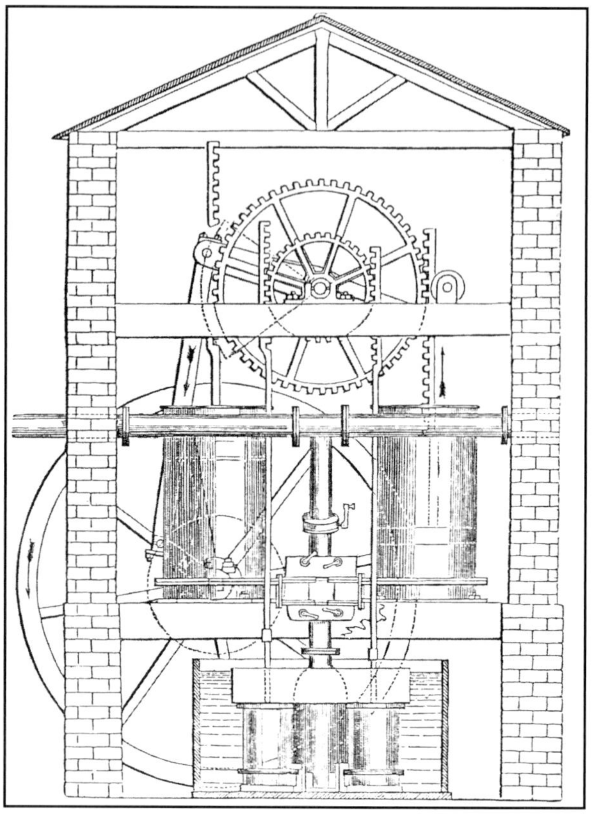

Plate 39: Twin-cylinder rotative engine of the type built by Bateman and Sherratt (reproduced from Farey 1827)

(1795, 176) considered William Sherratt to be a 'very ingenious and able engineer, who...brought the steam engine to great perfection', and the partnership wasted little time in exploiting this new market as it opened up during the 1790s.

Some of their first engines were single-cylinder atmospheric models, adapted from the Newcomen type, but capable of producing rotary power. Whilst they were certainly inferior to Boulton and Watt's engines, not least in the amount of power they could produce, they were nevertheless cheap to build, reliable in performance, and reasonably economical (Hills 1970, 151). Bateman and Sherratt also produced a two-cylinder version of the atmospheric engine, to which they fitted separate condensers and air pumps (Pl 39). It is thought that the first engine of this type was set up at Thackeray's cotton mill at Garratt on the river Medlock in *c* 1794 (Dickinson and Jenkins 1989, 320). It is possible that an engine of this type was installed in New Islington Mill, given the size and internal features exposed within the excavated engine room (Fig 14).

The Engine Room

The original steam plant for New Islington Mill was evidently housed in a dedicated building, which abutted the south-eastern end of the main block (Fig 13). This building measured some 14.5 x 6.8 m and had been divided by a substantial brick-built

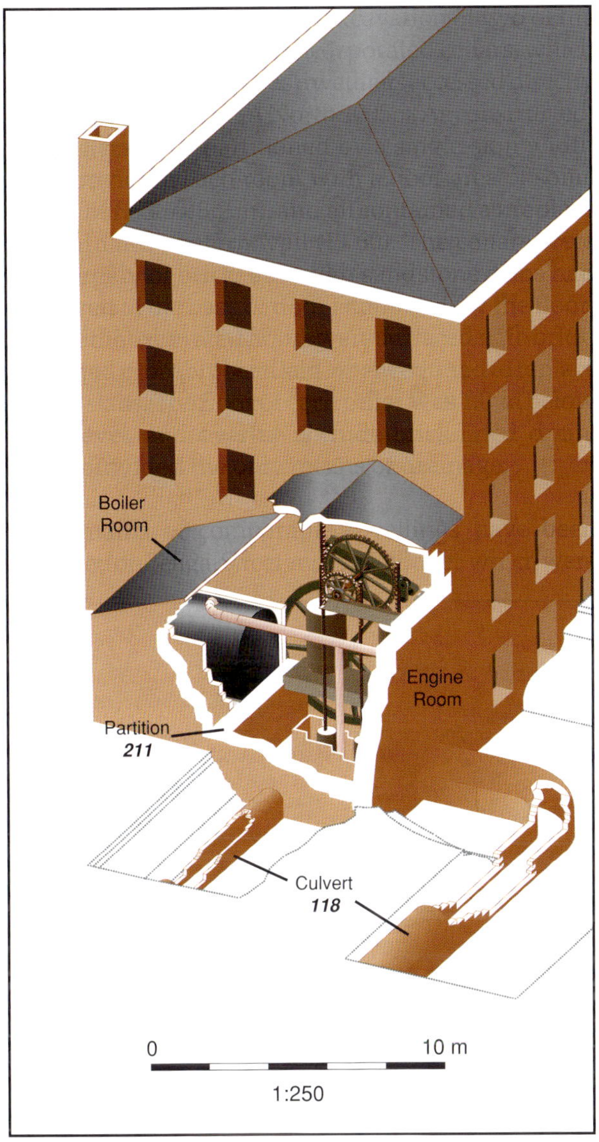

Figure 14: Isometric reconstruction of the engine and boiler rooms, and the projected route of the culvert

Plate 40: Reused stone block incorporated within the original engine room at New Islington Mill

partition (**211**), forming two separate areas (Fig 14). The northern part, with internal dimensions of 5.2 m^2, had contained the beam engine, which was housed upon two substantial bench walls (**103** and **123**), set 1.92 m apart. Several square-sectioned iron rods that had been used to restrain the engine cylinders and framing protruded vertically through the bench walls, their position suggesting that the engine had been placed transversely across the mill.

The uppermost course of the eastern bench wall (**103**) incorporated a row of large stone blocks, including one that retained clear evidence of a wheel scar (Pl 40). The projected circumference of this scar would not fit within the layout of the engine room (**100**) as excavated, indicating that it was reused, possibly from the putative waterwheel. Evidence for the operation of the steam engine was provided by worn recesses within the inner face of one of the engine-house walls, and small, evenly spaced square sockets within the upper course, which possibly represented housings for the timber engine frame. A circular pit with a diameter of 0.6 m, formed within two large sandstone blocks, was exposed within the south-eastern corner of the engine room. These stone blocks had been carved carefully to receive part of the engine mechanism.

During this period, the original culvert (**118**) beneath the engine room floor was deliberately blocked-off along the eastern edge of the room to form a 1 m^2 pit. This contained water, and may have been used by the engine for condensing purposes. The engine-room floor was made up of randomly patterned bricks, thin flagstones, and ashlar blocks. The ashlars were located along the eastern edge of the floor, supporting a large iron plate that sealed culvert **118** (Pl 41). A

Plate 41: General view across the original engine room, showing the bench walls, restraining rods, and culvert

cast-iron pipe, with an internal diameter of 0.16 m, protruded through bench wall ***123***, and terminated adjacent to this plate, and probably represented the main steam pipe from the boiler to the engine. The boiler had seemingly been placed to the south-west of the engine, beyond partition ***211***, and was housed in a dedicated room, measuring some 7.3 x 5.2 m.

Early Expansion
In 1800, a second factory was erected on the site, contiguous to the original building (Royal Exchange 170024; 180501). This is depicted on a map published by Bancks and Thornton in 1800, which also shows a detached long narrow range to the north (Fig 13), and both mills are also shown on a plan of the Mosley Estate that is dated 1805-8 (MLSU 25671). Interestingly, the course of Shooters Brook immediately downstream of the mill is shown on the latter map to be straight and narrow, in contrast to the meanders upstream, and appears to form a small pool adjacent to the mill. This implies that the brook was being utilised as a water supply, presumably in association with power production.

The mill is shown in *Plans of All the Cotton-Spinning Mills Within the Township of Manchester* of *c* 1822, which annotates the two factories as being of five storeys, and the long range to the north as a two-storey 'batting shop'. Excavation within the footprint of the mill revealed a basement with a stone-flagged floor, but otherwise this part of the site furnished little detail of significance. Similarly, initial evaluation of the 'batting shop' revealed that it had been wholly destroyed during demolition in the 1970s, and did not merit further investigation.

Phase 3, Johnson and Brookes (1815 - *c* 1830)
The mill was occupied from 1815 by the firm of Gallimore, Johnson & Brookes, identified as cotton spinners at New Islington in contemporary trade directories (*eg* Wardle and Bentham 1815, 151). John Gallimore is listed in earlier trade directories as a manufacturer of 'muslinet, dimity, etc', based at Swan Court in Manchester (Dean and Dean 1809, 67). By 1811, he had evidently formed a partnership with Johnson and Brookes, and commenced business as cotton spinners and twist dealers, based at 'Johnson's Buildings' with a factory at 'Garratt' (Dean and Dean 1811, 66).

The firm's move to New Islington Mill is confirmed in the Manchester Rate Book for 1815, which assessed the rateable value of the factory as £85 (MLSU M9/40/2/79), suggesting it to have been of above-average size. It seems that the partners retained their premises at Johnson's Buildings for a short period, and are entered at that address in a trade directory under the heading of 'calico printers and print warehouses' (Wardle and Bentham 1815, 145). Entries in subsequent trade directories indicate that Gallimore left the firm within a few years, whilst Johnson & Brookes continued their partnership as 'spinners, manufacturers and printers' (Pigot and Dean 1817, 139), implying that they were engaged in weaving in addition to cotton spinning. This is reinforced by the evidence given by Thomas Brookes to a Parliamentary Commission in 1833, which states that the firm had carried out cotton spinning and power-loom weaving at the mill for approximately 18 years (PP (HC) 1834 [167] XX, A1). This would represent a pioneering application of power looms and an early appearance of the combined spinning and weaving mill, which proved to be a condition of success and growth for many textile businesses during this period (Jewkes 1930, 95). Ure (1836, 430) considered that the early association of spinning and power-loom weaving was partly an attempt to avoid bankruptcy during depressions in the cotton-spinning trade, and it is perhaps of note that Gallimore, Johnson & Brookes' entered New Islington Mill in a year (1815) of economic crisis (*Ch 5, p 70*).

Installation of a Supplementary Engine
Pigot's small-scale *New Plan of Manchester and Salford*, published in 1819, shows that a formal reservoir had been constructed immediately to the east of the mill, evidently associated with the installation of a second steam engine. This appears more clearly on Thornton's map of 1824 (Fig 15), which also shows the batting shop to have been extended, with the main access to the site at the western end via Pot Street.

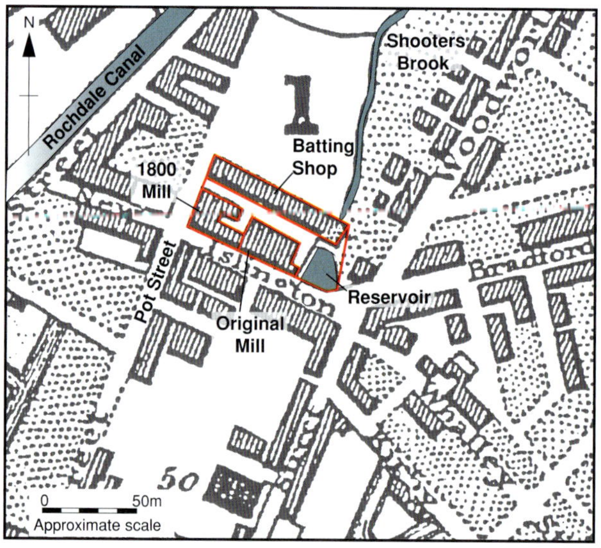

Figure 15: Extract from Thornton's map of 1824, showing New Islington Mill and its reservoir

The new engine was supplementary to the existing beam engine, and was placed immediately to the north of the original mill, within a rectangular-shaped building. Excavation of this structure (***141***) exposed the remains of a small waterwheel pit and associated steam-powered pumping engine of the type known to have been developed during the late eighteenth century by the Manchester-based engineer, Joshua Wrigley (*Ch 2, p 21*).

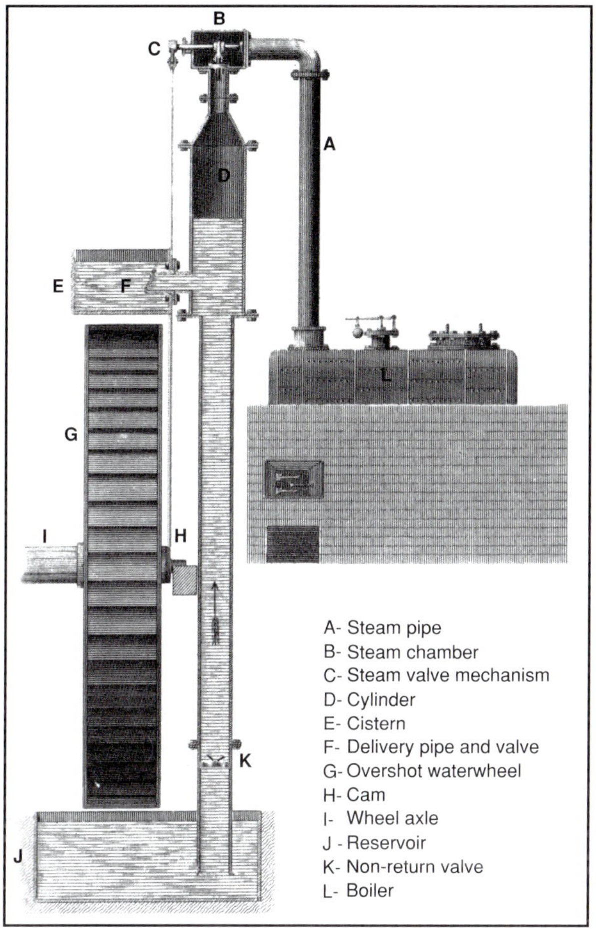

Plate 42: Section across a Savery-type engine developed by Wrigley for driving waterwheels (reproduced from Rees 1819)

Wrigley's engine was a simple device that had few working parts (Pl 42), and was applied 'to impel the machinery of some of the earliest manufactories' (Farey 1827, 122). It was cheap to build as it did not require the precision engineering demanded by machines comprising a piston and accurately bored cylinder, and no premiums were charged for its use (Hills 1970, 138); in 1790, an engine of this type cost just over £200, including the waterwheel (Tann 1970, 85). The fact that water power remained as the prime motive source was also reassuring to manufacturers who had reservations about rotative beam engines. A boiler supplied steam to the cylinder, which was placed on top of a pipe leading down to a reservoir of water. The water was forced by atmospheric pressure from the lower reservoir into the vacuum created in the cylinder when the steam was condensed. The water in the cylinder then flowed out by gravity into a higher reservoir, from where it was released over the waterwheel. The number of engines that Wrigley supplied to the new factories is unknown, although it is likely that they were widespread. The market for these engines was not restricted to Manchester; at least 35 industrial sites in Yorkshire used pumping engines before 1800, including some of the most prominent textile mills of the period (Giles and Goodall 1992, 133).

Whilst it remains uncertain precisely what use this engine was applied to, it is nevertheless remarkable that this type persisted into the second decade of the nineteenth century, despite having been 'outclassed by others of improved design' by the 1790s (Hills 1989, 48). The relatively low power that the pumping engine was capable of producing would certainly have been insufficient to drive the most up-to-date spinning mules, and may perhaps have been applied to power looms, or machinery in the two-storey batting shop.

The steam-pumping engine and the waterwheel were contained within wheelhouse ***141***, which had maximum plan dimensions of 6.9 x 5.5 m (Fig 16). The floor was split-level, with a small lower area within the south-eastern end. The waterwheel pit (***165***) was situated within the approximate centre of the wheelhouse, with an overall length of 3.50 m and a width of 0.68 m (Pl 43). It was of brick construction, although parallel rows of large stone blocks lined the top of each long

*Plate 43: Waterwheel pit **165** at New Islington Mill*

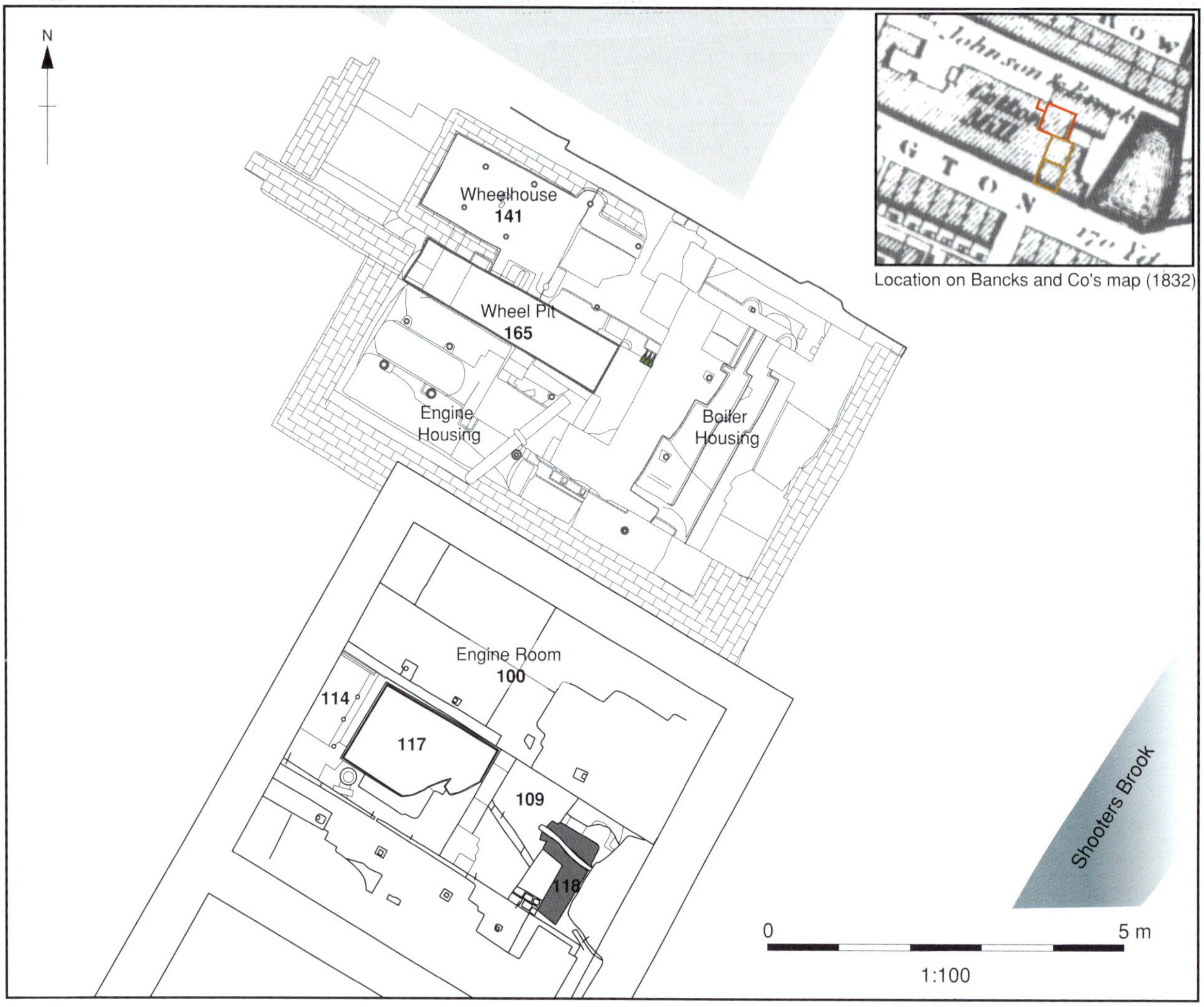

*Figure 16: The excavated remains of the wheelhouse (**141**) at New Islington Mill*

Plate 44: Bearing housings for the waterwheel at New Islington Mill

wall. Two opposing blocks had semi-circular rebates cut into them, each with a diameter of 0.26 m, clearly representing the housing for the waterwheel's axle bearings (Pl 44). The projected centre of the axle was 1.8 m above the base of the wheelpit, allowing for a waterwheel of some 3.6 m (11 ft 10 in) diameter.

The waterwheel pit (***165***) was connected at its base by two culverts, which acted as a conduit for water from the reservoir (Fig 17). This was used to power the waterwheel and its associated pumping engine, and was also channelled to engine room ***100*** for condensing purposes.

The pumping engine had seemingly been placed immediately to the west of the waterwheel pit, its position marked by two parallel rows of large stone blocks. These were pierced by a series of vertical iron rods, which had presumably been used to restrain the engine mechanism. A series of large worked stone blocks on the opposite side of the waterwheel pit probably formed part of the power-transmission system. The stone blocks incorporated

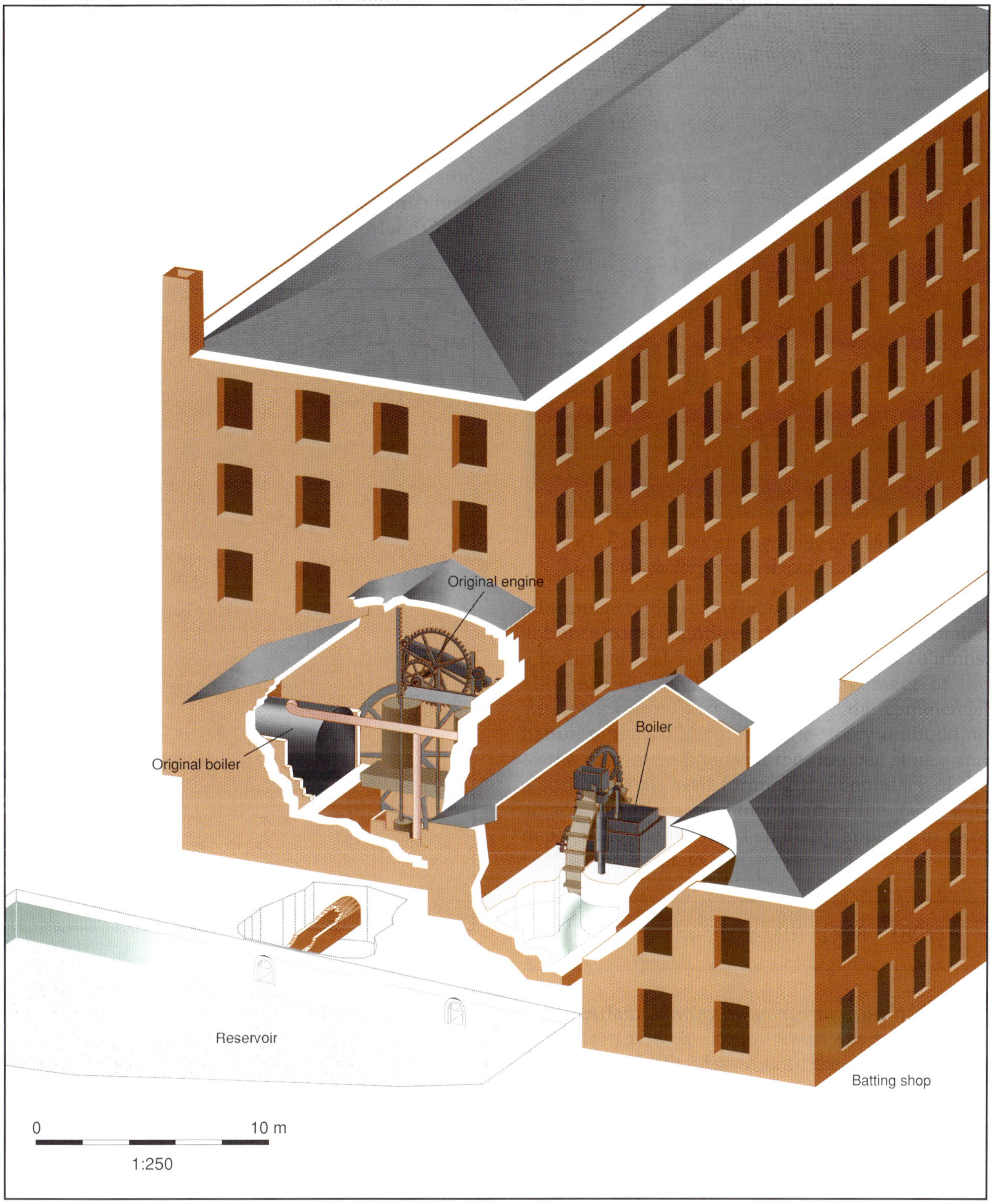

Figure 17: Isometric reconstruction of the pumping engine and culverts

several threaded vertical iron bars, which may have restrained the transmission drive bearing. The threads cut into the iron rods were of various, but coarse, gauges, each having been mould-thrown.

The southern part of wheelhouse ***141*** contained two rectangular-shaped pits that had been sunk into the floor. Pit ***174*** incorporated an arched aperture in its north-west-facing elevation, which may have connected with one of the culverts within engine room ***100***, although this could not be corroborated. The adjacent pit (***175***) incorporated a narrow channel or drain, which passed through the eastern wall of the building; these features are likely to have been associated with the boiler for the engine, although its precise mechanism remains uncertain.

Phase 4, Remodelling and a New Engine (*c* 1830 - *c* 1837)

Archaeological excavation demonstrated that the mill had been remodelled and fitted with a new engine, which was probably installed during the early 1830s. This engine was placed transversely across the south-eastern part of the original mill (Fig 18), which had necessitated a remodelling of the north-western edge of waterwheel pit (***165***), signifying its disuse. The interior of the new engine room (***128***) was defined by a series of four brick piers, situated adjacent to the south-eastern wall, and six piers against the north-western wall. Each of the piers was set at an interval of 0.45 m from the next, with a distance of 2.10 m between the two rows. Two of the piers supported a large stone ashlar block, which contained an iron restraining rod, indicative of it having acted as a foundation for a beam engine (Pl 45). Some details of this engine are implicit in the evidence given by Thomas Brookes to a Parliamentary Commission in 1833 (PP (HC) 1834 [167] XX, A1). Brookes stated that the provision of power in his factory was reliant exclusively on steam, using an engine of 20 hp, which was also used to turn a 'small mill adjoining' that was occupied by a tenant.

Plate 45: Foundation blocks for a replacement steam engine

The remodelling of the steam-power plant involved the adaptation of the culvert from the reservoir into the southern part of a flue leading to a new chimney. This section of the flue comprised vertical walls of mould-thrown bricks that had clearly been abraded by running water, whilst the arched capping of refractory bricks was a modification (Pl 46). The chimney was erected adjacent to the reservoir, which had been abandoned, infilled, and subsumed by an expansion of the front factory block (Fig 18). The chimney was of a circular plan, with an internal diameter of 2.50 m, and had been set on a square brick plinth; it is marked as being 150 ft (45.72 m) high on the 1932 revision of Goad's insurance plan. The northern extent of the flue was evidently a new-build, composed entirely of refractory bricks set between parallel retaining walls (Pl 47), which connected with the new boiler house. A curious element of the flue was a 1.9 m diameter circular chamber (***151***) attached to its eastern side,

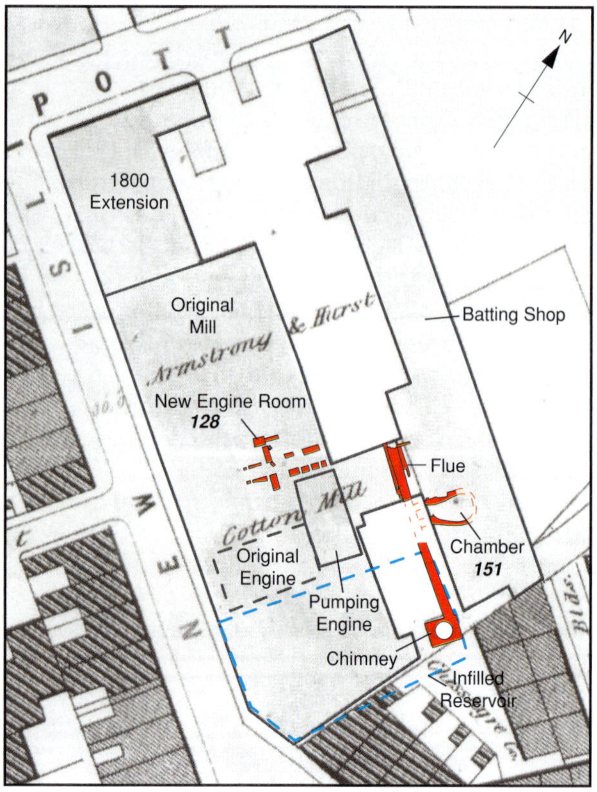

Figure 18: The excavated remains of New Islington Mill (Phase 4), superimposed on Adshead's map of 1851

which was connected to the flue via two channels that were constructed of refractory bricks. It is uncertain what function the circular chamber served, other than that it was associated with high temperatures, presumably by utilising the heat of the flue gases. It is possible that it represented elements of the textile-finishing processes, such as the foundations of a bleaching vat.

Plate 46: View along the former culvert modified as a flue for the new chimney

In 1833, Thomas Brookes reported to a Parliamentary Commission that his firm employed a total workforce of 105, or which three were mechanics, and 42 were engaged in preparation and spinning; in contrast to

Plate 47: *Section of newly built flue at New Islington Mill*

many of Ancoats' spinners, Johnson & Brookes spun coarse yarns with counts between 17 and 20 (PP (HC) 1834 [167] XX, A1). The weaving department, however, employed 60 people, representing more than one half of the total workforce.

Phase 5, New Occupants (c 1837 – 1893)

The firm of Johnson & Brookes is listed as cotton spinners and manufacturers at New Islington in trade directories for most of the 1830s, although it is not entered in an edition for 1838 or later (Pigot 1838), suggesting that it may have been bankrupted by the serious depression of trade in 1837 (*Ch 5, p 77*). Adshead's map of 1851 identifies the firm of Armstrong & Hirst as the occupants of the mill (Fig 18), whilst a trade directory published two years later lists the firm of Scott & Holden, 'spinners and manufacturers' (Slater 1852, 373), although their association with New Islington Mill appears to have been short-lived. In 1858, the mill was occupied by William Sharp, who is curiously described in a directory as a 'cotton spinner, grocer and sugar refiner (New Islington Mill)' (Kelly 1858, 1362). By 1861, William Sharp had been joined in partnership by William Galloway, and the firm of Sharp & Galloway is listed in trade directories until the early 1870s as cotton spinners, manufacturers, and sugar refiners, based at New Islington Mill (*eg* Slater 1872, 282). The firm is also listed as having a subsidiary grocers' company, known as Sharp & Scott. By 1874, the site was occupied by the firm of J & G Walthew and Mayor, which is listed as a cotton doubler and manufacturer of sewing cotton at New Islington Mill (Slater 1874, 64). This firm left New Islington Mill during the 1890s and relocated to Stockport where, in 1893, it commissioned the firm of Stott and Sons, mill architects of considerable repute, to erect a doubling mill at Brinksway (Holden 1998, 235). Any remodelling of New Islington Mill undertaken by this series of occupants, however, was not represented in the archaeological record.

Phase 6, Late Developments (1893 - 1970s)

The Ordnance Survey plan published in 1891 shows the site to have contracted slightly, with the removal of elements of the buildings, particularly at the western end of both ranges, and the engine house in the centre of the mill complex appears to have been demolished. By 1905, the mill had been partially converted for use as an engineering works, although the building in the south-western part of the site continued to be associated with the textile trades through its use as a cotton-reeling factory. This is shown on the 1932 revision of Goad's insurance plans, which indicates the building to have comprised by that date two storeys plus a basement, with brick-arched ceilings supported by cast-iron columns; the building is depicted on a photograph taken in 1967, when it was occupied by '*Permanoid*' electric cable manufacturers (Pl 48). It is impossible to ascertain whether this component of the building was a reduced element of the original structure, but the use of brick-arched ceilings nevertheless point to fireproof construction.

Plate 48: New Islington Mill in 1967 (reproduced courtesy of Manchester Archives and Local Studies)

The Emergence of the Steam-Powered Mill: McConnel & Kennedy's Mill

Whilst the water-powered textile mills in Ancoats appear to have adopted steam power in one form or another by the end of the eighteenth century, the earliest purpose-built steam-powered mill in Manchester was that established by Peter Drinkwater in Piccadilly during 1789 (Chaloner 1954). This was the first mill in the town to have employed a Boulton and Watt engine, and was also the first to have been fully independent of the site requirements of a water-power system, reflecting its design as a steam-powered factory. This attribute was crucial to the subsequent development of Manchester as a manufacturing centre, with mills being established across the town, with a significant concentration in Ancoats (*Ch 8, Fig 58*). By their very nature, these mills represented a new wave of textile factories that incorporated several innovative design features, not least a new type of power house. Surviving physical evidence for these buildings is scant across Manchester; archaeological excavation of Drinkwater's Mill, for instance, demonstrated that its earliest fabric had been almost wholly destroyed (OA North 2005a).

The complex of spinning mills that was to become the largest in Manchester by the 1820s was established in the final years of the eighteenth century by James McConnel and John Kennedy, who became one of the best-known firms in the Lancashire cotton industry (Williams 1993, 30). Both McConnel and Kennedy had migrated to Lancashire from the New Galloway area of Scotland, where they had been well acquainted with Adam and George Murray (*Ch 5, p 61*).

Upon completing his apprenticeship as a textile-machine maker with William Cannan in Chowbent, near Leigh, James McConnel took up employment in February 1788 with Alexander Egelsom, a Manchester weft and twist dealer (Lee 1972, 10). Egelsom maintained premises for cotton spinning on Newton Street in Ancoats, possibly in the same building as that used by Adam Murray. Three years later, in 1791, McConnel formed a partnership with John Kennedy and Benjamin and William Sandford, and the new firm moved subsequently to Salvins' Factory (*p 36*). In March 1795, McConnel and Kennedy established their own business, and relocated from Salvins' Factory to rented premises on Derby Street in Ancoats (McConnel 1861, 139).

Old Mill

By 1797, the McConnel & Kennedy partnership was ready to build its own mill, which was possibly the first to have been designed to house steam-powered spinning mules. The site chosen was on undeveloped land in Ancoats adjacent to the line of the proposed Rochdale Canal, but separated from it by Union Street (Fig 19).

The new mill was a seven-storey structure, with a loft. It was 16 bays long and four bays wide, with plan dimensions of some 54 x 12 m. An early engraving of the mill shows a cupola on the roof (Pl 49), which would presumably have contained a bell. A 16 hp steam engine was ordered from Boulton and Watt in June 1797, with two long boilers to supply the steam. Unusually for a mill of this period, the engine house and boilers were external, attached to the south-east corner of the building. The steam plant was, however, built over subsequently, incorporating the engine and boilers within the mill (Pl 50), with the intention of providing heating in the spinning room (McConnel 1913, 39).

Despite continuing to rent premises on Derby Street and space in a factory owned by a Mr Lane on Union Street, where six spinning mules were operated, McConnel & Kennedy did not occupy the whole of their new mill immediately, but rented out half of

Plate 49: McConnel & Kennedy's Old Mill in 1800, viewed from Cotton Street and showing the north-facing elevation (reproduced from McConnel 1913)

Plate 50: McConnel & Kennedy's Mill in c 1820, showing (from left to right) Long Mill, Old Mill, and Sedgwick Mill (reproduced from McConnel 1913)

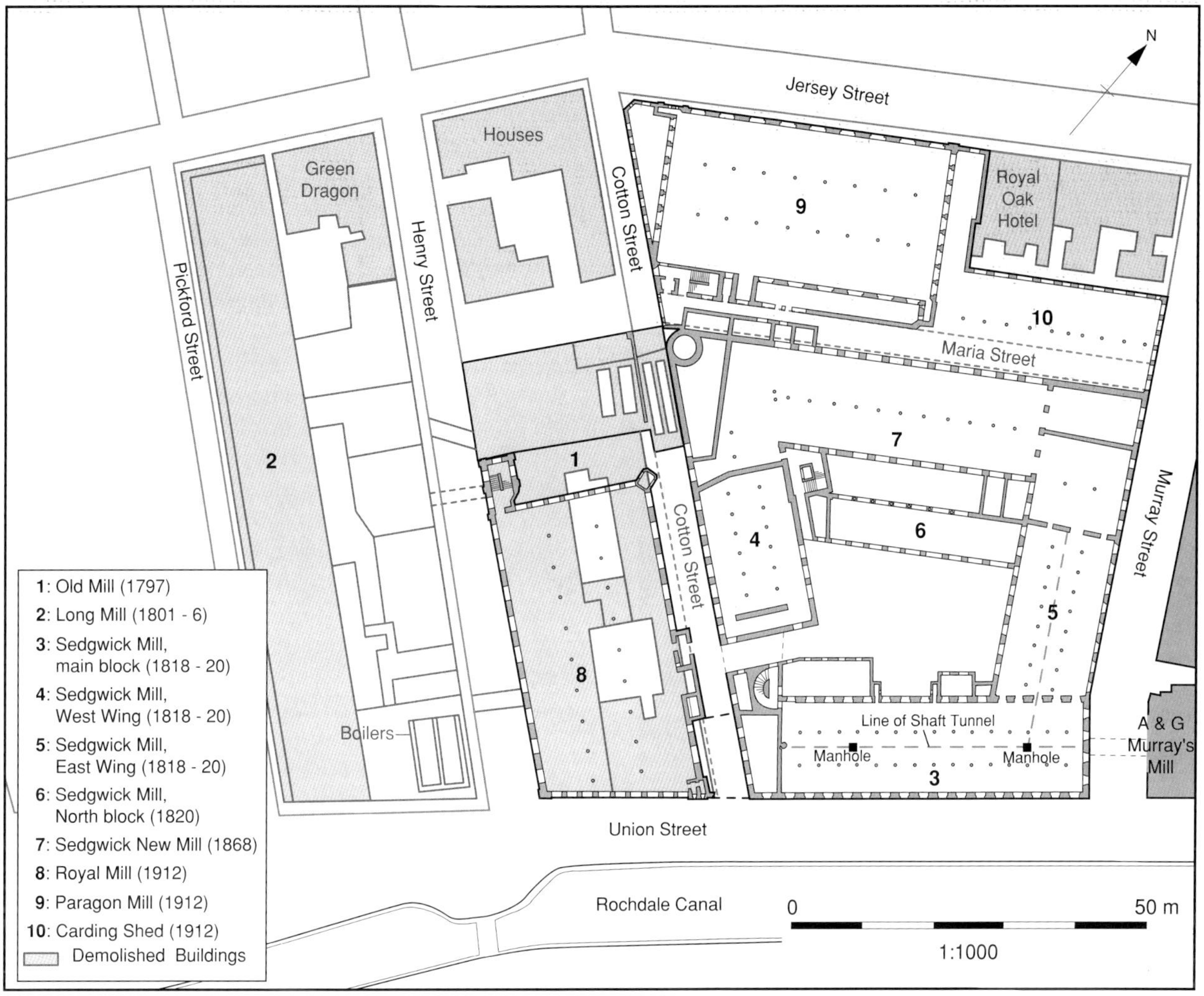

Figure 19: Composite plan of McConnel & Kennedy's Mill complex

the floor space to Peter and Andrew McCandish at £370 per year until 1802 (McConnel 1861, 140).

Long Mill

The firm expanded its premises in 1801 when land was purchased on the opposite side of Henry Street to their first mill, and a second factory was commenced (Fig 19). This was built in two phases, and was not totally completed until 1806 (Lee 1972, 102), but when finished it was eight storeys high and 30 bays long. Known originally as the New Factory, the long narrow profile of the building gave it the name of 'Long Mill' in 1819 (McConnel 1861, 144). It was powered by a Boulton and Watt engine, a 45 hp model, which was purchased in 1802 and placed in an internal engine house in the south end bay of the mill. Two-storey offices and ancillary buildings, including the boiler house, were placed against the east wall of the mill, adjacent to Henry Street (Pl 50), and a bridge and tunnel were built to connect the two mills. The layout of the mill respected the Green Dragon public house situated on the corner of Henry Street and Jersey Street (Pl 51). Research has shown that McConnel & Kennedy came to own the Green Dragon, and it seems that the mill operatives' wages may have been paid out there.

In 1809, a gas-making plant was added to the site, and a gas-lighting system supplied by Boulton and Watt was installed (BWA 3147/3/478/21). This system was one of the earliest to have been installed in a cotton mill, and also one of the most ambitious, as 1500 gas burners were required, which were hung from the beams (Tann 1970). The gas was generated in a large bank of retorts, and stored in six gasometers (Smith 1932, 27), from where it was delivered to the burners via ¾ in (19 mm) pipes attached directly to the beams (BWA 3147/3/478/21).

Sedgwick Mill

Some ten years after the completion of the Long Mill, McConnel & Kennedy was offered land to the north of their first mill by a Colonel Sedgwick, for £5500. In the event, the property, which included a factory and several cottages, was bought in 1817 for £2700 (Lee 1972, 102). The existing buildings were all demolished, and the new factory was erected, which was named after the Colonel, becoming Sedgwick

Plate 51: The former Green Dragon public house on Jersey Street, a Grade II listed building (now demolished)

Mill. Construction began in 1818 and was completed by the mid-1820s, comprising four buildings round an internal courtyard (Fig 19). The largest component was a 17-bay spinning block, eight-storeys high, fronting Union Street, with an internal engine house at the western end. Two wing mills were erected to the north, the eastern of which was also built to a height of eight storeys, whilst the western was only five-storeys high. The central courtyard was enclosed by a four-storey block to the north.

The buildings were of brick and slate and of 'fireproof' construction, comprising cast-iron pillars and beams, and the floors were supported on brick arches built between the beams. The mill was built by John Lowe (Lee 1972, 102-3), to a design that allowed for little architectural adornment, although some quoining was added to the covered entrance on Cotton Street, beneath a gate-tower into the courtyard, and a stepped parapet of dressed stone embellished the main wing of the mill. The first 16 courses of brick above ground level were in English bond, and the courses above were in Flemish bond.

The internal engine house was three-storeys high, with rooms above to the height of the mill (Fig 20). There was originally no direct access to the spinning floors from these rooms, and they were therefore probably used for storage. The engine house contained a 54 hp

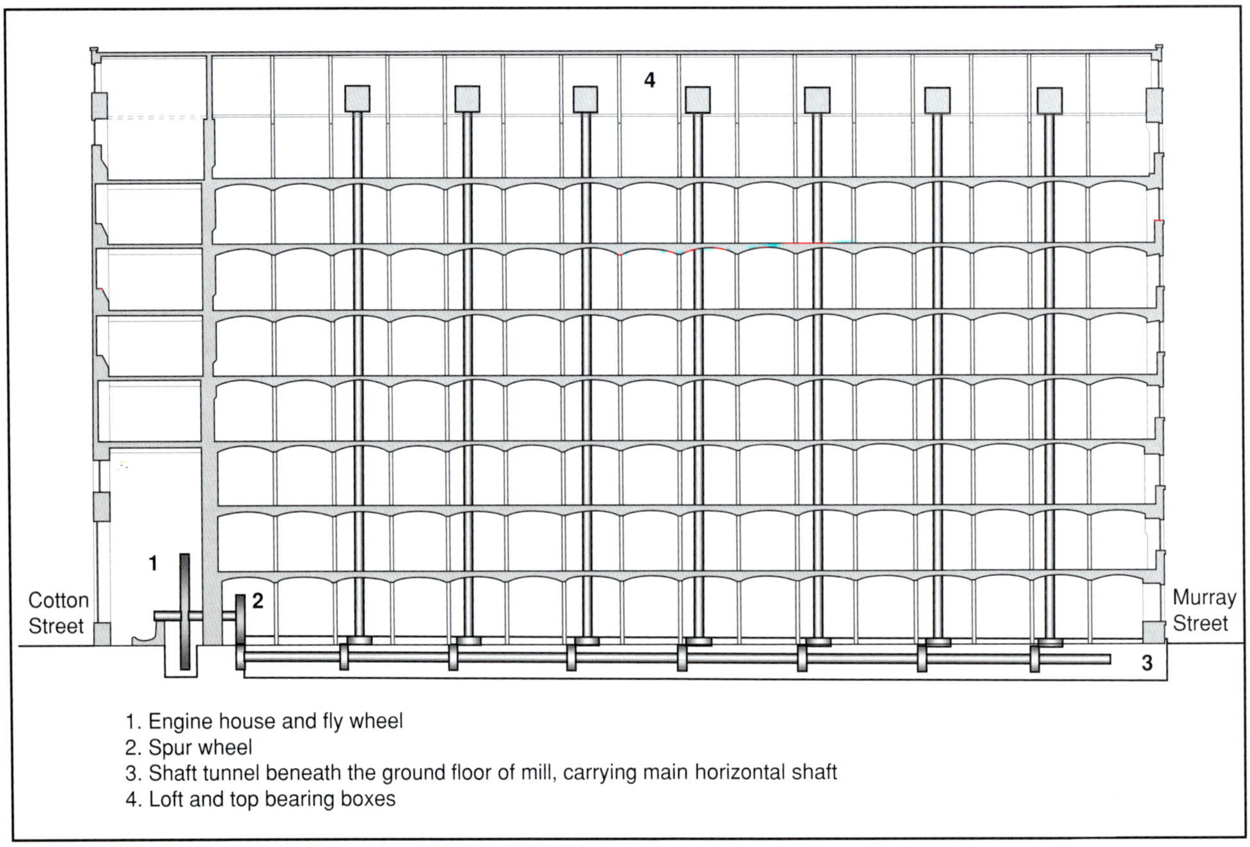

Figure 20: Longitudinal section through Sedgwick Mill, showing the configuration of the power transmission

Boulton and Watt beam engine, which was described by an eyewitness in 1821 as 'the best finished of any I have ever seen' (Smith 1932, 27). It was fitted with a 24 ft-diameter (7.31 m) flywheel and a 12 ft (3.66 m) toothed spurwheel, which connected to the main horizontal drive shaft.

A full set of drawings of the engine exist at the Boulton and Watt Archive at Birmingham (BWA 3147/5/465), but the only remaining physical evidence exposed during the watching brief was the drain of the engine's air pump and a rebate for the flywheel. However, the nature of the original transmission system, designed and installed by William Fairbairn and James Lillie, was elucidated. Fairly unusually, the main shaft ran under the mill and was housed in a purpose-built tunnel that lay beneath the main block and the East Wing (Pl 52). A feature of Fairbairn and Lillie's design is the way in which they dealt with the fact that axis of the East Wing is not at 90° to the axis of the main mill block (Fig 19). The shaft tunnel and hence the shaft was at 15° from the right-angle, and the gearing that enabled this to happen would have had to have been precisely cut to achieve a difficult engineering problem. The main shaft powered a series of vertical shafts in every other bay of Sedgwick Mill (Fig 20). Physical evidence for this was provided by cast-iron bearing boxes that were embedded in the brick-arched ceilings of each floor (Little 2007).

It is clear from the archives that the company moved into the mill in stages, so that it was partially working before construction was complete. When the mill was finished, McConnel & Kennedy emerged as the largest single employer of labour in Manchester,

Plate 52: View of the purpose-built shaft tunnel beneath the main block and the East Wing of Sedgwick Mill

having overtaken their rivals and friends A & G Murray, and for some years the company was the most extensive spinner in the country. John Kennedy retired from the firm in 1826, selling his share to James McConnel for £85,000, who appointed his two eldest sons, Henry and James, as partners in the business. The firm traded thereafter as McConnel & Co (McConnel 1913, 11).

Mid-Nineteenth-Century Alterations

Whilst some of the larger spinning firms in Manchester that wished to expand to cater for larger machinery chose to relocate to the fringes of the town, McConnel & Co and A & G Murray altered their existing factories to accommodate new machines. This meant that the main spinning blocks within the mills had to be altered, and McConnel & Co contracted William Fairbairn and James Lillie to undertake the required modifications during the early 1860s (Fairbairn 1866, 182).

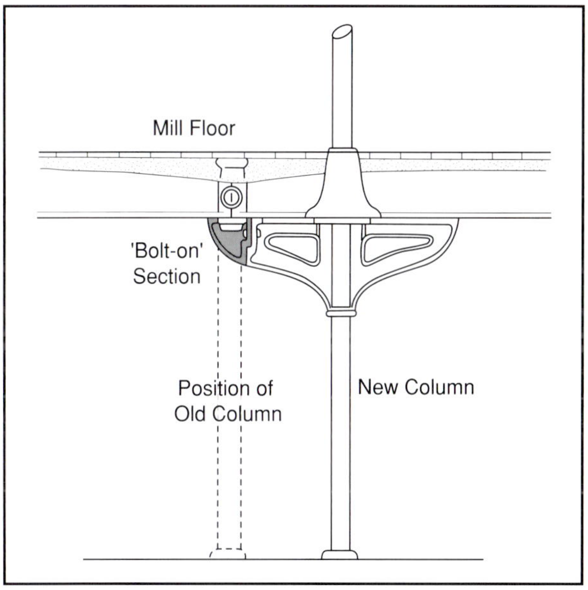

Figure 21: Column replacement in Sedgwick Mill

Fairbairn and Lillie's alteration involved moving a whole row of columns on each floor of Sedgewick Mill, which was carried out whilst the mill stayed in production. Each of the new columns had a winged capital, one side of which had a missing bolt-on section. The old column was then cut and removed, and the missing bolt-on section was keyed in and bolted tight; the engineering was absolutely precise, and needing no packing (Fig 21).

Fairbairn was also commissioned to modify the column layout in the Sedgwick West Wing. The McConnel instructions were precise; they only wanted one column on the top three floors, but were not too worried about the lower levels. The method Fairbairn used was not as successful as the work he had carried

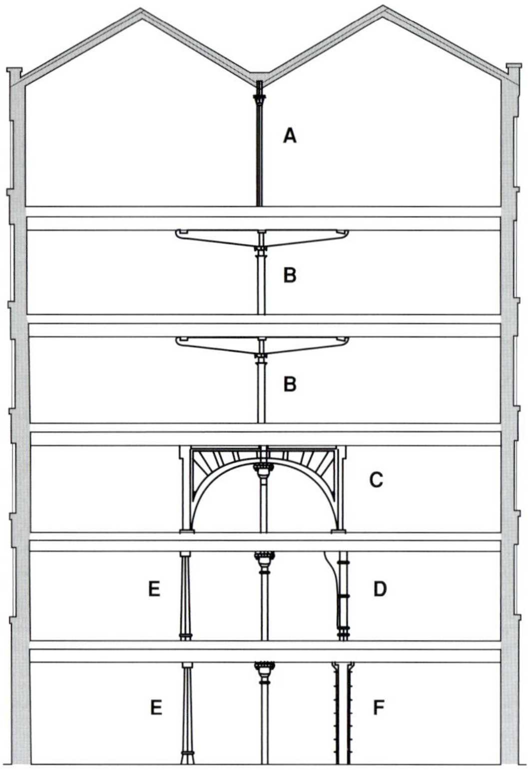

A. Fifth floor

B. Fourth and third floors. The length of the winged capital to the central column is fixed by the heads of the original columns

C. Segmental brace fixed between the two original columns on the second floor, with a central coumn added subsequently

D. The original cruciform column with added winged half sleeve

E. The original cruciform column

F. The original cruciform column encased within an added sleeve

Figure 22: Section across Sedgwick West Wing, showing the configuration of columns installed by Fairbairn and Lillie

out on the main block and East Wing, and involved putting a segmental brace between the columns on the second floor to carry the single column above. This had the effect of putting a great deal of lateral tension on the columns below, which began to show signs of stress. The remedy was to add a row of columns between the existing rows on these lower floors, creating a 'forest' of pillars (Fig 22).

Sedgwick New Mill

Further expansion took place on the site when Sedgwick New Mill was added in 1868 (Fig 19). This five-storey structure was built on an 'L-shaped plan, joined to the West Wing of the earlier Sedgwick Mill, and had larger bays, bigger windows, and higher ceilings than its predecessors. Built by AH Stott, Sedgwick New Mill was unusually narrow for the time, reflecting its design as a doubling mill for the making of sewing thread. It was only the first or second mill built by Stott, who went on to become one of the premier mill architects in Lancashire as Stott and Sons (Holden 1998). The mill was powered by two horizontal steam engines built by Goodfellows of Hyde, the remains of the engine house being exposed during the refurbishment work, including the flywheel pit (Pl 53). The primary drive was geared to a main upright shaft in an external stair tower, an unusual layout that was probably a symptom of the limited space available.

Plate 53: The exposed remains of the flywheel pit in the engine house of Sedgwick Mill

Plate 54: View of the partial internal collapse of Sedgwick New Mill

The mill was not a great success as far as McConnel & Co was concerned, articulated in a stream of letters of complaint to Stott and Sons in the company's archives: 'It is a sad reflection to us writing so many letters before we can convince you of mis-attention to our interests and neglect of duties on your part' (JRL MCK/2/2/23). The complaints were evidently founded, as the mill partially collapsed internally in 1994, at the point where there was an inherent weakness in the design (Pl 54).

Fine Cotton Spinners' and Doublers' Association Limited

In 1898, McConnel & Co became part of the Fine Cotton Spinners' and Doublers' Association Limited (FCSDA), which comprised 31 concerns with a share capital of £4,000,000 and an issue of debenture stock of £2,000,000 (Fine Cotton Spinners' and Doublers' Association Limited 1909). The remit of the combine was summarised in its prospectus: 'while no endeavour to create a monopoly is contemplated, it is expected that the centralisation of office work, and of buying, selling, and distributing arrangements, will lead to considerable economy'. Some ten years after amalgamation, McConnel & Co decided to expand the mill complex in Ancoats, and take advantage of the newly introduced technology of electric drives. This involved the building of two modest mills adjacent to the existing factories, which were both completed in 1912 (Pl 55).

Paragon and Royal Mills

These two mills were designed by H S Porter, who created structures in Edwardian Baroque, of Accrington brick with stone and terracotta embellishments, typical of the period (Pragnell 2000, 109-11). The advanced design used reinforced-concrete floors, supported by transverse steel beams and cast-iron columns, power being provided by electric motors that were housed in external towers. The adoption of this new technology followed its partial application to the rest of the site, which had been electrified in *c* 1909, the supply coming via a transformer house in the mill courtyard, although it was superseded by a sub-station built on Jersey Street in 1915. During this period, Sedgwick New Mill and Long Mill were 'practically rebuilt from bottom to top, so as to be fitted with the weight and power of the most modern machinery' (McConnel 1913, 16), hinting that ring-spinning frames were installed.

Paragon and Royal Mills were designed initially as five storeys, but were ultimately of six storeys and nine bays long. Paragon Mill was placed to the north of Sedgwick New Mill and formed an extension to the site (Fig 19), which necessitated the demolition of houses along Maria Street. It had an attached carding shed which, unusually, incorporated a partially flat and partially pitched glazed roof, because of the 'light rights' of the Royal Oak Hotel and other buildings that still stood on the corner of Jersey Street and Murray Street (Building Control Plan 4454).

Royal Mill was a rebuilding of the Old Mill, and was known originally as the New Old Mill, but was renamed Royal Mill in honour of a visit by King George VI and Queen Elizabeth in 1942 (Williams with Farnie 1992, 167). The mill was attached to the Sedgwick Old Mill by an extension that bridged the line of the former Cotton Street, and created a new entrance to the site (Pl 56).

Plate 55: McConnel & Co's Mill following the addition of Paragon and Royal Mills in 1912 (reproduced from McConnel 1913). Long Mill, on the left, connected with Royal Mill via a roof-level gangway over Henry Street. The Sedgwick Mills are shown to the right, with Paragon Mill visible to the rear

Plate 56: McConnel & Co's Royal Mill, showing the new entrance over Cotton Street

Late Developments

Spinning on the site ceased in *c* 1959, and most of the machinery was scrapped, although the ring-spinning frames may have been sold abroad (J Schofield *pers comm*). The buildings were sold to Leslie Fink, who let the space to a multitude of companies, many involved in the making of clothes, thus maintaining some connection with textile manufacturing. The Long Mill was taken over by the Flatley Drying Company, although their tenancy was short-lived: the mill caught fire one night in February 1959, and was completely destroyed (*News Chronicle*, 10 February 1959).

The site of Long Mill was redeveloped in 2001, and all associated earth-moving works were monitored by an archaeological watching brief. Two subterranean tunnels and the foundations for an engine that had been installed during the late nineteenth-century were exposed during this work (UMAU 2002).

The last of the small companies occupying the other mills had vacated the site by the mid-1990s, and the buildings became derelict and vulnerable to attack by vandals and arsonists. Several schemes for their refurbishment were proposed during the late twentieth century, but none came to fruition until the site was sold to the Dutch bank, ING, in 2001. The mills have since undergone structural repairs, and have been converted for mixed use that will ensure their long-term future.

The Emergence of the Steam-Powered Mill: Other Examples

Waller's Mill

The buried remains of other early steam-powered mills have been excavated elsewhere in Ancoats, including the factory referred to as Waller's Mill (Fig 12). This was built during the final years of the eighteenth century, and is shown on contemporary maps of the area, such as that published by Bancks and Thornton in 1800, as having comprised a rectangular building along the south side of New Islington. An archaeological investigation of the mill, carried out in advance of redevelopment, concluded that the original mill had measured some 48 m long with an internal width of 8 m (OA North 2004), and it was thus somewhat narrower than other Manchester factories. Indeed, its dimensions were more typical of the design associated with Arkwright-type mills of the late eighteenth century (Aspin 2003), suggesting that it was not intended to house spinning mules.

Documentary evidence for the initial development of the mill is scant. It can be speculated that an early occupant was John Lees, who is listed in Scholes' trade directories for 1794 and 1797 as a 'cotton manufacturer'

Plate 57: Flue at Waller's Mill, with the foundations for a boiler, probably of the long or wagon-type, to the rear

at New Islington, although the exact address of Lees' mill is not given. Similarly, the Boulton and Watt Archive contains a portfolio of 12 engine drawings relating to an unidentified mill in Ancoats, drawn up in April 1799 at the request of J Lees. Initially, a 16 hp engine was specified, although further correspondence in August 1799 requested plans for a 20 hp engine (BWA 3147/5/182). The absence of any further communication suggests that Boulton and Watt were not commissioned to supply an engine, although archaeological evidence has demonstrated that the mill was steam powered at an early date (OA North 2004).

Excavation also revealed that the mill had contained a single boiler, which had evidently been placed at ground-floor level in the western part of the building (Fig 23). The associated flue was 0.3 m wide and of brick construction, with a level-capping of stone flags (Pl 57). In contrast to most early nineteenth-century mills, which had attached or internal chimneys, that associated with Waller's Mill was free standing at some distance from the factory building. Parallels to this may be drawn from the late eighteenth-century Shude Hill and Garratt mills, which similarly had free-standing chimneys (Williams with Farnie 1992, 67-8).

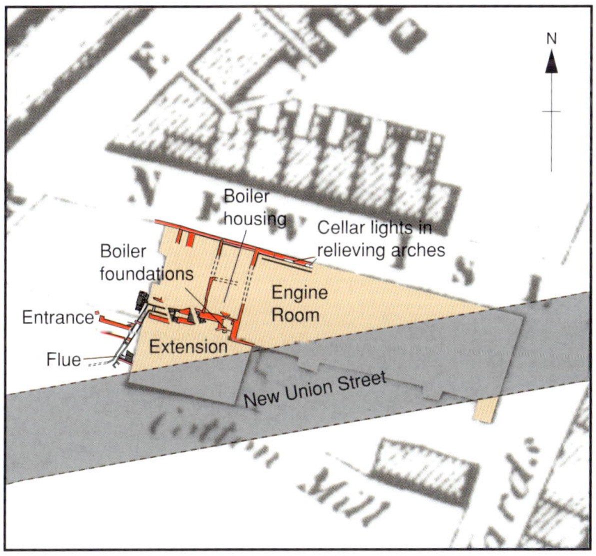

Figure 23: Excavated elements of Waller's Mill, superimposed on Bancks and Co's map of 1832

The exact position of the engine within the mill is not entirely certain, although the surviving elements of a basement, with a floor level some 2.3 m below the contemporary ground surface, incorporated at least three relieving arches in its build (Pl 58). The presence of these arches implies that the wall had been designed to support an increased load, such as the weight of a beam engine; parallels for this design may be drawn from the broadly contemporary engine house at A & G Murray's Mill (*Ch 6, p 105*).

Plate 58: Relieving arch in the basement of Waller's Mill, remodelled subsequently as a cellar light

The earliest specific entry for the mill within trade directories appears in an edition for the year 1815, which lists the cotton-spinning firm of S and R Waller as the occupant (Wardle and Bentham 1815, 152). It is upon this information that the mill is referred to as 'Waller's Mill': there are no contemporary documents referring specifically to the mill by this name. The Waller family is also named as the occupant of the mill on *Plans of All the Cotton-Spinning Mills Within the Township of Manchester* of *c* 1822, which identifies the building as comprising a factory and machine-makers' shop of four storeys at the western end, and the remainder of the factory being of six storeys with a loft. Bancks and Co's map of 1832 depicts an extension added to the western end of the mill, forming an L-shaped building (Fig 23). Excavation revealed that the entrance to the mill, at this time, was from the north-west via an enclosed courtyard, which presumably afforded a degree of security.

The 60": 1 mile Ordnance Survey map, published 1850, depicts much of the site of the mill as vacant land, with the north-western part having been completely redeveloped as a 'machine manufactory'. The relative paucity of demolition material associated with the mill was notable, implying that it had been dismantled with some care, presumably with a view to reusing the materials; the absence of any structural elements of the former power systems remaining *in situ* was particularly noticeable.

Moore's Mill

The well-preserved remains of a boiler house of a similar type to that within Waller's Mill were recorded during the excavation of an early nineteenth-century cotton-spinning factory on Mill Street in Ancoats (OA North 2005c). Erected in 1804 (PP (HC) 1834 [167] XX, A1), it was amongst the first of the large steam-powered mills

Plate 59: The excavated remains of the boiler house

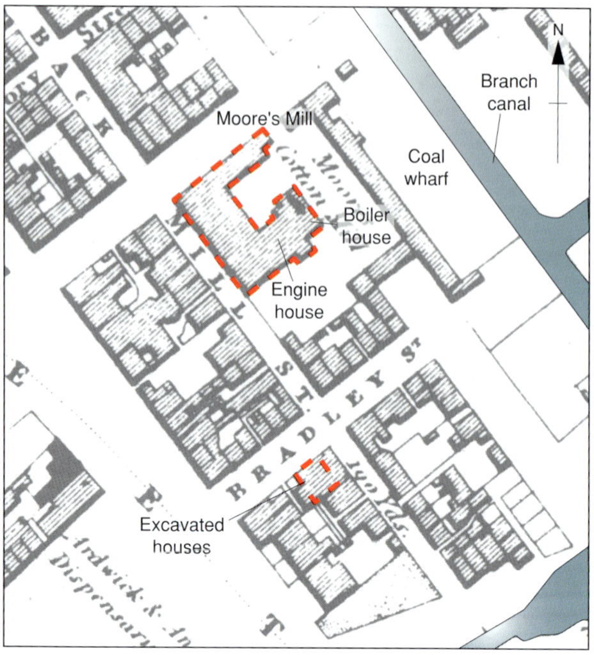

Figure 24: Location of excavated dwellings on Bradley Street, superimposed on Bancks and Co's map of 1832

in Ancoats built to the south of Shooter's Brook, and formed part of the initial industrial development along the Ashton Canal corridor (Fig 8). The mill was placed a short distance to the south-west of a newly opened branch of the canal and an associated coal wharf (Fig 24). Cartographic evidence indicates that the original mill comprised a single rectangular block, measuring some 27 x 12 m, with a smaller building attached to the south-east corner, which housed the steam-power plant.

The steam plant was replaced during the mid-1820s (*ibid*), with a new boiler house measuring 12.5 x 6.6 m (Pl 59). This contained a long or wagon-type boiler that, remarkably, does not appear to have been updated before the mill was closed in the mid-1870s (OA North 2005c). The character of the boiler house mirrored that of Waller's Mill, although it incorporated a greater proportion of refractory bricks in its build.

Workers' Housing in Ancoats

The construction of Moore's Mill in 1804 coincided broadly with an expansion of the housing stock in the immediate area, forming an integral component of the emerging urbanised industrial landscape. These houses included a row of back-to-back workers' dwellings erected along Bradley Street (Fig 24), which were eventually demolished during the late twentieth century, having been occupied

Plate 60: The remains of two early nineteenth-century cellar dwellings excavated on Bradley Street, Ancoats

for more than 150 years. The excavation of two of the houses revealed that they incorporated cellars, which had been used originally as dwellings accessed directly from Bradley Street (OA North 2005c). As constructed, both cellars were partitioned by a single-skin width wall, providing each room with a floor area of some 11½ x 10½ ft (3.5 x 3.2 m), and all contained a fireplace built into the western wall (Pl 60). The cellars were built largely of brick, although sandstone slabs had been used at the base of door jambs and for the floor; parts of the excavated floors were surfaced with brick, which had probably been laid when required to replace broken slabs. The floor of each cellar was 1.8 m below street level, and overlay a crude brick-lined drain, which provided the only means of drainage.

The remains of comparable dwellings have been excavated on Bengal Street and Jersey Street, which were some of the earliest workers' housing in Ancoats. These are depicted on Green's map of 1794 as a row of buildings along Bengal Street, with a short block fronting onto Jersey Street and two parallel rows to the rear (Fig 25). Excavation revealed that each of the properties fronting onto Bengal Street and Jersey Street incorporated two-roomed cellars (OA North 2007a). The dimensions of those on Bengal Street were typically 10½ ft (3.2 m) wide, but varied between 10 ft (3.05 m) and 12½ ft (3.81 m) long, and were somewhat smaller than the contemporary housing recorded in the 1980s on nearby Portugal Street (Roberts 1993, 17). The excavated cellars on Jersey Street were of a similar width, but each room was some 16½ ft (5.03m) long, providing comparatively large accommodation. The size and layout of these dwellings compared closely with an early nineteenth-century block of two-roomed cellars excavated some

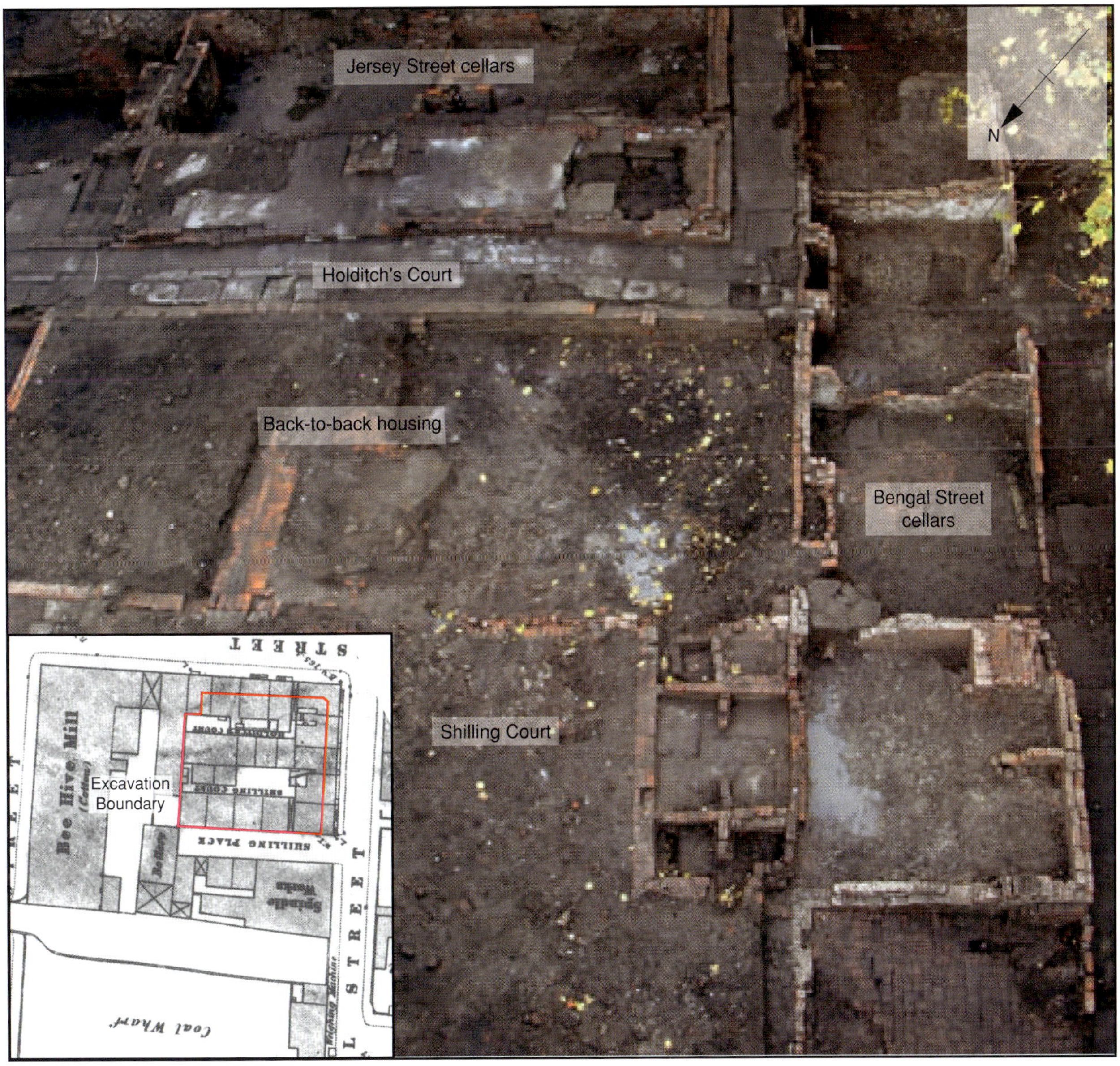

Figure 25: The excavated dwellings on Bengal Street / Jersey Street, with inset showing their location on the Ordnance Survey map of 1850

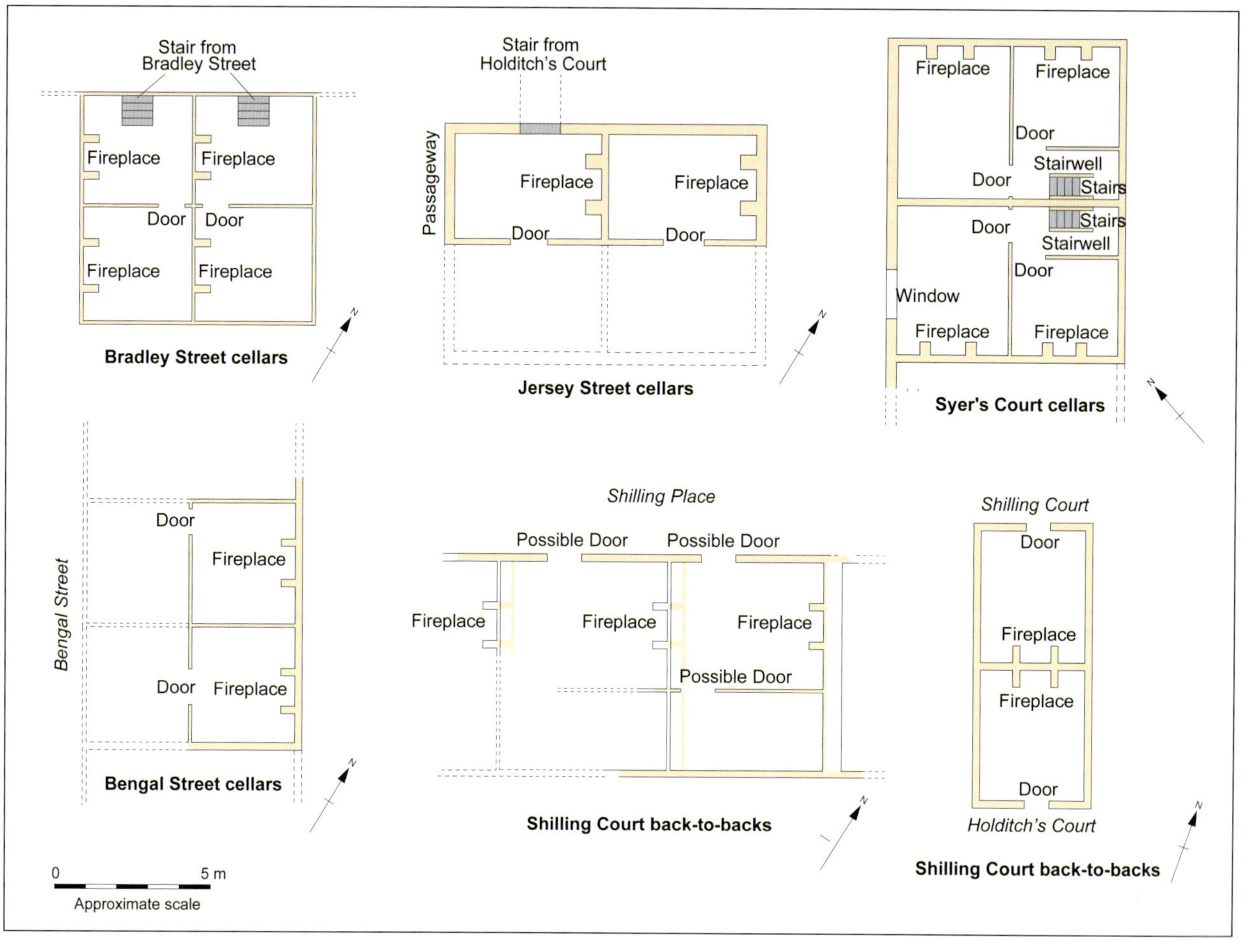

Figure 26: Plans showing the internal layout of excavated dwellings

500 m to the south-west at Syer's Court in Piccadilly (OA North 2006).

The back-to-back housing behind the street frontage did not incorporate cellars, and was entered from enclosed courtyards, named on historical mapping as Shilling Court and Holditch's Court (Fig 25), with narrow passageways affording access to Bengal Street and Jersey Street. The size of these single-roomed dwellings was broadly consistent with the individual cellars that fronted onto Jersey Street, although the total accommodation space was considerably reduced (Fig 26). Green's map depicts another parallel row of houses to the north, fronting onto Heath Street, which actually became a cul-de-sac known as Shilling Place. Excavation demonstrated that the ground floor of each of these houses contained two rooms of unequal size, with a total internal floor space slightly larger than the cellars along Jersey Street (Fig 26).

The varying size of these workers' dwellings reflects their unregulated construction by different property speculators, designed without the benefit of an architect. This is similarly reflected in the diversity of the internal layout employed in their build, clear variation being noted in the positioning of fireplaces and means of access (Fig 26). These factors perhaps highlight that urban workers' housing was a new element of the townscape, although the rows of back-to-back dwellings and numerous small alleys and blind courtyards came to typify working-class accommodation throughout the industrialised North of the nineteenth century (Muthesius 1982, 107).

5

THE RISE AND PROGRESS OF AN ICONIC COTTON-SPINNING FIRM: THE HISTORY OF A & G MURRAY

Ian Miller

Introduction

George and Adam Murray grew from a childhood in the middle strata of eighteenth-century Scottish society to become owners of one of the largest pioneering cotton-spinning firms in the world (Howe 1984, 9). Hardly any of the company records have survived, however, and in their absence a wide range of other archive sources, including published maps, contemporary newspapers and magazines, eyewitness descriptions, rate assessments, leases, commercial trade directories, and deposited building plans, need to be used to produce a coherent account of the origin and progress of the company. Much of this material was collated as part of the *Greater Manchester Textile Mill Survey* (RCHME and GMAU 1989), and a documentary archive generated from that project is curated within GMAU.

The development of the A & G Murray company can be divided into eight broad phases, which correlate with significant documented events. The account, though, cannot be seen in isolation, as the changing market conditions provide a vital context against which the success of the company can be judged. Similarly, whilst the adoption of cutting-edge technology was a fundamental component of the early success of the company, its efficient use was dependent upon the personnel employed to operate the machinery (Kennedy 1831b, 26-7), and thus an overview of the physical conditions endured by the workers is an important element in assessing the influence of the Murray brothers in the development of both the cotton industry and the industrial community of Ancoats.

From Scottish Origins to Cotton Spinning in Manchester

George and Adam Murray, born in 1761 and 1766 respectively, originated from the small town of New Galloway in Kirkcudbrightshire, Scotland. Their father was a shopkeeper in the town and was well acquainted with the Kennedy family, who lived on the nearby country estate of Knocknalling. George and Adam Murray, together with their two brothers and sister, paid numerous visits to John Kennedy at Knocknalling during their youth 'by way of seeing country life' (Kennedy 1849, 8-9), and developed a firm friendship that was to last throughout their lives. The Murrays were also good friends with James McConnel, a close neighbour in New Galloway, with whom they were also to become closely connected in business. Another local family with whom the Murrays were to become associated in Manchester was the Coates, who lived at Woodfoot of Knocknalling, and similarly migrated to Lancashire to become involved in the textile trade (D Hilton *pers comm*).

Apprenticeship in Lancashire

Despite being the younger brother, it was Adam Murray who was first to migrate to England in search of a career when, in 1780 and at the age of 14, he travelled to Chowbent (now Atherton) near Leigh in Lancashire. His destination was the workshop of William Cannan, an uncle of James McConnel, where he was to be apprenticed as a textile machine-maker (Lee 1972, 12). William Cannan originated from the parish of Kells in southern Scotland, where he had been trained as a carpenter before moving to England during the 1760s 'for the sake of improving himself' (Kennedy 1849, 9). Dorning Rasbotham, an eighteenth-century travel writer, described Chowbent in 1787 as a place where 'several families have acquired fortunes by making spinning jennies and carding machines which they send into Scotland, Ireland and different parts of the kingdom' (quoted in Lunn 1971, 131). Upon arrival in Chowbent, William Cannan took advantage of this lucrative trade and applied his carpentry skills to making textile machines, and soon employed more than 30 apprentices making spindles, jennies, and looms (Wood and Wood 1992, 117).

Adam Murray was not the first Scot to be apprenticed under Cannan, and was by no means the last: he was joined in 1781 by James McConnel, then George Murray, and 14-year old John Kennedy in 1784 (*op cit*, 116). For all of these young men, the *c* 170 mile journey to Chowbent would have presented

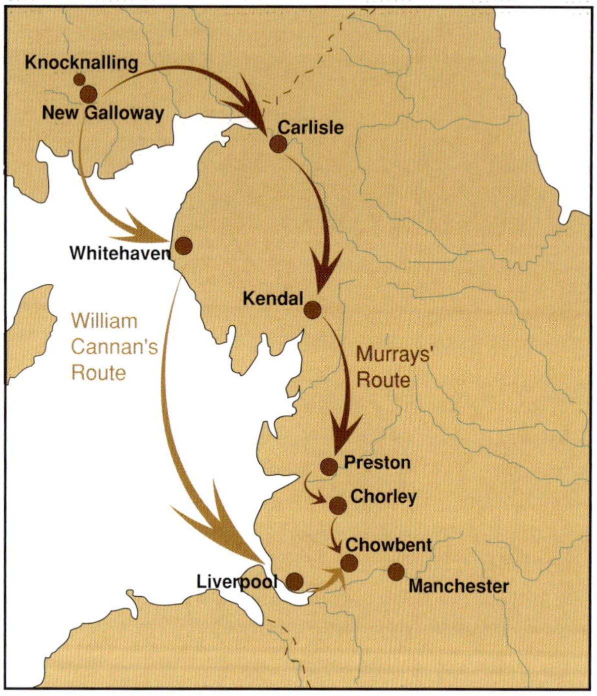

Figure 27: Map showing the routes from New Galloway to Manchester

a challenge in itself: William Cannan appears to have travelled by boat via Whitehaven and Liverpool, whilst the Murrays, McConnel, and Kennedy made the journey overland (Fig 27). James McConnel walked the entire distance, whilst John Kennedy completed the journey in six days on a pony (Kennedy 1849, 12). Their route may have been influenced by the long-standing link between Galloway and Newton-le-Willows (a short distance to the east of Chowbent), where generations of Scottish drovers had taken their cattle to market (Wood and Wood 1992, 115).

This was an exciting time to be undertaking such an apprenticeship, as the rapidly expanding cotton industry was placing increasing demands upon the machines required for factory-based production. The earliest of these machines had reached their first stage of maturity during the 1780s (*Ch 2, p 13*), but they required continual improvement to satiate the growing demand for output. The introduction of gearing and finely engineered rollers in Arkwright's water-frame, for instance, relied heavily upon the skills of the clockmaker rather than the carpenter and the blacksmith, who had traditionally been charged with manufacturing simple spinning wheels. This trend was reinforced by the invention of the mule, the gearing and motion of which were more complex than for any earlier machine. Moreover, its growing predominance created the demand for a textile-machinery industry that was capable of building to much more precise engineering standards. Against this background, it is of note that Samuel Crompton is said to have used a workshop in Chowbent, and possibly that of Cannan's, during the 1770s to solve a problem he encountered in developing his spinning machine (Lunn 1971, 170). It was perhaps through this connection that, some years later, Crompton ordered a small carding engine from William Cannan. John Kennedy was dispatched to deliver the machine and attempted to take the opportunity to inspect Crompton's workshop. Whilst Kennedy failed in this desire, he was later to become a 'friend, benefactor and biographer' of Crompton (French 1859, 103).

Whilst at Chowbent, the Murrays, McConnel, and Kennedy all developed their expertise in the manufacture and operation of spinning machinery, which undoubtedly gave them a distinct advantage over other cotton spinners in the years to come. This association of machine-builders-cum-cotton-spinners certainly appears to have been an important route of entry into the spinning industry for several of the major manufacturers in Manchester (*Ch 2, p 17*). Indeed, it seems to have been a characteristic of Manchester's early factory-based textile trades, and has been recognised as a combination alien, for instance, to the Midlands' spinning industry (Chapman 1967, 216).

Starting a Business in Manchester

Upon completing his seven-year apprenticeship with William Cannan in 1787, Adam Murray wasted little time in establishing a machine-making business of his own; by 1790, he had accumulated sufficient capital to relocate to Manchester and invest in land in the developing district of Ancoats. A deed between Messrs Sedgwick and Adam Murray, dated 24 June 1790, refers to the release in fee of a plot of land on Bengal Street, at the western side of its junction with Union Street (Fig 28), subject to an annual chief rent of £19 2s 1d (RCHME and GMAU 1989). This land was to be developed during the late 1790s for Adam Murray's first spinning mill, suggesting that he had anticipated the building of a purpose-built factory at a very early stage, and pre-empted McConnel and Kennedy's decision by several years (*Ch 4, p 50*). In the interim, however, he dedicated himself to making textile machinery, based nearby on Newton Street, and appears to have focused upon developing improvements to the spinning mule. Notably, he applied 'double speed motion' to some pairs of hand-powered mules for 'customers in Derbyshire, who had artificial power' (Kennedy 1831a, 342), implying that he had improved the design and operation of powered mules before establishing a spinning factory of his own. Moreover, he was evidently engaged in cotton spinning during this period, presumably using his own machines, as a sideline to machine-making (*ibid*).

Adam Murray thrived in business and, by 1797, had expanded to occupy space in three premises in Ancoats, on Newton Street, Henry Street, and Union

Street, where he had machinery and stock insured to the value of £2000 (Royal Exchange 7253/32A/157421). The insurance document identifies Adam Murray's Union Street premises as having been within 'Mr Lane's Factory', which was probably situated on the eastern side of Bengal Street at its junction with Union Street (Fig 28). This factory may have been owned by Aaron Lane, who is listed in trade directories as a cotton spinner on Union Street, with a warehouse at Half Moon Court (*eg* Scholes 1794, 79).

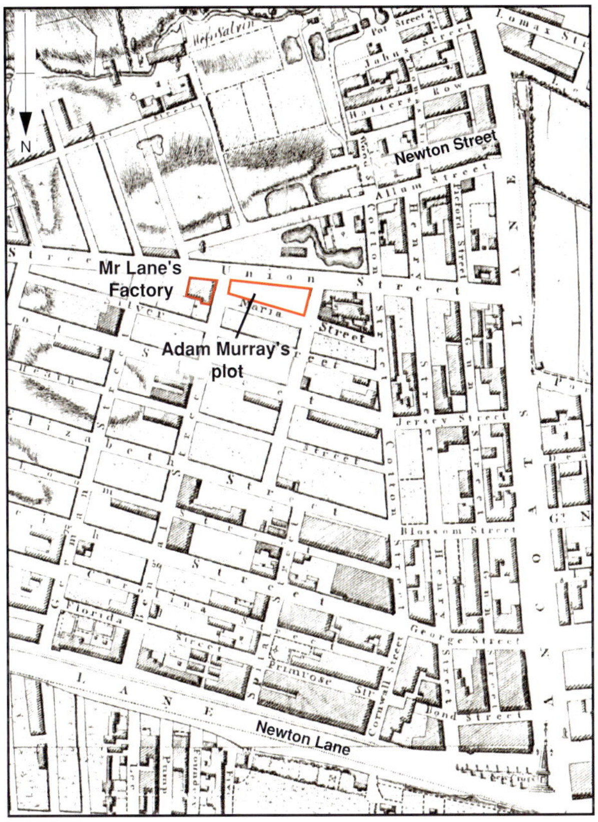

Figure 28: Extract from Laurent's map of 1793, showing Adam Murray's land and 'Mr Lane's Factory'

Adam Murray continued to occupy this building for some years, and is listed as such in the Poor Rate Assessments for the area during the early nineteenth century (*eg* MLSU M9/40/2/67). The layout of the site is shown on the *Plans of all the Spinning Factories within the Township of Manchester*, compiled in *c* 1822, which annotates a three-storey 'counting house', a single-storey 'lumber room', a small yard, and a three-storey factory comprising some 268 square yards (245 m^2). It was evidently steam-powered by that date, as it is included in a list of factories, compiled in 1820, that used the Rochdale Canal as a supply of water 'for the purposes of working the steam engines' (GMCRO B2/10/6).

The buildings are depicted partially on an engraving published in 1831, which features the 'counting house' (Pl 61). This three-storey, four-bay structure is shown to have had a gable roof, and architectural

Plate 61: Extract from an engraving of c 1829, showing 'Mr Lane's factory' (reproduced from Pyne 1831)

adornment typical of the late eighteenth century. The entrance from Union Street, for instance, incorporated a pediment that was flanked by engaged columns, although the asymmetrical arrangement of the windows on the first floor betray the commercial nature of the building. A single-storey outbuilding to the east corresponds to the 'lumber store', and a section of the wall forming the boundary of the adjacent yard is also shown. Part of the 'factory' is depicted to the rear, and similarly appears to have been of three storeys.

Phase 1, The First Mill (1798 - 1801)

When Adam Murray secured the lease of land in Ancoats in 1790, the cotton trade was experiencing a boom period that lasted until the end of 1792. By then, war with France was considered inevitable, and confidence in trade dipped accordingly, whilst the declaration of war in 1793 resulted in a contraction of trade with Europe. The problems were offset by increased exports to North America, however, and the cotton trade emerged from the crisis by the end of 1793 (Edwards 1967, 12-27). Exports continued to expand until the autumn of 1796, when problems occurred as the markets were well-stocked and merchants became reluctant to give large orders until they knew the outcome of peace negotiations with France. This was coupled with a growing scarcity of cash, as holders of paper currency tried to convert it into gold and silver coinage, forcing the Bank of England to suspend such transactions in February 1797 (Holland 1976, 79). These difficulties continued into 1798, when many Manchester spinners went into 'short time' working. In the midst of this uncertain economic climate, McConnel & Kennedy managed to establish their first multi-storey spinning mill (*Ch 4, p 50*), although they were forced into selling yarn at great discount because of the lack of cash.

The cotton trade improved during the second half of 1798, by which time Adam and George Murray were engaged in building their first mill. Their early production benefited from the remarkable recovery the trade had achieved by the middle of 1799, although a short-lived slump in the cotton market, and resultant low prices towards the end of the year, was triggered by a bad harvest and financial upheavals in Hamburg and other European towns central to the cotton export trade. It was, however, Scotland that provided the main market for the fine yarn spun by A & G Murray and McConnel & Kennedy at this time, and particularly the expanding muslin-weaving industry in Paisley and Glasgow, which demanded yarn in counts above 100 (Lee 1972, 23-7).

The Murrays' First Mill

By 1798, Adam Murray had formed a business partnership with his brother George, who had completed his apprenticeship with William Cannan, and had also married Cannan's daughter, Jane. Entries in trade directories for this period list the Murrays' commercial address as Newton Street (Bancks 1800, 33), but after forming a partnership, the brothers commenced immediately with financing a purpose-built, steam-powered spinning mill on the land secured in Ancoats. This multi-storey factory, originally called Union Mill but referred to subsequently as Old Mill, was erected along Union Street at its junction with Murray Street (known at this time as Pit Street), and parallel to the proposed line of the Rochdale Canal. The canal, however, would be to the south of Union Street, leading the Murrays to adopt an innovative approach to obtaining a canal-side location for their mill (*p 71*).

Old Mill is likely to have been the first cotton-spinning factory ever built to a height of eight storeys, although taller commercial buildings had been erected previously, including some of the Goree Warehouses of 1793 in Liverpool that were reputedly 13 storeys high (Liverpool City Council 2005, 123). Old Mill probably took at least one year to build, although the actual date at which construction began is uncertain. Those responsible for the design and erection of the mill are unknown, but it was clearly a specialist undertaking that would have required the skills of several professions, including builders, stonemasons, and iron-founders. Of great importance was the role of the millwright, whose remit at Old Mill would have been designing the system of power transmission from the steam engine to the machinery on each floor.

The influence of the millwright on factory design increased greatly during the nineteenth century, and it is no coincidence that Manchester-based firms came to dominate this specialist trade (Fitzgerald 1988, 137). A notable exception was Thomas Lowe of Nottingham, an influential millwright during the late eighteenth century, to whom William Fairbairn attributed all the important early factory millwork: 'as cotton mills were then in their infancy he was the only person qualified from experience to undertake the construction of the gearing' (Pole 1877, 121). Lowe had been involved in the planning of Arkwright's two earliest factories, and was appointed as a millwright by at least three other cotton spinners in Nottingham (Tann 1974, 84). His first commission in Lancashire was provided by Peter Drinkwater, who required Lowe to execute the millwork in his Piccadilly Mill in 1789, and was followed by similar requests from Samuel Oldknow at Stockport in 1791, Robert Owen at Chorlton-on-Medlock in 1795, and George Lee at his Salford Twist Mill in 1801, Lancashire's first fireproof factory. The other millwright specialising in steam-powered factory millwork in Manchester during the 1790s was Peter Ewart, whom Tann considered to be of equal importance with Lowe, along with William and Henry Creighton (*ibid*).

Figure 29: Extract from Bancks and Thornton's map of 1800, showing the Murrays' Old Mill and the incomplete canal

In its original form, Old Mill had plan dimensions of 105 x 42 ft (32 x 13 m), and each of the eight floors were of 11 bays. Its construction required an estimated 400,000 bricks, all of which were hand-made. These will almost certainly have been produced locally, if not on the actual site, using the clay excavated during the construction of Old Mill; late eighteenth-century maps of the area show several brick fields in the vicinity, whilst an advertisement in the *Manchester Mercury* on 17 December 1799 offered for sale 'a quantity of good clay for making bricks in Prussia Street. Part of the clay is already cast, and the purchase may be accommodated with land sufficient for working four or five stools'. McConnel & Kennedy are known to have taken advantage of the local natural clay resource, and the bricks for their mill were manufactured on the firm's land in Ancoats (Lee 1972, 102).

Old Mill was largely completed in 1798, and attention had turned to installing the steam-power plant by September of that year (BWA 3147/2/10/35). The earliest cartographic depiction of the mill is upon a map of the area that was published in 1800 by Bancks and Thornton (Fig 29). This was produced at a scale that lacks detail of individual buildings, but nevertheless shows a single rectangular factory block on the site, and an apparent boundary wall to the north, forming an enclosed yard. The map also shows the Ancoats section of the Rochdale Canal as being unfinished; prior to the completion of the canal in 1804, all raw materials and finished goods would have been carried to and from the mill by cart.

The Steam-Power Plant

The mill was powered initially by a steam engine supplied by the firm of Boulton and Watt, the builders of the most advanced machines at that time (*Ch 2, p 22*). In accordance with an agreement of 1 August 1798, Boulton and Watt undertook to supply a 12 hp engine at a cost of £620, with the promise to provide '...all necessary directions in writing and with proper plans & drawings for the erecting, completing, using and working the said Engine in the most useful & beneficial manner' (BWA 3147/5/167).

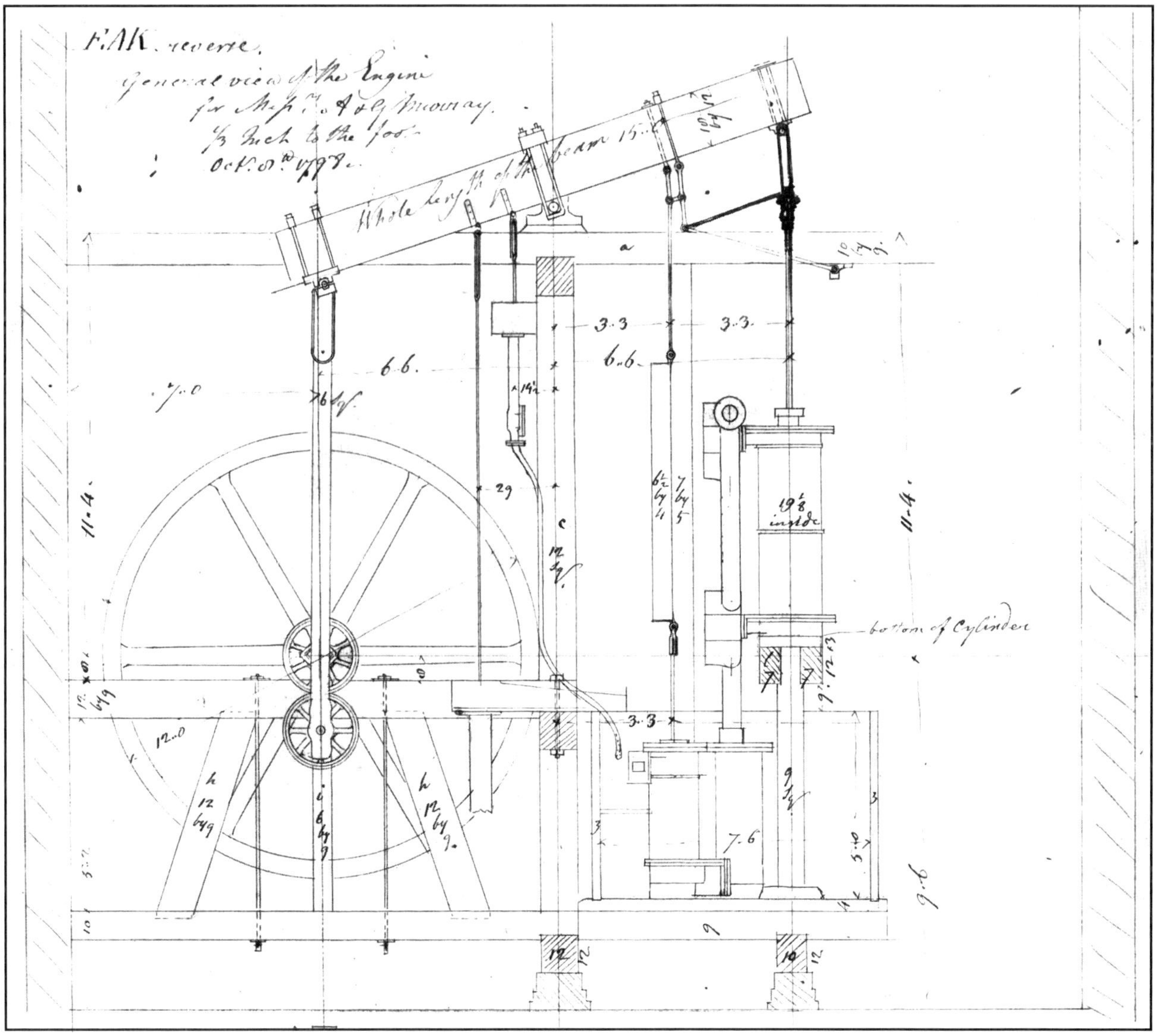

Plate 62: Boulton and Watt design drawing of the engine for A & G Murray, 1798 (reversed view) (reproduced courtesy of Birmingham City Archives)

Boulton and Watt draughted the initial drawings for the engine in June 1798, although these were seemingly not finalised until October of that year (Pl 62). It was to consist of a timber-framed, double-acting beam engine with 'sun and planet' gearing, which characterised Boulton and Watt's engines of that date. The beam was to be constructed of 'straight grained oak', and all other structural components were of deal. The flywheel, seemingly of cast-iron construction, was of 12 ft (3.66 m) diameter, and the power transmission was taken directly from the flywheel shaft. The drawings appear to indicate that the steam for the engine was to be generated by a single long-type boiler, which is shown on original plans to have been placed adjacent to the engine, although separated by a full-height cross-wall. A note on one of the plans states that 'they have the boiler that was first intended for Mr Bound' (BWA 3147/5/167).

A letter addressed to Matthew Boulton from the Murrays, dated 26 September 1798, states: '...the Engine materials sent up per Worthington & Gilbert, are all laid down here in good order agreeable to your letter and have only to beg you send a Man of your approving to put it up. We hope it will be convenient for him to be here on or before the 8 October' (BWA 3147/3/416/74). This implies that the mill was not fitted with mechanical power until the end of 1798, although this would not have precluded the installation and use of hand-powered machinery.

It is not clear from Boulton and Watt's drawings precisely where the first engine was to be situated, but it may be deduced that its housing was to occupy an area measuring 28 ft long by 9 ft wide (8.5 x 2.7 m), and over 25 ft (7.6 m) high. The drawings also indicate the engine was to be placed transversely across the building, suggesting that it was sited at the eastern end of the mill. Whilst Bancks and Thornton's map of 1800 should not be relied upon for precise measurements, it is notable that the single block representing Old Mill is seemingly larger than the mill, again hinting that the engine house may have been attached to the eastern gable. The position of the chimney is similarly unknown from documentary sources, although it would undoubtedly have been in close proximity to the boiler.

The Machinery

As with any textile factory, Old Mill was a functional building that was designed to house a range of machinery in the most efficient manner. The production of yarn required several successive operations, which may be summarised into three main stages: the opening and initial preparation of cotton bales; carding and the production of a roving; and stretching, drawing, and spinning to produce the yarn. Some spinning mills also contained winding machines, which transferred the spun yarn onto bobbins before dispatching. A summary of these processes is presented in *Appendix 1*.

The archive sources provide few references to the layout of the machinery within Old Mill, although it may be relevant to draw comparison with McConnel & Kennedy's first mill, for which there is considerable surviving documentation (McConnel 1913, 38-9). The initial processes of opening the cotton bales and cleaning the raw cotton were undertaken manually. Known as 'batting', the cleaning involved spreading the cotton on a raised mesh of cords and beating it with sticks of hazel or holly to remove seeds and other impurities (Pl 63). This produced considerable amounts of dust, presenting a health hazard to the workers and a serious fire risk. Consequently, this process was often undertaken in detached ancillary buildings, or even at a separate site, which may have been an option taken by the Murrays. The initial processing was mechanised with the invention of a scutcher in *c* 1800, although this machine was not introduced to the Manchester area until 1808-9, and even then cotton of fine quality continued to be processed manually (Tomlinson 1861, 453); an eyewitness account published in 1832 noted that the cleaning of the raw cotton at A & G Murray's Mill was still carried out by hand (Allen 1832, 129).

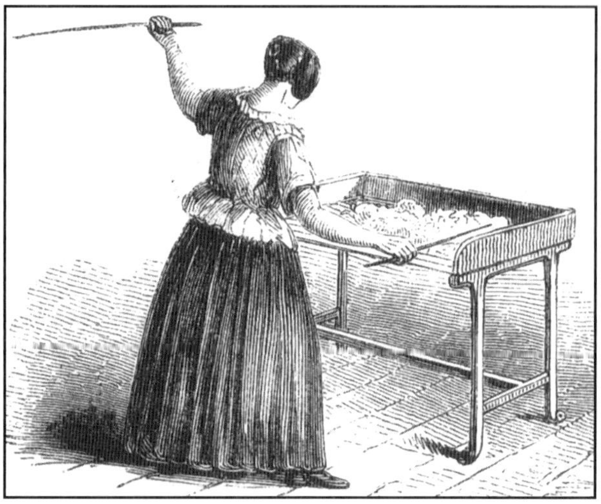

Plate 63: Batting the raw cotton by hand with sticks (reproduced from Tomlinson 1861)

The first mechanised stage in the production of cotton yarn was carding, which combed the cotton fibres into parallel lengths (Pl 64). For fine spinning, the cotton normally passed through two carding engines. Montgomery (1833, 20) considered that the optimum position for the carding rooms in a multi-storey mill was nearest the centre of the building, on the third or fourth floor. McConnel & Kennedy, however, installed their heavy carding engines in the lower storeys of their first factory (also known as Old Mill), from where the prepared cotton was transferred to the upper storeys for drawing (Pl 65), roving, and finally spinning. This layout was adopted increasingly by other firms, and

Plate 64: Engraving showing a set of double carding engines (reproduced from Barfoot 1840)

Plate 65: Engraving of drawing frames (reproduced from Barfoot 1840)

remained standard practice throughout the later part of the nineteenth century (Thornley 1907, 187). The plan of *c* 1822 provides the earliest documentary reference for the installation of carding engines on the lower floors of the A & G Murray's Mill, and it is likely that this had been the internal layout for some years previously.

It is probable that at least some, if not all, of the machinery within Old Mill was built by the Murrays themselves at their Newton Street premises. Insurance records from 1799 (Royal Exchange 7253/169894) refer to the Murrays providing cover for machinery to the value of £3000 in their new factory, which may equate to approximately 50 mules; at this time, James McConnel was selling spinning mules with 180 spindles for about £57 each (Lee 1972, 20). This factor in itself suggests that the mill was not filled entirely with machinery in 1799, a situation that was commonplace amongst new factories. By way of illustration, Peter Drinkwater stated in correspondence with Boulton and Watt in 1789 that Arkwright's factory at Shude Hill 'has been more than seven years filling with machinery and I am doubtful whether with convenience it could have been filled much sooner' (BWA 3147/5/44).

Phase 2, The Second Mill (1801 - *c* 1804)

The temporary cessation of war with France brought about by the signing of the Treaty of Amiens in 1802 resulted in a rapid increase in trade (Edwards 1967, 15), stimulating a burst of mill building in Manchester over the following 12 months. Prior to this boom, however, A & G Murray completed what was an effective doubling of the size of their mill with an extension to the east, referred to as Decker Mill, and McConnel & Kennedy began the construction on their 'Long Mill' (*Ch 4, p 51*). The resumption of war with France in 1803 caused another slump in the market; the frenzied activity of the boom period had created a glut of goods and resulted in a downturn in trade. Nevertheless, the spinning sector fared rather better than the rest of the textile industry, stocks of yarn being cleared by the end of 1803 (Edwards 1967, 15).

A & G Murray and McConnel & Kennedy continued to dominate the Scottish market for fine yarn during this period, which probably reflects the superiority

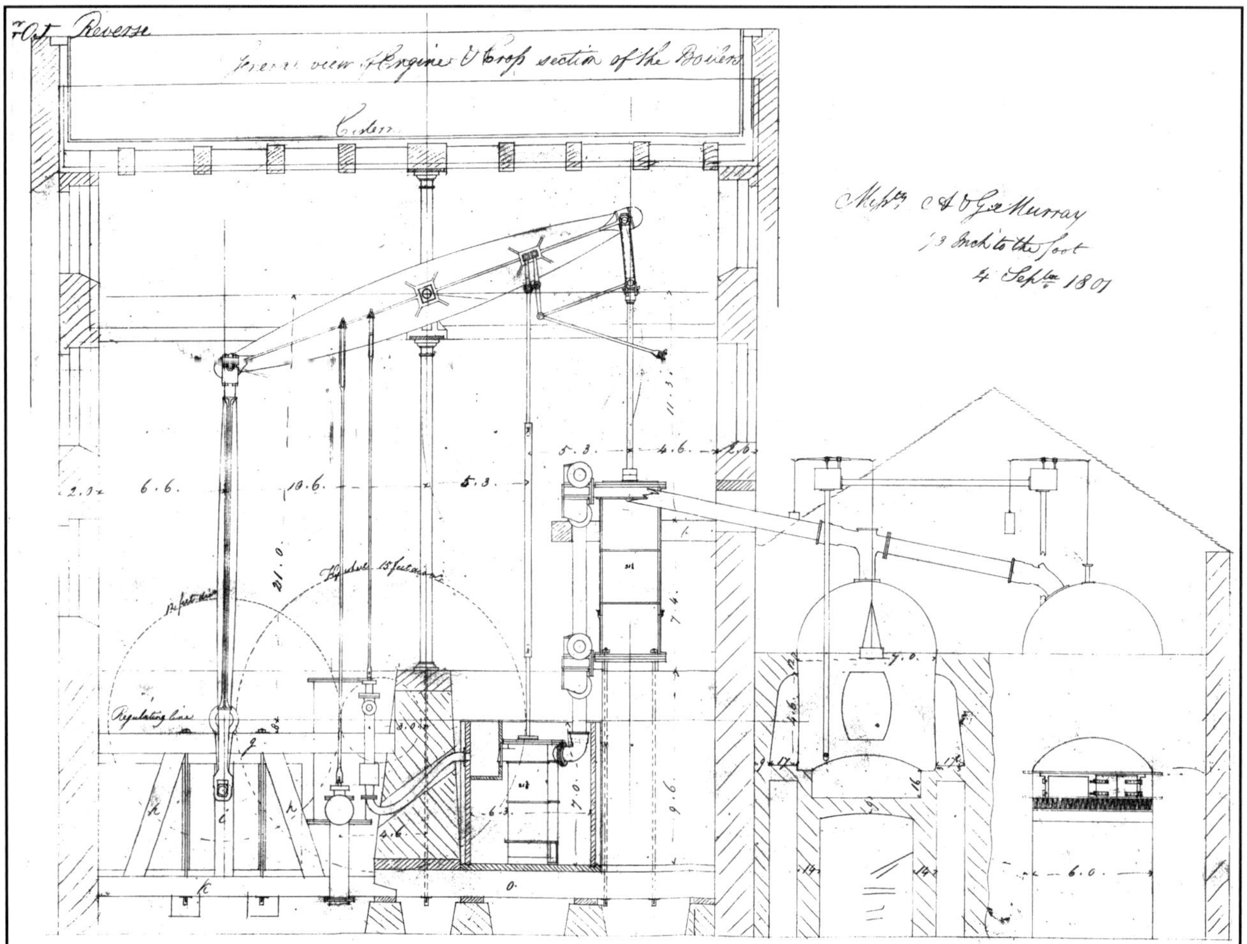

Plate 66: Boulton and Watt design drawing, showing section across the 1801 engine and boilers (reversed view) (reproduced courtesy of Birmingham City Archives)

of their machinery, coupled with high productivity resulting from the adoption of steam power. It is perhaps also likely that both firms exploited their Scottish origins and family connections to secure contracts. Indeed, their yarn reached the markets via agents working on commission, and amongst the agents used by McConnel & Kennedy during the early 1800s was John Kennedy's brother, Robert (Lee 1972, 23-7).

Decker Mill

By 1801, A & G Murray was actively engaged in erecting Decker Mill, which occupied the space between Old Mill and Bengal Street, and was similarly built to a height of eight storeys. It was ten bays long, and was therefore slightly shorter than Old Mill, but a little wider (*Ch 6, p 103*). The architecture largely mirrored that of Old Mill, resulting in what was visually a single building range. The origin of Decker Mill's name is obscure; it may perhaps have been named after a financial backer, or simply referred to an additional level to the firm's spinning capacity.

Access to Old and Decker Mill was afforded by an external tower of brick construction with stone stairs around a central C-section newel. The stair tower was placed against the northern elevation of the buildings, with an entrance from the mill yard at ground-floor level.

Updated Steam-Power Plant

Whilst the installation of powered machinery in Decker Mill is likely to have been gradual, as it would have taken some time to build, the Murrays updated their power system at the earliest opportunity. The original 12 hp engine was sold to a Mr Gaskell of Newton Heath and replaced with a 40 hp model, which was also supplied by Boulton and Watt. The design plans for this engine, dated 1801 (BWA 3147/5/295), show that it incorporated several design improvements, notably the replacement of the 'sun and planet' gearing with a crank (Pl 66). It was housed in a new building, placed against the stair tower in the mill yard, and steam was provided by two long boilers, which were placed in a dedicated two-storey building immediately adjacent to the engine house (Pl 67). Correspondence within the Boulton and Watt Archive, dated to March 1802, requested a quotation for extra materials, such as the cost of pillars, connecting wheels, crank shaft, and plummer blocks, and also for calculating the difference between a cast-iron beam and a wooden beam for a 40 hp engine (BWA 3147/5/295). This implies that the engine had not been installed by March 1802, but

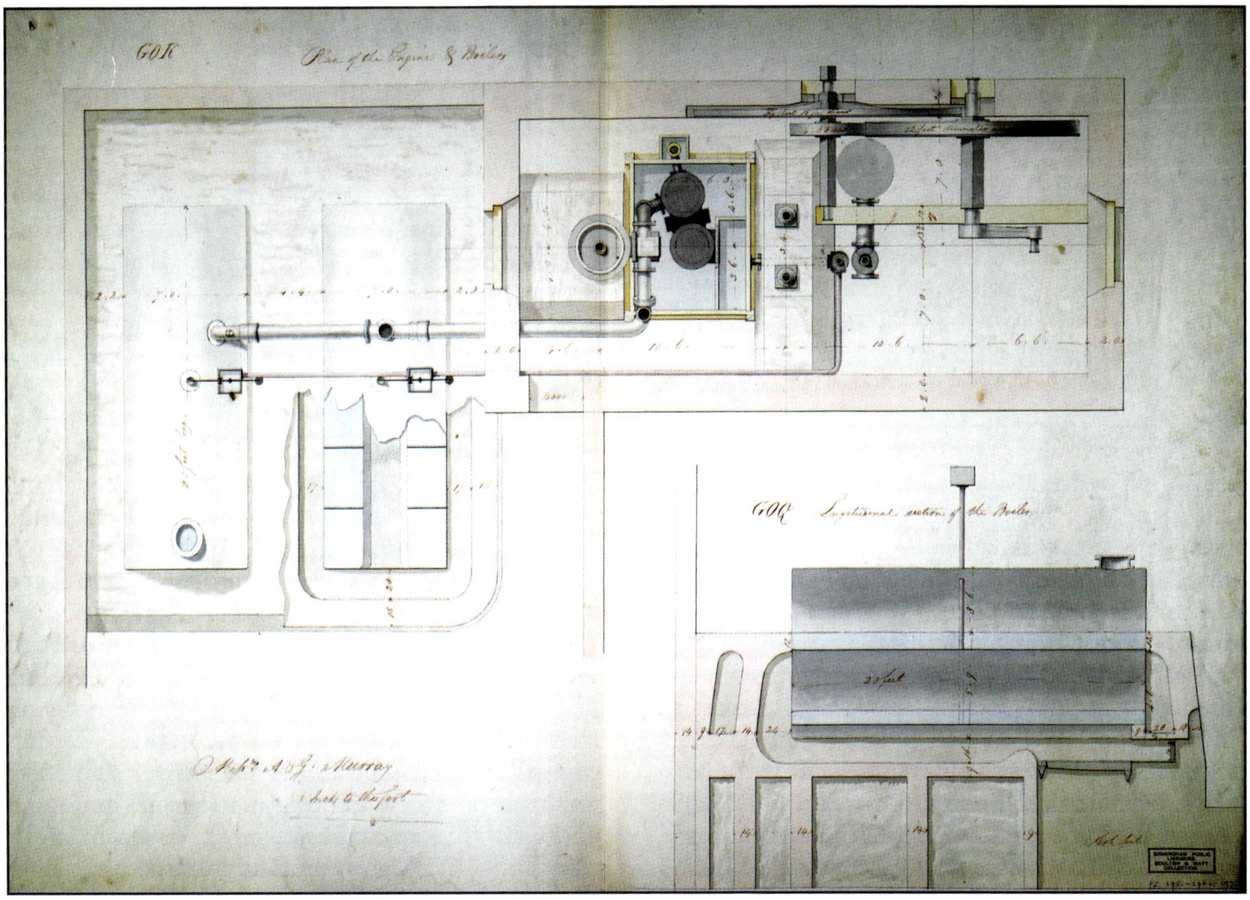

Plate 67: Boulton and Watt drawing, showing the plan view of the 1801 engine and boilers, and a longitudinal section of a boiler (reproduced courtesy of Birmingham City Archives)

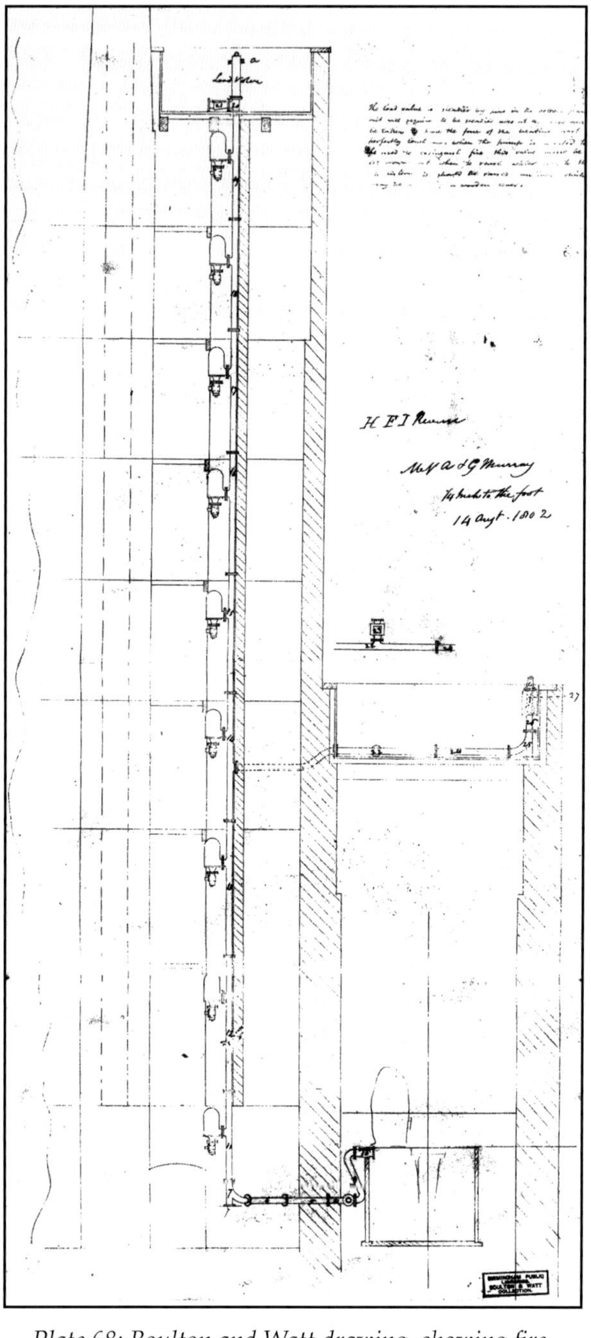

Plate 68: Boulton and Watt drawing, showing fire-fighting equipment of 1802 (reproduced courtesy of Birmingham City Archives)

progress was such that in June 1802 James Watt junior was able to report to Matthew Boulton that:

> A & G Murray's [engine] is working delightfully and they are perfectly pleased and satisfied...They are working about the same quantity of machinery as was driven by their Little Engine & with the same expenditure of Coals. They would like to have an Estimate of the Extinguishing apparatus, which I have promised to send with Acct. (BWA 3147/3/51/13).

Design plans for the requested fire-fighting equipment were drawn up by August 1802 (BWA 3147/5/295), and these show that the apparatus was intended to be housed within the stair tower, and was therefore original to Decker Mill (Pl 68).

The successful operation of the new engine as reported by James Watt junior did not result in a quick payment by the Murrays, perhaps reflecting the economic slump of 1803. On 27 June of that year, James Watt junior reported to Matthew Boulton: 'When looking over our Stock of bills here to see what others we might have of a Suspicious Nature, I find another from A & G Murray of £205 drawn by Mitchell & Constable on Smith and Lindsey & Co, which as both the partners have suspended their payments, I shall take with me and endeavour to precure (*sic*) some better security' (BWA 3147/3/52/18). By 30 June, James Watt junior had reached Manchester to pursue the matter and received assurances from George Murray: 'He says he expects to be able to take up both the Bills when due; and should they not be able so to do, he pledges his word to give Security upon the Engine, which as well as the Mill is free from any present incombrances (*sic*)' (BWA 3147/3/52/19). A & G Murray claimed to have debts owed to them amounting to £9000 in Glasgow, and a further £6000 of funds available (*ibid*). By August 1803 £300 had been paid, and a further £205 was settled in late October of the same year. This left a balance of £500 outstanding, bringing the total cost of the engine to £1005 (BWA 3147/3/52/32).

Phase 3, Completing the Original Complex (*c* 1804 - *c* 1817)

The foreign market for British cotton fluctuated throughout 1804-5, although yarn exports continued to grow and soared to record levels in 1805. Following the Peace of Tilsit in August 1807, however, Napoleon tightened his blockade of continental markets, causing a rise in the price of cotton and a depression in trade that persisted throughout 1808 (Edwards 1967, 16). Following a short-lived boom in 1809, renewed depression reduced many of Lancashire's industries to short-time working in 1811 (Holland 1976, 80). Many cotton-spinning firms experienced difficulties, and McConnel & Kennedy even took the unusual step of stopping their works for a time in the middle of the year.

There was an upturn in trade in autumn 1812 and, by July 1813, spinners throughout the region were receiving increased wages on demand as the trade boomed. A crisis following the end of the Napoleonic Wars in 1815 was succeeded by a short boom before another slump in 1819, which was almost certainly caused by post-war speculation (Lee 1972). Each of these crises brought more businesses to failure, although economies of scale probably offered the larger firms such as A & G Murray better protection from fluctuations in the market.

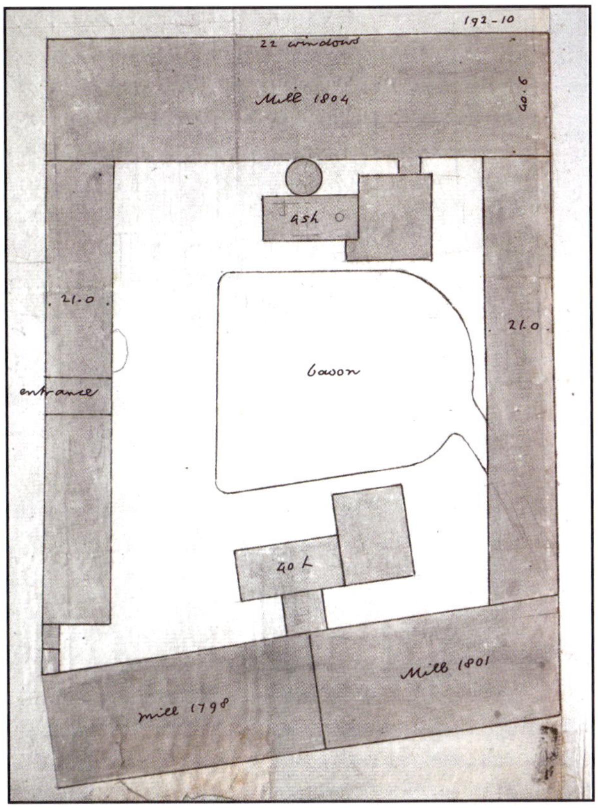

Plate 69: Boulton and Watt plan of A & G Murray's Mill in 1805 (reproduced courtesy of Birmingham City Archives)

During this period, the position of A & G Murray, McConnel & Kennedy, and other large firms was strengthened by engaging directly in the export trade of yarn, rather than depending upon merchants (Lee 1972, 57); an entry in a trade directory even lists Adam and George Murray as 'cotton spinners and merchants' (Pigot and Dean 1815, 146). Nevertheless, the Scottish market remained the principal destination for the fine yarn produced by McConnel & Kennedy, and it is most likely that this was the case for A & G Murray. The large volume of sales provided by this market, coupled with reliable payment, was an important factor in the stability and growth of Manchester's two largest fine-spinning concerns. Linen weaving and the production of muslin in the Belfast and Larn Valley areas of Northern Ireland also provided a market for fine yarn, especially during the Napoleonic Wars, although this was never as significant as the Scottish trade. Curiously, A & G Murray and McConnel & Kennedy were only slightly involved in the Lancashire market during this period, reflecting their specialist production of fine yarn: Lancashire manufacturers tended to use coarser yarn, and did not have the weaving skills commanded by the Paisley and Glasgow manufacturers (Lee 1972, 79).

Despite economic fluctuations and uncertainties in the cotton trade, A & G Murray managed to expand their site dramatically to become, by 1806, the largest mill complex in Manchester (Williams 1993, 28). An initial stage in this process was achieved on 29 September 1802, when Adam and George Murray obtained from John Buckley a lease of the land between their existing mills and Jersey Street (RCHME and GMAU 1989). It seems that they wasted little time in developing this land, and by 1806 the New Mill, the Murray Street and the Bengal Street blocks, and the canal basin and link with the Rochdale Canal had all been constructed. A plan in the Boulton and Watt Archive, dated 1805 (BWA 3147/5/364), illustrates that the new additions formed a quadrangle arrangement enclosing a central yard and canal basin, with an entrance off Murray Street providing the sole access for pedestrians (Pl 69).

The Rochdale Canal

The completion of the Rochdale Canal in 1804 was vital to the site, and the incorporation of a private canal basin within the enclosed courtyard of the Murrays' complex was a remarkable innovation that contributed greatly to the success of the spinning enterprise, representing a new level of integration between the canal network and the factory. The canal facilitated the delivery of raw materials in bulk and, more importantly, it provided the water required by the steam-power plant, and a ready supply of water for fire-fighting. This factor was a key attribute of the Ancoats' mills, which negated the requirement for dedicated reservoirs and allowed numerous mills to be packed together in a comparatively small area. This characteristic feature proved to be a restriction to expansion after the mid-nineteenth century, however, and was a factor in many firms, such as Thomas Houldsworth & Co, relocating from Ancoats to the periphery of Manchester (Williams with Farnie 1992, 178).

Plate 70: Blocked entrance to the tunnel from the Rochdale Canal

Access to the Murrays' basin from the canal was via a tunnel below the Bengal Street block (Pl 70), facilitated by a short arm on the opposite side of the canal that allowed boats to negotiate the sharp turn. The tunnel was too small for the barges that operated on the canal, and access would have been restricted to specially designed craft or narrow boats, such as those that plied the Ashton Canal, which connected Manchester with the coalfields of Oldham, Ashton, Dukinfield, Hyde, Newton, and Denton (Hadfield 1994, 88). Moreover, height restrictions and the absence of a towpath through the tunnel would have left the boat crews with no alternative but to haul the laden vessels by 'legging'.

There is no reference to the construction of the canal basin in any of the surviving Rochdale Canal Company's records, implying that it was entirely the responsibility of A & G Murray, although they would have been liable to an annual fee for the provision of water. The Rochdale Canal Company allowed steam engines within 20 yards (21.89 m) of the canal to condense by its waters (Rees 1819, 389), and A & G Murray is named in a list of factory owners who used the canal for such purposes (GMRO B2/10/6).

New Mill

The annotated Boulton and Watt plan of the site (Pl 69) marks New Mill with the text '1804', which may indicate the year that the building (excluding the installation of the steam-power plant) had been completed. Surviving physical evidence shows the mill to have been largely extant before the erection of either the Murray Street or Bengal Street blocks had begun (*Ch 6, p 117*). It was erected as a single unit adjacent and parallel to Jersey Street, and was built to a height of eight storeys (including a basement), with plan dimensions of 193 x 46 ft (58.98 x 14.17 m), forming the largest building within the Murrays' complex. Indeed, it is likely to have been the largest single cotton mill ever constructed in Manchester at that time.

The dimensions of New Mill broadly mirrored the combined Old and Decker Mill range, reflecting its primary function as a steam-powered cotton-spinning factory. It seems likely, however, that the basement at least was used for preparatory purposes. A beam engine placed in a detached engine house within the courtyard supplied the power for the mill. This abutted a circular stair tower, which provided the only access from the central courtyard to all floors (Pl 71).

Design plans within the Boulton and Watt Archive, drafted during 1805 (BWA 3147/5/364), show the proposed layout of the engine and boiler houses associated with New Mill. The engine was a 45 hp model that incorporated a cast-iron flywheel of 18 ft (5.49 m) diameter, located on the primary shaft. The

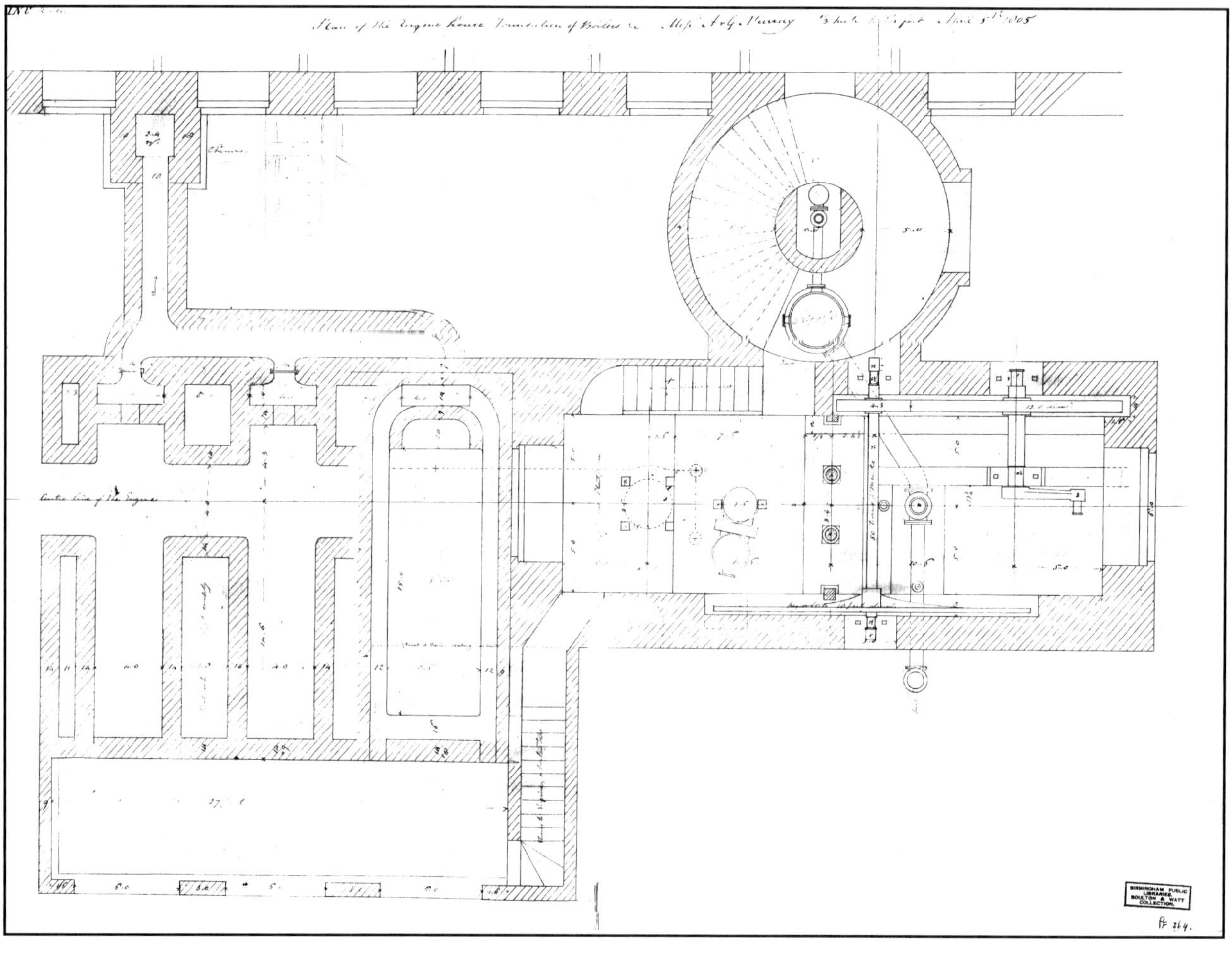

Plate 71: Boulton and Watt 1805 plan of New Mill engine house (reproduced courtesy of Birmingham City Archives)

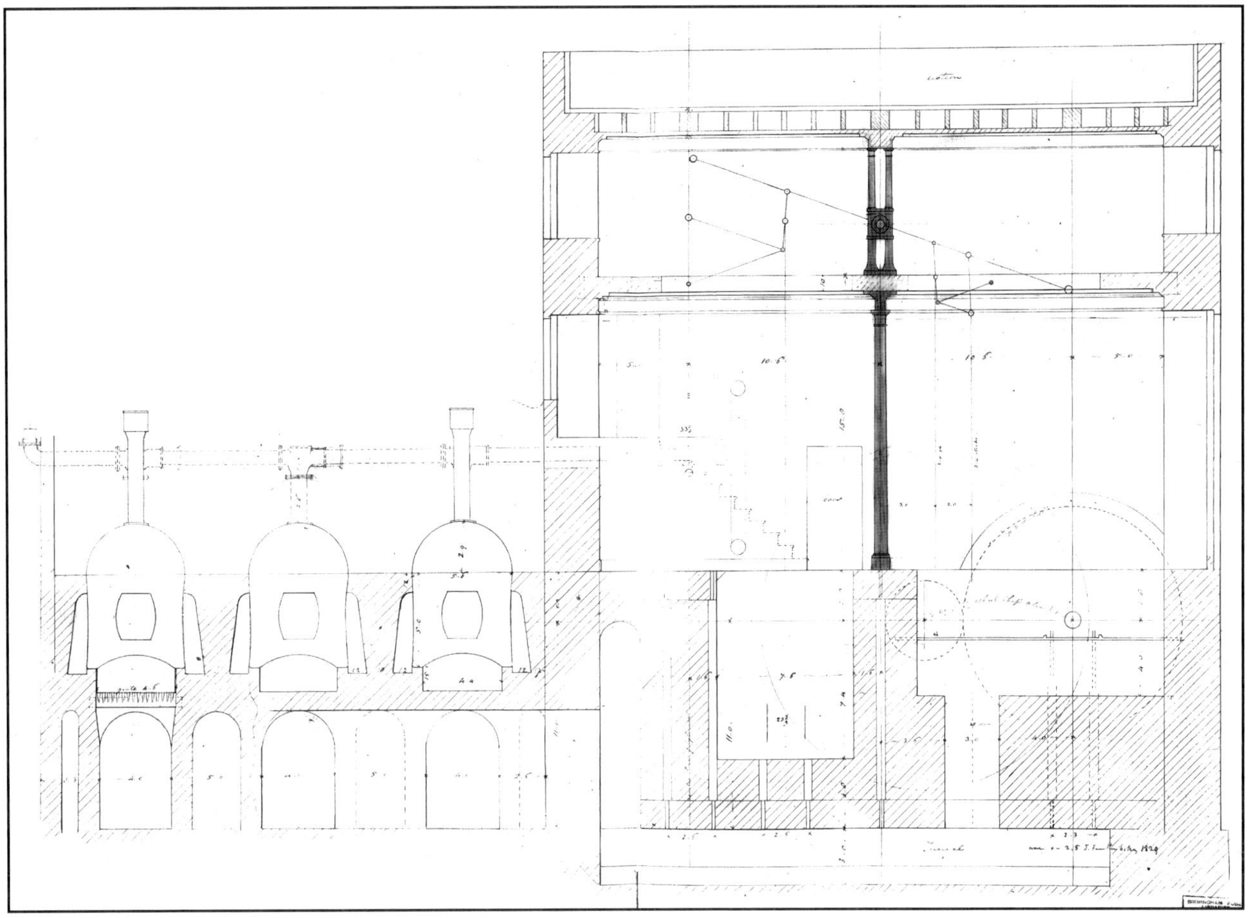

Plate 72: Boulton and Watt drawing of the 1805 steam plant for New Mill (reproduced courtesy of Birmingham City Archives)

primary shaft entered the mill through the base of the stair tower, and was driven via a crank shaft and two spur wheels attached to the north wall of the engine house (Pl 71). The steam for the engine was to be provided by three long boilers (Pl 72), the flues from which led to a square-section chimney attached to the south side of the mill. The proposed layout allowed for the boilers to be built to the west of the engine house, although the final design placed them to the east. As with Old and Decker Mill, fire-fighting equipment was situated in the central recess of the stair tower, and comprised a stand pipe, which was fed with water from the canal basin by a pump that was driven directly from the engine's main beam. The pressure for the fire-fighting equipment was provided by a water tank situated on top of the stair tower, which was augmented by a large cistern, or header tank, on the roof of the engine house.

Correspondence dated to 1806 in the Boulton and Watt Archive concerns an enquiry regarding the difference in cost between a wheel with iron teeth over one with wooden teeth (BWA 3147/3/42/23). A small note saying '45 Horse' suggests that this referred to New Mill, implying that the steam plant was not fully operational before 1806.

The Wing Blocks

Archive sources contain few direct references to either the Murray Street or Bengal Street blocks, and information regarding their development is based largely on cartographic evidence. The Murray Street block was erected as a single unit, although it incorporated three components. The northern part was originally ten bays long, two bays wide, and built to a height of four storeys, and is thought to have been used primarily for warehousing purposes (RCHME and GMAU 1989, 16). The central section of the block incorporated a covered entrance passageway, which provided the only pedestrian and wheeled-vehicle access to the mill complex, and controlled movements to all parts of the site; an eyewitness noted that a porter at the 'great gate' was 'always in attendance to refuse admission to intruders from without' (Allen 1832, 129). The entrance utilised rusticated stone voussoirs in its build, representing modest architectural embellishment that was largely absent from the rest of the mill complex. The stone blocks were not procured locally, and may have been delivered to the site from East Lancashire or Yorkshire by the newly completed Rochdale Canal.

The southern end of the block was originally similar to the north end, comprising a four-storey structure, two bays wide, that is also thought to have been used for warehousing (RCHME and GMAU 1989, 17). It was slightly shorter than the northern end, being only nine bays long. Part of the Murray Street block was certainly used for offices from the 1830s, although it is uncertain whether this had been an original function; entries in trade directories throughout this period, and up to the late 1820s, list A & G Murray's office at Union Street (*eg Anon* 1828, 109), which may refer to the 'counting house' on the eastern side of Bengal Street. Subsequent directories list the firm at 2 Murray Street (*eg* Pigot and Son 1836, 380), perhaps reflecting the completion of purpose-built offices within the Murray Street block (*p 82*).

The Bengal Street block was originally 19 bays long, three bays wide, and four storeys high. The outer façade mirrored that of the Murray Street block by incorporating the distinctive arrangement of stone-arched openings, although these did not relate to any internal walls and were bricked-in during original construction. As with the Murray Street block, the original function of the building is likely to have included warehousing, although the second storey may have been used for powered processes, perhaps yarn winding (RCHME and GMAU 1989, 15-6). All power requirements would have been provided by the engine that served Old and Decker Mill or New Mill, however, as the Bengal Street block did not house its own engine.

The result of these additions was, by contemporary standards, an enormous cotton-spinning complex with an unprecedented number of mule spindles and operatives; by 1811, A & G Murray was operating 84,300 mule spindles, and a survey in 1815 noted that the firm employed 1215 operatives (Lloyd-Jones and Le Roux 1980, 74). This placed A & G Murray as one of the largest cotton-spinning firms in Manchester, and probably the country, at that time. This is highlighted by a valuation of the town's factories that was compiled in *c* 1809 (Table 2), which clearly demonstrates that

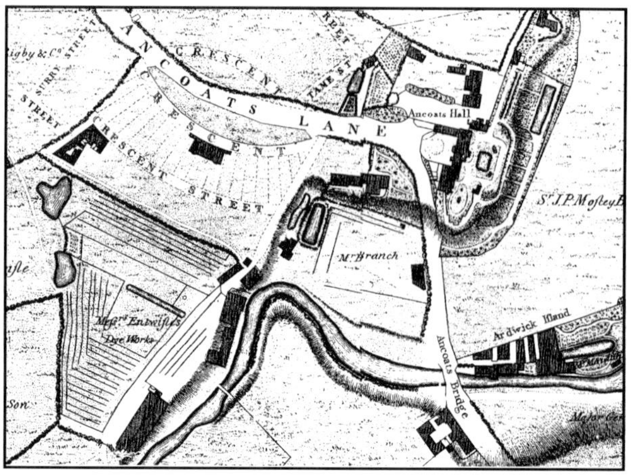

Plate 73: Extract from Green's map of 1794, showing Ancoats Hall and the initial development of the Crescent

A & G Murray and McConnel & Kennedy were the leading firms by a significant margin.

The large profits that A & G Murray had accrued by this time are reflected in George Murray's choice of residence; by 1808 he had moved from his house at 60 Great Ancoats Street, where he had been a neighbour of John Kennedy (McConnel 1861), to a fashionable address at the Crescent in Ancoats (Pl 73). By 1813, however, he had purchased the medieval timber-framed Ancoats Hall (Pigot 1813, 178), which he converted into a stone-clad mansion during the 1820s. Adam Murray's residence is not clearly documented, although entries in trade directories for the early years of the nineteenth century imply that he was living on Newton Street (*eg* Bancks 1802, 125).

Employment Structure

The management and day-to-day control of the business throughout this period was in the hands of the Murrays, and this was one reason why they lived near to their mills, as did many of the early nineteenth-century factory owners. The physical operation of the mill was the responsibility of the engineer, whose remit was to ensure that power was

Name of Firm	Value	Name of Firm	Value
A & G Murray	£20,456	Appleton & Ogden	£3967
McConnel & Kennedy	£18,153	Robert Schofield	£2660
Late J Simpson	£10,130	B & W Sandford	£2161
Jonathan Pollard	£9564	Archibald Carruthers	£1436
William Robinson	£9547	Smith & Townley	£1269
T & J Houldsworth	£9279	Thomas Grocott	£891
Joseph Thackeray	£4440	John Pass	£871
James Kennedy	£4225	Scott & Walker	£584

Table 2: Relative value of some cotton-spinning firms in Manchester in c 1809 (after Daniels 1915a, who provides a complete list)

Plate 74: Engraving of a mule-spinning room, showing the machinery arranged transversely (reproduced from Barfoot 1840)

transmitted to the machines without interruption. This was a skilled occupation, which was reflected in the comparatively high wages paid to engineers. At the opposite end of the pay-scale were the unskilled workers who unpacked the cotton bales, and those responsible for the initial cleaning and carding operations. In these preparatory processes, women were generally engaged in machine-minding, and men undertook handling and lifting operations (Bullen and Fowler 1986, 3). The intermediary processes, such as roving and drawing, prepared the cotton for the spinner, and were tasks dominated by female workers.

Cotton spinning had traditionally been women's work, but the introduction of the spinning mule and factory-based production led to the appropriation of the trade by adult men (Mason 1987, 3). During the early nineteenth century, the mule spinner was required to manoeuvre the physically-taxing machine through the winding and putting-up stages, implicit in contemporary engravings (Pl 74), and pay close attention to the drawn-out threads. They acquired craftsman status and became regarded as the 'elite of the cotton labour force' (Kidd 1996, 82), the so-called 'barefoot aristocrats'. This was reinforced to a degree by the employment structure; mule spinners were paid for the yarn they produced, and were left to recruit, train, and pay their assistants, which normally comprised a big and a little 'piecer', whose roles were to rejoin broken threads, and a 'scavenger' to clean the machinery. These assistants were frequently children, and often relatives of the spinner. During the early nineteenth century, the spinners who worked for A & G Murray each employed four piecers, although this number grew to eight with increases in the size and operating speed of the machinery (PP (HC) 1833 [450] XX, D1).

In the absence of any surviving company records for the firm, it is difficult to establish the exact number of operatives employed through time, although other primary documentation provides some indication for specific years. Similarly, whilst extensive records for the firm of McConnel & Kennedy do survive, they do not state how many people were employed. One of the earliest references to the operatives within the Ancoats' mills is provided by the returns on the employment in cotton factories taken in September 1802, when McConnel & Kennedy claimed that they employed 312 people in their mill (Lee 1972, 114). The workforce comprised 160 males and 152 females, all of whom were paid operatives, and it is likely that the size and structure of the Murrays' labour force was similar.

By 1815, McConnel & Kennedy had increased their workforce to 1020, whilst A & G Murray had 1215 operatives, representing the largest single employer in Manchester at that date (Lloyd-Jones and Le Roux 1980, 74). These figures serve to highlight the scale of the Murrays' and McConnel & Kennedy's mills: only two other textile firms in the Manchester area at this time employed more than 700 workers (Lee 1972, 114); during 1815, the median size of a labour force in cotton factories has been calculated at 54 employees (Lloyd-Jones and Le Roux 1980, 74).

Working Conditions

Much has been written about the fearsome working conditions in early textile factories, often based on eyewitness accounts, which frequently present an emotive picture of brutality and exploitation, particularly with respect to children (*eg* Brown 1832; Aspin 1995). Charges of 'child slavery' were levelled against many early factory-masters, reflecting their 'apprenticeship' of pauper children from workhouses across the country (Pl 75). As early as 1784, however, the magistrates of Manchester had decided to refuse their sanction to indentures of parish apprentices if it appeared that they were expected to work more than ten hours daily (Hopwood 1969, 63); McConnel & Kennedy and A & G Murray claimed that they had never used such apprentices (PP (HC) 1834 [167] XX, A1), reflecting the widespread availability of labour in Manchester. Thus, although data for conditions in the early factories in Ancoats are lacking, and whilst workers undoubtedly suffered some hardship, there is evidence to suggest that conditions in these textile mills were better than elsewhere. An official enquiry in 1818, for instance, was able to report that 'the results then of our investigations justifies a conclusion that the persons who work in the mills of Messrs McConnel & Kennedy enjoy for the most part a good state of health' (quoted in Lee 1972, 127).

Phase 4, Remodelling and Expansion (*c* 1817 - 1855)

In broad terms, the first half of the 1820s saw the cotton market steadily increasing in prosperity (Farnie 1979), although the markets became overstocked during 1825-6, and many manufacturers were forced to sell 'at a ruinous loss' due to excessive competition. Thomson (1966, 319) considered this period to have been one of the worst trade depressions in Manchester's history, noting that some 6000 Irish workers had been repatriated to Ireland through a lack of work. Normal conditions had resumed by 22 May 1827, when a report in the *Manchester Mercury* claimed that 'the market for manufactured goods was the briskest which there has been for a very long time'. This situation persisted until supplies of raw materials became short during 1836, causing prices to rise. This led to a serious depression of trade in

Plate 75: Cartoon by Robert Cruikshank (1832), depicting brutality to pauper apprentices in a cotton factory

Plate 76: An engraving of Manchester, emphasising the density of textile mills (reproduced from The Builder *1853)*

1837, which resulted in 'the vigorous weeding out of inefficient firms' (Howe 1984, 12), although the sheer scale of A & G Murray's business is likely to have afforded the firm immunity from economic fluctuations. Normal conditions had returned by 1842, but a serious downturn in 1847 resulted in a temporary commercial crisis. Boom conditions reigned between 1848 and 1853 as the effects of the repeal of the Corn Laws in 1846 were realised, and the number of cotton mills in Manchester reached a peak of 108 at the close of 1853 (Williams with Farnie 1992, 21). Coincidentally, it was during the same year that Manchester was designated a city (Briggs 1971, 32). The density of the mills at this date is captured vividly in an engraving published in *The Builder* (Pl 76).

During this period, A & G Murray and McConnel & Kennedy were increasingly involved in supplying fine yarn to the expanding lace- and hosiery-manufacturing industries centred on Nottingham. These trades demanded doubled fine yarn, and provided a lucrative new market for Manchester's fine spinners. Indeed, James McConnel commented that all the large firms in the town 'doubled more or less' (Lee 1972, 86).

Fairbairn and Lillie

Significant modifications to the mills were undertaken during 1817, when William Fairbairn and his partner James Lillie offered the Murrays' their services as engineers. In response, Adam Murray took Fairbairn and Lillie around the mills, and enquired if they could '...renew, with horizontal cross-shafts, the whole of his millwork that turned the mule spinning'. One of the conditions of the contract was to execute the alterations without stopping the machinery, unless absolutely necessary. The work was completed within the time specified, 'and in such a manner as to satisfy Mr Murray and his friends' (Pole 1877, 112-4). This was William Fairbairn's first contract to undertake engineering works within a textile mill, and undoubtedly gave him valuable experience in what was to be an illustrious career. Fairbairn's account of the project provides a valuable insight to the working of a cotton mill in the early part of the nineteenth century:

> I discovered great defects in the principle as well as the construction of the millwork. All the cotton mills that I had seen were driven with large square shafts and huge wooden drums, some of them four feet in diameter. The main shafts seldom exceeded 40 revolutions per minute; and the couplings were so badly fitted that they might be heard creaking and groaning a long way off. The speeds of the driving-shafts were mostly got up by a series of straps and counter drums, which not only crowded the room, but seriously obstructed the light where most required for conducting the delicate operations of the different machines. Another serious defect lay in the construction of the shafts, and in the mode of fixing the couplings, which were constantly giving way, so that a week seldom passed without one or more break-downs. The repairs were usually made on Sundays, which were the millwrights' hardest working days... (*ibid*).

Fairbairn addressed these problems by using '... lighter shafts driven at double or treble the velocity, smaller drums to drive the machinery, and the use of wrought-iron wherever practicable, because of its greater lightness and strength compared with wood'. He also provided for 'the simplification of the hangers and fixings by which the shafting was supported, and introduced the "half-lap coupling" so well known to millwrights and engineers' (*ibid*). Fairbairn implies that he was responsible for the introduction of wrought-iron shafts in textile mills, although it is of note that Peel, Williams & Co of Manchester was probably manufacturing wrought-iron shafting as early as 1806 (Tann 1970, 103).

Death of Adam Murray

On 26 June 1818, Adam Murray died as a bachelor at the age of 52 (*Manchester Mercury*, 7 July 1818), and was buried at St. Mark's Church in Cheetham, north Manchester. He died intestate, and the responsibility of settling his affairs resided initially with his brother, James, who had followed Adam and George's lead and established himself as a cotton spinner in Manchester; a plan of the mills in Ancoats that extracted water from the Rochdale Canal, compiled in February 1820 (GMRO B2/10/6), identifies James Murray as the occupant of the factory on the corner of Union and Bengal Streets, known formerly as 'Mr Lane's Factory'. The firm of James Murray & Co is listed there in a trade directory for 1825 (Pigot and Dean 1825, 120), although James Murray had died in July 1821, leaving his brother's affairs unsettled (LRO WCW 1821). The responsibility of administering Adam Murray's estate was then passed to his sister, Margaret, who was similarly residing in Manchester and was connected to the textile industry through her marriage to Archibald Carruthers (LRO WCW 1818), an established cotton spinner in the town (Table 2). It seems that Carruthers had also spent an early part of his career renting 'room-and-power' in Mr Lane's Factory (Pigot and Dean 1815, 39), but had acquired sufficient capital by 1818 to establish his own factory on Allum Street, on the opposite side of the Rochdale Canal to McConnel & Kennedy's Mill.

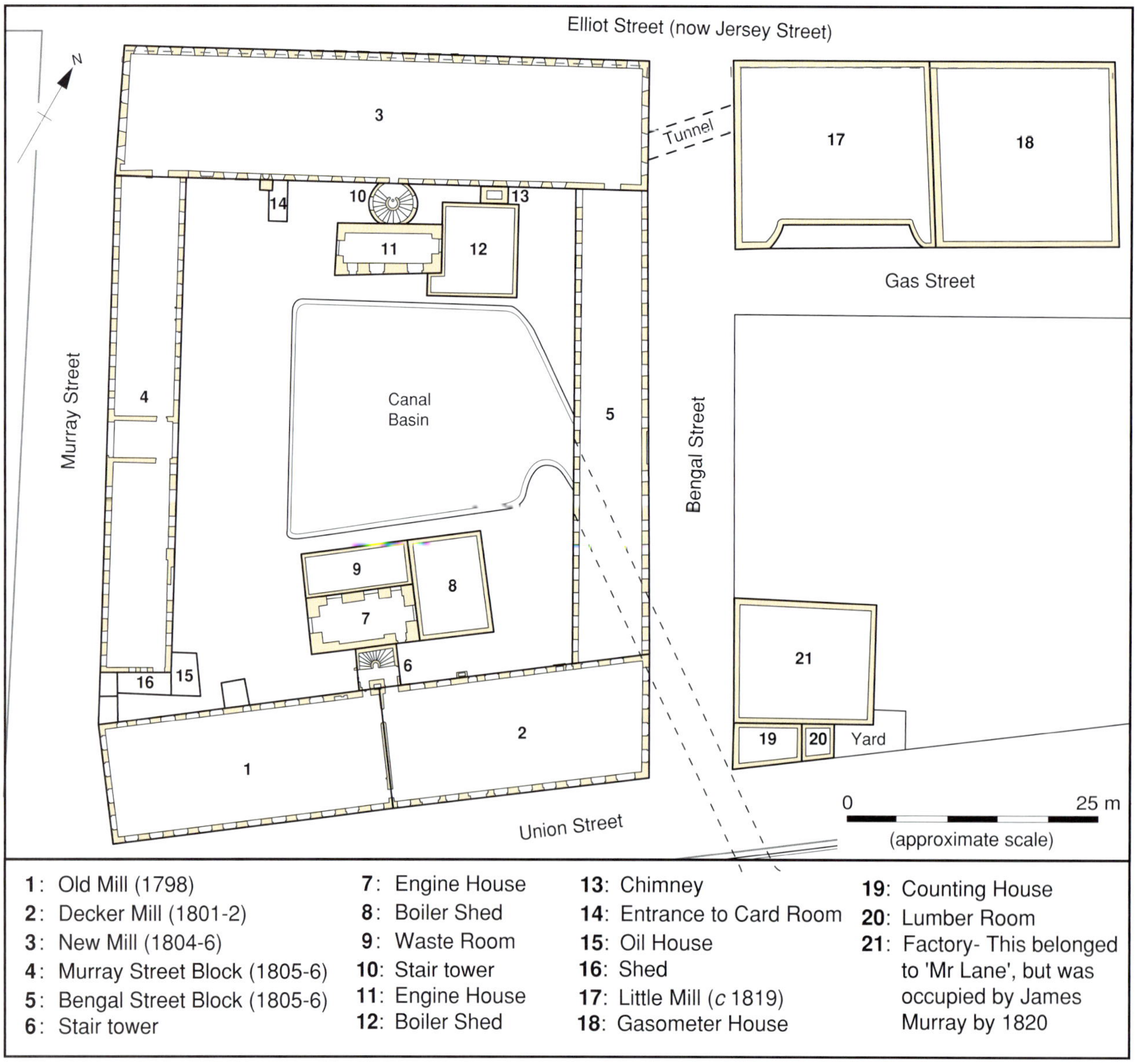

Figure 30: The layout of A & G Murray's Mill, based on a plan of c *1822*

Little Mill and Gas Street

Upon Adam Murray's death, the mill complex was independently valued at £59,000, representing nearly a three-fold increase of the valuation taken in 1809 (Lee 1972, 104). Thereafter, the business was managed by George Murray, but continued to trade as A & G Murray. It seems that one of his earliest decisions as sole partner was to develop the plot of land to the east of Bengal Street, with the erection of what was called the Little Mill and a terrace of 15 cottages (MLSU M9/40/2/100), shown as blocks on Pigot's *New Plan of Manchester and Salford*, which was published in 1819.

The earliest detailed survey of Little Mill is provided by an annotated plan of *c* 1822, which identifies the building as a factory of six storeys with a loft (Fig 30); the mill was increased in height subsequently to nine storeys, but the date at which this was completed is unknown. The footprint of the factory is shown to have occupied 704 square yards (644 m^2), although slightly more than half of this area comprised a large gasometer house. This will almost certainly have contained several retorts that supplied the entire mill complex with gas for lighting purposes, and will also have provided the impetus for the naming of the adjacent Gas Street. The Murrays had certainly installed gas lighting in their mill by 1819, as it is referred to specifically in an insurance policy of that date (Sun Insurance 945442/11937).

The plan of *c* 1822 also annotates Old, Decker and New Mills as being eight storeys in height, with external staircases, and the Murray Street and Bengal Street blocks are shown as factories of four storeys. Several smaller structures within the courtyard include the two engine houses and their associated steam-raising plant, an oil house and shed attached to the Murray Street block, a waste room attached to the Old Mill engine house, and the entrance to the carding room on the west side of New Mill. Little Mill is shown to have been linked to New Mill via a tunnel beneath Bengal Street, which may have provided a conduit for a pipe from the gasometer to the main complex. The possibility that power was transmitted from the main site via the tunnel cannot be discounted, as the documentary material provides no evidence that Little Mill contained its own engine. The cottages on Gas Street are omitted from the plan, although these are shown on a map published by Bancks and Co in 1832 (Fig 31). This map also shows the factory on the corner of Bengal Street and Union Street and, fronting German Street to the east, an iron foundry that also appears to have been owned by George Murray before 1855 (*p 86*).

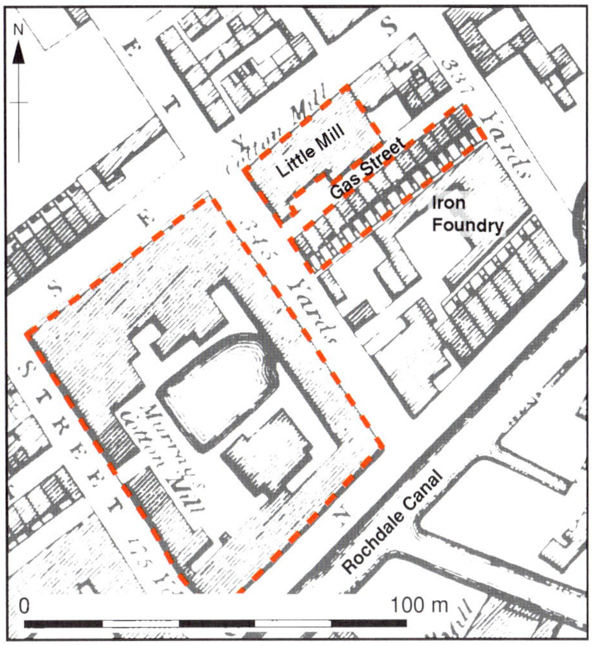

Figure 31: Extract from Bancks and Co's map of 1832, showing A & G Murray's entire mill complex

Modifications to New Mill Engine House

Correspondence within the Boulton and Watt Archive, dated March 1829, includes a drawing for a proposed replacement engine for New Mill (BWA 3147/5/364). Although a new engine was almost certainly installed at some point during this phase, an absence of further correspondence with Boulton and Watt on this matter suggests that George Murray had commissioned a different engine builder to fulfil his requirements. This not only represented a break in the long association between A & G Murray and Boulton and Watt, but also reflects the growing domination of local engine builders such as Hick Hargreaves (established in 1832) and Musgrave & Sons (1832), both of Bolton, W & J Galloway (1835) of Manchester, and Goodfellows (1838) of Hyde (Buchanan and Watkins 1976, 116-9).

Contemporary Observations

The scale of Manchester's mills was a marvel of the Industrial Age, which throughout the nineteenth century excited comments of the kind made by the French writer, historian, and politician, Alexis de Tocqueville, when he approached Manchester and observed 'thirty or forty factories rise on the tops of hills ... their six stories tower up; their huge enclosures give notice from afar of the centralisation of industry. From this foul drain the greatest stream of human industry flows out to fertilise the whole world' (de Tocqueville 1958, 106-8). An earlier visitor from the Continent, the Prussian court architect Karl Friedrich Schinkel, noted in 1826 that 400 new factories had been founded in Lancashire since the end of the Napoleonic Wars. He paid particular attention to the mills on Union Street (Pl 77), which he considered to be as big as the Royal Palace in Berlin, but had been 'erected without the benefit' of an architect (Bindman

Plate 77: Schinkel's sketch of Union Street in 1826, featuring the mills of McConnel & Kennedy and A & G Murray

and Riemann 1993, 175). The most pertinent comment was perhaps that made by the Swiss engineer, Johann Escher, who had noted some 12 years previously that 'in a single street in Manchester [Union Street] there are more spindles than in the whole of Switzerland' (Henderson 1968, 35). Indeed, it has been calculated that the 170,000 spindles operated jointly by A & G Murray and McConnel & Kennedy equated to 12% more than those in Escher's native country in 1814 (Williams with Farnie 1992, 19).

The earliest published account of a visit to the Murrays' complex is provided by Joshua Field, who visited the site in August 1821, and noted that whilst the factories were built 'upon the old plan, they spin the finest thread' (Smith 1932, 28). Field appears to have been particularly impressed with the canal basin and the attendant barges; the boats 'discharging their freights of raw cotton and coal' and 'receiving the packages of yarn' were similarly noted emphatically by an American visitor to the mill complex in 1832 (Allen 1832, 129). Joshua Field also observed that one of the steam engines had been fitted with a 'smoke burner', patented by Josiah Parkes in May 1820. This device was ostensibly to 'lessen the consumption of fuel in steam engines', but Joshua Field also remarked that

Plate 78: A & G Murray's Mill in c 1829 (reproduced from Pyne 1831)

it had 'considerable effect' in reducing the smoke emitted from the chimney. Unfortunately, Field had called on the Murrays before midday, when work stopped for the dinner hour, and thus 'hardly saw the mill to advantage' (Smith 1932, 28).

Some details of the machinery operating during this period may be elucidated from George Murray's evidence given to a Parliamentary Commission on child employment in June 1833 (PP (HC) 1833 [450] XX, D1). In this document, George Murray stated that recent improvements to the firm's machinery had resulted in a reduction of the workforce to approximately 850, implying that larger spinning mules had been installed. This reinforced the eyewitness account of 1832, which observed that A & G Murray's Mill contained some 90,000 spindles and that the 'labour of three persons at a mule of 300 spindles is required' (Allen 1832, 130). George Murray also stated in 1833 that most of the spinning mules contained 324 spindles, although some carried 372 spindles, two pairs carried 492, another two pairs were equipped with 816 spindles, and he was currently 'putting up some more which will be a little larger' (PP (HC) 1833 [450] XX, D1).

In 1831, George Pyne published his '*Lancashire Illustrated in a Series of Views*', which contained an image of A & G Murray's Mill derived from a steel engraving by McGahey after J Harwood (Pl 78). Considered to be 'one of the stock images of the Industrial Revolution' (Stratton and Trinder 1997, 33), this classic engraving depicts the Murrays' complex at the peak of its early development. The exact year that the engraving was produced is uncertain, although it is likely to date from the late 1820s, and shows the Bengal Street block to have been expanded with two additional storeys relative to the plan of *c* 1822.

Doubling and Fireproof Mills

During the early 1840s, A & G Murray expanded their complex further with the addition of two new factories, referred to as Doubling Mill and Fireproof Mill (although together known as Waulk Mill since the mid-twentieth century), situated to the south of Little Mill on the eastern side of Bengal Street. It is tempting to credit the growth of the mill complex at this time to the increased demand for doubled fine yarn resulting from an expansion of the Nottingham lace and hosiery markets, coupled with the introduction of the mechanical sewing machine, which greatly increased the demand for thread (Berg 1979, 227-31).

Doubling Mill was built on the site of the small, original factory and counting house, which is not listed in trade directories from 1838 (*eg* Pigot and Slater 1841), whilst Fireproof Mill was placed immediately to the north. The two mills were separated by a narrow alley, which led to another subterranean passage that connected with the Bengal Street block on the main site. Doubling Mill was erected to a height of five storeys, eight bays long and four wide. As was the case for the majority of mills built at this time, it was not of a fireproof construction, containing timber floors supported by timber beams and a single row of cast-iron columns (Freeman 1891, 177). A full height, stone circular stair tower was attached to the north side of the mill, with a privy tower adjacent to the north-east corner. The mill contained an internal engine house in its western end, the position of which was marked by two tall arched windows in the west end bay, overlooking Union Street (Pl 79). A series of drawings prepared by Boulton and Watt between 1840 and 1843 shows design proposals for this building and the engine (BWA 3147/5/524). The engine house was of a trapezoidal plan, which reflected the existing street pattern, and was designed to contain a single cylinder 40 hp beam engine. Steam was provided by a single wagon-type boiler, placed in a dedicated building to the north, and connected with an octagonal-section chimney at its eastern end (Pl 80). It is perhaps of note that the Boulton and Watt drawings do not depict Fireproof Mill, suggesting that Doubling Mill was built first.

Plate 79: The view north-east along Union Street in 1903, featuring Doubling Mill (reproduced courtesy of Manchester Archives and Local Studies)

Fireproof Mill was built to a height of four storeys and was eight bays long, aligned parallel to Bengal Street. It was the first building within the Murrays' complex to have been of 'fireproof' construction, incorporating Hodgkinson-type cast-iron beams supported by a single row of centrally placed cast-iron columns, and brick-vaulted ceilings. This type of construction suggests that the mill may have been used, at least in part, for warehousing purposes, a theory reinforced by the incorporation of three wide-arched entrances to the street in the ground floor (Nevell and Hradil 2002). Moreover, there is no evidence, either physical or

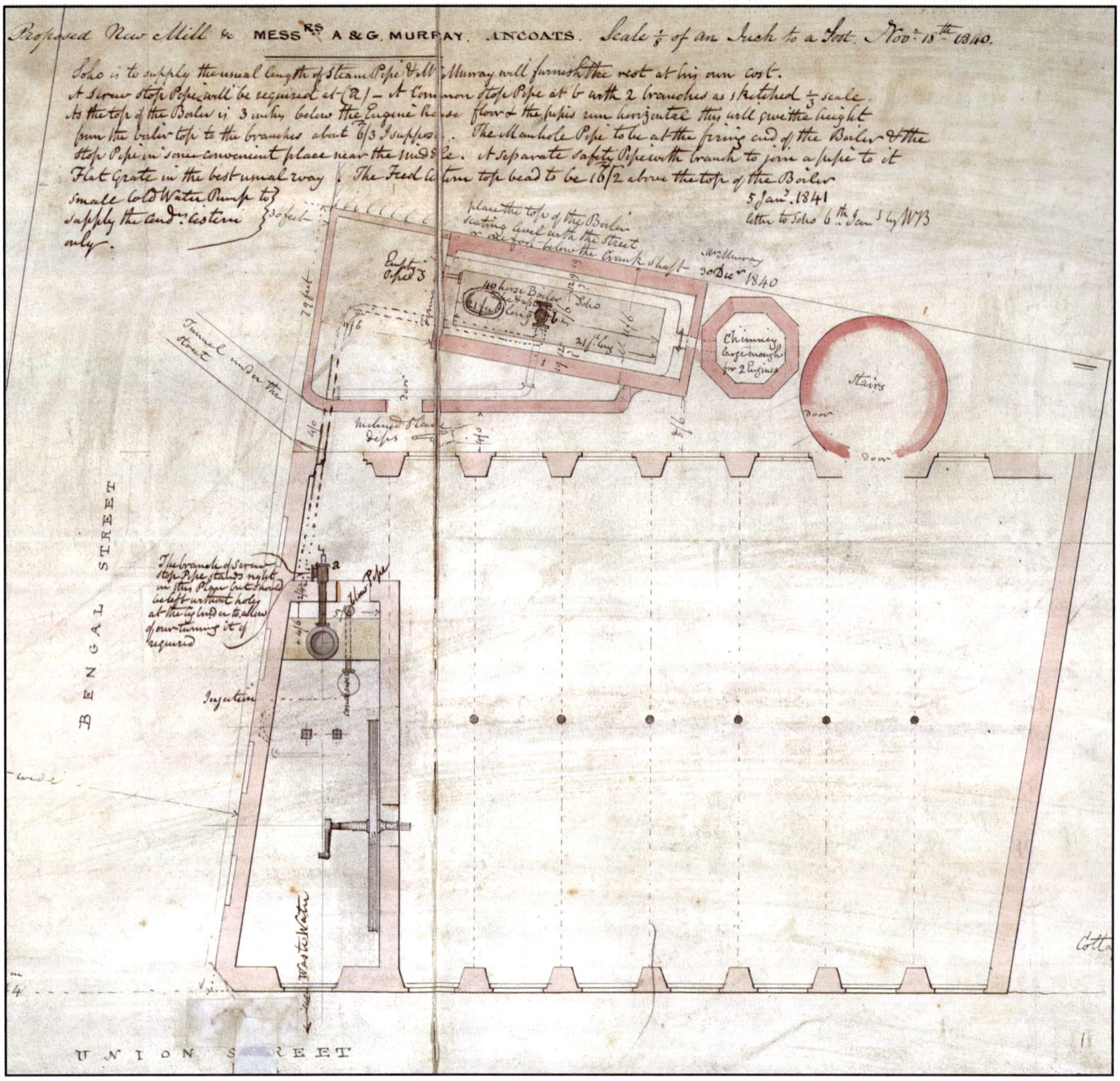

Plate 80: Boulton and Watt drawing of the proposed steam-power plant for Doubling Mill, draughted in 1840 (reproduced courtesy of Birmingham City Archives)

documentary, to indicate that Fireproof Mill originally contained its own steam-power plant.

Modifications to the Main Site and Changes to the Company Structure

The Ordnance Survey 60 in: 1 mile map of the area, surveyed in 1848-9 and published in 1850, is the first detailed map to depict the layout of these new mills. It also shows some modifications to the main site, including extensions to the east and north of the engine and boiler houses that served Old and Decker Mill, and a stair tower added to the Bengal Street block, presumably associated with the addition of two extra storeys to the building. This suggests a change in use, or perhaps even the addition of fire-fighting equipment, which had previously been reserved for the spinning floors. The map also marks the line of the two tunnels beneath Bengal Street. One tunnel is shown to connect the northern end of the Bengal Street block with Little Mill, and the second runs parallel to the canal tunnel beneath the block and then turns beneath Bengal Street to emerge in the yard between Fireproof and Doubling Mills (Pl 81).

The same map also shows that the southern end of the Murray Street block had been extended to its present size of three bays wide by 1848-9. The extension incorporated a bow window overlooking the yard and the entrance to the site, implying its use as an office. Another bow window is shown to have been inserted within the northern part of the block,

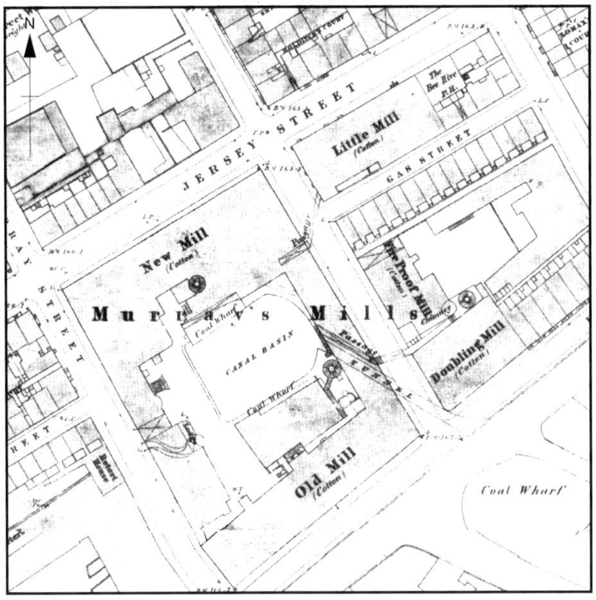

Plate 81: Extract from the 1850 Ordnance Survey map, showing A & G Murray's Mill

again overlooking the courtyard, with a flight of steps immediately to the north, suggesting that this portion of the building was also used as offices.

Despite the boom conditions of the cotton market in the late 1840s, A & G Murray was reported to be experiencing financial difficulties by 1850, perhaps reflecting the considerable capital that the firm had invested in expanding their mill. It seems that Sir W H Houldsworth, another leading Manchester manufacturer of fine cotton yarn and a relative by marriage to the Murrays, assembled a committee to discuss how financial assistance to George Murray might best be provided. This resulted in the raising of an emergency fund that was intended to tide over the firm's financial problems (Fine Spinners' and Doublers' Ltd 1948). Some four years later, on 2 January 1854, and at the age of 93, George Murray relinquished his role of managing director and leased the entire mill complex to his two sons, James and Benjamin Rigby Murray. The lease was for a period of seven years at an annual rent of £3250, and included all of the buildings, steam engines, gas apparatus, and millwright work (RCHME and GMAU 1989, 7).

Working Regime

Following the introduction of the Cotton Mills Regulation Act of 1825, A & G Murray reduced the time worked in its mills to 69 hours per week; George Murray stated to the Parliamentary Commission in 1833 that his operatives had worked longer hours prior to the 1825 Act, although he failed to elaborate. James McConnel, however, specified that they worked a 72-hour week before 1825, and it is likely that A & G Murray had kept the same hours. After 1825, the working week comprised 12 hours on five days and nine hours on Saturdays, the maximum permitted legally (PP (HC) 1834 [167] XX A1). The 12-hour day was kept by most operatives, regardless of age or department, with the exception of 'the younger children employed to clean the machinery,' who worked fewer hours (*ibid*). Both George Murray and James McConnel claimed that they did not knowingly employ children under the age of nine in 1833, and did not consider it necessary to employ anyone younger than 12, although George Murray conceded that parents sometimes employed their own children below that age (PP (HC) 1833 [450] XX, D1). Moreover, in the absence of compulsory registration of births, which was not introduced until 1837, it was difficult to confirm the age of children with confidence.

The working day included three breaks: half an hour was allowed for breakfast and an hour was allocated for dinner time, for which periods the mill engine was stopped. Operatives were free to go home during these periods, should they so choose. Tea was delivered to the workrooms between four and five o'clock in the afternoon and was taken at the operatives' convenience, although the machinery was not stopped. These breaks appear to have been standard practice for most of the fine-spinning mills in Ancoats, whilst some spinning firms in other parts of Manchester did not give the afternoon break (PP (HC) 1833[450] XX, D1).

Numbers Employed

In his evidence given to a Parliamentary Commission in June 1833, George Murray stated that he had reduced his workforce from 1215 to 841, as a result of 'recent improvements to the firm's machinery' (PP (HC) 1833 [450] XX, D1). Those employed at this time included 36 engineers and mechanics, and 805 engaged in the preparation and spinning of cotton (Ure 1836, 391). Of these, more than 60 people worked in the preparatory room (Allen 1832, 129-30).

It seems that most of those rendered unemployed by improvements to the machinery were adults, with children forming a larger proportion of the workforce. To a degree, this is likely to have reflected a diminishing requirement for skilled labour with each technological advancement. Indeed, George Murray noted that he had a room 'in which there are two men, formerly there used to be five'. A recent study of the employment structure in early cotton mills, however, argued that factory managers in the early nineteenth century, and particularly the fine-cotton spinners, considered child labour to be an important means of securing a skilled adult workforce for the future; the proportion of children employed in cotton mills had declined by the mid-1830s with the maturing of generations of child workers (Galbi 1997).

Wage Levels

A comparison of the wages paid to those in the cotton-spinning industry with other trades demonstrates that the wages in cotton mills were relatively high. The gulf between the wages of the mule spinners and the weavers became particularly marked, highlighting the disastrous effect of the power loom on the socio-economic status of the weavers after the 1820s (Engels 1973, 88).

Fine spinning was dependent upon export markets and was therefore much more liable to fluctuations in trade, which were reflected in the fluctuation of wages. Moreover, it seems that there were fairly wide differences in the rates paid by different firms engaged in fine spinning; analysis of the returns to the Parliamentary Commission in 1833 has shown that the average weekly net earning of each individual employed by A & G Murray was slightly less than 12s (60 p), whilst those working for McConnel & Co received just under 11s (55 p) (Ure 1836, 391). Whilst this discrepancy may reflect a slightly different employment structure, with McConnel & Co employing more people in the preparatory processes, the operatives of B & W Sandford only earned 9s 6d (47 p), despite maintaining a similar division of labour to A & G Murray (*op cit*, 393). These inconsistencies may have arisen in part from variable machine efficiency, as many operatives were paid on piece rate.

Wages were not the only means of payment, and many Lancashire manufacturers offered their employees benefits in kind, such as the 'truck system', whereby workers were given credit to purchase goods at company-owned stores, referred to as 'tommy shops' (Aspin 2003, 108-11). Neither A & G Murray nor McConnel & Co, however, ever operated this system. Another type of benefit in kind was the provision of housing for employees, most evident in the 'factory colonies'. In his response to the Parliamentary Commissioners in 1834, however, the owner of a factory on Mill Street in Ancoats, Samuel Moore, asserted that 'in Manchester, the hands generally do not live under their employers, as tenants' (PP (HC) 1834 [167] XX, A1), a comment that is corroborated by the answers given by other factory owners. Nevertheless, James McConnel and George Murray both owned a few residential properties in Ancoats; the Poor Rate Assessments for 1832 list 14 houses owned by James McConnel on Maria Street (MLSU M9/40/2/106), with other tenants located in Great Ancoats Street, Jersey Street, Henry Street, Cotton Street, and Union Street,

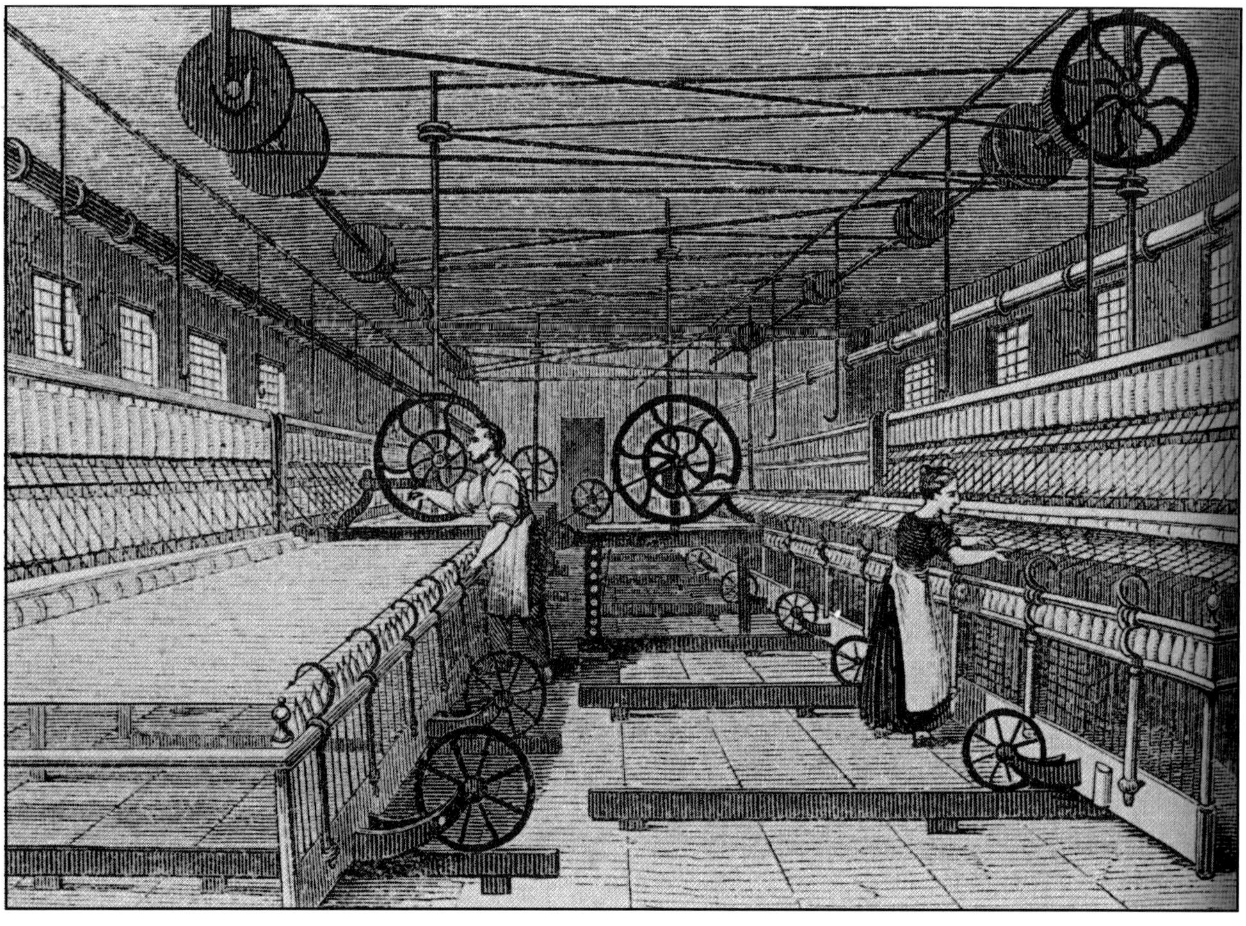

Plate 82: Engraving of a mule-spinning room, showing the steam-heating pipes below the ceiling and the spinning mules arranged longitudinally (reproduced from Redding 1842)

whilst George Murray owned the row of 15 cottages on Gas Street, situated immediately to the rear of Little Mill. George Murray stated that his workers did not live in company-owned properties, 'with, perhaps, five or six exceptions' (PP (HC) 1834 [167] XX, A1), hinting that his houses were reserved for key workers, such as overseers and engineers. Whilst the Census returns for this period list several 'cotton mill employees' on Gas Street, precise occupations are not divulged, although three 'machinists' are specified in the returns for 1851 (MLSU 107/2225 Folio 390-402).

Physical Conditions

The temperatures maintained on the spinning floors were dictated by the need to create a humid environment, and varied slightly according to the count of cotton being spun. George Murray stated to the Parliamentary Commissioners on the topic of heating the factory that 'we endeavour to keep the rooms at 75° Fahrenheit; our directions are that no steam be put into the mills if the rooms are at that temperature' (PP (HC) 1834 [167] XX, A1). The evidence given by mill owners to the Parliamentary Commission in 1833 shows that 70-75° F (21-24° C) was the average temperature maintained in most of the spinning mills, although some workers in the combined factories experienced up to 85° F (29° C) in the dressing plant (*ibid*), where loose filaments were removed from the spun yarn.

The desired temperatures were achieved via a combination of solid-fuel stoves and pipes carrying steam though all the working areas. A visitor to the Murrays' complex in 1832 noted that the steam from the engine boilers was 'conducted through cast-iron pipes, in some cases arranged near the floor, with the design of distributing the heat more uniformly' (Allen 1832, 130). This was not an unusual arrangement in spinning mills, and heating pipes may be seen in contemporary engravings (Pl 82).

Ventilation of the spinning floors was provided by a casement in every window. The opening and closing of these windows was 'under the control, and at the discretion, of the persons employed', although it may be assumed that this was not allowed to affect spinning temperatures. In terms of sanitation, every floor had access to a closet, and buckets of water were taken into each room several times daily for washing purposes (PP (HC) 1834 [167] XX, A1).

The most adverse working conditions in the mill were almost certainly endured in the cotton preparation rooms, especially those areas where batting was undertaken. Indeed, a visitor to A & G Murray's Mill noted that 'the dust and small particles of cotton floating in the air in this room are almost suffocating...' (Allen 1832, 130).

Phase 5, The Later Generations (1855 - 1898)

In general terms, the second half of the nineteenth century saw a considerable development of the world economy and a large increase in international trade. Despite increasing competition from the cotton industries of America and industrialising Europe, Lancashire maintained a major share of overseas markets. The period did have some economic crises, notably the 'Cotton Famine' of the early and mid-1860s, which was triggered by shortages of raw cotton as a result of the American Civil War, coupled with the massive over-production of textile goods during the late 1850s and early 1860s (Timmins 1996, 46). The fine spinners, however, probably suffered least from the ensuing economic hardships. Indeed, it was reported some 20 years later that A & G Murray had never worked short-time (Historical Publishing Company 1888, 89).

Plate 83: The first cotton ship at Manchester, unloading 4170 bales on 17 January 1894 (reproduced from Tracey 1901)

The early 1870s were particularly prosperous for the cotton industry, resulting from a surge in the economy coupled with a sharp rise in the European demand for British cottons. Notwithstanding the 'Great Depression' of 1873–96, the average spinning firm expanded from operating 16,872 spindles to 36,504 between 1870 and 1890 (Marrison 1996, 241). The operating capacity of A & G Murray, however, was listed in manufacturers' directories as being nearly three times the size of the average firm, with 100,000 spindles in 1891 (Worrall 1891, 125).

Trade was given a substantial boost with the opening of the Manchester Ship Canal in January 1894, making Manchester a port of international stature (Hartwell *et al* 2004, 262). By 1900, over 500,000 bales of raw cotton per year were being shipped up the canal (Pl 83), reducing freight and port charges to Manchester's business community (Timmins 1996, 61).

The Death of George Murray and the Limited Liability Company

George Murray died at the age of 94 on 18 April 1855. In accordance with his will of December 1852, the entire mill complex, valued at some £75,000, was conveyed to two of his sons, James and Benjamin Rigby Murray (LRO WCW 1855); George's other son, William Cannan Murray, does not appear to have had an interest in the family business. James, as the eldest son, was also bequeathed £8000, whilst a codicil stated that his three nieces, the daughters of his eldest brother John, were each to receive an annuity of £100. James and Benjamin Murray were also given the option of purchasing George Murray's foundry yard on German Street, and his cottages on Gas Street. Within one month of George Murray's death, Benjamin purchased McConnel's house in the Polygon, Ardwick (McConnel 1861, 141), whilst James resided at Ancoats Hall with his mother, Jane Murray. They both remained at Ancoats Hall for at least another ten years, when James took possession of a fashionable address in London and, by 1868, Jane had moved to Benjamin Murray's house in the Polygon. She died on 13 October 1878, leaving an estate valued at under £45,000, which was administered by James and Benjamin Murray (National Probate Calendars 1878, 22/59). Ancoats Hall was described at this time as 'a most perfect picture of desolation, neglect and misery…the sooner the place is pulled down and the land disposed of the better' (Heathcote 1876, 57) (Pl 84). The hall was, however, purchased by the Midland Railway Company, and converted for use as an art museum in 1886 (Harrison 1993, 93-6); it was eventually demolished in the late 1960s.

Plate 84: Ancoats Hall in 1903 (reproduced courtesy of Manchester Archives and Local Studies)

Following the death of his mother, Benjamin moved to Parton in Scotland, leaving the management of the family firm to his sons, George and John Rigby Murray. This appears to have been a short-lived measure, however, as Herbert Dixon became managing director in 1881 (Burnett 1899, 135), by which time A & G Murray had been registered as a limited liability company.

Numerous textile firms in Lancashire became limited liability organisations during the late nineteenth century, representing a significant change in industrial structure and practice. In particular, the authority within the day-to-day regulation of business was passed to managerial personnel, and the civic role that had been assumed by many nineteenth-century employers diminished; 'a civic elite was being lost, to be replaced by a more bureaucratic managerialism orientated more to the pursuit of profit than to a recognition of wider social responsibilities' (Griffiths 2001, 148). It is certainly clear that the Murray family had little direct involvement in the management of the mill after *c* 1880, and that Herbert Dixon was probably responsible for modifications to the mill complex during the late nineteenth century, ensuring the firm's survival into the twentieth century. In 1888, a description of the firm noted that 'during recent years the mills and machinery have undergone a complete remodelling, and the internal arrangements are upon the most modern and approved principle' (Historical Publishing Company 1888, 89). Indeed, the ability of the firm to keep apace with modern technological developments was cited as a primary reason for the continued success of the firm, allowing it to 'forge ahead of many more modern and recently constructed establishments' (*ibid*). A consequence of technological improvement was a reduction in the number of operatives employed, such that by 1897 A & G Murray Ltd only employed 500 hands (Biographical Publishing Company 1897, 59).

A significant alteration undertaken during the late nineteenth century was the replacement of the steam-power plant with a new engine and boiler house and a detached chimney, which were all placed within the courtyard adjacent to Old and Decker Mill (*Ch 6, p 127*). There are no references within the archive sources to furnish a precise date for the erection of these structures, although the size of the engine house, and the brick embellishment to the eaves, points to a date of around 1870-80. The new detached engine house abutted the structure that it was to supersede, with the front wall of the older structure forming the rear wall of the newer one. The form of the new engine house indicates that it contained a beam engine, which will almost certainly have been compounded to provide sufficient power. The associated boiler house was placed to the east, and contained a bank of four Lancashire-type boilers, which were connected to a common flue (*Ch 6, p 130*). This took a route along the southern elevation of the new engine house, terminating in an octagonal-shaped chimney, which reached a height of 135 ft (41.2 m). The date of the chimney is uncertain, and whilst chimneys of this type became common during the 1860s, that built for the Atlas No 4 Mill in Bolton, erected after 1875 (Williams with Farnie 1992, 113), is a good parallel to the one at A & G Murray's Mill.

Plate 85: Late nineteenth-century engine house at the north end of Bengal Street block, with the electricity transformer house in the foreground (reproduced courtesy of MRIAS)

By 1891, when the Ordnance Survey published their 10 ft: 1 mile plan, the steam-power plant for New Mill had been replaced, perhaps in connection with the adoption of larger mules. This involved the installation of a new engine in a dedicated building, which was placed at the northern end of the Bengal Street block and necessitated the rebuilding of the three end bays. The proportions of the engine house are shown on a photograph taken during the 1960s, and suggest that it contained a vertical-type engine (Pl 85). Whilst the traditional beam engine had been largely superseded by compound engines with horizontal cylinders by the 1870s, those with vertical cylinders were introduced during the 1880s (Williams with Farnie 1992, 114-5). The limited space available within A & G Murray's site would have precluded the choice of an horizontal engine, rendering a vertical type the only realistic option. This powered a rope drive, whereby the main line shafts on each floor of New Mill were driven from the engine flywheel by several cotton ropes, providing a more efficient, reliable, and quieter drive than the traditional geared system. Developed initially in America, the installation of rope-drive systems became widespread in England during the 1880s (Dickinson 2002, 97).

The Ordnance Survey plan of 1891 shows that New Mill's boiler house had been removed, implying that the steam for the new engine was generated in Old and Decker Mill's boiler house. This map also depicts the short arm on the southern side of the Rochdale Canal, opposite the entrance to the canal tunnel, as having been infilled. This arm had provided boats entering the Murrays' basin with the space required to negotiate the sharp turn into the tunnel, and its infilling reflects the demise of the canal as a means of transporting goods to and from the mill complex. Whilst the basin is marked on the 1891 plan, it is labelled as a 'reservoir', reinforcing the suggestion that it was by then used solely for supplying water to the steam-power plant and fire-fighting equipment.

Leasing Doubling and Fireproof Mills

A & G Murray Ltd is documented as having been engaged directly in cotton doubling in addition to spinning during the 1870s, and is listed as such in trade directories for the 1870s and 1880s (Hosking 1877, 24; Slater 1883, 76). On 10 February 1887, however, Fireproof Mill and Doubling Mill were leased to C E Bennett for a period of 12 years, with an option to purchase. The lease itemises some of the infrastructure on the site, which included steam pipes, mains gas, shafting, and engine power 'for effectual turning and working of such and so many doubling frames to be set up in the said mills' (RCHME and GMAU 1989, 7). The wording in the lease implies that gas to the mills was supplied via the city main, suggesting that the gasometer house in Little Mill was redundant by this date. The lease also stated that new doubling frames were to be installed in the mill within two months, and a separate clause specified that the mills were to be used only for the doubling of cotton.

The configuration of the mills at this time is depicted on a plan that was drawn up to accompany the lease (Fig 32). The detail of this plan appears to confirm that Fireproof Mill did not have its own steam engine.

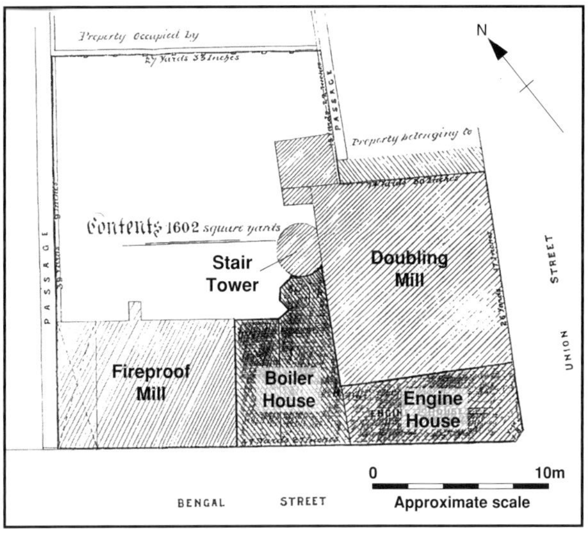

Figure 32: Plan of Doubling and Fireproof Mills accompanying the 1887 lease

In February 1891, a deed supplementary to Bennett's lease of 1887 mentions offices, a waste house, a warehouse, and a new boiler house that had been erected on the site, for which Bennett was charged extra rent. The firm's lease of Doubling and Fireproof Mills was renewed in 1897 for a term of 15 years (RCHME and GMAU 1989), and by 1910 was accredited with operating 16,000 spindles to produce 'extra strong super lace yarn' (Worrall 1910, 203). Despite leasing these mills, A & G Murray Ltd continued to double cotton itself; during this period, A & G Murray Ltd invested in a new factory at Cross Heath, near Newcastle-under-Lyme in Staffordshire, which appears to have been intended specifically for doubling. The firm's rationale in choosing a site in Staffordshire is uncertain, although proximity to the hosiery industry in the Midlands may have been a factor. An illustration of the Cross Heath Mill is included as an inset to an engraving of A & G Murray's Mill that was published in 1909 (Pl 86), and shows a large mill block of at least six storeys with two-storey ancillary buildings. The associated steam-power plant was supplied by the Bolton firm of Hick, Hargreaves & Co Ltd (BA ZHH/6).

Plate 86: Engraving of A & G Murray's Cross Heath Mill, Staffordshire (reproduced from the FCSDA 1909)

Phase 6, Fine Cotton Spinners' and Doublers' Association (1898 - *c* 1947)

The Fine Cotton Spinners' and Doublers' Association Limited (FCSDA) was formed in 1898, and for the next 30 years remained the largest and most successful cotton-spinning concern in the world, expanding to operate in excess of 60 mills and employing some 30,000 operatives. The initial years of the FCSDA coincided with a period of renewed growth in the Lancashire cotton industry, with expansion of the spinning sector being especially marked in towns such as Oldham, Rochdale, Middleton, and Farnworth (Williams with Farnie 1992, 46). This boom did not stimulate renewed growth of the spinning mills in Manchester, however, where the number of mills declined under the continuing inflation of land values. Indeed, in reference to the mills in Ancoats, Charles Rowley (1899, 4) noted that they were 'nearly all antiquated, and many of them are not now in use'.

The Great War (1914-18) caused severe difficulties for the textile industry, initially due to manpower shortages, and latterly as a result of restricted shipping space that led to scarce supplies of raw cotton. The immediate post-war period saw remarkable recovery as prices and profits rose sharply, although this boom collapsed in 1921 (Timmins 1996, 74). The succeeding years were characterised by a contraction of the industry and, in 1926, the last cotton mills to be built in Lancashire were completed as the industry reached its maximum productive capacity. Thereafter, 'what had been the world's greatest manufacturing industry was quietly but effectively dismantled' (Williams with Farnie 1992, 17), as attempts were made to address problems of excess capacity. A significant step in this process was the formation of the Lancashire Cotton Corporation in 1929, which took control of firms crippled by banking loans that could not be repaid, and embarked on a programme of rationalisation. Support for this initiative was provided by the Cotton Spinning Act of 1936, which was designed to reduce capacity by levying all employers and compensating those who agreed to break up machinery (Fowler 2003, 98).

Amalgamation

In 1897, Herbert Dixon resigned from A & G Murray Ltd in order to co-operate with Scott Lings in the formation of the FCSDA (Burnett 1899, 135). In September of the following year, and after exactly a century of independent production, A & G Murray Ltd was voluntarily wound up and conveyed to the FCSDA. Together with the firms of McConnel & Co, Houldsworth's, and C E Bennett & Co, A & G Murray Ltd were amongst the first to amalgamate with the FCSDA, although the separate firms retained their own identities within the framework of the association (Lee 1972, 153). The FCSDA, undoubtedly representing attempts at modernisation to counteract the effects of increasing foreign competition, instigated several episodes of remodelling of A & G Murray's complex. One of the first improvements was the installation of an automatic fire sprinkler system throughout the mill in 1902 by Mather & Platt Ltd (*Ch 6, p 134*).

A revealing illustration of the mill at this time is provided by an engraving published by the FCSDA in 1909, which features the north-facing elevation of New Mill, part of Old Mill, and the Murray Street block at its original height of four storeys (Pl 87). The engraving depicts New Mill as six storeys high, including the basement, indicating that the building had been reduced from its original height of eight storeys. Similarly, Old Mill (and presumably Decker) had been reduced by a single storey. The rationale for this remodelling is unclear,

Plate 87: Engraving of A & G Murray's Mill in Ancoats, featuring New Mill, Little Mill (Jersey Street), and the Murray Street block (reproduced from the FCSDA 1909)

although it is likely that structural factors were a major consideration, coupled with the installation of new machinery (*Ch 6, p 134*).

Replacement of Little Mill

The engraving of 1909 depicts Little Mill as having nine storeys, demonstrating that extra floors had been added to the original construction, making it 'one of the highest buildings in Manchester' (*Manchester Guardian* January 1908). On 28 January 1908, however, a catastrophic fire in the mill, attributed to 'friction in some part of the machinery on the second floor', resulted in its demolition (Pl 88). Whilst fighting the blaze, which broke out shortly after midday and raged for at least 12 hours, the fire-tender blew over in high winds, resulting in a fireman losing his life (Pl 89). The damage caused by the fire was estimated at £20,000, and some 200 operatives were put out of work (*Cotton Factory Times*, 31 January 1908).

Proposals for a replacement mill were devised rapidly, and architect's plans for New Little Mill were deposited with Manchester City Council in June 1908 (Building Control Plan 19038). These show the new building as

Plate 88: Photograph of Little Mill immediately after the fire in 1908 (reproduced from the Manchester Guardian, *29 January 1908)*

Plate 89 : Little Mill immediately after the fire, January 1908 (reproduced from Manchester Guardian, *29 January 1908)*

five storeys high, ten bays long, and five bays wide, occupying a larger footprint than its predecessor, and necessitating the demolition of the company-owned houses along Gas Street. The architecture and structural engineering inherent within New Little Mill was typical for its date, utilising reinforced concrete for the construction of the floors and roof. It was of especial significance, however, as it was one of the earliest, if not the first, purpose-built electrically-powered textile mill in Manchester; the first such mill in the wider region was probably Acme Mills, Pendlebury, which was built in 1904 (Williams with Farnie 1992, 134). This technology appears to have met with widespread approval; it was estimated in January 1908 that the rate of adopting electricity for power was such that by the middle of the year, 6% of the total spindles in Lancashire would be electrically driven (*Cotton Factory Times*, 31 January 1908).

Some steam-powered mills in the area that were converted to use electricity during this period, including Kearsley Mill near Bolton and Welkin Ring Mill near Bredbury, produced their own power using generators driven by steam-turbine engines (Williams with Farnie 1992, 134). Brunswick Mill, on Bradford Road in Ancoats, was converted to electric drive in 1908, but obtained its power supply directly from the Manchester Corporation main at 6500 volts, and was transformed down to 400-40 volts for machinery and 220 volts for lighting purposes in a transformer house (*Illustrated London News* 1909) (Pl 90). It is likely that A & G Murray Ltd used a system similar to that installed at Brunswick Mill. Electricity was supplied by Manchester Corporation, via a single-storey transformer house situated in the courtyard adjacent to the Bengal Street block (Pl 85). Group-drive motors were sited on each floor of New Little Mill to power the spinning machinery, and these motors were housed in a full-height external tower, attached to the Jersey Street elevation, as a precaution against the fire risk that this new technology presented (Pl 91).

Plate 90: Electric drives powering the carding engines in Brunswick Mill (reproduced from the Illustrated London News, *July 1909)*

Plate 91: New Little Mill, showing tower for electric motors

A & G Murray's use of electric drives was not restricted to their newest factory, and its adoption subsequently within the main complex was a significant modification to the mills (*Ch 6, p 136*). The archive sources have not furnished a precise date for this modification, although it was not before the late 1920s as it is not marked on Goad's insurance plan of the site for 1927. When it was adopted, electricity not only powered the textile machinery, but facilitated the installation of new infrastructure, such as lighting and a small cage hoist that was added to the north-east corner of New Mill. The successful application of electricity to power New Little Mill was adopted subsequently by McConnel & Co, when they erected Royal Mill and Paragon Mill in 1912 (*Ch 4, p 55*).

It is tempting to associate this latest technology with the introduction of new machinery, perhaps ring-spinning frames, although firm documentary evidence is lacking. Ring-spinning frames were smaller and heavier, but exceeded the yarn output of spinning mules, which in many cases resulted in the installation of additional preparation machinery (Williams with Farnie 1992, 123). The origins of the ring-spinning frame may be traced to the USA, where Messrs Addison and Stevens patented a device in 1829 that was effectively the first ring-spinning machine (Catling 1986, 184). Despite efforts to introduce this new invention to Britain in 1832, it was widely rejected by the Lancashire manufacturers and the trades unions, and it was not until the mid-1870s that it was re-introduced to the region. Even then, the adoption of this improved machinery was slow, and spinning mules continued to account for over 70% of total spindleage in Lancashire as late as 1939 (Griffiths 2001, 16).

The installation of ring-spinning frames in A & G Murray's Mill during the twentieth century has been suggested by anecdotal evidence; several such frames were reportedly removed from the mill by J & H Schofield Ltd, who exported them to Budapest during the 1950s (J Schofield *pers comm*). It remains unknown what year they were first used, how many were installed, and which buildings housed them, although a group of spindles found on the ground floor of New Mill during the archaeological survey (*Appendix* 2) may have derived from ring-spinning frames. It may be surmised that the floors in the upper storeys of the original buildings would have required modification to take the increased loading.

Canal Basin

The canal basin was filled in during the early twentieth century, although the exact date at which this happened is uncertain. The canal tunnel beneath the Bengal Street block is shown on a plan of the site, dated March 1902 (MLSU MC 3834M 892), and may have been used to supply water to the steam plant after the basin had been abandoned. Whilst this function will have been made largely redundant by the adoption of electric drive, the boilers remained in operation as part of the heating system within the mills, which continued to use canal water until the 1950s (RLSU C/RCC/1/3).

Minor Modifications

A deposited building plan of August 1926 (Building Control Plan 17927), proposing the conversion of New Mill engine house to a first-aid room and office, and the 1927 revision of Goad's insurance plans, provide useful snapshots of the site's layout during the second decade of the twentieth century (Fig 33). The former is the first plan of the site to show the electric transformer house, and marks the adjacent part of the Bengal Street block as a dynamo house with a mechanic's shop to the south. Goad's plan also identifies New Mill engine house as a bobbin store. Other modifications included the addition of a larger toilet block to Old and Decker Mill.

In 1930, the Bengal Street block was reduced in height by two storeys, in accordance with a deposited building plan (Building Control Plan 20366). The plan also indicates that timber floor beams had carried a boarded floor and, whilst the lower storeys were fitted with cylindrical columns, the upper floor retained columns of cruciform cross-section with load-transfer boxes around the beams.

At some point during this phase, the northern end of the Murray Street block was reduced in height to two storeys. Kelly's directory of 1937 indicates that the building was still of four storeys at that date, but it is annotated as being of two storeys on a deposited building plan of 1950 (Building Control Plan 30000).

Doubling and Fireproof Mills

It seems that C E Bennett & Co Ltd vacated Doubling and Fireproof Mills upon expiry of their lease in 1912, and relocated to Union and Bengal Mills on Cambrian Street in Ancoats, where they were accredited with operating 50,000 doubling spindles (*eg* Skinner 1930, 962). It is assumed that, after 1912, the Fireproof and Doubling Mills reverted back to A & G Murray Ltd. By the 1930s, a new section that linked the two mills had been inserted, and the mills were re-named as Waulk Mill, as marked on the Ordnance Survey plan of 1933. A & G Murray Ltd had evidently vacated Waulk Mill by the 1940s, as it was occupied by Sutherland & Bowley Ltd, bedding manufacturers (Kelly 1942, 690), and subsequently by The London Waterproof Company Ltd (Goad's Insurance Plan, 1943).

Phase 7, The End of Spinning (*c* 1947 - 1950s)

In 1946, the FCSDA was reconstituted as the Fine Spinners' and Doublers' Ltd. This coincided with the start of a five-year period that saw a sustained boom in the textile industry, reflecting a world shortage of cotton goods. Yarn production increased by 50% during these years, although output fell by 28% in 1951, signalling the final collapse of the Lancashire industry (Miles 1968, 24).

During this period, A & G Murray's Mill was conveyed to two or more separate companies, marking the beginning of the end of cotton spinning on the site. Old and Decker Mill appear to have been the first elements of the complex to have been sold. The deed of conveyance, dated 6 February 1948, was between the Fine Spinners' and Doublers' Ltd and Messrs F and SS Hurst, who purchased the two mills for £5800. The Murray Street block was sold for £2500 to Fred Beech & Co Ltd, yarn merchants, in December 1950, but the Bengal Street block was not sold until December 1960, when the Fine Spinners' and Doublers' Ltd conveyed the premises to Trownbay Property Co (RCHME and GMAU 1989). The Bengal Street engine house was evidently out of use by this date as a deposited building plan, dated 14 March 1950,

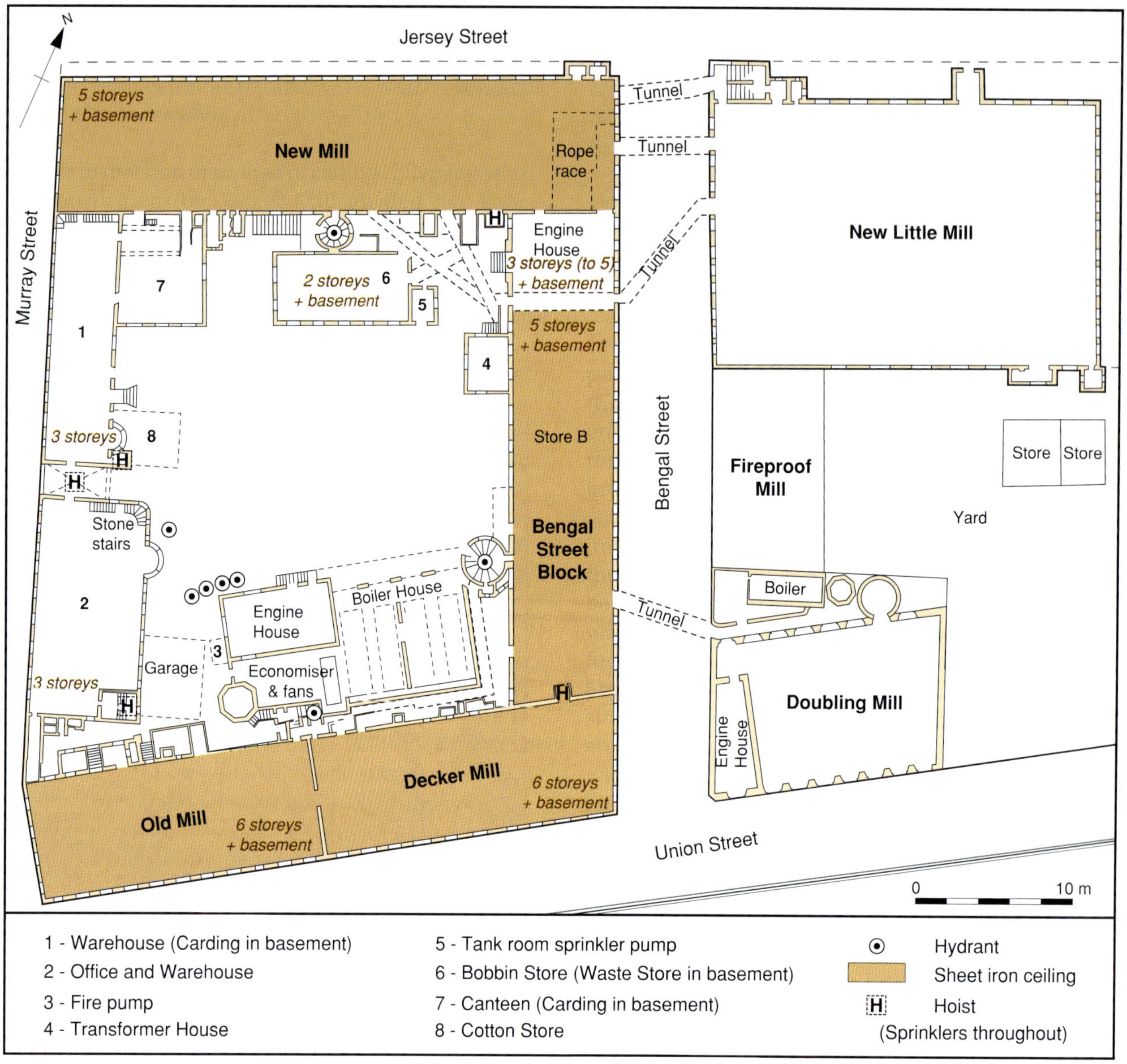

Figure 33: The layout of A & G Murray's Mill, based on Goad's Insurance Plan, 1927

proposed the conversion of the rope race to a stair tower (Building Control Plan 30000).

Despite the fragmentation of the complex, A & G Murray Ltd is listed in trade directories until 1954, accredited as cotton spinners in Ancoats, producing yarn of counts between 40 and 220, and 'rayon specialities' (Kelly 1954, 1766). This provided the final reference for the firm's activities in Manchester, although their mill at Cross Heath in Staffordshire continued to produce 'high-class folded cotton yarns for all purposes' (Collinson 1956, 131); correspondence dated October 1965 confirms that A & G Murray's Cross Heath Mill outlived the firm's premises in Ancoats by at least a decade (GMRO B/CTLD/1/48).

It was also during this period that an aerial gangway above Murray Street linked the sixth storey of Old Mill with the fifth storey of McConnel & Co's Sedgwick Mill (Pl 92). After more than a century of close association, Manchester's two largest mill complexes finally became linked physically, albeit after they had ceased cotton spinning.

Phase 8, The Final Days of Manufacturing

During the second half of the twentieth century the mills were used for a variety of functions, but retained their association with the textile industry. After 1954, Old and Decker Mill was used as a warehouse for Baxendale & Co Ltd, plumbers' merchants (Kelly 1959, 654), but was occupied subsequently by various clothing manufacturers, with the basement being used as a carpet warehouse (Goad's Insurance Plan, 1966). Limited strengthening work and improvements to

Plate 92: Bridge linking A & G Murray's Old Mill with the McConnel & Co complex (© Crown Copyright NMR)

sanitation had been carried out to the mills during the early 1960s (Building Control Plans 45761; 53792), but in general terms the buildings failed to receive the maintenance and repair they required. The engine house at the north end of the Bengal Street block was destroyed by fire in August 1964, and Old Mill engine house was vacant by 1966 (Goad's Insurance Plan, 1966). Doubling and Fireproof Mills are not listed in trade directories for the 1960s, suggesting that they were also vacant. New Mill remained in commercial use, and was occupied jointly by Rainclipper Ltd (rainwear manufacturers), Glamyre Ltd (clothing manufacturers), and Chorlton Warehouses Ltd (credit drapers), whilst the Bengal Street block was occupied at this time by the London Waterproof Co (Silkimac) Ltd (Kelly 1965, 69).

The boiler house for the Old Mill engine house was still standing in 1985, but had been demolished by 1990 (RCHME and GMAU 1989, 18). New Mill engine house suffered fire-damage during the 1990s (Pl 93), whilst the remnants of the Bengal Street block were destroyed completely in a fire in 1996, leaving only the stub walls at the south end. Further acts of vandalism and arson that would have led ultimately to the complete loss of the site were averted by the timely regeneration initiatives that focused on Ancoats (*Ch 1, pp 3-5*). These were coupled with recognition of the immense historical significance of the area's surviving large mills, and the proactive steps taken to ensure their long-term future.

Plate 93: View north across the New Mill engine house, showing the damage and dereliction of the 1990s

Conclusion

Adam and George Murray established one of the most important cotton-spinning factories in Britain. The rise and progress of their firm is a testimony for the development of Ancoats as an urban centre of manufacturing, whilst their mill became an iconic example of technology employed in the new steam-powered spinning factories.

Notwithstanding the exceptional commercial success achieved by Adam and George Murray, their route to prosperity in Manchester's textile industry was not uncommon. Indeed, their entrance to the trade via the fabrication of textile machinery was an option taken by several of Manchester's eighteenth-century entrepreneurial manufacturers, and became a trait of the town's early factory-based textile industry. This was an important factor in the Murrays' rapid rise to become the largest cotton-spinning firm in Manchester by the early nineteenth century, combined with favourable economic conditions, the inception of the canal system, and the application of steam power. The Murrays' entrepreneurial vision drove them to create a mill complex on an unprecedented scale, utilising developing technology and providing employment for more than 1000 people in the expanding suburb of Ancoats. Their huge mill epitomised the emergence of a new type of urban landscape, and became an iconic symbol of the steam-powered factory system. This remains the case in the twenty-first century; textile manufacturing has disappeared from Ancoats, but the monumental mill of A & G Murray provide testimony to the former importance of the industry. The fabric of these buildings encapsulates a remarkable physical record of the evolution of the steam-powered textile mill, allowing its major stages of development, from inception to demise, to be charted.

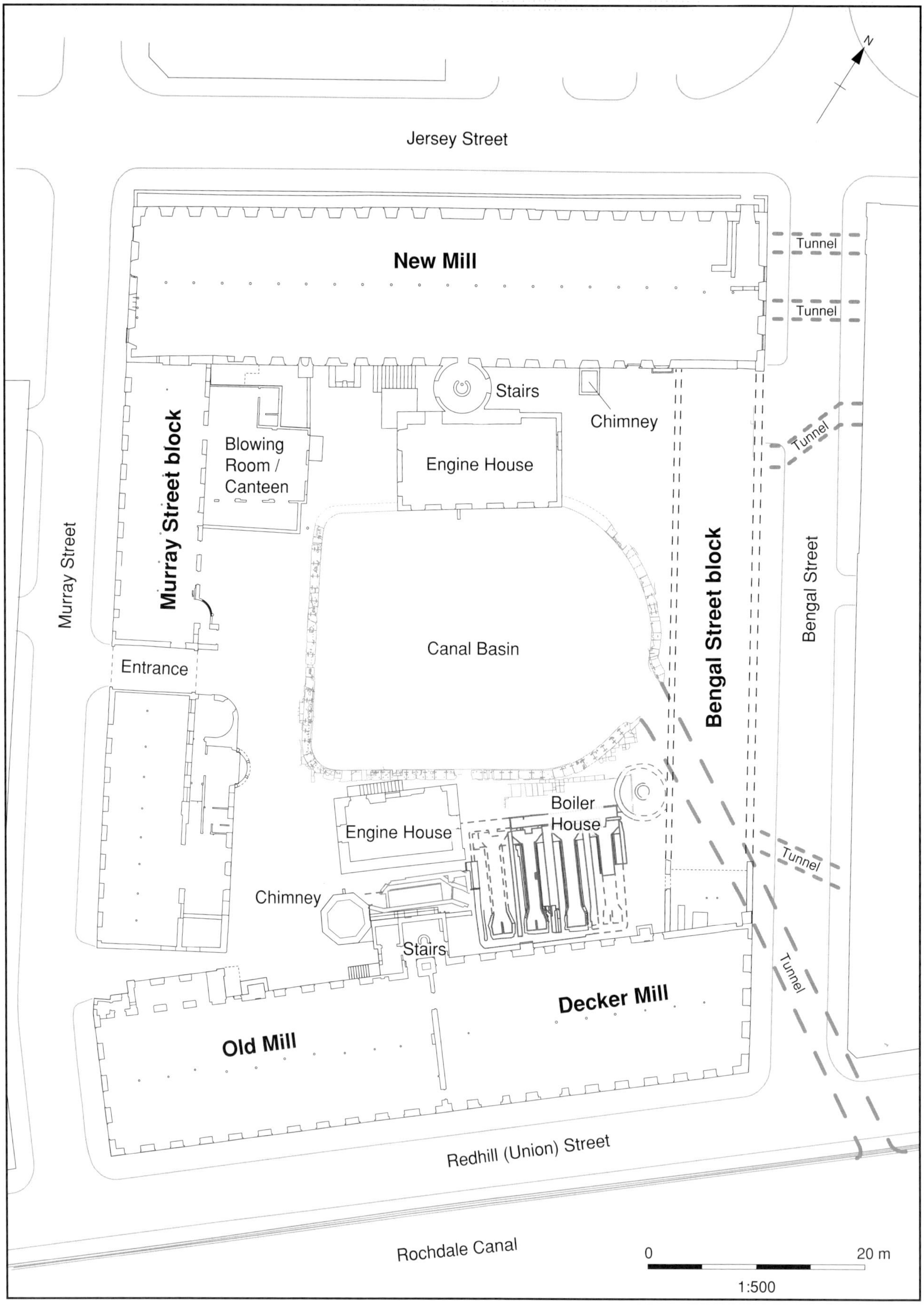

Figure 34: Site plan showing location of the main structures

6

A & G MURRAY'S MILL: THE ARCHAEOLOGICAL SURVEY

Chris Wild

Introduction

Between October 2003 and June 2006, OA North carried out a comprehensive archaeological survey of A & G Murray's Mill in advance of, and concurrent with, the structural repair work (*Ch 7*). The archaeological work comprised a detailed fabric survey, targeted excavation, and recording of the various buildings in conjunction with their structural repair. This facilitated access to parts of the mill complex that were previously unavailable, and has allowed a comprehensive record of the buildings to be generated. In many instances, this has confirmed and expanded upon the results obtained from earlier studies (*e.g.* RCHME and GMAU 1989; Donald Insall Associates and Structural Perspectives 2002), but has also allowed for the re-interpretation of some of the conclusions drawn from previous research. The work focused on the historic core of the site to the west of Bengal Street, omitting three mills which once formed part of complex: Doubling Mill; Fireproof Mill; and New Little Mill.

Of the structures recorded, the most striking are the two large spinning blocks fronting Redhill (formerly Union) Street and Jersey Street (Fig 34). The former actually comprises two factories, Old and Decker Mill (Pl 94), whilst the latter is a single build (New Mill). All were originally eight storeys high, but were reduced in height to seven and six storeys respectively in *c* 1902 (*Ch 5, p 88*). The Murray Street block links the two spinning mills along the western boundary of the site, whilst the Bengal Street block forming the eastern boundary was almost

Plate 94: South-facing elevation of Old and Decker Mill in 2005

completely demolished following a devastating fire in 1996 (*Ch 5, p 93*). Within the courtyard enclosed by these four structures are two engine houses and their associated chimneys, and archaeological excavation exposed the remains of the associated boiler house and the distinctive canal basin visible on nineteenth-century maps.

In order to create an overview of the development of the complex, the description of the buildings has been organised chronologically, with the dates being tied into the sequence of available historic maps and other archival sources. For clarity within the descriptive text, the individual bays within each structure have been assigned numbers, which run either from west to east, or south to north, and are continuous through Old and Decker Mill.

Phase 1, The First (Old) Mill (1798 - 1801)

Old Mill was largely completed in 1798 (*Ch 5, pp 66-7*), and comprised an eight-storey building, plus a loft. It was orientated approximately east/west along Union Street, bounded by Murray Street on its western side, and measured 42 ft (13 m) wide and 105 ft (32 m) long, excluding the attached engine house. Typically for a late eighteenth-century mill, it was not of fireproof construction; the earliest known use of iron-framed fireproof construction in the area was in an extension to the Salford Twist Mill in 1801 (Fitzgerald 1988). The load-bearing walls of Old Mill were up to 3 ft (0.92 m) thick, constructed in mould-thrown brick and bonded in a pale grey lime and sand mortar, but had no foundations, sitting directly on the natural clay.

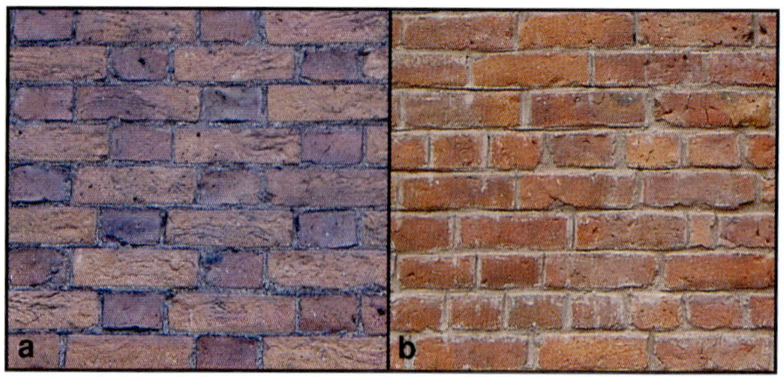

Plate 95: Brick bond types within the Murrays' Mill: a) Flemish bond b) English Garden Wall bond

The south and west external walls of Old Mill were built in Flemish bond, whilst the north and east walls were in the less decorative English Garden Wall bond, as were all internal elevations (Pl 95). The use of different bonds was also applied subsequently to Decker Mill, New Mill, and the blocks on Murray Street and Bengal Street. Flemish bond was the fashionable decorative brickwork during the Georgian period, but was unsuited to walls over one and a half bricks thick (Lynch 1994, 220), explaining why the internal elevations of the four-bricks thick walls were constructed in a different bond. Whilst English Garden Wall bond and Flemish bond require the same quantities of brick (96 yd^2), more facing bricks are required for Flemish bond (63 compared to 60 (*op cit*, 205)), and facings in a stretcher course require lower quality, less precisely manufactured brick than those comprising headers and stretchers within a patterned wall. It is also noteworthy that English

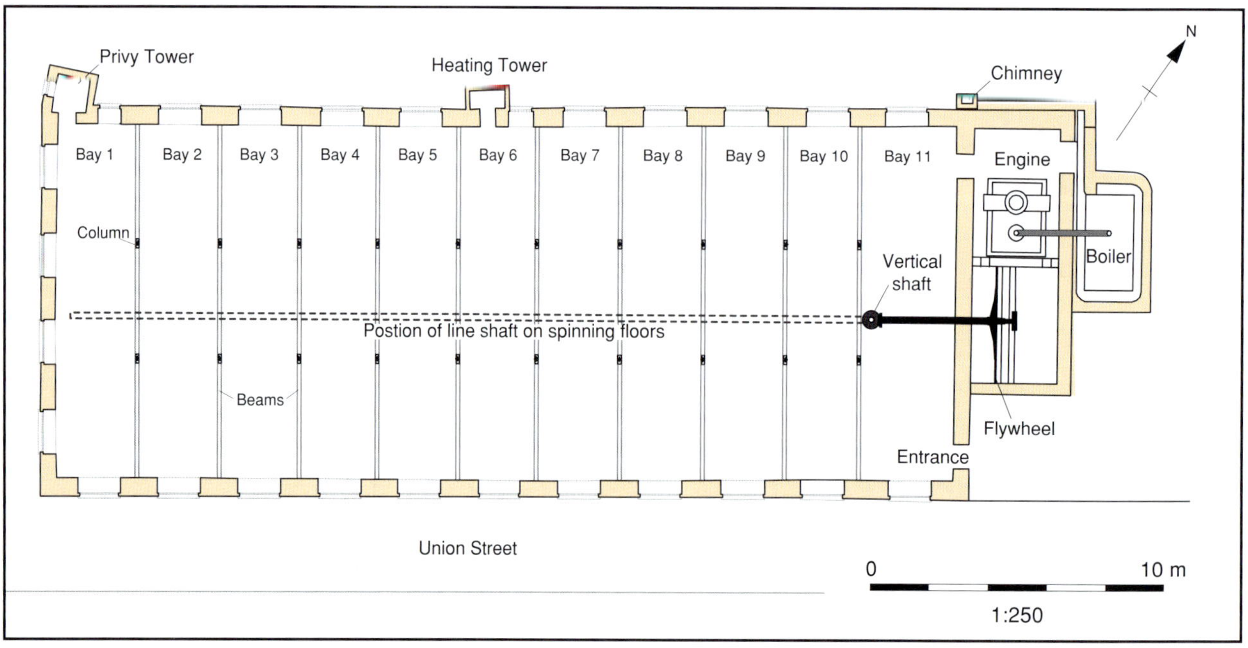

Figure 35: Ground floor plan of Old Mill, showing the layout of the power transmission and position of original columns

Plate 96: Baltic timber shipping marks on the underside of beams in Old Mill

Garden Wall bond is stronger than Flemish bond (Brunskill 1990, 52), suggesting that whilst Flemish bond was preferable stylistically, construction in English Garden Wall bond was more practical. The dimensions of the bricks used are generally 9 x 3 x 2¾ in (229 x 98 x 70 mm), slightly less deep than typical bricks of the period, which tended to measure 4¼-4½ in (10814 mm) (Harley 1974, 76).

Old Mill comprised 11 bays, all of slightly different widths, typically around 9 ft (2.75 m), with wider end bays, especially to the east, which was 11¼ ft (3.43 m) wide (Fig 35). The mill also had tapering wall thicknesses and diminishing floor heights, with each floor about 95% of the height of that below. The shorter, narrower walls in the upper floors required considerably less bricks; the construction of the basement required around 65,000 bricks, whilst the top floor used almost half that amount, approximately 34,000 bricks. This dramatically reduced the load of the upper floors, giving the stability to build to a height of eight storeys, and also significantly reduced the cost of materials.

Each bay had windows in the long north and south elevations, with shallow brick-cambered arches, and sandstone sills that projected slightly externally. Windows at street level afforded light to the basement, with the ground floor situated some 6 ft (1.83 m) above. The internal apertures varied slightly in width, probably reflecting the rapid and functional construction rather than a need for precise symmetry. The end walls of the mill also had similar windows, four on each floor, with the exception of the basement, ground, and first floors of the eastern end, signifying the position of the original engine house.

The bays were divided by large-scantling, chamfered timber beams, each almost 40 ft (12.19 m) in length. Rather than using oak, which might have been difficult to procure locally in the lengths required, Northern European softwood was imported for use throughout the mill, with several beams, joists, and rafters exhibiting Baltic timber shipping marks (Pl 96). In total, 25 original beams survive within the main floors, and several retain evidence of the original line shafting.

The beams supported timber board floors, overlying joists, also of Northern European origin, attached at either end by simple square-housed joints. Brick-vault ceilings were beginning to be employed for fireproofing in textile mills by this date (Fitzgerald 1988), but the expense and additional weight of brick-arched floors made them uneconomical, and thus impractical, for a mill of this type. Instead, the timber floorboards in Old Mill were under-drawn with lath and plaster in an attempt at fireproofing.

The large, heavy timber beams were supported by cast-iron columns. Whilst the originals were replaced during the early nineteenth century (*p 117*), their positions are represented by several compression marks and scars on the soffits of the beams. The original structure probably had two rows of columns, positioned approximately 13 ft (3.96 m) from each of the long elevations (Fig 35). These will have been slender, solid cruciform-section, cast-iron columns, similar to those surviving within the upper floor of New Mill (*p 113*) and the Murray Street block, and typical of the period (Falconer 2001, 19-24). Within the basement, every column was supported on a sandstone block, each approximately 3 ft (0.92 m) square and 2 ft (0.61 m) high.

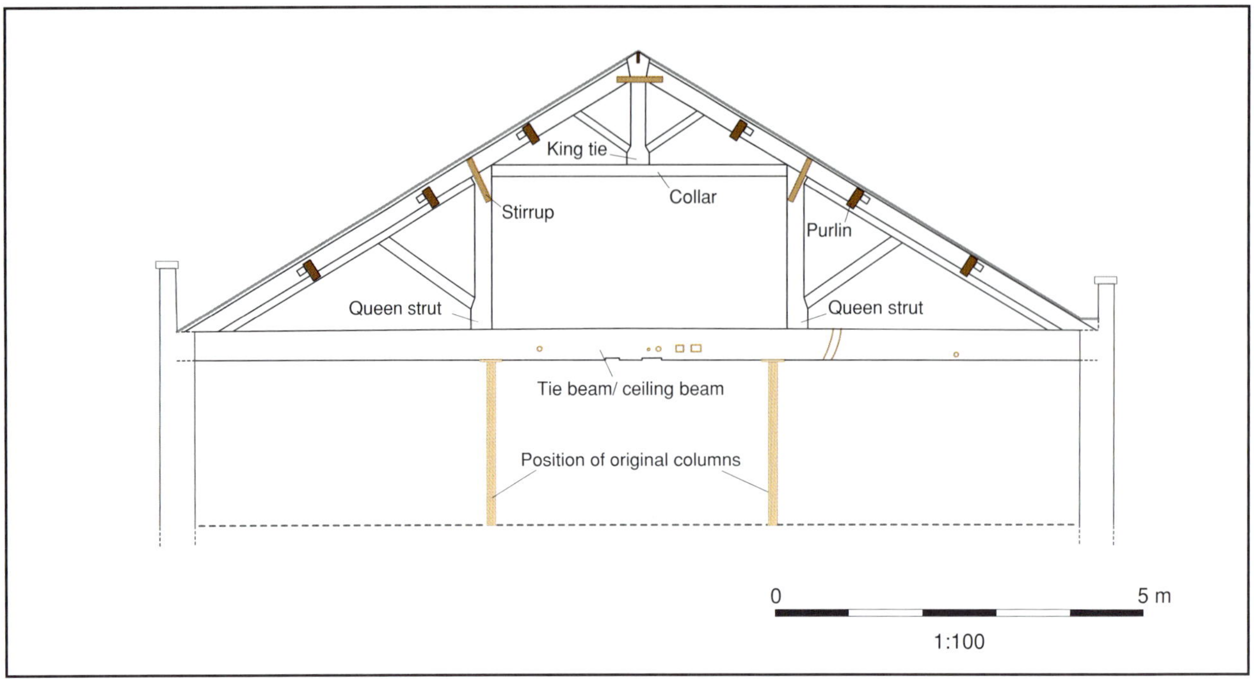

Figure 36: Roof truss detail, Old Mill

The Roof

Although the mill was reduced in height by a single storey around the turn of the twentieth century (*p 134*), the roof structure appears to represent the form of that used in the original build. Indeed, the inconsistency of the numbering of the trusses in the present roof (shown by carpenter's assembly marks), implies that the original timbers were reused. The roof was probably hipped at both ends, each with a longitudinal half-truss of similar style to those in the main roof. Several reused round-headed Cumbrian slates survive on both pitches of the roof, suggesting that this was the original roofing material, and the variance in their size implies that they were laid in diminishing courses.

The existing roof comprises queen strut trusses with king ties above the collar (Fig 36). Both the queen struts and the king tie have jowled feet, housing straight braces, with the king tie also having a jowled head, clasping the ridge board. All joints are tenoned, with additional iron stirrups at either end of the queen struts, held in place with gibs and cotters. The principal rafters are bolted through the tie beam, whilst the king ties are bolted into the collar in a more sophisticated manner. This type of timber truss, strengthened with wrought-iron bolts and stirrups in an attempt to stop truss members from separating, became popular during the late eighteenth century (Brunskill 1994, 74), and similar examples were used in the Arkwright-type mills of the 1770s.

The tie beams of the trusses all have dovetailed joist sockets, implying that the upper floor had a ceiling, rather than being open to the rafters. This hints that the roof space may have been used, perhaps for storage, although this cannot be confirmed. Each pitch has three tusk-tenoned purlins (Pl 97), which provide increased rigidity to the roof structure, but are more commonly associated with floor construction (*op cit*, 143). The rafters are aligned on 18 in (0.46 m) centres, and are mainly the full length of each pitch. At their lower ends, the rafters are birdsmouth-jointed to the wall plates, which sit on the inner face of the external walls.

Most of the trusses bear chiselled assembly marks on the eastern face, usually in the form of Roman numerals, but occasionally letters (Pl 98). Several different marking systems appear to have been employed simultaneously within the roof of a single structure, probably denoting the work of different carpenters.

Plate 97: Tusk-tenoned purlins in Old Mill roof

Plate 98: Carpenter's assembly marks scored on the roof truss in Old Mill

During the survey, a small woman's shoe or slipper was found to have been concealed in the roof of Old Mill (Fig 37). Intended for the left foot, it is plain in design with no evidence of decoration, but is clearly more than a workaday shoe, having a low front and slightly pointed toe; there is a fabric lining. It is heavily worn and all trace of the outer sole is missing, removing any indication as to whether there was originally a 'lift' or heel. The configuration of the remaining insoles and stitching, however, suggest not. It is not easy to date plain shoes such as this with any precision, but a late eighteenth- or early nineteenth-century date would not be unreasonable, bearing in mind that the shoe was already worn out before it had deliberately been placed in the roof of the building. Another worn shoe was found concealed in the northern end of the Murray Street block, and is also likely to have been secreted during the construction of the building (*Phase 3, p 114*). This was similarly of a late eighteenth- or early nineteenth-century date, but had evidently belonged to a child (Fig 37).

The hiding of old shoes within buildings is not unusual, being a long-established superstition well known by the seventeenth century and continuing into the twentieth. Opinions differ as to their purpose, but Merrifield (1989) suggests either a link with builders (often the shoes are left somewhere normally inaccessible), or with a more general belief that shoes could contain or ward off evil spirits and were thus placed at significant potential points of entry, not least the roof. It is especially interesting to note that the shoe had evidently been replaced when the roof was rebuilt during a reduction in the height of the building (*Phase 6, p 134*).

The Machinery

The floor space in Old Mill was certainly dominated by spinning mules, eventually with the basement and ground floor being used for preparatory processing. The layout of Old Mill is consistent with transversely arranged mules, given the use of a double row of columns, which would not have permitted the full extension of the carriage of longitudinally arranged mules. Although some earlier mules were beginning to be operated in pairs, such as those supplied by McConnel & Kennedy to Ainsworths of Preston in 1797 (Catling 1986, 45), the uneven number of bays in Old Mill suggests that they may have been operated individually, although the extra bay may have been used for temporary storage. The advantage of operating mules in pairs is that it required less skilled labour, as one operative could tend two mules.

The internal width of Old Mill is 38 ft (11.58 m), of which around 3 ft (0.92 m) would be required for access along one side. In the upper floors, some 2½ ft (0.76 m) would be taken up by the headstock and framing of each mule, suggesting a carriage length of *c* 32½ ft (9.91 m) for each. Correspondence between McConnel and Kennedy and Messrs Taylor and Heywood of Derbyshire in 1795 concerns the provision of mules with spindles of 1¼ in spacings, although those supplied to Ainsworths two years later had spindles at 1⅜ in spacings (Catling 1986, 45). Assuming a similar spindle separation in the original mules in Old Mill, this would give a total capacity of 282 spindles per mule.

Power Production and Transmission

The mill was powered initially by a 12 hp steam-powered beam engine supplied by the firm of Boulton and Watt in Birmingham (*Ch 5, p 65*). This engine is unlikely to have been of sufficient power to drive machinery throughout the mill, suggesting that it did not operate at maximum capacity at this time. The exact position of the engine and its associated boiler is not clear on the design plans, although it may be deduced that they were placed transversely across the eastern end of the mill. The surviving physical evidence within the former eastern end wall reinforces this view, being the only end wall within the complex missing windows in the basement, ground, and first

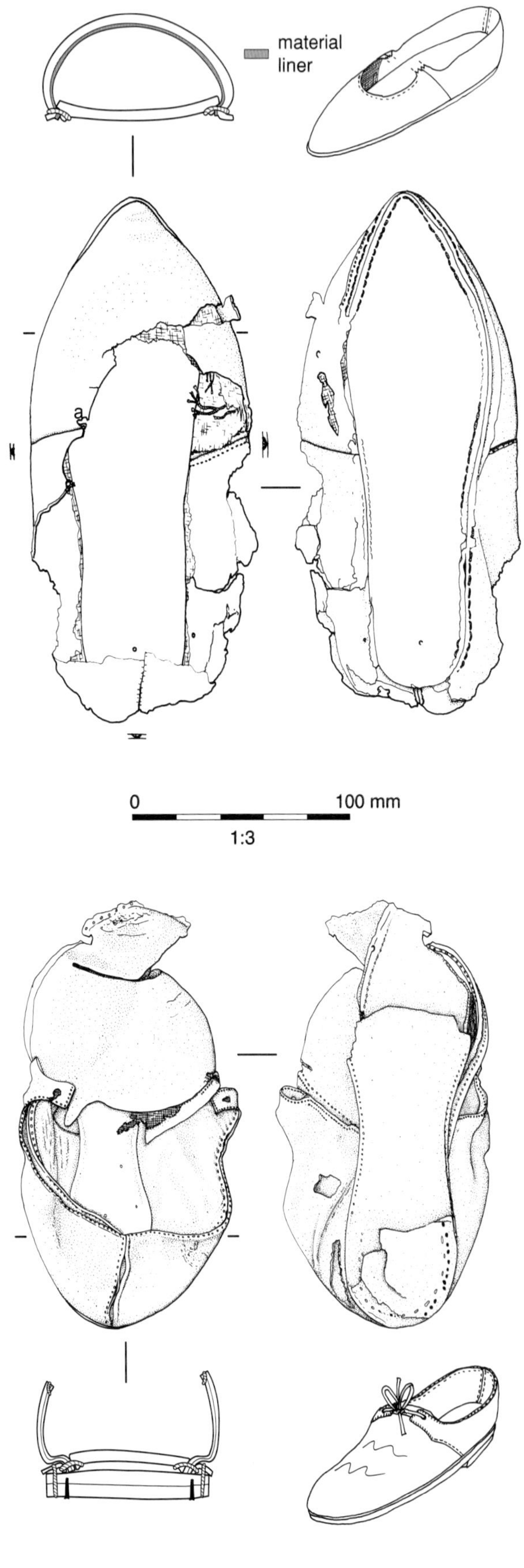

Figure 37: Shoes discovered in the roof of Old Mill (top), and the heating flue in the Murray Street block (bottom)

Plate 99: Blocked doorway into the original 1798 engine house from Old Mill

Figure 38: Isometric reconstruction of Old Mill (1798 - 1801)

floors. This wall also incorporated two brick-arched apertures at ground level, the northern of which is likely to have provided access into the engine house (Pl 99). The southern aperture, which has a more rounded arch, and what appears to be a broken-out sill just above floor level, probably represents a window positioned immediately south of the engine house. The physical evidence also demonstrates that the engine house was flush with the northern elevation of the mill, and that it was constructed to the depth of the mill basement, rather than standing at ground level (Fig 38).

The steam for the engine was generated in a single long boiler, which was placed adjacent to the engine, although the exact position of the original chimney is uncertain; the Boulton and Watt plans do not show the chimney, although this was probably placed against the north-facing elevation. The method of water supply to the engine and boiler is similarly uncertain. Subsequent engine houses within the complex incorporated header tanks on the roofs (BWA 3147/5/295; BWA 3147/5/364), although no such feature is shown on the design plan for the original engine house (BWA 3147/5/167). Whilst adequate boiler-feed water was vital to their operation, the steam engines themselves also required large quantities of cold water for condensing purposes. Boiler feed could be recycled, but condenser-feed water would have to be allowed to cool before recycling. Thus, prior to the completion of the Rochdale Canal through Ancoats in 1804, a reservoir had to be constructed of sufficient capacity to hold at least one day's supply of cooling water. The logical position for such a structure would be within the part of the site that was occupied subsequently by the canal basin, although there is no surviving evidence to confirm this. However, a well with a 3 ft (0.91 m) internal diameter, situated close to the southern end of the Murray Street block, possibly furnished the water supply. Two drains, each approximately 5 ft (1.52 m) below ground level, linked into the shaft of the well on its eastern and south-western sides, the former possibly representing a supply to the boiler.

The original power transmission from the engine entered the building at basement level, immediately south of the centre of the east elevation, and turned an upright shaft that extended between the floors of the mill. It is likely that the vertical shaft was situated in the eastern bay of the mill, which would account for the extra width of this bay, although no indication of vertical shaft brackets survives within the joist layout. Bevel gears connected with the vertical shaft powered a network of horizontal line shafts on each floor. The individual machines were powered by belts or ropes, attached to fixed drums rotating on the line shafts.

Semi-circular rebates in the soffits of the beams represent the positions of the original line shafts, although these are only present above the second floor, implying that powered mules were installed initially solely on the upper floors. The positions of these rebates suggest that the line shaft on each floor was placed 21 ft (6.41 m) from the northern elevation, just south of centre (Fig 35). The position of the rebates also correlated with the point at which the main drive shaft entered the mill, as shown on the original design plans for the engine (BWA 3147/5/295).

Heating System

Given the external position of the engine and boiler house, the warm and humid atmosphere required on the spinning floors had to be generated by other means. The use of steam was suggested as a means of factory heating as early as 1745, but there is scant evidence of its uptake prior to patents being granted in 1791 and 1793 (Tann 1970, 105). During the 1790s, several experimental systems were devised, most appearing to have involved a large stove at the lowest floor level of the mill, with vents into each floor from a main flue. A good example of this system was operated in the first mill at New Lanark, built in 1789, which had a simple stove at each end of the cellar. Warm air passed through a vertical iron pipe, with vents that could be opened and closed on each floor (*op cit*, 109).

Plate 100: Heating tower attached to the north-facing elevation of Old Mill

The construction of Old Mill incorporated a rectangular heating tower, measuring 8 ft (2.44 m) wide and projecting 4 ft (1.22 m) from the northern external elevation (Pl 100). Unlike at New Lanark, internal apertures suggest that the original system of heating used here provided for a stove on each floor, with warm air being circulated through a vent above the stove, and the exhaust being carried through the main flue of the tower. Externally, the tower was remodelled subsequently, obscuring any original detail, but the internal face has blocked floor-level recesses, many retaining top-hung timber vents, some with evidence of metal sheet coverings. Physical evidence in Old Mill suggests that a single large stove in the basement had at some point replaced the stoves on each floor, providing a safer and more efficient system. Indeed, this approach became common during the early nineteenth century after pioneering work by William Strutt at Belper Mills in 1792, and the uptake of the design by Boulton and Watt in 1808 (Tann 1970).

Another small, 4 ft (1.22 m) square, tower projects from the western end of the north elevation, on an angle to the north-east, following the line of what is now Murray Street. This appears to have been a privy tower, and whilst not included within every mill (even into the twentieth century (Catling 1986, 170), they were time-efficient features, reducing the time spent away from the spinning floor by employees. It is likely that the tower housed simple ash closets, which would have filled an ash-box in the basement, a type of privy installed subsequently in the Murray Street block (*Phase 3, p 114*).

Original Access

The fabric survey of Old Mill provided no firm evidence for the original access into the building, although this may have been at the southern end of the eastern elevation. There, a blocked doorway within the basement survives, which may have connected with the external ground level via a set of steps. The blocked doorway has a shallow-curved sandstone lintel, which was unusual within the original construction where arches were typically of brick.

Unfortunately, removal of the lath and plaster ceilings during consolidation of Old Mill provided no physical evidence for the position of the original stairs between the floors. Such features often took the form of simple ladders between floors, but no evidence of associated trimmers for apertures between floors or repaired joists was observed. If the access comprised a straight stair, however, a wider ceiling aperture would be required, and it appears that complete replacement joists were added only a few years later, and thus were indistinguishable from the originals (*p 104*).

Phase 2, The Second Mill (1801 - *c* 1804)

With the success of the initial cotton-spinning venture, a period of rapid expansion of the premises had commenced by 1801 (*Ch 5, p 69*). A new factory, known as Decker Mill, was erected immediately to the east of Old Mill, filling the remaining frontage of Union Street up to the junction with Bengal Street and effectively doubling the size of the mill complex (Fig 39). Decker Mill is of similar construction and height to Old Mill, although it is some 3 ft 8 in (1.12 m) wider, having an internal width of *c* 42 ft (12.69 m). This increased width would have allowed for larger mules to be installed; with the rapidly increasing technology of the period, the maximum size of mules then available carried well in excess of 300 spindles (Catling 1986). It is possible that these were operated in pairs, allowing one spinner to control two machines. The increase in power, from 12 hp to 40 hp, also allowed for further mechanisation within Old Mill at this time, and output is likely to have expanded dramatically, with the number of powered spindles increased from around 12,500 in the original mill, to approximately 38,500 in less than five years.

The base of each wall forming Decker Mill incorporated a single brick foundation plinth, contrasting with the total lack of foundations in Old Mill. The bay

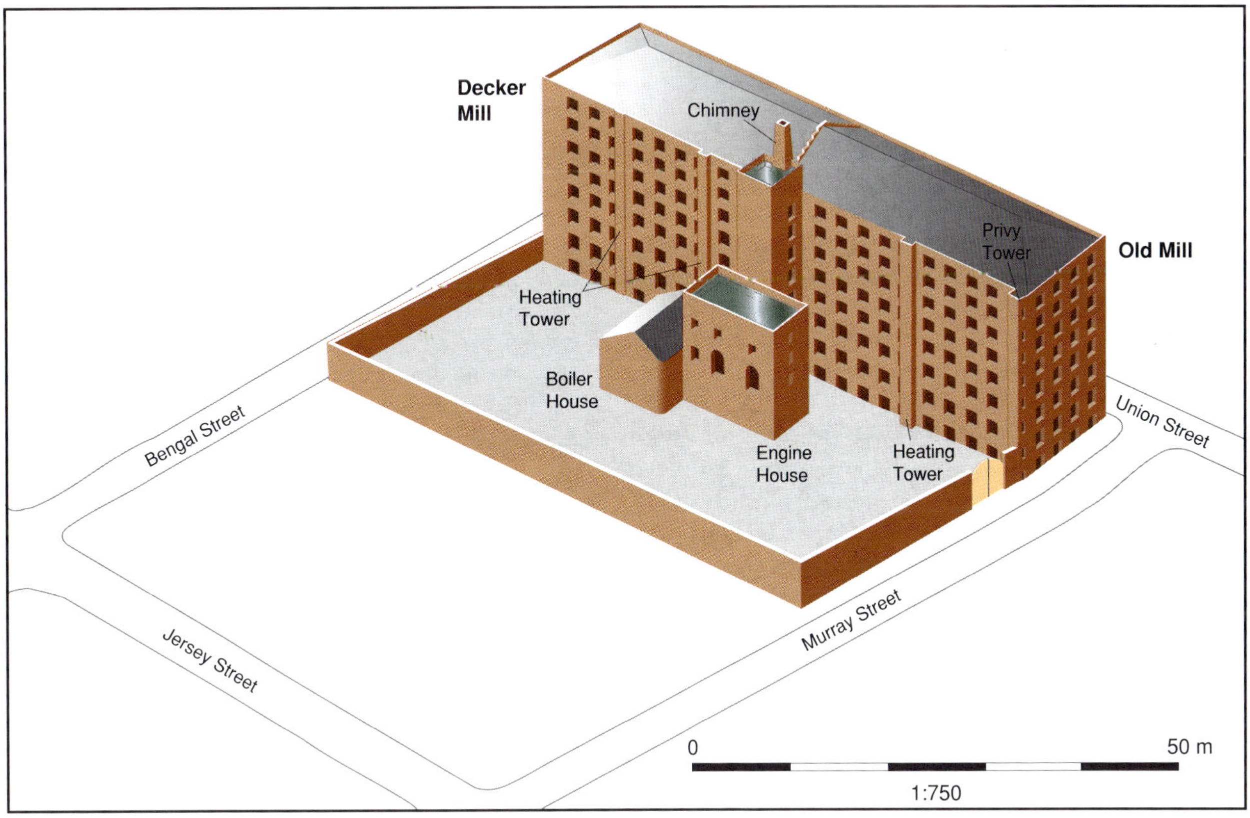

Figure 39: Isometric reconstruction of Old and Decker Mill (1801 - c 1804)

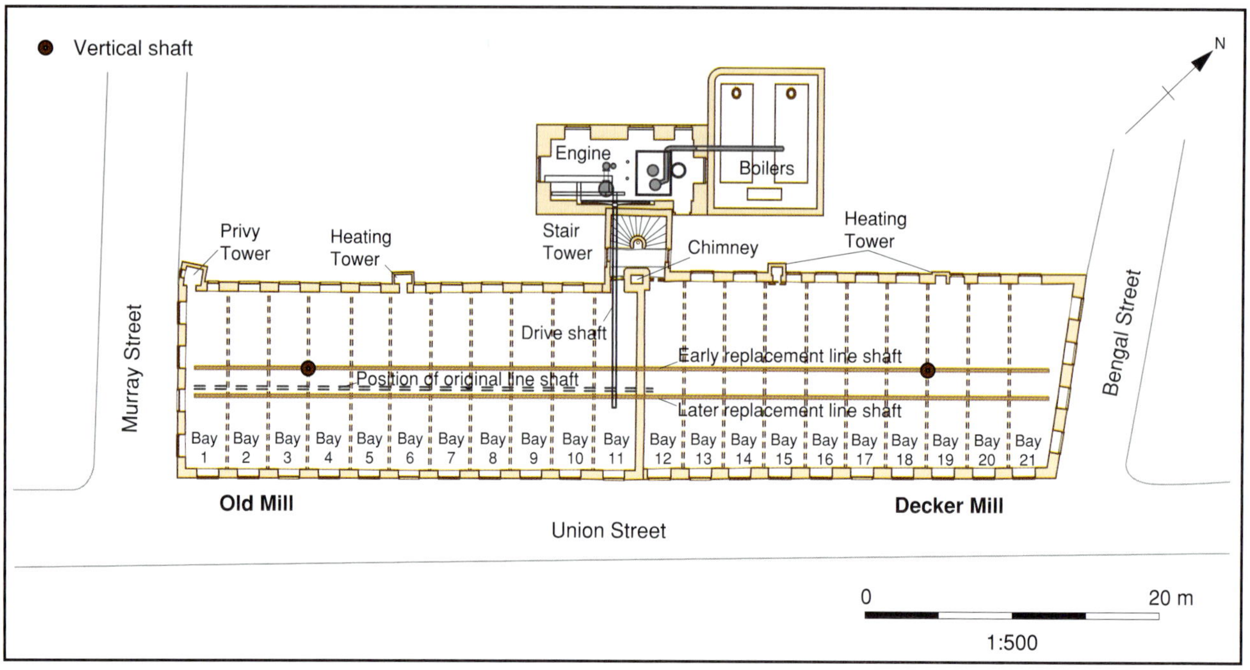

Figure 40: Ground floor plan of Old and Decker Mill, showing the layout of the power transmission

widths of Decker Mill are more regular, each being 9 ft (2.74 m) wide, with the exception of the eastern bay (Bay **21**), which was wider at the northern end, since Bengal Street is not parallel to Union Street (Fig 40). The windows are of the same proportions, being as variable in their internal width as those in Old Mill, but they incorporate straight-angled internal sills, as opposed to the curved ones of the earlier structure.

The construction of Decker Mill necessitated the demolition of the original structure housing the engine and boiler. In order to keep power transmission to the machines undisrupted during the majority of the construction works, however, a new engine house was built prior to the demolition of the original. The erection of the new engine house, and the adjacent stair tower, formed an early element of the expansion programme.

The Stair Tower

Access into Decker Mill was afforded from a new stair tower, rectangular in plan, projecting 13½ ft (4.11 m) from the northern side of the building, and spanning the offset junction with Old Mill (Fig 40). The surviving fabric indicates that it was begun prior to the construction of the mill, as its lower courses formed part of the new engine house. The tower was of fireproof construction, with slender T-section, fish-bellied, cast-iron beams supporting a spiral stair of roughly-dressed sandstone blocks, capped with sandstone flags, in contrast to the timber floors and beams used in the mills it served. The spiral stair incorporated a C-section stone newel in it centre, which housed fire-fighting equipment supplied by Boulton and Watt on each floor (*Ch 5, p 79*); much of this equipment remains *in situ*. It is likely that the stone was sourced from the East Lancashire Pennines, possibly from around the Rossendale area, where 'Haslingden Flags' were being quarried in the late eighteenth century (LUAU 1997). The design drawings for this equipment show a water tank atop the stair tower, the only physical evidence for which is a timber water gauge at the top of the eastern elevation.

The tower was lit by 2 ft (0.61 m) wide windows, positioned slightly to the north of those now present. Although much altered by later remodelling, the base of the stair tower retains significant *in situ* original detail. The floor level landings were supported on T-section cast-iron beams, with two flat anchor-ties into the sandstone newel. Below the ground level landing, however, the northern beam is supported by an original A-framed column, comprising two 3 in (76 mm) diameter cruciform-section members, set at an angle of 15°, with a lateral supporting rib (Pl 101).

With the construction of this new stair tower, the original access and stair within Old Mill became redundant. The putative access from Union Street within the original east gable was subsumed within the expanded structure, but was probably retained to allow communication between the two basements.

New Power Plant

Some of the fabric of the 1801 engine house survives *in situ* within both the stair tower and the south elevation of the replacement engine house, which was built in the later nineteenth century (*Phase 5*).

Plate 101: A-frame cruciform-section column and stone newel at the base of the stair tower

Plate 102: Timber sole plate and cast-iron bearing box that housed the drive shaft from the 1801 engine

A large timber sole plate and associated cast-iron bearing box within the north elevation of the stair tower is of especial interest, as they represent the rare surviving remains of early nineteenth-century power transmission features (Pl 102). It supports a cast-iron bearing box, which framed the horizontal drive shaft that passed through the stair tower and into the eastern bay of Old Mill. The sole plate is formed of box-sectioned heartwood, with the upper and lower faces retaining the natural curves of the timber. It has a roughly cut, semi-circular rebate in the centre, with a chamfered outer edge, which included well-preserved tool-marks on the northern face. The sole plate sits on a course of greenish Cumbrian slates, similar to those used for the roof, overlying a course of header bricks and a badly-rotted timber rail. These appear to have acted as a dampening rail, reducing the vibration from the drive shaft through the structure.

What appears to be the full extent of the northern elevation of the 1801 engine house survives intact within the fabric of the later nineteenth-century replacement (*Phase 5*; Fig 41). A wall-scar shows the original wall head, above which sat a header tank, depicted on the design plans (BWA 3147/5/364). At approximately first floor level are the remains of two round-headed, blocked windows. The western is better preserved by far, and comprises a segmental arch, and projecting rolled-edge sandstone sill. Below the sill the arch is mirrored, but is infilled with contemporary brickwork, acting as a relieving arch, spreading the load of the aperture through the wall below. A sub-rectangular blocked feature between these two large apertures is aligned directly opposite, and slightly above, the sole plate opening in the north side of the stair tower. At its base it has a cast-iron plate, which may have been associated with the fixing of the timber framing for the original engine. At a similar level, towards the eastern end of the elevation, is another sub-rectangular aperture, with a well-defined eastern jamb, and the sill replaced with a soldier course-blocking. This may relate to a window shown in a similar position on the Boulton and Watt plan of 1801 (BWA 3147/5/295).

The original chimney probably also lay within the footprint of the new mill, and therefore had to be replaced. A new, rectangular chimney, approximately 6 x 5 ft (1.83 x 1.53 m), was constructed in the north-eastern corner of Old Mill, the butt joint between the two structures being clearly visible at the south-east corner of the chimney. It must have been at least 72 ft (22 m) high, although the Boulton and Watt drawings show a tapering stack extending above the mill, suggesting that the chimney was intended to be significantly higher. This is reinforced by the detail within an engraving that was published in 1831 (*Ch 5, Pl 78*), which clearly shows the chimney rising above the roof line of the mills. Modelling of the survey data, combined with the aspect of

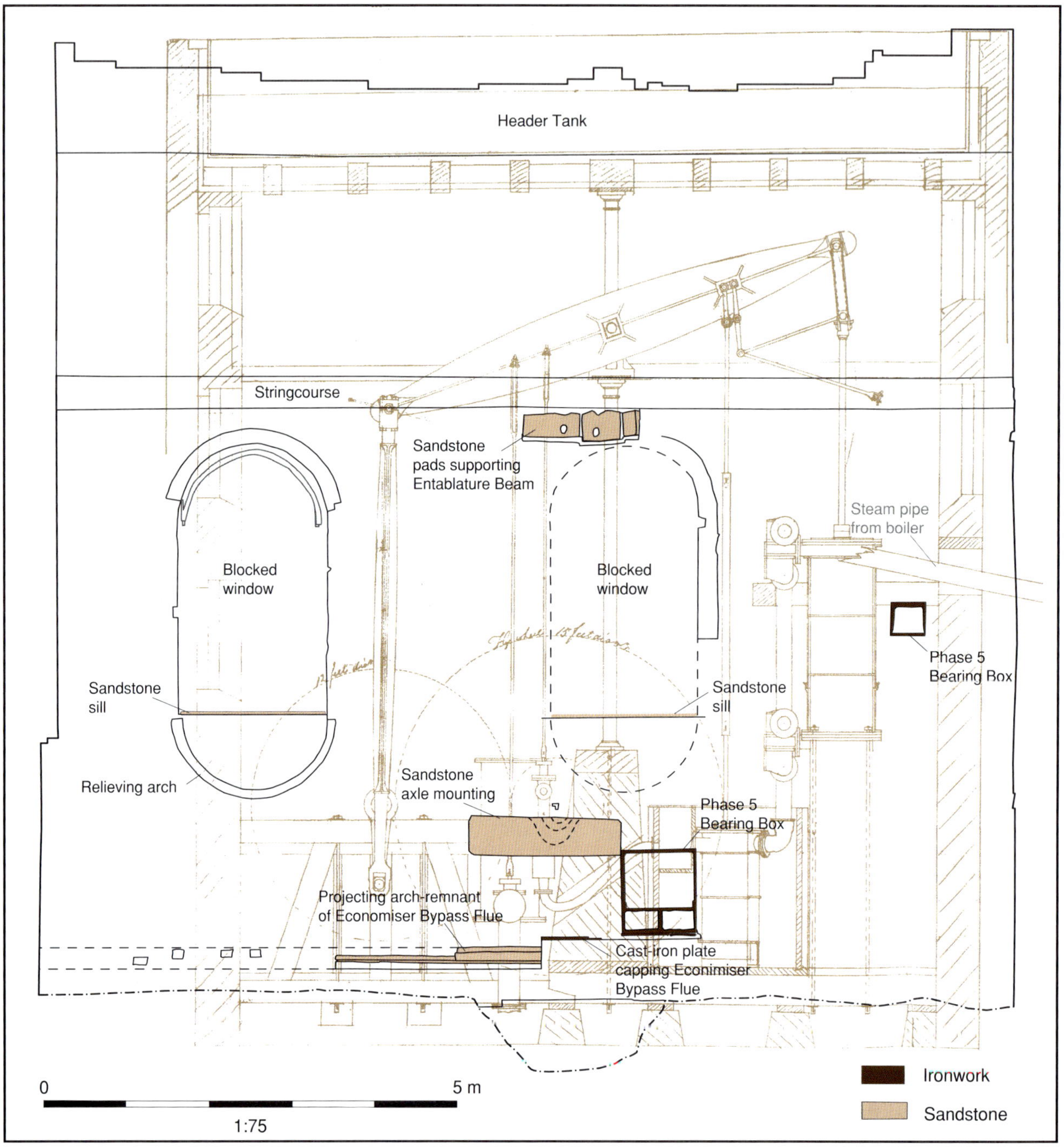

Figure 41: South-facing elevation of the extant Old and Decker Mill engine house, showing the surviving fabric of the 1801 structure, superimposed onto the Boulton and Watt design plan

the 1831 engraving, suggests that the chimney was approximately 100 ft (30.50 m) high (Fig 39).

Whilst nothing survives of the associated boiler house, the remains of the flue to the chimney were exposed during the consolidation of the stair tower. This lay to the east of the engine house, and comprised a 2 ft (0.61 m) wide flue with one-brick thick walls of refractory brick, which led into the northern face of the chimney around the south-eastern corner of the stair tower (Pl 103). The position of the flue is also apparent in the western bay of Decker Mill (Bay **12**), where the thickness of the northern elevation was increased locally at basement level.

Power Transmission

With the removal of the engine house from the gable end of Old Mill, the power transmission system required alteration. The main drive shaft from the new 40 hp engine entered the eastern bay of Old Mill at basement level, via bearing boxes within the north and south elevations of the stair tower. This connected with a vertical shaft in both Old and Decker Mill, the positions of which may be deduced from surviving features. The position of the vertical shaft in Old Mill is marked by rebates on the western face of beams in Bay **3** on the ground, first, second, and fifth floors. In Decker Mill, ogee-moulded timber support-bearing

Plate 103: View of the 1801 flue rising to the chimney, with its nineteenth-century successor in the foreground

pads were attached to the western side of the beams of Bay **18**, immediately to the north of the horizontal shafts (Pl 104). A top-steady bracket, which would have housed the upper end of the vertical shaft, also survives within Bay **18** on the top floor of Decker Mill.

The vertical shafts powered single line shafts, located slightly to the north of centre, allowing the original shafting to continue in use during their construction. Bolt-holes and rebates in beam soffits in Decker Mill, and a rebate in a comparable position in the beam of Bay **9** on the ground floor in Old Mill, suggest that the new horizontal shaft was to the north of the original shaft by approximately 4½ ft (1.42 m). This corresponds to a blocked aperture in the east wall of

Plate 104: Sole plate for vertical transmission bearing, Decker Mill

Plate 105: Bevel gear scar, Old Mill basement

Old Mill, immediately above a 3 ft (0.91 m) diameter, 2 in (51 mm) deep circular gouge in the wall (Pl 105). This was probably associated with a bevel gear on the line shaft relating to the transfer of power from the main drive shaft.

Evidence of two further early line shaft mountings survive within Old and Decker Mill, which were removed subsequently for the insertion of cantilever brackets (*Phase 4, p 117*). Both were to the south of the main horizontal shaft, and comprised either rectangular or semi-circular rebates on the beam soffits, some also having blocked bolt-holes through the beam faces. The first was situated 15½ ft (4.73 m) from the southern elevation, with the second shaft 2 ft 4 in (0.70 m) to the north, perhaps representing a displacement of the same shaft.

The Roof

There are slight differences between the trusses in Old and Decker Mill, the latter being slightly wider, and having wider-set queen struts. The assembly marks also differ, in that they are on the western faces of the trusses, whilst those in Old Mill are on the eastern faces. The Decker Mill cotters also differ slightly, in that the protruding spikes have been bent into a curl rather than cut off. These differences confirm that the two roofs were constructed at different times, and also adds weight to the suggestion that the *in situ* roof structure was reused when the height of the mill was reduced at the turn of the twentieth century.

An internal rainwater downpipe, seemingly an original feature, survives *in situ* in the north-east corner of the mill, providing evidence for internal guttering within the roof space. It seems likely that water was drained from behind a parapet wall, which projected above the upper floor.

A close inspection of an area of ceiling collapse within the fourth floor of Decker Mill yielded two coins of George III, dated 1799. The coins were identical issues and displayed little wear, implying that they had been deposited within ten years of minting. As with the shoe recovered from the roof of Old Mill, it seems likely that these coins had been deliberately concealed during the construction of the building.

Plate 106: External heating tower aperture, Decker Mill

Heating System

In contrast to Old Mill, the north elevation of Decker Mill housed two heating towers, effectively dividing the elevation into three (Fig 39). Internally, each floor had a sandstone hearthstone, suggesting that individual stoves were still being used, although the incorporation of two towers represents an attempted improvement of heat circulation within each room. The upper timber vents, present on most floors, appear similar to those in the basement of Old Mill, and the internal flues are not heavily sooted, suggesting that pipes ran through the flue, between the stove and the vent. The western tower (Bay **15**) appears to have undergone similar alteration to that in Old Mill, to allow for the addition of a single stove, whilst a large aperture at basement level in the eastern tower was located on the external face (Pl 106), implying that the stove was housed within an external structure. This may have been simply to reduce the risk of fire in the working rooms, but could represent evidence for the evolution in the technology of stoves.

Phase 3, Completing the Original Complex (*c* 1804 - *c* 1817)

In 1802, the Murrays obtained the lease for the entire parcel of land to the north of Old and Decker Mill (*Ch 5, p 71*), and implemented a further episode of enlargement. Within the next three to four years, the Murrays' complex was to expand to form a group of four multi-storey mills around a central courtyard (Fig 42). Uniquely, the enclosed courtyard incorporated a large canal basin that was linked to the newly constructed Rochdale Canal via a tunnel beneath Union Street. The largest of the new buildings was a massive spinning mill that occupied the entire Jersey Street frontage between Murray and Bengal Streets. The structure, named New Mill, was eight storeys high, including a basement, and measured an incredible *c* 195 ft (59.5 m) long and 46 ft (14 m) wide, probably representing the largest single mill building in Manchester at that time (Pl 107). Although no documentary evidence describes the erection of the two wings flanking the large spinning mills, it is most probable that their construction was concurrent, both being largely completed by 1806 (*Ch 5, p 73*).

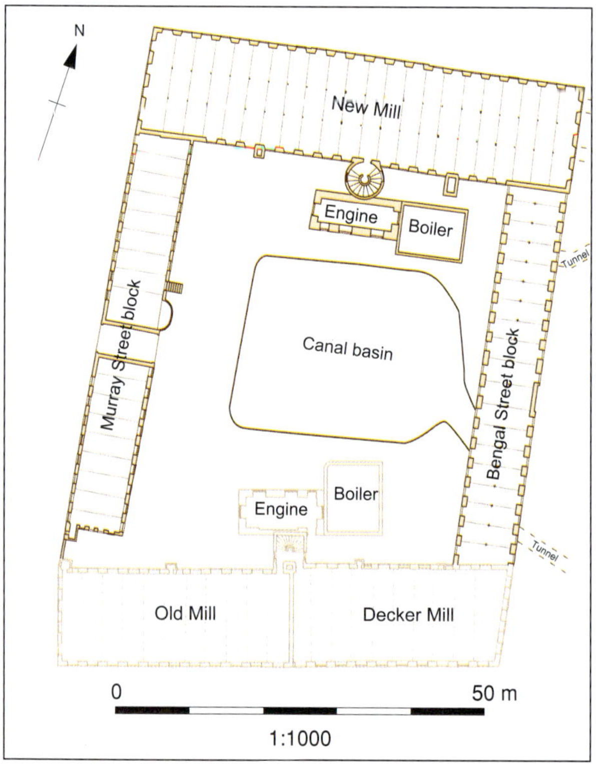

Figure 42: Site plan, Phase 3

Plate 107: The Jersey Street elevation of New Mill in 2004

New Mill

Construction of New Mill appears to have followed similar techniques to those in Old and Decker Mill, with Flemish bond being used in all but the external elevation facing onto the courtyard. In contrast to the earlier structures, however, a three-brick deep stepped foundation was included at the base of each wall.

The mill walls taper, but floor heights are uniform above the basement level, making the original building taller than Old and Decker Mill. In the lower floors, it is the northern elevation that is the thickest, with the southern elevation only slightly wider than the end elevations. The reason for this bias towards the northern elevation is unclear, but above second-floor level all walls are approximately the same thickness. The northern elevation also has a central, six-bay wide, single skin projection on the external face. This may have formed part of a pediment, representing an element of architectural embellishment often incorporated into mills of the period (Giles and Goodall 1992, 24). The architectural expression of the northern facade was further enhanced by a low dressed-sandstone wall, constructed along the pavement edge of Jersey Street, and capped with square-section iron railings.

A brick-built culvert capped with sandstone flags formed part of the drainage system, and was placed beneath the centre of the basement floor. The drain was carried through the south elevation of the mill via a double-skinned round-arched opening (Pl 108). Ground floor level within the original structure corresponds to those in Old and Decker Mill, lying some 6 ft (1.83 m) above street level. Each floor was divided into 22 bays by chamfered timber beams, supporting the floor above. These were similar to those used in Old and Decker Mill, but of increased length, with several displaying shipping marks relating to their Northern European origins. Bay widths are of a uniform size, but are significantly narrower than those in Decker Mill; bay widths in New Mill are typically 8 ft 3 in (2.52 m) wide, as opposed to 9 ft (2.74 m) in Decker Mill. Both end bays are asymmetrical; the western bay (Bay **1**) is wider than average, especially at the southern end, reflecting the offset angle of Murray Street from Jersey Street, whilst the eastern bay (Bay **22**) is narrower, although wider at its northern side, as Bengal Street is parallel to Murray Street.

Plate 108: Drain below New Mill

All of the original columns supporting the timber beams in New Mill were replaced subsequently (*Phase 4*), although eight cast-iron load-transfer, or 'crush' boxes (Pl 109), survive on some of the beams on the fourth floor and in the basement, indicating the position of the original columns. Most were situated 14 ft 9 in (4.50 m) from the north elevation, 14 ft 3 in (4.34 m) from the south elevation, with a central space of 13 ft 3 in (4.04 m). The columns in the basement, however, were situated closer to the north elevation, due to the increased wall thickness, and sat on large sandstone pads. The load-transfer boxes were formed as a single casting, and therefore had to be slid onto the beams from the end, prior to the beams being built into the long walls of the structure. Their purpose was to transfer the vertical load from the floors above the timber beam, which rested on the base plate of the box but was free of the top plate, therefore avoiding crushing damage to its fibres. It is noteworthy that load-transfer boxes were not used during the construction of either Old Mill or, more interestingly, Decker Mill, the erection of which immediately preceded that of New Mill. They were incorporated, however, into the design of later

Plate 109: Load-transfer box, fourth floor, New Mill

columns inserted into the Murray Street block. Each load-transfer box had three-sided flanges on their upper and lower surfaces, thereby securing both the column head of one floor level, and the base of that above.

It has been suggested (*e.g.* Donald Insall Associates and Structural Perspectives 2002) that the single row of cruciform columns that survive on the fourth floor of New Mill represent the repositioning of original columns. The size of these column heads, however, is more consistent with those in the Murray Street block, which fit into a 3½ in (89 mm) wide socket in the cap, whereas the socket in the base of the load-transfer boxes on the fourth floor of New Mill are significantly larger, measuring 7 x 5 in (178 x 127 mm). Whilst it was not uncommon for columns to reduce in scantling vertically through a mill, the similar size of the load-transfer box flanges in the basement to those on the fourth floor, and the fact that New Mill does not have diminishing floor heights, would suggest that column thickness was consistently larger throughout the original construction.

The ceilings on all floors were covered with lath and plaster / metal sheet fireproofing, except on the fourth floor where it is now absent. This was presumably removed during the life of the mill, with the exposed ceiling having been covered with many layers of white lime wash, maximising the light within the spinning floor. The ceiling comprised north / south-aligned floorboards above east / west-aligned joists (including many waney-edged timbers), positioned on 18 in (0.46 m) centres. Several display Baltic timber marks, similar to the timbers of the roof.

The Roof

The roof of New Mill was lowered when the building was reduced in height during the early twentieth century, but appears to have been rebuilt largely to the original design. It is likely to have had the same basic form as that of Old and Decker Mill, being hipped at both ends, each with a longitudinal half-truss of similar style to those in the main roof. The queen struts were set narrower than at either Old or Decker Mills, despite the increased span of New Mill. Each pitch has three tusk-tenoned purlins, supporting rafters that were mainly the full length of each pitch, and nailed onto the purlins and wall plates, which are themselves jointed with bridled scarf joints, many displaying assembly marks (Pl 110). This differed from those in Old and Decker Mill, which appear to have been birdsmouth-jointed to the wall plates. Several reused round-headed Cumbrian slates present on both pitches of the roof suggest that this was the original roofing material.

Plate 110 : Detail of wall plate scarf joint in New Mill roof

The tie beams of the trusses all display dovetailed joist sockets, indicating that the upper floor had a ceiling, rather than being open to the rafters. The joist sockets stop 3 ft (0.93 m) from each long wall, revealing that significant loads were not applied to the floor within the eaves, as the floorboards would have been unsupported in this part of the roof-space. This suggests that the roof-space was not used for warehousing, as only the central section would have been fit for such purposes.

Stair Tower

Access into New Mill was afforded via a circular stair tower, 15 ft (4.58 m) in internal diameter, which was placed in the centre of the southern elevation of the mill. This incorporated a larger internal space than the rectangular tower serving Old and Decker Mill, with a similar quantity of bricks providing a more stable, load-bearing structure. This represents an early improvement to mill design, and it is interesting to note that the stair tower that was erected during the mid-nineteenth century to serve the Bengal Street

Plate 111: Boulton and Watt fire-fighting cistern

block (*Phase 4*) was of a similar design. The tower was constructed in a fireproof manner as was that for Old and Decker Mill. It incorporated a central C-section stone newel, which housed a stand-pipe and fire-fighting equipment on each floor, identical to that in Old and Decker Mill (Pl 111). Unlike that in the earlier stair tower, however, the newel incorporates an offset brick plinth at its base. The main light source within the tower was provided by windows similar to those used throughout the rest of the mill. The stair tower was accessed at ground-floor level via a flagged landing above 12 sandstone steps from the courtyard, the entrance to which had a round-arched brick doorway, comprising a double-header arch, with a moulded sandstone keystone, supported on projecting imposts.

Heating System

A heating tower similar to those in Old and Decker Mill projected from the southern elevation, to the west of the stair tower. Internally, segmentally arched a floor level aperture on all floors above the basement. These apertures were much smaller than those in Old and Decker Mill, suggesting, that the tower was furnished with a single stove in the basement.

Steam-Power Plant

Power for the mill was generated within a new detached engine house, abutting the stair tower, with an attached boiler house to the east. An annotated plan of the site by Boulton and Watt in 1805 dates New Mill to 1804, but the proposals for the associated 45 hp steam engine were not draughted until 1805 (BWA 3147/5/364). Internally, two rows of large sandstone blocks, which had formed a solid foundation for the engine, were exposed during consolidation works. Between them, the east/west-aligned access tunnel, allowing the engine to be bolted to the supporting bed, survived *in situ*.

Centrally within either end elevation of the engine house were tall arched windows, comprising different coloured brick, below a triple-skin brick arch. Access into the engine house was provided from within the stair tower of New Mill, which survives as a blocked doorway with a flat sandstone lintel and offset immediately to the east of the north/south axis of the tower.

Nothing remains of the original boiler house and flue, although the aperture for the steam pipe from the boilers survives to the south of the window in the eastern elevation, just above sill height. This demonstrates that the associated boiler house was constructed to the east of the engine house, rather than to the west, as shown in the original Boulton and Watt plans (*Ch 5, Pl 71*), and that the boilers were positioned at ground level, unlike those in the two earlier boiler houses. The flue from the boilers led into a square-section chimney, which abuts the external face of New Mill between Bays **16** and **17** (Fig 43). Access into the flue was provided at third-floor level on the western face, through a fish-scale patterned cast-iron grille. As with the slightly earlier chimney that served Old and Decker Mill, it is unclear precisely how far above roof level the chimney originally projected. Although unproven, it is probable that the hot gases passing through the chimney were utilised to heat the eastern part of the spinning floors within New Mill.

Power Transmission

The original drive shaft from the engine entered New Mill at basement level through the stair tower, immediately to the west of the C-section central stone newel. The surviving bearing box in the southern elevation of the stair tower comprises large, roughly dressed sandstone blocks, which formed the sill and jambs of the aperture, below a rectangular-section cast-iron lintel. Evidence for the original power transmission within New Mill is scant, as later remodelling replaced or obscured much of the original apparatus, although elements survived within the ceiling structure of the fourth floor.

A longitudinal beam ran the entire length of the fourth floor, offset slightly south of the centre line. It comprised an additional timber nailed onto the underside of the central joist in each bay, and each had a mixture of rebates and sockets of varied sizes, which all appear to represent housings for features related to the original mules, possibly supports for pulley drives. Many were blocked with lime-based plaster, containing large quantities of

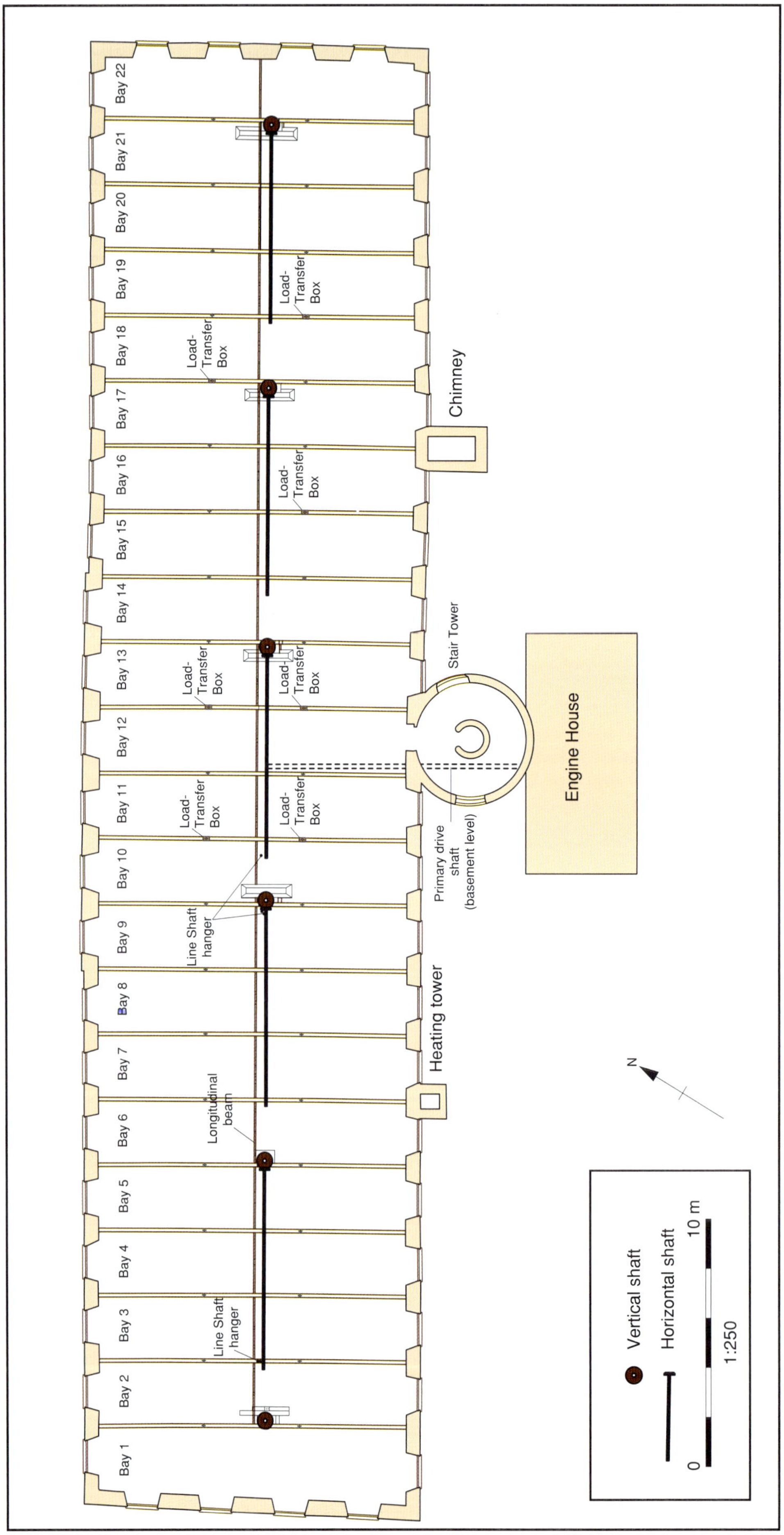

Figure 43: Fourth floor of New Mill, showing the layout of the power transmission

Plate 112: Framing for vertical drive shaft, fourth floor, New Mill

horse hair, suggesting an early date of disuse. The most significant surviving elements of the original power transmission, however, are six timber-framed apertures within the ceiling of the fourth floor (Pl 112), presumably representing housing attachments for vertical transmission brackets. Circular drum scars on the soffits of adjoining beams in Bays **5**, **9**, and **13** represent the position of bearings on the vertical shafts. A similar scar in Bay **13** of the third floor provides the only evidence of the earliest transmission below the upper floor. Two pairs of bolt-holes, and several rebates in the adjoining beams of the fourth floor, represent the remains of support bearings for the vertical transmission. The vestiges of several cast-iron base plates, presumably relating to contemporary line shaft hangers, also survive. Only one had a complete base plate, cruciform-shaped in plan, with a broken cruciform-section shaft projecting from it.

The layout of the transmission shafts on the fourth floor of New Mill suggests that power transfer was based on a vertical system. The original power-transfer system in Old, and later Decker, Mill utilised horizontal line shafts, positioned just below ceiling level on each floor, with belt drives to the individual mules below. In the original layout of New Mill, however, half of the mules appear to have been driven directly from vertical shafts, with each of the six vertical shafts directly driving those in the bays on either side (Fig 43). Between each pair of vertically-driven mules was a further pair, which appear to have been powered from an horizontal shaft, positioned just below ceiling level, as in the earlier mills. The positioning of the flywheel scars associated with vertical transmission on the fourth floor demonstrate that the horizontal drive shafts within the original layout of New Mill were situated approximately 2 ft (0.61 m) south of the centre-line of the mill, which appears to mirror that of the primary line shafts in Old and Decker Mill at the same period.

Many features visible within the internal northern elevation above ground-floor level appear to represent the layout of spinning mules, including cut-outs in the wall, presumably to accommodate larger machinery (Pl 113). The shape of the cut-outs appears to show the profile of the end of a spinning mule, and indicates that the mules were arranged in pairs, one per bay, for the entire length of each floor above the ground floor.

Plate 113: Fourth floor of New Mill, showing cut-out wall sections for machine pairs

Murray Street Block

Shortly after the completion of New Mill, work commenced on the wing blocks along Murray Street and Bengal Street, creating an enclosed courtyard. The Murray Street block was built as a single range, comprising four storeys of 20 bays (Fig 44). The western elevation, fronting Murray Street, was faced in Flemish bond, whilst the eastern face was in English Garden Wall bond, consistent with the earlier structures. Access to the entire mill complex was via the Murray Street block, through a two-storey, 12 ft (3.66 m) wide arch, immediately south of the centre. The arch itself is a shallow, three-centred, or basket arch, allowing the maximum width possible for load height. Access to the building itself was afforded via doorways in the western elevation on either side of this arch. North of the arch, the structure had a basement, similar to Old, Decker, and New Mills, whilst to the south there is a split level. Communication between the Murray Street block and New Mill was facilitated by doorways on all floors. Those on the upper three floors were placed flush with the eastern elevation of the new structure, with those in the basement offset slightly to the west.

The block is depicted as butting the tower projecting from the north-west corner of Old Mill on the 1805 Boulton and Watt plan (*Ch 5, Pl 68*), thereby completing the external wall of the courtyard. A privy tower that extended beyond the southern extent of the Murray Street block, however, would not have been large enough to fill the intervening gap, as depicted on the plan of 1805, suggesting that a boundary wall completed the enclosure. Internally, narrow brick-blocked doorways into the privy tower survive at first- and second-floor levels, with a low brick-arched aperture at the base of the southern internal elevation, most likely representing access to the base of the tower, presumably to empty an ash-box serving the closets above.

At its northern end, the Murray Street block abutted New Mill, which was partially remodelled to allow for the keyed-construction of the new building. The windows in the three bays of the southern elevation of New Mill were covered by the new buildings to a height of four storeys. The solution was to block the windows and re-face the internal and external elevations at the junction of the new structures. The main reason for this appears to relate to the inclusion of further heating flues within the thickness of the remodelled wall. During the consolidation works, a child's shoe was recovered from this flue (Fig 37), where it had probably been deliberately concealed when the Murray Street block was built.

Projecting timber-framed vents into these flues survived on all floors, similar to those into the heating towers in Old and Decker Mill. The top of each vent projected slightly from the brick wall face, suggesting that the internal elevation had a plaster covering. Blocked apertures, similar in style to those within the internal face of the heating tower in New Mill, but much larger in size, survive at first- and second-floor level in the northern elevation of the Murray Street block, suggesting that stoves were originally present on each floor.

Externally, the majority of bays have windows similar to those present elsewhere within the complex. One aperture, at lower ground floor level in the eastern side of Bay **9** (Fig 44), retains an original iron window

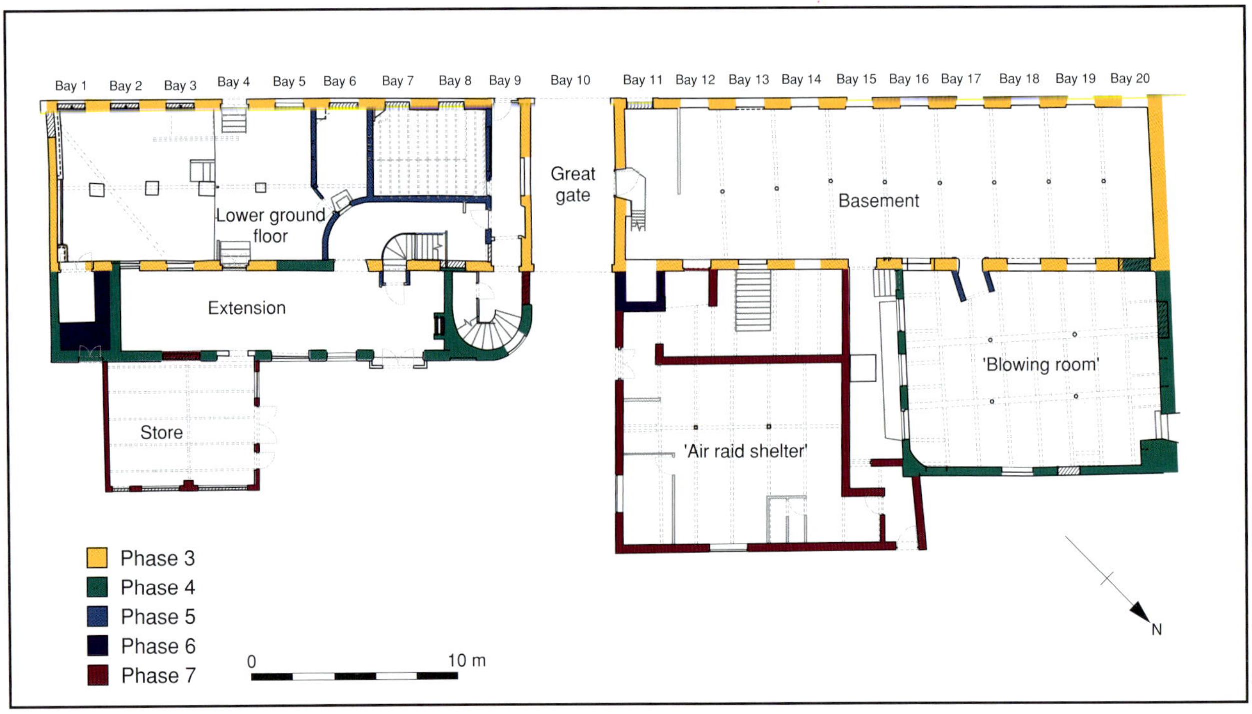

Figure 44: Multi-phase plan of the Murray Street block

Plate 114: Original window frame, Murray Street block

frame, comprising six rows of six lights (Pl 114), which was preserved as a result of later blocking. Several bays have differently styled windows and door apertures, reflecting varied use of different areas within the Murray Street block, compared with the uniformity of the spinning blocks.

Internally, bays were typically 8 ft 6 in (2.59 m) wide, with narrower bays at the southern and northern ends. At ground-floor level, the southern part of the block appears to have been a single room originally, with windows in each bay in the western elevation, except in the northern bay, where the wall was continuous behind a quarter-turn staircase. The symmetry of the external elevation was maintained with the incorporation of a blind window in this position.

Access to the ground floor was afforded by both a stair from the courtyard, within Bay **13**, and by a stair directly from Murray Street in the western part of Bay **11**. The first floor was accessed via the stair in the north-west corner of the ground floor, and also via New Mill. There is no evidence for original internal access to the second floor, other than from New Mill. A door in the western elevation to the south of the arch in Bay **10** led into the lower ground floor of the southern part of the block. There is no surviving physical evidence for an original staircase for access from street level to the ground floor in this part of the block. A 3 ft (0.91 m) square hatch, cut through the western end of a joist in Bay **8** of the lower ground floor may, however, represent the position of an internal ladder or stair.

The presence of a bow window in the eastern elevation in Bays **11** and **12**, with an external stair to the north, implies that part of the ground floor contained offices. The window was partly destroyed by the insertion of a lift shaft during the twentieth century, although the surviving northern window jamb appears to be an original feature, with a curved sandstone lintel built into the wall face. Internally, the window is panelled with decorative beading, incorporating recessed circles at either end, identical to that in a similar window in Bay **7** (*Phase 4, p 122*). An arch to the north of the bow window (in Bay **13**) also appears to be an original construction, and comprises a double-row brick arch. Similar arched openings exist in the eastern wall of the original construction in Bays **6** and **7**, perhaps representing a doorway and a loading hoist towards the southern end of the block.

At first- and second-floor level, the internal cross walls on either side of Bay **10** butt the western elevation, suggesting that both the upper floors were originally open rooms. At second-floor level the ceiling forms the under-drawing of the roof trusses above, which appear original. These comprise braced king-post trusses jointed with iron fittings, similar to those used in the queen strut trusses in Old, Decker, and New Mills. The southern end of the roof is hipped, behind a parapet wall, in a similar style to the earlier structures.

A plan of A & G Murray's Mill dated *c* 1822 (*Ch 5, Pl 71*) shows a 'shed' and single storey 'oil house' at the southern end of the Murray Street block, butting the privy tower. The lack of windows in the southern elevation below first-floor level, and a blocked rectangular aperture at lower ground-floor level, which presumably afforded access between the two structures, suggest this may have been part of the original construction of the Murray Street block. The 'oil house' must have been demolished prior to the extension to the southern part of the Murray Street block during the mid-nineteenth century (*Phase 4, p 122*).

Bengal Street Block

The erection of the four-storey Bengal Street block was broadly concurrent with the Murray Street block, although, as it was largely demolished in 1996, its description and analysis relies heavily upon the work undertaken as part of the *Greater Manchester Textile Mill Survey* (RCHME and GMAU 1989). The construction of the Bengal Street block abutted Decker Mill to the south and New Mill to the north, necessitating slight remodelling of these earlier buildings. In both cases, the windows at the eastern end of the north elevation up to the fourth floor were remodelled into doorways or blocked.

Plate 115: Crown of canal link tunnel beneath Bengal Street block, showing twentieth-century concrete infilling

The surviving two bays at the southern end of the block have window apertures at ground-floor level on both elevations, similar in style to those in the Murray Street block. Ground floor level is consistent with that in the other buildings in the complex. At lower ground-floor level, window apertures exist only in the western elevation, as the surviving eastern elevation housed the tunnel linking the canal basin to the Rochdale Canal. The tunnel has a shallow three-point centred, or basket, arch of single brick thickness (Pl 115). A one and a half brick relieving arch in the internal eastern elevation was constructed to deflect stress from the tunnel crown. This implies that the Bengal Street block was constructed concurrently with the canal tunnel.

Canal Basin

The innovative adoption of a canal basin within the courtyard represented a new advance in fully integrating a cotton-spinning site with a canal (Pl 116). Excavation demonstrated that the basin was well preserved, although the installation of an electricity sub-station to the west of the Bengal Street block (*Phase 6, p 136*) had caused some localised damage. The walls of the basin comprised mould-thrown bricks, similar to those used in the buildings, bonded in a pale lime and sand mortar, and laid in English Garden Wall bond to a depth of *c* 7 ft (2.14 m), curving slightly into the basin as it deepened. The foundation of the wall appeared to be set up to half a course wider, and it was capped with dressed yellow sandstone blocks, several of which were laid upon slate packing. The blocks had been carefully worked to fit the curve of the canal basin, and all were joined by two iron strips set into lead flashing. Horizontal rebates cut into the surface of several of the capping stones may have housed a large timber that would have acted as a fender, affording some protection to boats. Many capping stones retained sockets and other cut features in their upper faces, including an iron mooring-ring and a narrow U-section channel that had been gouged through the sandstone capping in the curve at the south-west corner, presumably acting as a drainage channel into the basin. A row of lead-filled, sub-rectangular, sockets was observed along the western side, and may have housed vertical iron bars, perhaps railings around the basin.

Plate 116: Excavation of the canal basin in 2006

Three alcoves were built into the basin wall, two on the southern side of the basin, outside the Phase 5 engine house, and one positioned centrally on the southern elevation of the Phase 4 extension to the New Mill engine house. These were almost certainly associated with water supply to the steam-power plant.

Phase 4, Remodelling and Expansion (*c* 1817 - 1855)

With the advances in technology during the early nineteenth century, and an increasing demand for cotton, larger spinning mules became available. This was coupled with the development of more powerful steam engines, and an increase in the efficiency of the shafting around the mill, to allow the line shafts to rotate more rapidly. A & G Murray kept apace with these developments by updating their machinery and steam plant, and employing Fairbairn and Lillie to improve the power transmission in *c* 1817 (*Ch 5, p 77*). Surviving physical evidence in Old and Decker Mill suggests that Fairbairn and Lillie's work involved moving the line shaft to within 5 ft (1.52 m) of the north wall. It is not entirely clear whether a similar line shaft, the same distance from the south wall, was installed at this time, or after the re-orientation of the columns at a slightly later date. Physical evidence for the improvements in line shafting and associated linkage survives within the base of the stair tower, where the main drive shaft entered Old Mill. It comprised a 19 in (0.48 m) wide curved rebate on its southern side, presumably for a bevel gear, providing evidence for the replacement of timber drums with smaller wrought-iron examples.

There is also physical evidence within New Mill for modifications to the power-transmission systems undertaken in this phase, perhaps associated with the installation of a new steam engine after 1829 (*Ch 5, p 79*). The most visible surviving element pertains to a renewed vertical shaft, immediately to the west of the entrance to the stair tower. The original drive shaft from the engine through the basement of the stair tower was retained, but a new cast-iron carrier beam was inserted to reduce its unsupported length. A new footstep bearing and bevel gears were also installed within the basement, with supporting brackets (presumably also incorporating bevel gears for power transfer into each room) on the ground, first, second, and fourth floors. That on the fourth floor is the most complete (Pl 117), retaining the housing for the horizontal shaft into the room.

Plate 117: Transmission bearing, fourth floor, New Mill

Evidence for line shafting associated with the new power system in New Mill is difficult to distinguish from that associated with later modifications, as the system remained in use until the late nineteenth century, when it was replaced with a rope drive (*Phase 5, p 132*). Nevertheless, two large, square bearing boxes set in the east elevation on the third and fourth floors, which housed the eastern ends of the horizontal line shafts, are likely to have been installed during this phase.

Several T-section, fish-bellied, cast-iron beams within the ceiling of the fourth floor may also have been associated with this remodelling of the power system. Each bay contains six beams, all inverted, with those in Bay **6**, and the north and south examples in Bay **17**, being closed-web, the remaining four in Bay **17** open-webbed. The latter bear the initials 'A & G M', relating to Adam and George Murray.

New Columns in Old and Decker Mill

The double row of columns throughout Old and Decker Mill were replaced during this period with a single row down the centre of each building. It is likely that this was to allow for the installation of spinning mules longitudinally, probably with two pairs along the length of the building. The remodelling may also have been associated with the installation of gas lighting in the mills, which was becoming widely used to light textile mills and had certainly been installed in A & G Murray's Mill by 1819 (*Ch 5, p 79*). Whilst the gas for the lighting system installed in McConnel & Kennedy's mill in 1809 was routed independently (BWA 3147/3/478/19), hollow columns were used elsewhere to circulate gas around a building, as at Chorlton New Mill and Albion Mill in Manchester (Williams with Farnie 1992), and this may have been the solution adopted in Old and Decker Mill. All the columns in the mill were of hollow cylindrical-design cast-iron and interconnected between floors, bypassing the beams, appearing to have been designed specifically to allow gas to flow through them.

Column Types in Old and Decker Mill

The replacement of the columns appears to have been undertaken in several episodes, with six identified column types, and four associated types of cantilever brackets, surviving in both buildings. The Type I column (Fig 45) is the most widespread, with the beam-carrying bracket offset slightly to the front of the column. The gas passage through the column is reduced to half its diameter as it rises up past the beam, with the full diameter re-established in the socket connection between floors. On the opposite side to the beam-carrying bracket, the reduced section of the column is stiffened by a narrow vertical rib. The Type II column differs only slightly, in that it incorporates a double T-socket within the shaft, allowing transfer of gas between vertical columns. The Type III column shows the greatest variance from other column designs, in that the gas bypass of the beam is in the form of a separate off-take pipe. This type was only present on the fifth floor in Decker Mill, and sadly the mechanism of its re-attachment to the column above did not survive. The Type IV column actually comprises two very similar designs. Both vary from the Type I column in that, rather than reducing the column's diameter to bypass the beam, the whole shaft is displaced around the back of the beam, forming a pronounced bulge. The slight variance in Type IV columns is in the angle of the initial displacement of the shaft around the beam, with several examples being more abrupt than others. Type V columns are very similar to the Type II columns, but without the stiffening rib to the rear. Type VI columns do not have the interconnecting double T-sockets, making them similar to Type I columns, but without the strengthening rib. It is not clear whether this represents a modification of Type I or a precursor.

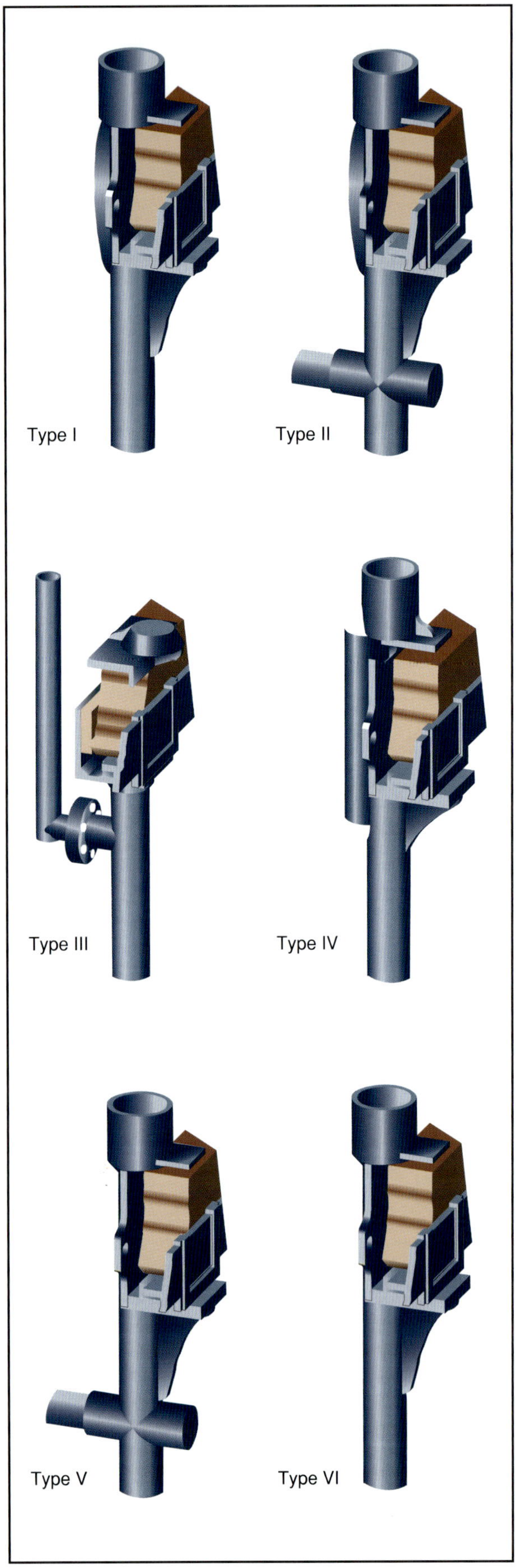

Figure 45: Column types within Old and Decker Mill

The method of gas supply within Old Mill appears to have comprised a single feed from the gas producers in Little Mill, and may have been directed into the central column in the basement. From there, it could have been distributed into a full-height vertical shaft, comprising Type I columns positioned between each bay, via interconnecting pipes between the Type II columns in the basement. The original method of gas supply appears to have been more complex in Decker Mill, with interconnecting Type V columns on the lowest three floors, suggesting that the original supply was to each floor. Alternatively, distribution between vertical columns may have been provided over several floors to allow for continuous supply whilst areas were undergoing replacement, or simply that it was easier, and probably cheaper, to create one mould and just cast a single type. Type VI columns would, therefore, appear to be a progression from Type V, with the socket removed. Type IV appears to represent the culmination of the technique, with no narrowing of the beam bypass within the gas pipe. This column type also has a better axial position for the beam, bringing its centre line closer to that of the column, although the load upon the column is still eccentric (Donald Insall Associates and Structural Perspectives 2002).

Whilst the same column types were utilised on different floors in Old and Decker Mill, each required a separate casting, due to the diminishing floor heights, which necessitated that columns were cast for a specific floor. The modification to each casting would not have been as simple as the reduction in the length of the shaft at the base, as each column incorporated a flanged foot, housing the head of the column below. This suggests that the mould for each column was created using a three-piece casting pattern, the head and foot being reused for each casting, with a new model of the shaft used for each floor.

Unlike the columns in Old and Decker Mill, those in New Mill had no obvious relationship with the gas lighting system. It is possible that the gas supply from the gasometer passed through a tunnel under Bengal Street, probably emerging adjacent to New Mill. Two T-section cast-iron beams across window apertures in Bays **16** and **17**, on the second and fourth floors of New Mill, may represent inlets for the gas supply, as each have sockets for housing pipes within the original castings.

The four types of cantilever brackets (referred to as Types A-D) are associated with every column from this period within Old and Decker Mill, and cantilever out along the beam from offset carrying brackets incorporated into the column designs (Pl 118). Each bracket has additional supporting points to the beam located at either end, effectively reducing the span of the timber beam, and presumably intended to replicate the support offered by the original columns. All bracket types differ in the

Plate 118: Cantilever bracket and replaced column on the fourth floor of Old Mill

style of decoration of the bracket face. In every instance, timber packing pads were inserted between the carrying bracket and cantilever bracket, demonstrating that the columns and brackets were not precision-cast for each position, and were not original features of the mill construction. The brackets were attached to the beams with bolts through the face of the heads of the cantilever brackets, secured by hand-made nuts (of different dimensions) on the rear of the beam.

The variety in columns and cantilever bracket types suggests that the process of replacement may have been somewhat experimental, and that new 'prototypes' were used in different positions, or alternatively that they were sourced from several manufacturers, to allow the job to be undertaken as rapidly as possible. All surviving columns from this period in Old Mill are of Type I, except in the basement, where they are Type II, allowing gas flow between bays. This suggests that the change of columns in Old Mill was a single planned episode, with columns all being cast in the same foundry and to the same specification. A variety of associated cantilever bracket types (A, C, and D) was utilised, however, suggesting that this was a more experimental technology, or possibly that many were replaced individually at a later date. The fact that nearly all the beams require pads to house them onto the cantilever brackets means that independent replacement of the columns would have been entirely feasible. The distribution of cantilever bracket types does not appear to follow any pattern, although Type B examples were found only in Decker Mill, and the basement and second floors of both mills had Type A brackets exclusively, where still present.

New Columns in New Mill

An internal re-orientation of New Mill similarly involved the replacement of the double row of columns with a single row, positioned slightly to the north of the centre line of the mill (Fig 46). Unlike Old and Decker Mill, however, there is limited survival of columns from this period, with only those used on the fourth floor remaining. These were cruciform-section solid cast-iron variants of 4½ in (114 mm) section. Both the column type, and engineering methodology used, differs markedly from that in Old and Decker Mill, where hollow cylindrical columns of a much greater section were used. Although the span in New Mill is slightly wider than that of Decker Mill, no additional support for the more slender, solid-section, columns was deemed necessary. The actual process of column replacement was much simpler than that adopted in Old and Decker Mill. In New Mill, the row of new columns was positioned to the north of the existing line shaft, and the original columns need not have been moved until the replacements had been installed and were supporting the load of the beam. The caps of the replacement columns were very similar to those

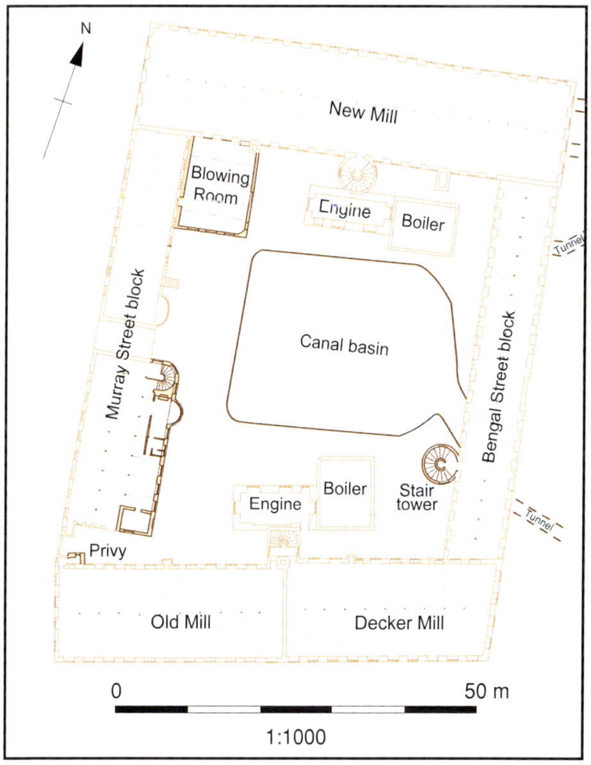

Figure 46: Site plan, Phase 4

extant on the first floor of the Murray Street block, which appear to have been later insertions.

Column replacement in New Mill appears to have been on structural grounds, or possibly related to the improvement in the power-transmission system. The dimensions of the mill are such that operating 11 pairs of 324-spindle mules transversely gave the maximum output per floor (7128 spindles per floor). Even if 492-spindle mules were operated longitudinally, there would only be 5904 spindles per floor, although the number of skilled operatives would be reduced from eleven to six. This was not the case during this restructuring work, however, as George Murray stated in 1833 that he only had 'two pair carrying four hundred and ninety-two spindles' (PP (HC) 1833 [450] XX, D1).

A secondary episode of column replacement appears to have taken place on the fourth floor of New Mill in the mid-nineteenth century. This comprised the replacement of the western two columns with 4 in (0.10 m) hollow, cylindrical cast-iron examples, similar in style to those used in the structural remodelling in the southern part of the Murray Street block, but without the decorative projecting rounded bead moulding (astragal). These two columns differ markedly in style from the later mass replacement of columns around the turn of the twentieth century (*Phase 6, p 136*), and perhaps represent the replacement of individual failing columns.

Modifications to the Wing Blocks

A major expansion of the Bengal Street block was undertaken during the second decade of the nineteenth century, increasing it in height from four to six storeys (*Ch 5, p 81*). A circular stair tower, similar to that adjoining New Mill, was added to the western side of the newly enlarged structure, affording access directly from the courtyard (Fig 47). A stone flag walkway from the Old and Decker Mill stair tower was also built at this time, connecting Old and Decker Mill to the Bengal Street block externally (Pl 119). The foundations of the circular stair tower, and the vestiges of the two bottom steps, were exposed by archaeological excavation. A circular structure with an internal diameter of 3½ ft (1.07 m), revealed at the centre of the stair tower footings, represented the remains of a vertical shaft. This housed an iron pipe of 5 in (0.13 m) diameter, which extended vertically

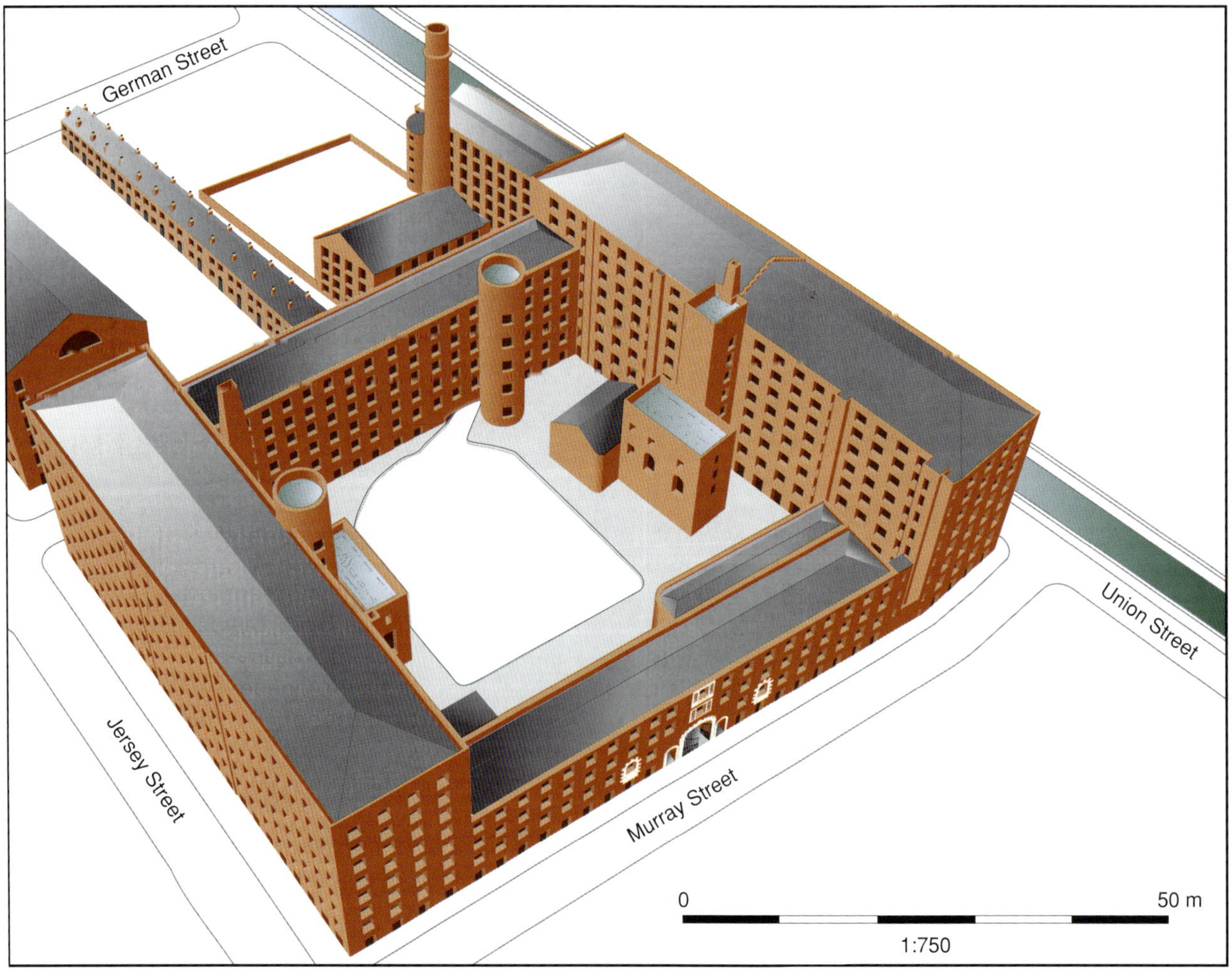

Figure 47: Isometric reconstruction of the Phase 4 complex (c 1817 – 1855)

Plate 119: Raised walkway between Decker Mill and Bengal Street block (© Crown Copyright NMR)

downwards to the base of the foundations to a stop end, representing part of the original fire-fighting system for the Bengal Street block. The shaft differs in style and fabric from those in the spinning mills, suggesting that a different system to that supplied by Boulton and Watt was used.

The first of two episodes of expansion to the Murray Street block can be dated to between 1824 and 1831 on cartographic evidence, and comprised the erection of a single-storey structure on the eastern side of the block. Known as the 'Blowing Room' subsequently, this is likely to have been intended as a primary processing area, where raw cotton was taken from the warehouse and broken out of its compressed, baled state and cleaned, and then passed to the adjacent card room. The building was constructed at the basement level, rising to the level of the ground floor, allowing the inclusion of cellar-lights in the eastern and southern elevations.

The Blowing Room had a structural impact within New Mill, both in terms of its construction, and also to allow its integration in the complex. The two western cellar-light windows in the basement of New Mill were blocked, whilst the easternmost window was remodelled to form a doorway into the new structure. This was a fireproof double-door, with three steps down into the Blowing Room. A doorway inserted in the western bay at second-floor level between New Mill and the Murray Street block also appears to relate to the improved communication between the structures in the north-west corner of the complex at this time.

It seems possible that this remodelling was coupled with a strengthening of the floors within the Murray Street block, which was undertaken shortly after the initial construction of the building. This was achieved in different ways in the southern and northern parts of the block, possibly at slightly different times, reflecting differing usage in the two parts of the building. The floors in the south were strengthened by the insertion of slender, cast-iron cruciform columns, at lower ground-, ground-, and first-floor levels (Pl 120), supporting a north / south-aligned spine of T-section, fish-bellied cast-iron beams, jointed over the column heads. Each 3½ in (89 mm) section column on the lower ground-floor has a square-section head and base, the latter fitted into a square pocket of a cast-iron base plate, cut into a sandstone pad. The column cap slid into a two-piece cast pocket formed at the ends of the T-section beams above. At ground- and first-floor level the column bases differ, in that the foot of the shaft bifurcates around the original transverse joist, to rest on thin timber packings above the fish-bellied spine beams. At first-floor level, the column head fits into a pad to a transverse timber bridging joist, but this may have been a later replacement of the cast-iron longitudinal beams present on the floors below. The columns were positioned at each bay division, with the southern five situated on the centre line of the building and the northern three positioned 2 ft (0.61 m) to the west.

Plate 120: Cruciform-section column, Murray Street block

A different approach to strengthening appears to have been adopted in the northern part of the block, where the open floor space was maintained by the addition of wrought-iron truss bars, attached to every fifth or sixth ceiling joist, supporting a central longitudinal timber spine beam. The truss bars were connected to L-shaped brackets, attached to the joists and the external walls, and supported a central spine beam via cast-iron pads (Pl 121). The second major remodelling to the Murray Street block

Plate 121: Truss bar detail in the Murray Street block

occurred sometime between 1831 and 1849 (*Ch 5, p 82*). This involved the addition of a 7½ ft (2.29 m) wide extension along the eastern elevation of the southern part of the block, to the full height of the structure. It was constructed of mould-thrown brick, in English Garden Wall bond, with its northern bay curving to meet the inner face of the arched entrance. A bow window was included in the eastern elevation at ground level in Bay **7**, its method of construction differing from the earlier example in Bay **13**, with the sill supported on a lath and plaster partition, itself supported on curved cast-iron beams (Pl 122).

Surviving physical evidence in the form of a wall scar in Bay **1** of the extension indicates that this area originally contained a staircase. A bull-nosed brick doorway with a brick arch in the eastern elevation afforded access from the courtyard, whilst internal access appears to have originally been from the northern side, with blocked doorways surviving at ground- and second-floor levels. The means of access from the stair to the first floor is uncertain, and it is not clear whether the southern three bays of the lower ground floor were reduced in floor level at this time to allow access to the stair, or whether this was a slightly later alteration during conversion to a hoist (*Phase 6, p 138*). The floor level was reduced by *c* 5 ft (1.53 m), with the column bases supported on concrete blocks. A central, brick-arched aperture in the southern elevation would appear contemporary with the change of floor level, extending to the full depth of the wall. This is likely to have afforded access to the 'shed' shown at the southern end of the structure on early maps of the site (*Ch 5, Pl 71*).

The eastern wall of the original block was retained within the extension, with several of the windows blocked, and others remodelled into doorways. The window in Bay **8** at lower ground-floor level was reduced in height, to three rows of six lights, by partially infilling the aperture. The original frame was retained, allowing light into the area beneath the new staircase in the extension. At first- and second-floor levels, only the southern 10 ft (3.05 m) was retained, forming the western wall of the staircase in Bay **1**. Support was provided to the north by a longitudinal beam, comprising several members, supported by hollow cylindrical cast-iron columns to each bay, aligned with the original east wall below. One of the beams (in Bay **6** on the second floor) has an intricate Baltic timber mark on its western face.

Plate 122: Eastern extension to Murray Street block

The second floor longitudinal beam supports the valley between the original pitched roof and the separate pitched roof of the extension, which comprised simple lap-jointed rafters. It was originally hipped at both ends, with a sandstone-capped parapet, but the southern hip was removed during early twentieth-century remodelling of the stair. Rainwater exited from the valley via a spout and hopper at the southern end of the roof, just below the height of the window lintel, which presumably replaced the rainwater goods of the original structure. A cast-iron downpipe survives *in situ*, which continues below ground, presumably exiting into the sandstone drain in the south-eastern corner of the original block in Bay **1**. A central lead-lined timber drain for the valley between the two roofs (Pl 123) was also constructed in Bay **5**, projecting below the ceiling, and venting into a hopper in the external elevation.

At second-floor level in the southern elevation of the extension is an original window-frame. The aperture is of similar proportions to those elsewhere in the mill complex, but the frame was not replaced during the later refenestration of the structure (*p 125*). It is similar to the earlier window in the eastern elevation of the

Plate 123: Double-span roof, southern part of Murray Street block

original block, comprising six rows of six lights, each with iron glazing bars. A later alteration included the insertion of a four-light horizontal pivot window, the original probably being fixed.

Architectural embellishment of the Murray Street façade was also undertaken at this time. The most striking feature is the central arch, which was re-faced with rusticated, chamfered sandstone voussoir dressings above similarly constructed jambs. Many of the original bricks forming the western elevation had been cut and reused to infill the indented quoins of the arch, which was cut through the external face at the outer diameter of the quoins. The inner face of the arch was rebuilt below first-floor level, in the same orangey-red brick as the extension to the block, which butts its southern side. This arch had projecting sandstone imposts and a moulded sandstone keystone, but was otherwise constructed in brick.

On either side of the archway, two doorways affording access to the building from Murray Street were similarly refaced with chamfered sandstone surrounds. It is unclear whether these doorways formed part of the original construction of the Murray Street block, or were inserted at the time of the remodelling of the western façade. The ground-floor windows, two bays on either side of the doorways (Bays **7** and **13**), also have dressed sandstone surrounds, which comprise stepped voussoirs and quoins. The quoins extend to the top of the street-level cellar-light windows, with the area between the ground floor sill and street level lintel infilled with an angled sandstone panel. The original lintel of the southern window was replaced with a curved cast-iron lintel, demonstrating that these architectural details were insertions to the original design. Similar architectural embellishments were also undertaken on the façade of the Bengal Street block (Pl 124).

The first- and second-floor windows above the archway in the western elevation of the Murray Street block are very different from those elsewhere in the complex, being horizontal, as opposed to vertical. Each comprises central nine-light windows, similar in proportion to those elsewhere, flanked on each side by flat sandstone columns, which form the mullion to a vertical, three-light window on either side. The window surrounds project, and have decorative mouldings, with rain hoods above and a sandstone frieze between floors, which has a central rectangular recess for a plaque. On the eastern face of the building, the windows above the archway were of standard type, but were significantly wider than elsewhere in the complex. As in the arch below, original bricks have been cut, and rebuilding around the window apertures is visible internally, demonstrating that the windows are insertions.

A doorway in the northern elevation of the extension, in Bay **9**, appears to be contemporary with the remodelling of the arch into the courtyard. It has dressed sandstone quoins, not chamfered as those in the western elevation, and a flat sandstone lintel, with curved lower face. This afforded access to a new staircase, situated in the quadrant at the north-eastern end of the extension (Fig 46).

Plate 124: Architectural embellishment to the Bengal Street block façade (© Crown Copyright NMR)

Little evidence survives of the internal layout of the Murray Street block at this time. The curved passage from Murray Street to the courtyard, shown on the Ordnance Survey map of 1850, pre-dates most of the internal divisions in the southern part of the structure. The east/west-aligned brick partition walls in the western part of the Murray Street block, on either side of Bay **6** at lower ground-floor (street) level, may well date from this time, surviving in truncated form. The ground floor of the extension, accessed via the staircase at its northern end, appears to have formed offices, with a fireplace in the northern wall of Bay **8**. Further indication of this having formed offices was provided by the incorporation of the bow window, and the use of sawdust as a packing material above the ceiling of the lower ground floor, which served to insulate the floor above, not only from noise, but also to reduce heat loss. Similar packing material was also observed within the fabric of the contemporary bow window.

It is probable that the internal dividing walls on either side of Bay **10**, at first- and second-floor level, date from this period, being constructed of mould-thrown brick, bonded in pale lime mortar. Both walls butt the outer elevations and had central doorways at first-floor level, with additional offset doorways at second-floor level, that in the northern elevation replacing the central door. The offset position of these doorways may be related to centrally positioned power-transmission brackets within the roof space of both north and south elevations in Bay **10**. The southern, timber, bracket has semi-circular rebates within its face, and is seemingly the top bracket for a vertical cable or belt, whilst the timber bracket attached to the northern elevation has a cast-iron end-bracket for an horizontal shaft mounted on its upper face. This implies that an horizontal axle extended across Bay **10** at second-floor level, presumably related to a hoist, and was driven by a vertical drive shaft in the southern part of the bay. The central doorway in the southern elevation has a rebate on its southern face, suggesting outwardly opening double doors.

During the internal remodelling of the southern end of the Murray Street block, it is probable that several of the windows in the western elevation were blocked, as a result of a change in function of the newly enlarged room-space. Only three of the nine windows remained in use, in Bays **2**, **4**, and **9**, the remainder being blocked flush with the internal face, and recessed one skin from the external face, in Flemish bond, to maintain the symmetry of the external façade.

Renewed Windows
The window casements throughout most of the mill complex were replaced at some point in the mid-nineteenth century, following the eastern extension to the Murray Street block, and prior to an enlargement of the privy tower at the western end of Old Mill, which is shown on Adshead's map of 1851. Replacement occurred throughout the entirety of Old, Decker, and New Mills, although it may have been more selective in the Murray Street block. The earlier windows were replaced with timber frames, each containing only nine lights, the central one partially opening on a central horizontal axle, with the uniformly sized frames requiring padding to fit many of the larger window apertures, particularly in the spinning mills.

New Facilities
The enlargement of the privy tower at the western end of Old Mill comprised an approximately 5 ft (1.53 m) square tower, built perpendicular to the earlier structure, adjoining the angled privy tower to the west. On its southern side, the tower covers the window of Bay **2**, which has the later style of window frame associated with the refenestration. Access to the extension was through the earlier tower. Given that it still retained only one access, it is unlikely that the enlargement reflects the introduction of divided separate-sex toilets. It is, however, probable that it represents the introduction of toilets flushed by a pipe, pumped from the engine.

The insertion of external fire escapes post-dates the refenestration, but probably by only a short margin. Cast-iron staircases were attached to the northern external faces of Old and Decker Mill, in Bays **5** and **18**, cutting through the western parts of the existing windows. Although both differ slightly in style, they bear similar makers' stamps of 'J & J H' and are probably contemporary in date. Whilst two fire escapes were installed on the courtyard face of Old and Decker Mill, New Mill only had a single fire escape, attached to Bay **4**. Although New Mill is a larger structure, the inclusion of the extra escape to Old and Decker Mill was presumably a result of the internal dividing wall between the two mills. That attached to New Mill is closer in style to that at Decker Mill, with similar cast-iron corbels at ground-floor level, although with slightly more elaborate examples above, containing the design 'AS Co' within the lattice (Pl 125).

Phase 5, Increased Power and New Technology (1855 - 1898)

Modifications to the Murray Street Block
Internal modifications to the northern end of the Murray Street block included strengthening works to all floors and the Blowing Room (Fig 48). New fireproof ceilings were also installed in the basement and the Blowing Room, using different technologies. Elsewhere within the complex, improved fireproofing of the structures was achieved by cladding the ceilings with metal sheeting, covering the original lath and plaster. Sheets were typically 6 x 4 ft (1.83 x 1.22 m), and damaged sheets were replaced when necessary until the mid-twentieth century. The technique of metal cladding was in use by the earlier nineteenth century (Williams with Farnie 1992, 58), but the large areas of exposed whitewashed lath and plaster ceiling within the Murrays' complex suggests that cladding was a secondary feature.

The fireproof ceiling inserted into the Blowing Room comprises shallow brick arches, 5 ft (1.53 m) wide, supported on seven east/west-aligned I-section iron beams, shown by previous studies to be of wrought iron, probably of a late nineteenth-century date (Donald Insall Associates and Structural Perspectives 2002). The ceiling of the basement of the Murray Street block is also of brick construction, but comprises flat rows of bricks supported on the flanges of inverted T-section beams. These act as bridging joists (29 per bay) and are lap-jointed into joists at each bay interval, which span the basement. Each is centrally supported by a 5½ in (0.14 m) diameter cast-iron column, with

Plate 125: Detail of fire escape ironwork, New Mill

Plate 126: Ground floor, northern part of Murray Street block

filleted astragal and double-flanged head. Similar but shorter columns were inserted at each bay division on the ground floor to support the longitudinal spine beam, replacing the earlier system of truss bars (Pl 126). Evidence for associated column insertion was exposed beneath the twentieth-century bitumen roof cover, and comprised four *in situ* column feet. These were aligned longitudinally on the upper surface of the ground-floor spine beam, each straddling the original transverse floor beams. A cruciform-section key on the upper surface jointed the foot to the column above, which was probably of hollow cylindrical section, and each flange contained a rectangular bolt hole. These holes were, however, redundant, the column feet resting on timber pads on the spine beam, possibly suggesting their reuse.

An internal reorganisation of the ground floor of the northern part of the Murray Street block appears to have coincided with the introduction of columns, which changed the structure from an open room to a series of divided bays. The original brick-arched apertures, seemingly associated with power transmission within the original structure, appear to have been blocked during this phase, and replaced with a small cast-iron bearing box, between Bays **19** and **20**, at window height. Two gallows brackets for drive pulleys survive in the eastern part of the room, that within Bay **18** retaining a slender pulley, grooved for a rope rather than a belt (Pl 127). Whilst this suggests that some form of light

Plate 127: In situ *pulley wheel, Murray Street block*

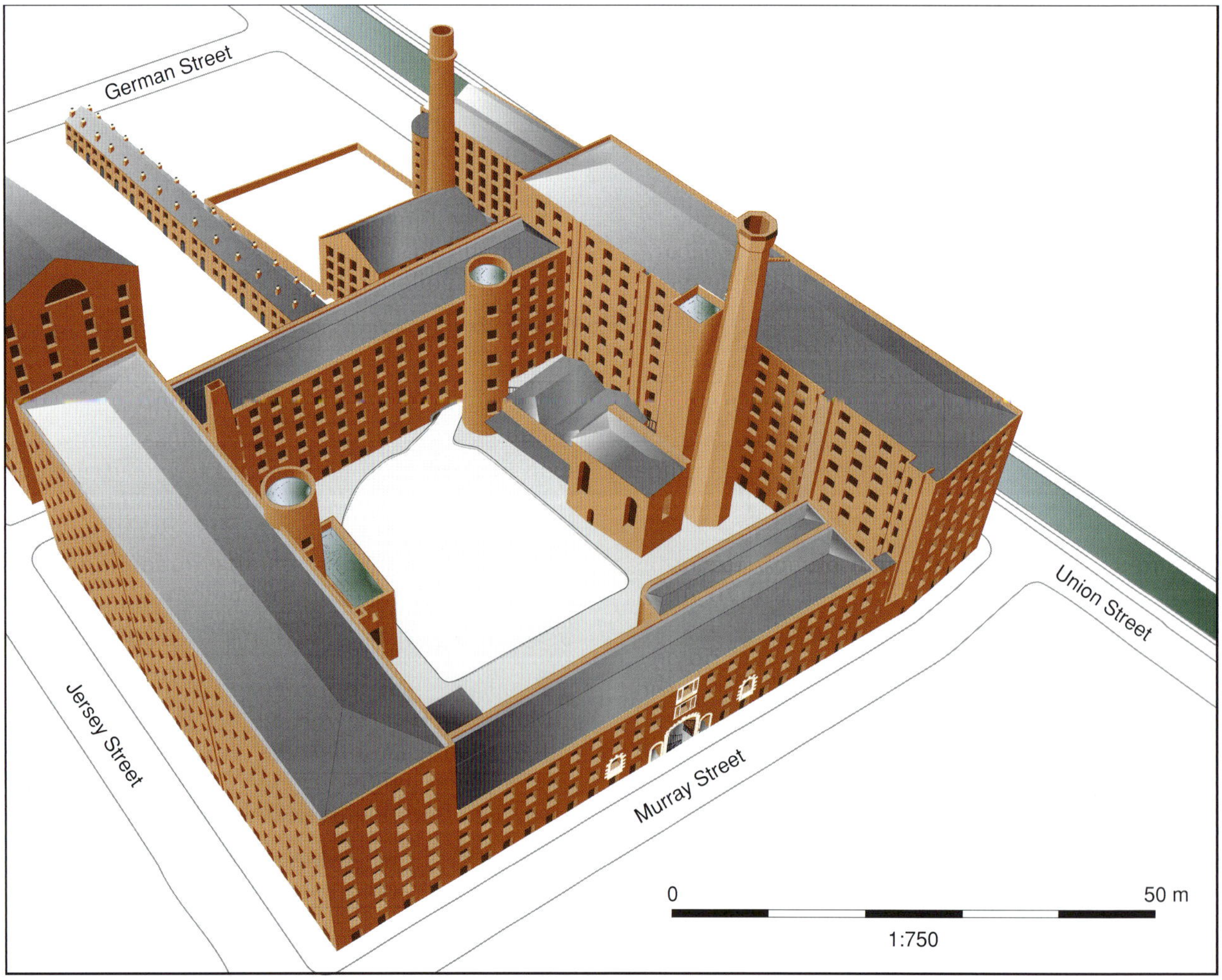

Figure 48: Isometric reconstruction of the Phase 5 complex (1855 – 1898)

Plate 128: Decorative door architrave, northern part of the Murray Street block

machinery remained in use during this period, the timber/lath and plaster partition in the eastern half of the room, which also dates from this period, implies that offices were created in the southern part. This is reinforced by the architectural detail used in the doorways through the partition, one of which has a panelled architrave with embossed flower designs at the corners (Pl 128). A further stud/lath and plaster partition in the western part of Bay **13** also probably dates from this period, suggesting that the offices flanked a central access to the archway in Bay **10**. The majority of the windows in this part of the block reflect this more polite architectural style, comprising 16-light balanced sash windows with panelled reveals and a flat projecting sill, above a moulded dado rail which encircles the room. The window apertures were reduced slightly at this time, with the lower part being blocked with four courses of brickwork, sealed with a 1½ in (38 mm) thickness of horse-hair lime/sand plaster.

Power was certainly required in the basement and Blowing Room; a large cast-iron bearing box at the southern end of the adjoining wall, slightly above floor level, appears to have been the main power transfer between the two rooms during this phase. To the north, 5 ft (1.53 m) long angled single-skin brick 'cheeks' were added on the Blowing Room side of the doorway from the basement, with a second fireproof door at the eastern end.

The interior of the southern part of the Murray Street block was also remodelled during this phase. The passage along the north side of Bay **9** appears to date from this period, and a rebate was cut at its western end to house the substantial panelled entrance door when fully opened. Lath and plaster partitioned washrooms and offices within the ground floor extension also relate to this period. Access to the first floor of this part of the block was afforded by a new staircase, entered from Bay **7** of the eastern extension. This had an associated brick-built passage, with flagstone floor, linking the corridor along the northern side of Bay **9** to the earlier extension in Bay **6**. It is noteworthy that this stair had no access to the ground floor, suggesting a clear division of function between the ground floor and upper floors, implying that, as in the northern part of the Murray Street block, the ground floor served as offices. The original staircase at the southern end of the earlier eastern extension was remodelled to form a hoist during these alterations.

New Steam Plant for Old and Decker Mill

The first major alteration to the power system in the complex during this period appears to have been the construction of an updated steam plant for Old and Decker Mill (Fig 49). It is unknown exactly when the new engine house, boiler house, and chimney were

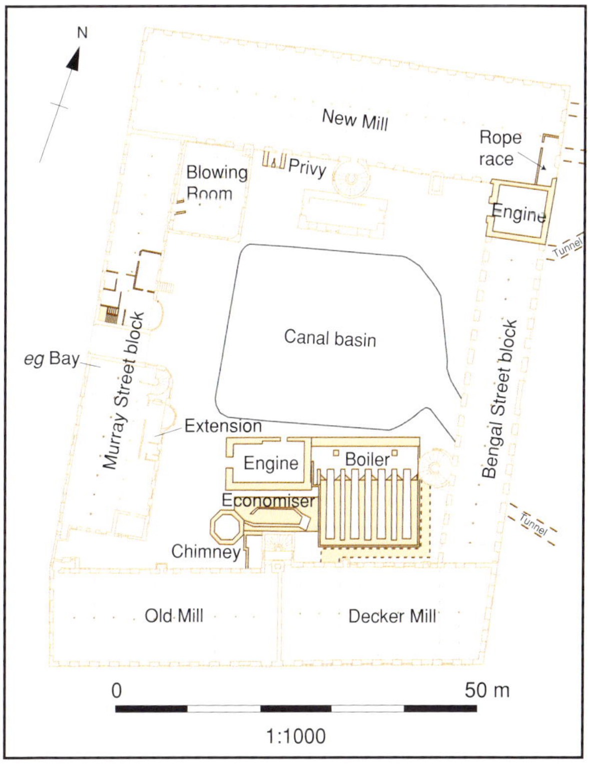

Figure 49: Site plan, Phase 5

constructed, although architectural embellishment points to a date of around 1870-80. Details of the engine are unknown, but the dimensions of the extant engine house are consistent with those required by a beam engine, which is likely to have been a compound type.

The new engine was probably installed prior to the disconnection of the existing engine, in order that power to the machinery might be maintained and disruption to production was minimised. This was accomplished by constructing a new engine house to the immediate north of the existing one (Fig 49), and offsetting the new drive shaft. Once the new construction had been completed, the internal power transmission could then be reconnected to the new main horizontal drive shaft, which still entered in the eastern bay of the Old Mill basement (Bay **11**).

Plate 129: Extant engine house for Old and Decker Mill

The new engine house (Pl 129), which survives intact, incorporates the northern wall of the earlier engine house. The joining wall was heightened by *c* 14 ft (4.27 m), with the raised section being one brick thinner. The new engine house was built of mould-thrown red brick, which externally was laid in English Garden Wall bond (with three rows of stretchers to one row of headers), with string courses picked out in yellow brick. It has hipped gables and a Welsh slate roof with ceramic ridge tiles. There is a central raised skylight, which may be a later addition, with a rolled lead ridge, and the wall tops have closed eaves above denticulated brickwork. Internally, the structure was of three bays, each divided by king-post trusses. The hips of the roof are constructed with a pair of purlins within each pitch, halved over the truss and mitred to the hip purlins. The roof space is finished with lath and plaster sealing the rafters.

The new structure featured larger arched windows than those in the north side of its predecessor, spaced slightly wider and deeper, and new windows were also included in the eastern and western elevations. On either side of the windows in the east and west gables are two pairs of large dressed sandstone blocks, each measuring *c* 6 ft (1.83 m) in length, representing load-bearing pads for the framing of the new engine. Two smaller sandstone blocks survive above the eastern window in the north elevation, and within the internal fabric of the south elevation. All contain bolt holes, suggesting that the upper part of the framing was attached across the engine house at this point. Single sandstone blocks in both north and south elevations represent the position of the entablature beam of the new engine. At ground-floor level, below the bearing blocks for this beam, similar blocks supporting the axle of the engine also survive, positioned centrally within the north and south elevations. That in the northern elevation had compression marks of two large oval plates in its external face, whilst that on the south elevation projected slightly, and has a semi-circular rebate cut into the centre of its face. This probably represents the position of a connector or drum on the external end of the axle. The western two bays of the north elevation were one brick thicker on the internal face than to the east, presumably reflecting the extra structural stability required to support the new engine, which, unlike its predecessor, was not a free-standing structure. The main stress of the engine would have been in the central and western ends of the engine house, and, therefore, materials could be saved by reducing the wall thickness towards the eastern end of the structure. Access to the engine house was afforded via a doorway from the contemporary large boiler house, constructed on its eastern side, and another doorway at ground level, which provided access directly from the canal wharf.

The drive shaft from the new engine lay immediately to the east of, and below, the axle pad in the south elevation, and was carried through the wall of the engine house by a large cast-iron bearing box. An opposing similar bearing box in the north elevation of the stair tower of Old and Decker Mill marked the position of the new drive shaft entry into the base of the tower. Both bearing boxes sat on inserted sandstone pads. The new drive shaft had to pass to the eastern side of the C-section vertical newel within the stair tower. Given the lack of space within the tower, and the desire to keep the old machinery working whilst the replacement system was constructed, led to a rebate having to be cut into the eastern wall of the newel, to allow the drive shaft to pass. A massive bearing was inserted in the southern side of the stair tower, the two huge cast-iron brackets being visible internally in the basement in Old Mill. The eastern of the two plates is L-shaped, bolted to both the north and east elevations, where it partially overlies the brick blocking of the original northern doorway, demonstrating that this had been blocked prior to the relocation of the line shafting. The 9 ft (2.74 m) wide bearing was the full height of the ground floor within the stair tower, and comprised three main bearings. The first housed an horizontal bevel gear, translating the north / south alignment of the drive shaft through 90°. A second housing to the immediate west again rotated the horizontal shaft, allowing it to pass into the basement of Old Mill, through the original aperture, allowing a simple transfer of connection from the old engine to the new. A third bearing, to the east, supported a continuation of the east / west-aligned shaft, which continued through the eastern elevation via a smaller bearing box. This allowed power from the new engine to be transferred along the northern external side of Decker Mill, into the basement of the Bengal Street block; this would not, however, have been possible until the associated new chimney became functional, as the drive shaft passed through the earlier flue. The subsequent insertion of a doorway in the western elevation appears to have removed a further bearing box housing the continuation of this shaft to the west. Evidence for the shaft, presumably providing the primary power supply to the southern end of the Murray Street block, survives at ground level in the heating tower projecting from Bay **6** of Old Mill. A deep rectangular cast-iron bearing box was inserted into the northern elevation of the tower (Pl 130), which appears to have been underpinned with a brick plinth, as part of this major intervention into its fabric. A further bearing must have housed a bevel gear, rotating the shaft to the north, and a smaller bearing box at a similar height in the southern elevation of the Murray Street block would appear to have housed this driveshaft, suggesting that the bevel gear was located in the position of the Phase 6 privy tower.

Plate 130: Bearing box inserted into the heating tower

Two further apertures in the eastern gable of the engine house relate to the contemporary boiler house to the east. A central small aperture, with three-course segmental brick arch, probably housed the condensate return pipe, whilst a slightly larger aperture to the south of the first floor doorway, with a two-course segmental brick arch, housed the steam pipe from the boilers to the engine.

New Boiler House

Whilst the building itself has since been demolished, substantial remains of the associated boiler house were revealed during excavations, which exposed approximately 75% of the original building (Pl 131). The excavation demonstrated that the boiler house had accommodated four Lancashire-type boilers. This revolutionary boiler design had two furnace tubes, each about one third of the diameter of the outer shell, and would measure typically 8 ft (2.44 m) in diameter by 30 ft (9.1 m) long (Watkins 1999, 218).

Plate 131: Excavated remains of the boiler house

Excavation of the boiler house revealed four parallel walls, lying on a broad north / south alignment, creating three adjoining bays of equal size, each to house a boiler (Fig 50). Each of the partition wall faces internal to the building were abutted by a low wall, creating a series of raised benches at a height of *c* 1 m, with a facing course of refractory bricks. A layer of thin slates bonded in clay was incorporated between the lower courses of each wall, presumably to protect the refractory bricks from rising moisture. The refractory bricks had evidently been obtained from different sources; 'Milnes Ltd Brighouse', 'B Gibbons Jnr Ltd Stourbridge', and 'Glenboig'

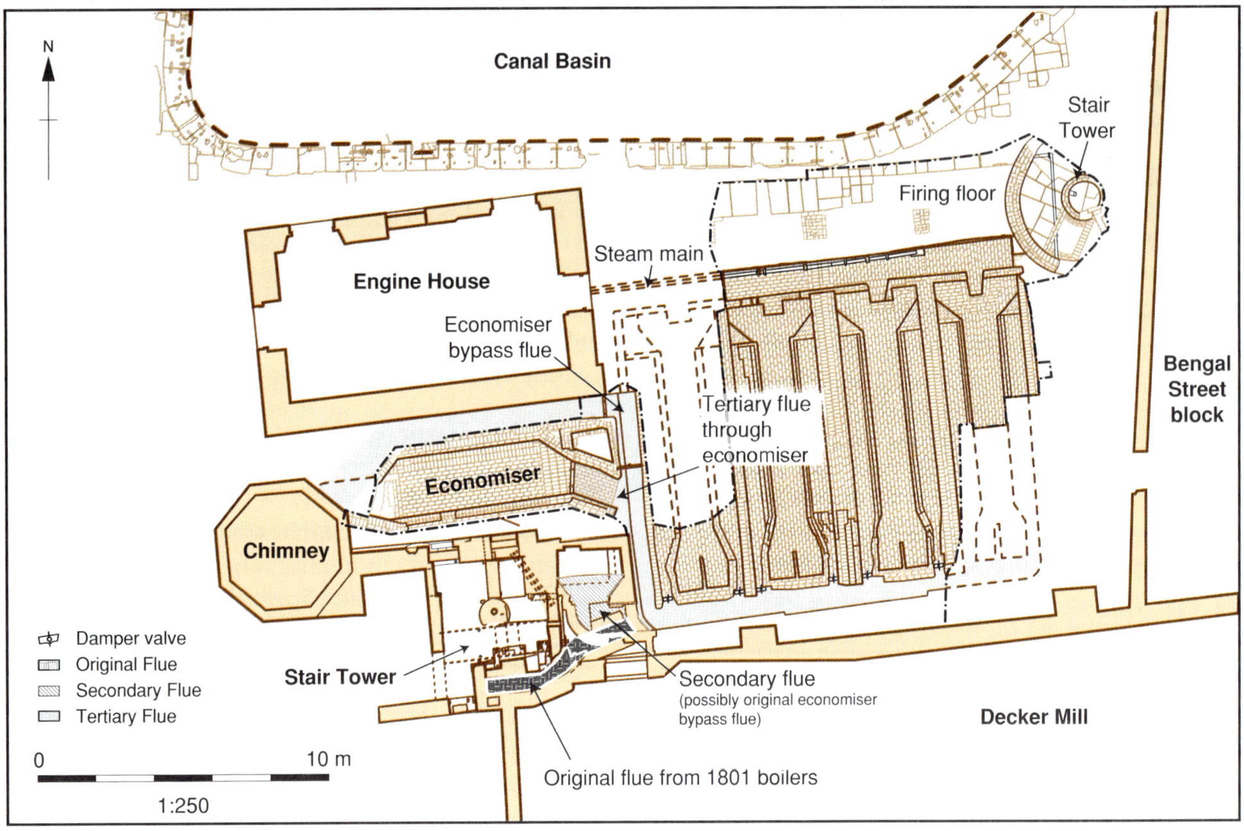

Figure 50: Boiler house, excavation plan

stamps were identified from different walls. A series of boiler mounting blocks, moulded from refractory clay, occupied the top course of each of the bench walls, although only a few survived *in situ*. These raised the boiler slightly to allow air to circulate around the body. The floors of each bay were composed of at least two courses of refractory bricks, aligned along the length of the building. At the northern end of each bay was a square-shaped cut-out in the floor, representing ash pits for cleaning out dirt within the boilers.

Immediately to the north of the boilers was the firing floor, which lay along the northern edge of the boiler house, and was situated *c* 2 ft 4 in (0.71 m) above the floor of the building, and 2 ft (0.61 m) below the level of the adjacent canal basin. Coal was transferred from boats directly onto the firing floor, from where the boilers were charged with fuel. The platform was composed of a type of concrete, which incorporated a large proportion of crushed bricks. An iron pipe that was aligned east / west along the foot of the firing floor probably represented the primary steam main from the boilers to the engine.

A photograph taken in October 1985 (RCHME and GMAU 1989) shows that the northern elevation of the boiler house comprised a double-span hipped roof with a central dividing wall, and four arched openings in the front, adjacent to the canal basin. The arched openings were supported on brick piers, the foundations of which were exposed on the firing floor.

Excavation at the rear of the boilers revealed the damper plates for the flue that were operated by iron rods, protruding through the ground-floor level paved walkway by Decker Mill, still visible during the 1980s (RCHME and GMAU 1989). The excavation also revealed a flue, leading from the rear of the boilers towards the eastern heating tower of Decker Mill, implying that the heating system was supplied by a steam pipe directly from the boilers. An eyewitness account, written in 1832, stated that 'the apartments are all warmed by steam from the boilers of the engine' (Allen 1832, 129), suggesting that this system was already in place, and the practice was continued with the construction of the new boiler house.

Excavations within the area of the earlier Phase 2 engine house contained the remains of the flue that had connected the boilers to a new chimney to the west of the stair tower. Within the flue, between the boilers and the chimney, were the foundations for a fuel economiser (Pl 132). At its junction with the economiser, the base of the flue was traversed by an iron plate, fixed down by two iron bolts, which most probably represents the remnants of a mechanism that regulated the flow of gases entering the economiser. The plate was retained *in situ*, obscuring the underlying bricks, although it seemed to overlie a butt joint between the flue and the economiser, suggesting these two elements were of slightly different dates.

Plate 132: Excavated remains of the economiser

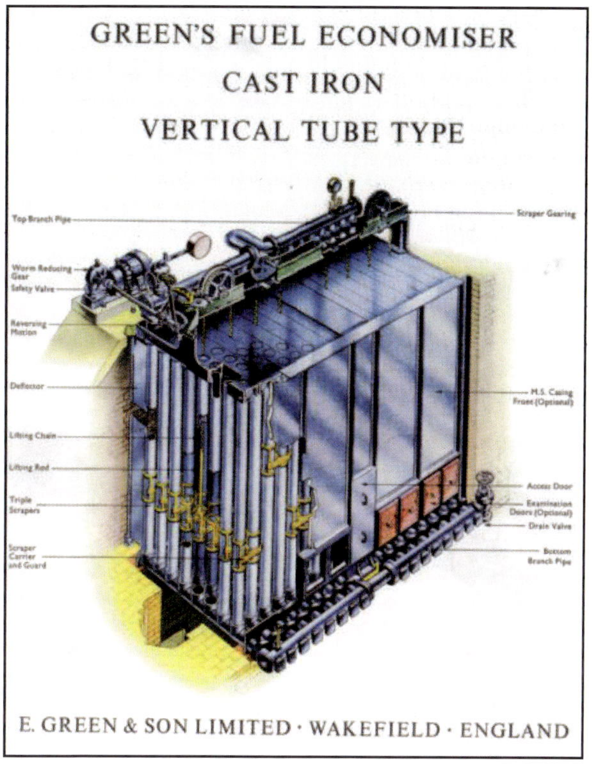

Plate 133: Green's economiser from an original advertisement

The remains of a bypass flue for the economiser were exposed immediately to the north, against the southern elevation of the engine house. An area of rebuilding at the base of the north-east elevation of the chimney represented the blocking of this flue, suggesting that it had been a temporary measure.

The fuel economiser, also known as a feed water heater, consisted of banks of cast-iron pipes, usually 4 in (0.1 m) in diameter and 9 ft (0.23 m) long (Pl 133). It could reduce the temperature of flue gases by as much as 150° C whilst increasing the temperature of feed water for the boilers from about 65° C to 120° C, thereby offering a considerable saving in the energy required to produce steam. Indeed, Watkins argued that the economiser 'undoubtedly saved more fuel for industry than any other single invention' (Watkins 1999, 218). It was normal practice for the feed water to be introduced at the end nearest to the chimney, so that the flows of water and gases were in opposite directions. In order that the feed water did not enter the economiser at too low a temperature, a National Circulator was frequently fitted. This device allowed the cold feed to mix with heated water, yet prevented furnace gases condensing on the tubes, which would have resulted in corrosion.

A new chimney was also constructed to serve the updated steam plant. It was placed to the south-west of the earlier engine house, and was built to a height of 135 ft (41.2 m). It is of octagonal plan, with iron straps attached all along its length and corbelled stringcourses at the top. A small aperture at approximately second-floor level, identifiable as a flat arch, presumably allowed access into the chimney, although it was blocked subsequently with red brick.

Power Transmission into the Bengal Street Block

In the south-eastern corner of the Bengal Street block, at lower ground-floor level, a massive cast-iron footstep bearing was cut into the eastern and southern elevations (Pl 134). It was bolted to a large sandstone pad, the full thickness of the wall, situated on a brick pier overlying the canal tunnel, and had two horizontal mounting brackets. The lower of these seemingly formed an end bracket for an horizontal shaft. The upper mounting would have housed a vertical drive-shaft bracket, transmitting power to the ground floor of the Bengal Street block, where a bearing box in the same wall above housed the end of an associated east/west-aligned horizontal shaft. Another mounting to the west, at lower ground-floor level, comprises a stepped brick pier, bonded in soft, dark mortar, typical of the late nineteenth century. This was capped with a 6 ft (1.83 m) long sandstone block housing two mounting bolts that ran through the full thickness of the brick pier. To the immediate west, a rebate cut into the southern elevation appears to represent a cut-away to house a drum.

Two large cast-iron bearing boxes in the western elevation are associated with this housing, and probably relate to the drive shaft from the Old and Decker

Plate 134: Footstep bearing, Bengal Street block

Mill engine house, which was driven through the eastern wall of the stair tower from the main bearing within the base of the stair tower. The window above has been blocked, and a rebate appears to have been cut into the southern end of the western elevation, to house the end of the line shaft in this position.

Replacement Engine for New Mill

A new engine house for New Mill was erected at the northern end of the Bengal Street block during the late nineteenth century (Fig 49). The precise date of construction remains elusive, although it is shown on Ordnance Survey mapping published in 1891. A photograph of the engine house taken during the 1960s, prior to its demolition (*Ch 5, Pl 85*), shows that it had probably contained a vertical-type engine, reflecting the restricted space available within the courtyard.

This engine powered a rope-drive system, which provided power for New Mill via a rope race inserted into the eastern bay. The huge innovation of the rope drive was that it removed the need for a primary vertical shaft, with power instead being transferred directly from the engine house to an horizontal line shaft on each floor, reducing the power loss caused by gearing in the old system.

The installation of the new engine rendered the earlier engine house redundant, which was modified for reuse. As part of this remodelling, it was extended to the edge of the canal basin, although the original south wall appears to have been retained as an internal partition. The building is shown in this format on a plan of the complex produced in 1902 for the installation of the automatic sprinkler system (MLSU MC/3834M/892).

Modifications to New Mill

The remains of tall, rectangular bearing boxes survive at ground- to fourth-floor levels in New Mill, situated in the eastern bay (Bay **22**), representing the apertures for the ropes from the rope drive (Pl 135). At basement level, a smaller bearing box in the northern elevation is offset to the west of the elongated boxes above, and represents the position of the horizontal rope into the basement of New Mill. The upper boxes are taller than that to the basement, due to the angle of the ropes to the upper floors, where they passed more obliquely through the external wall.

*Plate 135: Rope drive boxes, Bay **22**, New Mill*

At basement level, between Bays **21** and **22**, an additional 6½ in (165 mm) diameter hollow cylindrical cast-iron column was inserted to the south of the main column. A bracket on its north face houses a cast-iron carrier beam, with a mounting on its upper surface (Pl 136). This aligned with wall scars and projecting bolts in the west elevation of New Mill, which appear to relate to a carrier beam across the south central window, housing a terminal bearing for the line shaft. Bolt holes were observed through the beams of all bays, suggesting that line shaft hangers were positioned on every beam.

It is likely that self-acting mules had been installed by this date, perhaps in association with the new power system. Whilst these had become common much earlier in the nineteenth century, self-actors could not produce the fine-spun yarn produced by A & G Murray. Indeed, it was not until the end of the nineteenth century that

Plate 136: Inserted column and line shaft carrier beam, New Mill basement

self-actors had developed the complexity to be able to spin the finest counts, and it has been suggested that many fine spinners continued to use hand mules well into the twentieth century (Catling 1986, 51). It was noted in 1888, however, that A & G Murray had remodelled their mills 'in recent years' and that 'the internal arrangements are upon the most modern and approved principle', hinting at the use of self-actors (Historical Publishing Company 1888, 89).

Further alterations to New Mill included the addition of a rectangular privy tower, which projected from the southern side of Bay **8** (Fig 49). The tower was constructed of extruded red brick, frogged 'BC', most probably referring to the local Bradford Colliery brickworks (Donald Insall Associates and Structural Perspectives 2002). The tower was divided internally by a central partition wall, separating the cubicle on the western side from the cloakroom to the east. Cast-iron louvred vents in the east and west elevations serviced both elements on each floor.

Phase 6, Fine Cotton Spinners' and Doublers' Association (1898 - *c* 1947)

Sprinkler System

A & G Murray was conveyed to the Fine Cotton Spinners' and Doublers' Association (FCSDA) Limited

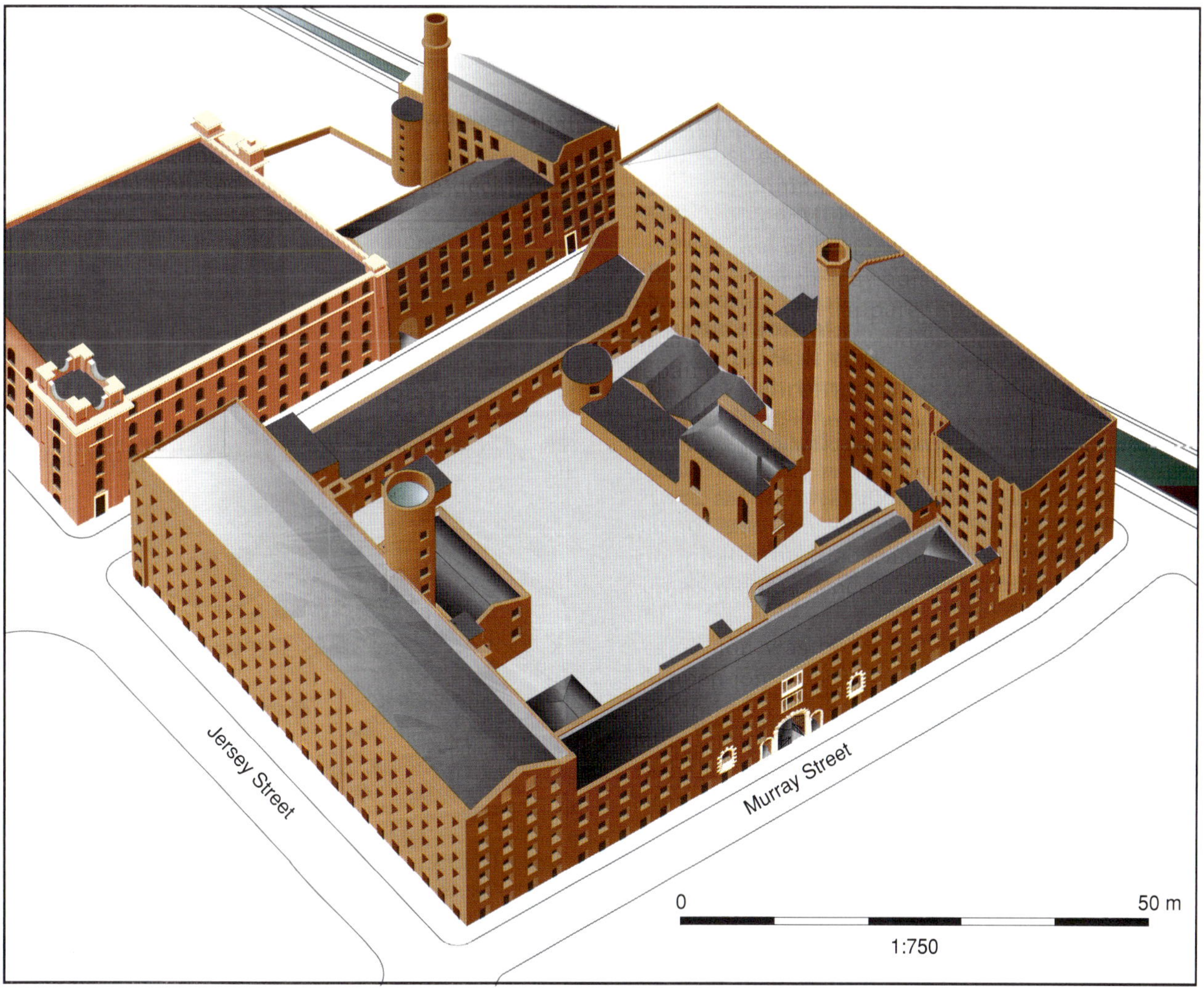

Figure 51: Isometric reconstruction of the Phase 6 complex, after 1909

in 1898 (*Ch 5, p 88*), and they implemented several improvements to the mills. These included reducing the height of the spinning mills, adopting electric drive, infilling the canal basin, installing internal hoists, and improving welfare facilities. The first improvement, however, was the installation of an automatic sprinkler system, which was fitted throughout the mill complex by Mather and Platt Ltd in 1902. Each sprinkler had an automatic heat-sensitive valve, which opened independently in the event of fire to discharge water and immediately sounded an automatic alarm, which was placed on the ground floor in Bay **12** of the Murray Street block. The supply of water to this system was via the mains supply beneath Murray Street, whilst tanks placed on top of the New Mill stair tower and the roof of the Bengal Street block provided the required head of water for the sprinklers.

Reducing the Capacity of the Spinning Mills

The most significant structural alterations to the complex during this period was the reduction in height of the spinning mills; Old and Decker Mill was reduced to seven storeys in height, and New Mill to six storeys (Fig 51). Surprisingly, this engineering feat is undocumented, and its rationale is therefore speculative. It is unlikely to have been for economic purposes, however, as the Lancashire cotton industry was expanding rapidly in the first years of the twentieth century (*Ch 5, p 88*), suggesting that the reduction in capacity was necessitated by structural considerations; around 100 years after their construction, the buildings were probably struggling to bear the load of increasingly heavy machinery. Indeed, there is evidence of strain on the upper surviving floor of New Mill, where the majority of the slender cruciform-section columns exhibit deflection to the north near their feet.

In both mills the trusses were reused during the reduction in height, although in Old and Decker Mill their repositioning was not in the same order, as shown by the discrepancies in the numbering of assembly marks (*Phase 2, p 107*). Relocating the trusses as complete entities in New Mill produced an extra horizontal beam, as the uppermost ceiling beam remained *in situ*. In the majority of bays, the solution was the same as that used in Old and Decker Mill, with short timber posts, at one third span points, propping the truss tie beam from the ceiling beam below. It is noteworthy in these truss types that the propping posts (or puncheons) sit directly on the floor beams of the fifth floor, demonstrating that the roofspace retained a floor, and also that the trusses could be repositioned with minimal disturbance to the floor below.

It is probable that further alterations to the majority of the roof trusses in New Mill were undertaken concurrently with their relocation to the fifth floor. Within each truss, the original queen struts were cut away, flush with the collar, and replaced with cast-iron

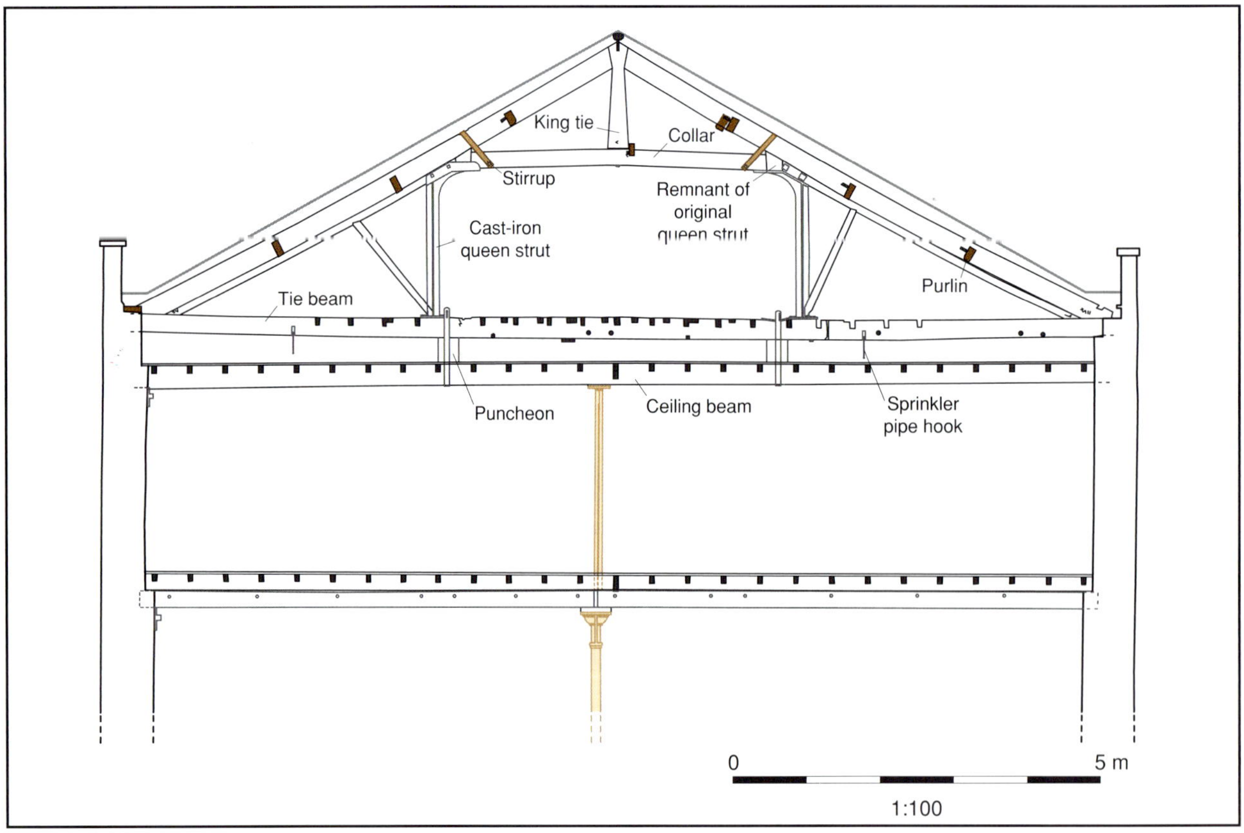

Figure 52: Remodelled truss, New Mill

Plate 137: Installation of a tramway on Union Street in 1903, showing the reduced height of Old and Decker Mill (reproduced courtesy of Manchester Archives and Local Studies)

struts that were set at a slightly wider spacing of 16 ft (4.88 m). Each strut comprises a single cast member, formed in cruciform-section (Fig 52).

On the majority of the reused trusses, eye-bolts survived, with attached hooks for supporting horizontal pipes associated with the automatic sprinkler system. These were similar to those on all floors below, and carried water to the sprinklers at ceiling level throughout both mills. Within both roof spaces many of the hooks hang to floor level, rendering them redundant, and demonstrating that the trusses were repositioned after the installation of the automatic sprinkler system. A photograph of Old and Decker Mill, taken in 1903, during the installation of the tramway along Union Street (Pl 137), clearly shows the mill as a seven-storeyed structure, dating the reduction in height to between the installation of the sprinkler system in 1902 and the photograph of 1903. Although no similar evidence exists for New Mill, which was reduced in height by two storeys, an engraving of A & G Murray's mills, published by the FCSDA in 1909 (*Ch 5, Pl 87*), shows the building to have been reduced before that date. During this remodelling, the western wall was reduced by one storey less than the others to produce a gable end, as opposed to the earlier hipped form of the roof. The windows within this gable wall were blocked within the new roofspace, although in both mills a framework of battens at collar level imply that suspended ceilings were added, suggesting the use of the attic space as storage (Pl 138).

Plate 138: Roof space, Old Mill

Electrification

Another important modification undertaken by the new association was the electrification of the mills. Electricity for lighting purposes had been introduced into cotton mills in the late nineteenth century, and was widespread in the larger mills by the 1890s (Williams and Farnie 1992, 119). The introduction of electric drive, however, was slightly later, and its adoption in the Murrays' complex was probably associated with the construction of New Little Mill, which was completed as a replacement for Little Mill in 1909 (*Ch 5, p 89*). This new mill employed group-drive motors, which were probably supplied with electricity from the sub-station adjacent to the Bengal Street block, and the cables routed via the tunnel beneath Bengal Street. The use of electric drive in New Little Mill was evidently a success, as the technology was applied to the main complex shortly afterwards, although the steam-powered rope drive in New Mill appears to have continued in use until at least 1926 (Building Control Plan 17927).

Infilling of the Canal Basin

By the early years of the twentieth century, the canal basin had been abandoned and infilled with clinker and brick rubble. It is shown on the Ordnance Survey plan of 1891, although it is marked as a 'reservoir' rather than a 'canal basin' as it had been on earlier maps, hinting that canal traffic entering the mill complex had ceased by this date. The fire services' plan of 1902 (MLSU MC/3834M/892) indicates the basin had been filled in, although the canal link apparently still contained water in August 1930 (Building Control Plan 20366).

Internal Remodelling of the Spinning Mills

The reduction in height of the buildings appears to have coincided with a programme of internal strengthening within Old, Decker, and New Mills, further suggesting its cause was structural. The detail differs between the two buildings, in that there was a much greater replacement of columns in New Mill but, whilst many of the original timber ceiling beams were removed from Old and Decker Mill and replaced with steel I-section beams, those in New Mill were simply strengthened with supporting steelwork. The I-section beams are unlikely to have been installed before 1890 and, in the absence of the British Steel mark, the sections were probably rolled before 1932. The supporting steelwork for the original timber beams in New Mill was in the form of two channel-section beams flitched onto either side of the original member. An 'LSW' stamp was present on the majority, the rolling mark of Leeds Steelworks, which was producing steel sections between 1888 and 1928 (Donald Insall Associates and Structural Perspectives 2002).

In New Mill, the columns from the basement to the third floor were replaced with hollow cylindrical double-flanged columns, similar to those used in the construction of New Little Mill in 1909. On the third floor the caps directly supported the ceiling beams, whilst on the floors below the caps formed the base of load-transfer boxes, which formed the feet of the columns above. On the ground to third floors the columns were of 5 in (0.13 m) section, whilst the taller columns in the basement were of 8 in (0.20 m) section. The basement columns were supported on concrete bases, similar in size to the sandstone examples used during the earlier column replacement in Old and Decker Mill. It is noteworthy that the load-transfer boxes associated with the replaced columns easily accommodate the additional steelwork, suggesting that this was a contemporary project. The central three bays of Old and Decker Mill also had replacement columns, demonstrating that electricity had replaced the need for gas supply. These central three bays were higher on the fifth, now the top, floor, with several transverse RSJs running across the central bay. These appear to have housed the top brackets of four steel ropes, which ran vertically through the building to the basement, with bearing boxes visible in the ceiling in Decker Mill.

Other Improvements

A cage hoist was added to the eastern end of the northern elevation of New Mill during this phase (Fig 53), and is first shown on a deposited building plan of April 1909 (Building Control Plan 3331). A doorway in its northern face, at street level, has a concrete lintel bearing the inscription 'Jersey House', with a projecting

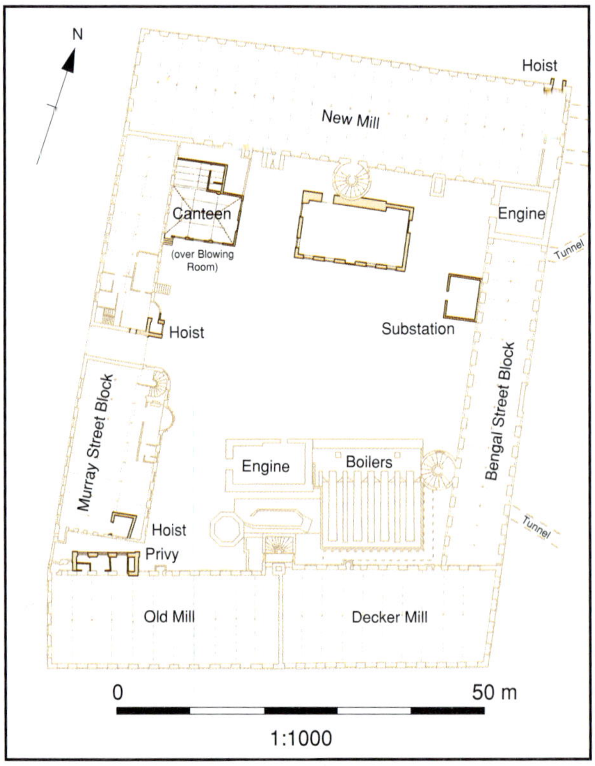

Figure 53: Site plan, Phase 6

concrete canopy and flat roof. This probably marked the first external access into the complex, since the courtyard was completed, that was not controlled through the gatehouse in the Murray Street block.

The addition of the hoist appears to relate to changes in the eastern end of the basement, and was probably associated with the erection of New Little Mill in 1909 (*Ch 5, pp 89-90*). The plan of 1902 (MLSU MC/3834M/892) shows a single tunnel between the basement of New Mill and Little Mill but, during the rebuilding, an additional tunnel was added, shown clearly on the deposited building plan of 1926 (Building Control Plan 17927). The new tunnel appears to have been directly linked to the cage hoist. Also in the early twentieth century, a much larger toilet block was added onto the eastern side of the existing privy tower on the northern side of Old Mill. The privy tower also had a personnel passage at first floor level into the southern end of the Murray Street block.

The deposited building plan of 1926 details the conversion of the upper floor of the New Mill engine house into a first aid room and office, with new access from immediately to the west of the stair tower, and two new windows in the western gable. Annotations on an associated section through the building describe the basement as a 'waste cellar' (*ibid*). The proposals appear not to have been quickly undertaken, as the 1927 revision of Goad's Insurance Plans describe the structure as 'Bobbin store....waste basement...2 [storey] + basement'. The internal partition in the first floor was also installed, suggesting that the Phase 6 engine house hoist went out of use at this time, although both survived to the abandonment of the structure in the late twentieth century (Pl 139).

It is uncertain precisely when the engine house servicing Old and Decker Mill went out of use for its intended purpose, although this is likely to have occurred during

Plate 139: New Mill engine house in 1986 (© Crown Copyright NMR)

the early twentieth century. It is shown to have been in service on the fire services plan of 1902, but had been removed by 1930, when a deposited building plan (Building Control Plan 20244) shows the engine house as having been converted to warehousing. The conversion of the building, which presumably resulted from the adoption of electrically-driven motors in Old and Decker Mill, included the insertion of two new concrete internal floor levels. The western gable was also remodelled into a loophole, with the insertion of full-height taking-in doors to each floor (Pl 140). A dormer roof was also added at the top of the elevation, housing an electric hoist. Whilst the engine house changed in function during this period, the associated Lancashire boilers remained in operation until the 1950s for the purpose of heating the mill complex (*Ch 5, p 91*).

Plate 140: Hoist doorways, west elevation, Old and Decker Mill engine house

Within the Murray Street block, an L-shaped single-storey building was constructed over the Blowing Room, in accordance with design plans approved in 1924 (Building Control Plan 16604). The new building was intended as a canteen, and its construction partially blocked many of the sash windows in the eastern elevation of the ground floor of the Murray Street block. The window frames were retained internally, whilst the window in Bay **19** was remodelled into a doorway.

Evidence within the surviving fabric for early twentieth-century activity within the Bengal Street block relates to the reduction in height of the structure to two storeys. A proposal to reduce the height was submitted in August 1930 (Building Control Plan 20558), and it would appear that large angled buttresses were constructed against Decker Mill at the southern end of the block during this work. A timber-framed hoist at lower ground floor level by the southern elevation probably relates to this phase. It provided a means of movement for materials between the lower ground floor and the basement of Decker Mill, which is *c* 4 ft (1.23 m) lower. The insertion of the hoist signifies the disuse of the horizontal shaft associated with the large mounting blocks for the earlier Phase 5 power-transmission system.

Several later alterations were carried out to the north of the archway through the Murray Street block. A hoist tower was added on the eastern elevation, its western side being partially formed by the original east wall of the Murray Street block. External access was afforded to the hoist at all levels, although the upper storey was completely removed at a later date.

Other alterations at this date included the installation of a new hoist crane, and the insertion of a weighbridge under the archway. The weighbridge, supplied by the local Manchester firm of William Hodgson, was installed within the cobbled surface of the entrance, with access to the below-ground mechanism provided from the basement to the north. A wide window and door were inserted into the elevation to the south of the weighbridge, creating a weighhouse. A hoist above the archway had double-battened flap doors inserted into the floor, opened by chains secured to the floor on either side.

Further hoist alterations were undertaken at the southern end of the Murray Street block, with the replacement of the stair in the south-east corner of Bay **1** (*Phase 4*). The work, according to a plaque within the cage, was undertaken by William Wadsworth of Bolton, in 1932. The orientation of the hoist was altered, with the external access blocked, and internal apertures all opening into the western face of the shaft. The eastern part of the earlier stairwell became redundant, and was partitioned from the retained shaft, with a personnel tunnel inserted at second-floor level, into the broadly contemporary privy tower of Old Mill. A small rectangular tower with a flat roof was inserted above the shaft, cutting the original hipped roof (Pl 141). At ground-floor level, within the Phase 4 extension on the eastern side of the Murray Street block, a straight timber stair was inserted, across the windows, to afford access to the first floor. This may reflect changes in the use of the hoist in Bay **1**, which may previously have been used to travel between the ground and first floors, as no other access appears to have been provided between these floors.

Plate 141: Hoist tower projecting above the Murray Street block roof

Plate 142: South-facing elevation of New Mill, showing late hoist platforms in Bays **16** *and* **17**

Towards the latter part of this phase, steelwork pertaining to two hoists was added to the southern elevation of New Mill in Bays **6** and **17**. Both comprised I-section steel beams, projecting through the elevation on either side of the original window apertures, with a similar beam projecting from the bay to the east, forming an external hoist platform (Pl 142). The hoist in Bay **6** accessed the structure on the fourth floor only, whilst that in Bay **17** serviced the first to fourth floors.

Phase 7, The End of Spinning (*c* 1947 - 1950s)

There is no definitive date at which cotton-spinning at A & G Murray's Mill ceased; the individual structures were rented out and sold in a piecemeal fashion during the final years of ownership by the FCSDA (*Ch 5, p 91*). During this period, several structural alterations were implemented to the mills, and some minor additions were made to the complex (Fig 54).

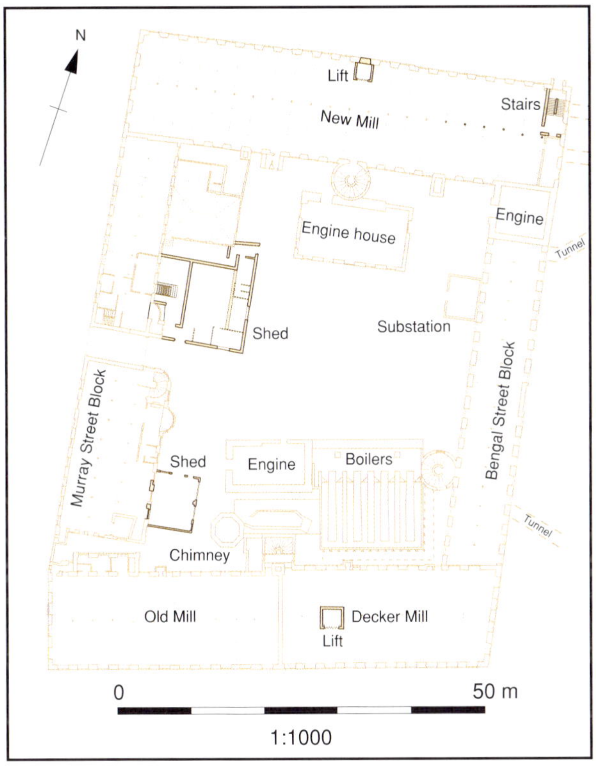

Figure 54: Site plan, Phase 7

A deposited building plan, submitted in 1948 (Building Control Plans 28486), proposed the addition of an internal lift shaft to Decker Mill, together with strengthening work in the basement. The lift had loading doors on the ground floor, with separate stair access from Redhill (formerly Union) Street. Access was further improved by the insertion of correspondingly larger doorways onto Redhill Street on the ground floor, and double-doorways between Old and Decker Mill were also inserted on each floor. A further lift shaft, in the northern part of Bay **12** of New Mill, is undated, but the similarity in style and materials would suggest that it was broadly contemporary.

Another deposited building plan, dated 14 March 1950, proposed the conversion of the Phase 6 hoist and former rope race within New Mill to a stair tower (Building Control Plan 30000). The access from Jersey Street was retained, and was the reason for the siting of the stairs in this position, affording access to all floors directly from outside the mill. A new stairwell was also inserted into the basement of Old and Decker Mill, adjacent to a new loading door in the eastern bay of Old Mill. This represented a change in delivery point to the mill, reflecting the multiple occupancy of the building at this time.

Several small structures, now demolished, were added to the eastern side of the Murray Street block, including a single-storey building referred to as an 'Air Raid Shelter' on a deposited building plan of 1950 (Building Control Plan 30059). Its appearance and construction technique, however, appeared most unsuitable for the purpose of an air raid shelter, especially as government guidelines concerning air raid shelter construction (*Colliery Guardian* 1939) suggested the preferred use of basements.

Phase 8, The Final Days (Post-1950s)

The final phase of commercial activity relates to the second half of the twentieth century. The most significant alteration to the complex was the removal of the upper two storeys of the northern part of the Murray Street block, with the addition of a flat roof to the ground floor (Fig 55). It is not clear exactly when this was undertaken, but it is shown as a four-storeyed structure on a Land Registry plan of 1950, prior to being sold by the FCSDA Ltd to Fred Beech & Co Ltd in December 1950 (RCHME and GMAU 1989).

Structural changes to the engine house serving Old and Decker Mill during this period relate to the insertion of toilet facilities. These were placed against the north elevation, and necessitated the shortening of the internal wall to allow the positioning of cubicles alongside the wall. Rectangular casement windows were inserted into the northern elevation on the first and second floors to light and ventilate these toilets. Partitions within the eastern end of the third floor appear to relate to offices associated with this late usage.

It is not known when the Lancashire boilers were removed, although the building was still standing in 1985 (RCHME and GMAU 1989), by which date it was being used as a receptacle for waste materials, including cloth cut-offs; it had been finally demolished by 1990. The external privy tower at the southern end of the Murray Street block was also removed after 1950, providing a further access point into the courtyard. Large timber gates were installed on a brick buttress added to the southern end of western elevation.

Further fires during the 1990s caused significant structural damage to the ground floor of New Mill,

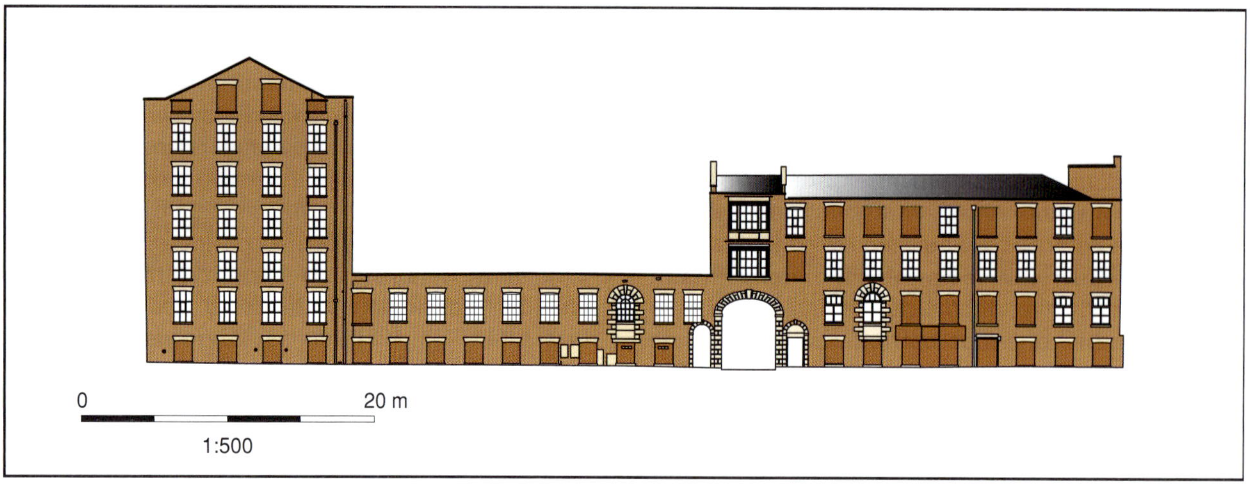

Figure 55: West-facing elevation of the Murray Street block in Phase 8

particularly towards the eastern end, and the majority of the Bengal Street block was demolished following a fire in 1996. Fire has always been a significant threat to the textile industry, with highly combustible materials being utilised alongside power-transmission systems. In the later history of these structures, however, the risk of arson has become an equal threat, as the abandoned buildings became landmarks of the rapid economic and social decline in the industrial areas of Manchester, as in most other industrial cities in the country. After the abandonment of the buildings towards the end of the twentieth century, a final act of blocking entrances to secure the building was undertaken. In addition, all the cellar-lights around the complex were sealed with clinker block, each aperture retaining brick vents. This work was funded by English Heritage in an attempt to reduce the rate of decay of the buildings, and the boards were painted externally in North West Development Agency colours (Pl 142).

7

A & G MURRAY'S MILL: THE MAJOR REPAIR PROJECT

Ken Moth

Background

It is perhaps self-evident that the historic environment is of fundamental importance to society. This importance has been established by numerous recent investigations and surveys, encompassing social, cultural, and economic benefits (*eg* DCMS 2001). In the immediate post-war period the historic environment was generally disregarded in the formulation of development strategies, but today a much more informed and rigorous approach is in place (DoE 1994), following many significant losses. In the post-war years, A & G Murray's Mill could easily have become one of these losses.

The Ancoats Buildings Preservation Trust (ABPT) first became involved with the Murrays' Mill in 1997. Two years later, a design team containing an array of professionals including architects, structural engineers, building services engineers, cost consultants, health and safety advisors, archaeologists, and architectural historians, was appointed for technical input and advice. Specialist contractors were required at an early stage to provide technical data, including measured surveys, contamination surveys, fungal and insect infestation surveys, materials testing, geotechnical surveys, and analysis. Finally, building contractors, sub-contractors, and suppliers were appointed to implement the proposals. Following a competitive selection and tendering process, Building Design Partnership (BDP) was appointed as project architect, structural engineer, and design team leader.

Conservation and adaptive reuse of historic sites and buildings remains a demanding area, which is in part due to a limited skills base in the design and construction fields. The process of conserving and adapting historic buildings is expensive. Apart from achieving social and cultural benefits, this expense can be justified by creating commercial value. Experience has shown that converted historic buildings become valuable assets, and this value extends to surrounding sites and buildings of previously low value. There are cases where the pioneering projects require financial subsidy, but this requirement declines as investors gain confidence. The key to successful projects is therefore to retain the significance of historic sites and buildings whilst creating value.

The process of securing the long-term repair of A & G Murray's Mill, and the adaptation of the component buildings to make them suitable for new uses, can be broken down into stages:

1. Understanding the buildings;
2. Preparing outline proposals;
3. Securing funding;
4. Preparing detailed proposals;
5. Obtaining statutory consents;
6. Identifying and selecting contractors and sub-contractors;
7. Administering the construction contract.

The first principle in the conservation and adaptive reuse of historic buildings is to understand fully the site and buildings. This understanding must cover the history of the site and buildings, why and how they were built, how they were used, and why they are significant. The process of research and analysis forms part of a *Conservation Plan*, a document which sets out the history and significance of a site, establishes the issues which will affect the future of that site, and the policies necessary to address the issues whilst protecting significance. Understanding must also be gained on the physical nature of the site and buildings, how they were constructed, and how they have been altered both by human intervention and by processes of weathering, ageing, and decay. This is established by physical investigation on site and laboratory investigation off-site. Finally, understanding must cover the potential future uses of the site and buildings, how these uses can be met, and how any deficiencies in the building fabric can be overcome. The *Conservation Plan* for the Murrays' Mill was prepared by Donald Insall Associates and Structural Perspectives Limited, and was completed in January 2002.

Physical Investigation and Surveys

Investigation begins with the procurement of a detailed measured survey of the buildings, which provides the design team with an accurate set of plans, sections, and elevations of the site and buildings as they stand. The surveys serve many purposes, and the drawings form the basis of archaeological recording and evaluation, helping archaeologists to understand, for example, how machinery was laid out, how power was transmitted from the engine houses to the production machinery, and where historic fixtures and artefacts are located.

The measured survey of A & G Murray's Mill provided detailed information on levels and alignments. Spot levels at close centres were given for floors, roofs, and soffits, and contour elevations showing deviation from true vertical were provided (Fig 56). Analysis of this information showed weaknesses in the overall building shape and structure, as well as identifying local areas of failure. In particular, it demonstrated that there was very little connectivity between floors and walls, and between roofs and walls. This, combined with the open-plan nature of the buildings, meant that they lacked stiffness and restraint to the extent that some walls had distorted to a point close to collapse.

Structural Issues

All the buildings in the Murrays' complex rely on the external walls to support both the internal floor construction and roofs, and are therefore load-bearing. Overall building stability is predominantly reliant on the configuration of these masonry elements. Old and Decker Mill and New Mill are tall structures with a rectangular footprint and have a relatively low lateral stiffness, and hence are weaker across the narrow width of the building in comparison with their length. The original internal structure of these mills comprised timber beams spanning across the width of the buildings, supported at one-third span by cruciform-section cast-iron columns. In the early nineteenth century, new machinery required a

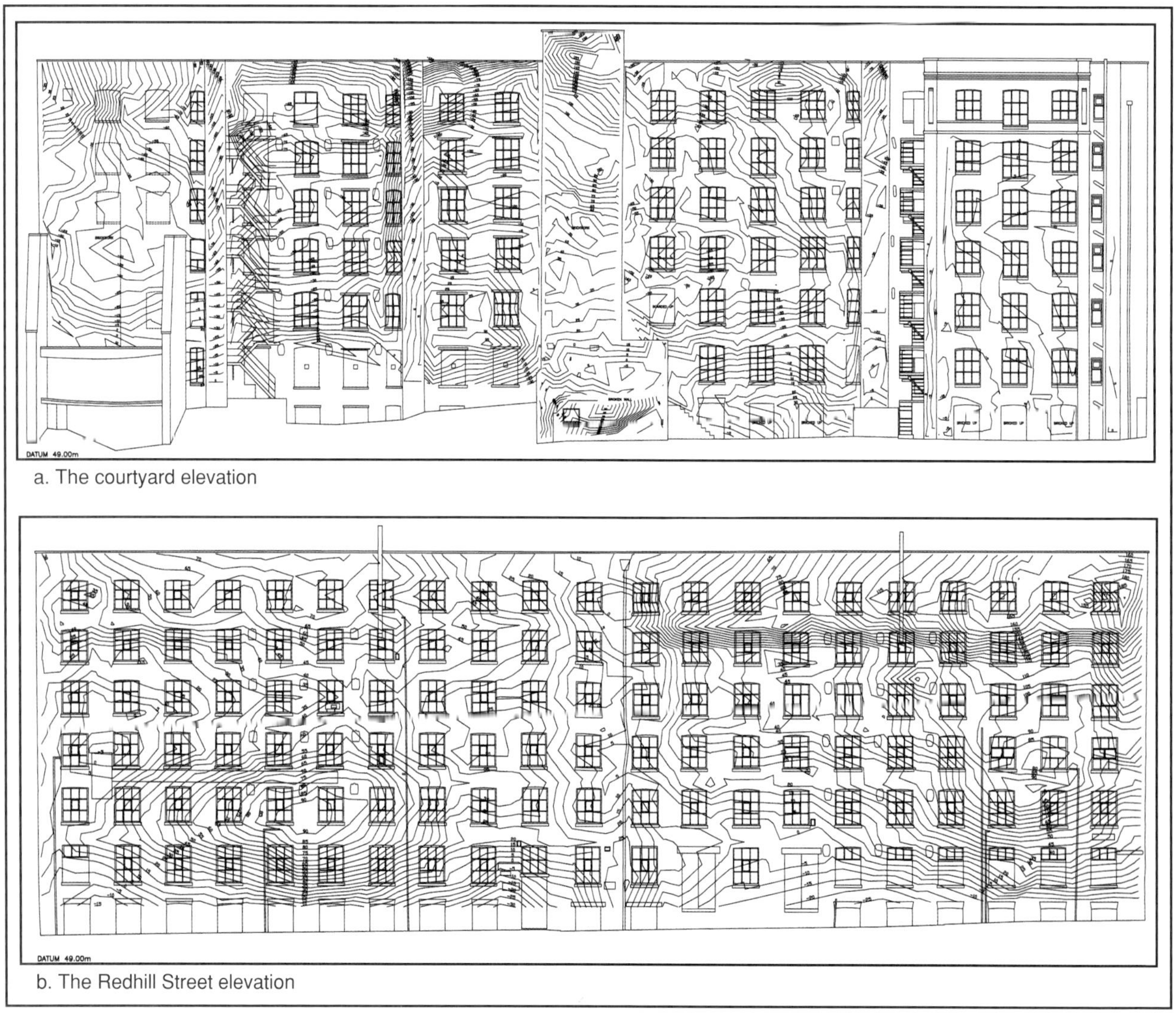

a. The courtyard elevation

b. The Redhill Street elevation

Figure 56: Contour elevations of Old and Decker Mill

wider column spacing, and so new cylindrical cast-iron columns were introduced at mid-span and the original columns at third points of the span were removed (*Ch 6, pp 117-20*). The new columns supported large cast-iron cantilever brackets, intended to give maximum support to the timber beams. The beams were over-stressed, however, and over time many of them failed and were replaced by steel beams. This was an ongoing process which, in Old and Decker Mill, resulted in a variety of columns and beams of varying dates, including some original timber beams and early circular columns. In parts of Decker Mill, replacement columns were not in true vertical alignment, producing eccentric loading. All the columns in New Mill, however, with the exception of the top floor, were replaced in a single exercise during the twentieth century (*Ch 6, p 136*), giving the building a robust structure capable of meeting office loading requirements.

Examination of the cast-iron columns in Old and Decker Mill showed that many were of poor quality. The columns had been cast in sand, the process involving the use of wooden cores to give the hollow section. In poor castings the core rises to the top of the mold during the casting process, giving an asymmetric section: a thick column wall on one side, and a thin column wall on the other side, substantially lowering the load-carrying capacity of the column.

Calculation of the load-carrying capacity of the existing Old and Decker Mill structure produced much lower figures than anticipated, falling short in some areas from even domestic floor loading. The BCSA publication *Historical Structural Steelwork Handbook* (1984) refers to an investigation of the load-carrying capacity of textile mills carried out in 1945, which also produced surprisingly low figures. This was explained by the lightweight nature of original spinning mules, which were timber-framed and, as a result of the drawing action of the thread by the carriage, covered a relatively large floor area. As larger and heavier iron-framed mules were installed, both column spacing and floor loading were increased, compounding the inherent weakness of the buildings.

Trial pits revealed that large parts of the complex were built without foundations. Walls rose directly from trench bottoms without any widening of the wall base. In Old Mill the wall bases were shallow, but as the later buildings were constructed, foundations became deeper. Geotechnical investigation of the clay-bearing strata showed that the clay was at the limit of its shear strength, and any increase in loading would have caused the bearing strata to subside (BDP and OA North 2007).

Decay of the building fabric, poor and failed structural framing, and inadequate tying of the structure inevitably led to distortions of the masonry and, in some cases, failure. Localised failures, particular above window heads, were associated with failure of brick arches and decay of embedded timber and metal elements (Pl 143).

Plate 143: Structural failure in the Murray Street block

In addition to the loads from floors and roofs, the buildings had also been subjected to external forces. These included loading from wind, environmental pollution, and expansion and contraction in response to temperature changes over many decades. The buildings were generally constructed from materials which had been reasonably tolerant of this exposure, considering their age. Nevertheless, it was evident that large sections of building fabric were at risk until repairs were completed (Pl 144). A series of invasive investigations of the masonry was undertaken, including the drilling of small-diameter holes through the piers to establish if any large voids were also present. Several brick headers were removed from both the external and internal elevations to establish the extent and adequacy of bonding of the masonry. These were subjected to laboratory analysis, which included brick compressive strengths, and mix constituents and sulphate content of the mortar.

An assessment of overall building stability showed that the central wall between Old and Decker Mill provided significant building stiffness (*ie* it acts as a shear wall). The gable walls also act as shear walls, but they are perforated by fenestration and, whilst they attract fewer loads, they are predominantly the weakest element. In the case of New Mill, significant stiffness is provided by the external central stair tower and engine house. There, the gable wall arrangement and function is similar to Old and Decker Mill.

The floors are important in that they provide a diaphragm for the loads to be transferred to the shear walls. The floors span perpendicularly on to the gable walls, the only floor tie to the gable wall being by

Plate 144: The canteen in 2003

friction between the floor joists and masonry. The friction tie force provided was minimal since the buildings were empty and consequently were not loaded. In most cases the walls had moved away from the floors, leaving a gap and reduced joist bearing. The window head and cill construction between piers was poor, and consequently distortions had occurred.

An assessment of the verticality survey revealed similar patterns of distortion on most elevations (Fig 56). The masonry elevations had been subjected to thermal and moisture movement over a considerable time. No movement joints were provided in the masonry walls, and consequently distortions were largest in areas of least restraint. In addition to this expansion process, there were localised distortions and damage attributed directly to either structural failure of other elements or by the action of wind loading.

An assessment of the most significant distortion profile on each elevation was undertaken, which showed the horizontal forces that had to be transferred by the floor diaphragm to the shear walls. In the majority of cases adequate tying of the floors to the walls was all that was required.

There were, however, several areas that needed bespoke solutions to address more significant failures. In most cases there was clear evidence of the damage and distortion. In other cases further investigations were required on site to understand the mode of failure and the necessary repair.

1. There was a large vertical crack located beneath the roof hip on the upper two storeys of the east gable of Old and Decker Mill. Inspection within the roof showed that the dragon tie and hip structure were producing significant horizontal forces that had moved the wall outward.

2. The upper two storeys of the southern elevation of Decker Mill had distortions which were not attributable wholly to expansion forces, and the magnitude and pattern of the distortions were of concern. The piers internally, approximately 700 mm above the top floor, had cracked horizontally, and, in some cases, the upper section of the pier had sheared outward. The building in this area had undergone significant alteration; not only had the building been reduced in height, but also the internal framing had been altered to provide strengthened bays for ceiling-hung machinery. The tying of the floors and roof were also factors, as was the construction of various piers, which required further investigation.

3. The west gable wall of New Mill had significant distortion, which was attributed to an inadequate tie to the floors. The top storey and gable pike leaned significantly into the building. This was due in part to the failure of the primary roof construction adjacent to the gable, and perhaps exacerbated by the re-roofing and introduction of a new lift structure in the early part of the twentieth century. Calculation of the horizontal forces demonstrated that transfer of these loads by the timber floors was inadequate.

4. The west elevation of the Murray Street block showed large distortions of the masonry in the basement storey. This was not the case in the larger buildings, and was attributed both to the ability of the walls to resist the retained material, and sliding of the base of the wall at founding level.

5. The distortion of the west wall of the Murray Street block was due primarily to expansion forces in the brickwork. The magnitude of the movement, however, had been exacerbated by the basement and foundation problem described above.

Fabric Decay

The buildings had slated roofs with lead parapet gutters, which had been repaired several times during the 200-year life of the mill. As the site decreased in value, low grade and more sporadic repair processes were adopted. Eventually, both slating and gutters were coated in scrim-reinforced bitumen. This short-lived repair precluded the future reuse of the roofing materials, and made

Plate 145: Rainwater pooling on the top floor of Decker Mill

leak detection more difficult. Material failure and structural movement had led to widespread roof failure, and consequent rainwater and moisture ingress. In Decker Mill, rainwater ponded on the floors at upper levels, eventually trickling down to basement level (Pl 145).

A primary cause of building decay is usually fungal infestation, commonly termed 'wet rot' and 'dry rot'. Fungal spores are present in the air, and given the appropriate moisture conditions will inevitably germinate and develop into established fungi, rotting timber to the point of failure and disintegration. Comprehensive investigation of the timber showed widespread infestation in New Mill, which had been unoccupied for many years, with lesser but serious infestation in other parts of the complex. Decay was most widespread at upper-floor levels, affecting truss and beam bearings, lintels, and wall plates. This had then spread to joists and floorboards, and several truss ends had collapsed. Some had been propped, others were held by the composite action of adjoining members. Large areas of flooring in New Mill were unsafe even for foot traffic, with propped beam ends, failed joists, and decayed boards. Many timber lintels and wall plates had also failed.

Examination of the external brickwork faces revealed a variety of conditions. On north- and east-facing elevations the brickwork was generally in good condition, with large areas of original pointing still sound and intact. Raking out joints for the full depth of the brick revealed no change in mortar from front to back of the bed, rather than the easily detectable change when joints have been repointed. On south- and west-facing elevations, the brickwork was more weathered. Unfortunately, large areas had been repointed in cement mortar, which accelerates brickwork decay, and causes internal dampness by restricting moisture evaporation on the external wall face. This in turn had led to areas of brickwork being painted with bituminous and cementitious paints to reduce internal dampness, but in fact having the reverse effect.

Client Brief

The commission from ABPT to the design team was to carry out the permanent repair of the buildings only, incorporating any necessary enhancements to facilitate their future use. Following the repair works, the buildings would then be acquired by a developer, converted, and fitted out for their chosen new uses. Whilst the new uses were not known at this preliminary stage, it was decided to base the repair works on either office or residential uses. This gave an imposed loading requirement for the repairs of 3.5 k N/m^2.

Whilst the *Building Regulations* set standards of construction for new buildings, they acknowledge that a different approach is needed for historic buildings. Here the intent is to come as close as is reasonably practicable to meeting the requirements of the regulations without adversely impacting upon the historic significance of the buildings. The key issues to be addressed in this regard were the structural integrity of the buildings, their thermal performance, particularly with regard to roof insulation, and the acoustic and thermal performance of replacement windows. These were considered to be areas of work which had to be addressed at the repair stage rather than the conversion stage to avoid abortive work.

Conservation Strategy

The *Conservation Plan* established that the mill complex and its component buildings were heritage assets of national significance, and that their significance lay in their form, layout, structure, and materials (Donald Insall and Structural Perspectives 2002). In discussion with the design team, the authors of the *Conservation Plan* set down an agreed *Conservation Strategy*, which can be summarised as follows:

- retain the maximum amount of historic fabric;
- repair primary structures so that each element serves its designated function and original load paths are followed where possible;
- repair building fabric on a like-for-like basis using matching materials and techniques, amplified where necessary with modern techniques to achieve the necessary performance requirements;

- reinstate missing elements where this can be done without conjecture within the cost constraints set down by the available funding;

- provide appropriate new elements where retention or reinstatement of the original would be incompatible with securing a long-term viable future for the complex;

- retain all fixtures, fittings and artefacts of archaeological significance as defined by the *Conservation Plan* and the appointed archaeologist.

As repair options for each element of the building fabric were investigated, the *Conservation Strategy* was used to assess these options. It was a specific objective of the project that each element of the historic structure and fabric should fulfil its original design function to its safe capacity. Where this left a shortfall in performance, new elements were carefully added to pick up that shortfall. This was in preference to replacing inadequate historic components with new components. The results were that most of the historic fabric present at the start of the project is still there and continues to serve its original purpose. Where new fabric has been introduced, for example replacement timber or cast-iron rainwater goods, these are stamped 'ABPT 2005'.

Scope

The project involved the repair of the standing buildings, namely Old and Decker Mill, New Mill, the Murray Street block, Old Mill Engine House, New Mill Engine House, and the Canteen and Blowing House. The chimney had been repaired previously and was not included in the scope of works.

The *Conservation Plan* called for the reinstatement of a building on the site of the Bengal Street block, although this did not form part of the shell repair works for two reasons. Firstly, it was felt that the nature of this building required the input of the selected developer (although recommendations governing its size and footprint are set out in the *Conservation Plan*). Secondly, the Heritage Lottery Fund was not able to contribute to the construction of a new building in this instance. The *Conservation Plan* called for the reinstatement of the missing upper storeys of the Murray Street block. This was included within the scope of the works, and was completed to a design based on historic illustrations, photographs, and archaeological evidence (Pl 146).

The reinstatement of the canal basin was also included within the scope of the shell repair works. The reinstatement of the canal tunnel which linked the canal basin to the Rochdale Canal was investigated by ABPT, but was not included within the scope of works because the ownership of the tunnel was not known, and therefore the necessary funding could not be provided by the Heritage Lottery Fund. The repair project involved the demolition of three small buildings: an air raid shelter; a garage; and a porch, all post-1940 structures of little historical value.

Plate 146: The Murray Street block in 2006, showing the reinstated upper storeys

Cleaning

A decision was taken to clean the interior of the building to remove accumulated layers of lime wash, which was in poor condition and seen to be an inappropriate finish for intended new uses. It was also decided to clean exterior masonry, both to remove harmful bituminous and cementitious paint, and to signify the regeneration of the area. Careful trials were carried out in each case to identify the most effective and least damaging cleaning techniques.

Sequence

A requirement of the contract was that the buildings should be fully scaffolded and provided with temporary roofs (Pl 147). As with most conservation projects, no scaffold fixings were to be made into the historic walls, and this, together with the temporary roof, required extensive scaffold tie members running across the building at the topmost floor level.

Plate 147: Scaffolding over the mills during the repair works

Foundations

It was anticipated that the new uses of the building would create significant additional loads on the bearing strata. As these were already at shear strength capacity, it was necessary to increase the width of column and wall footings to remain within the bearing strata shear capacity. Often this is achieved by underpinning wall and column bases, but this option was discounted at the Murrays' complex as there was restricted access to the wall bases on the street-side elevations of the building, and also because of the risks involved in undermining the wall bases. The chosen option was to cast ground beams alongside the existing walls at basement level (Pl 148). Concrete spine beams were cast at the same level, linking the isolated and inadequate column foundations. These beams were dowelled into the existing wall bases and column levels. In addition, concrete tie beams were cast linking the ground beams and spine beams to add a degree of robustness and counteract thrust forces at the wall bases. In this way substantial new foundations

Plate 148: Installing cast ground beams in the basement of Decker Mill

were provided with minimal impact on the historic fabric, whilst adding to the rigidity of the buildings.

Structural Frame

The structural frame in New Mill required little repair or enhancement. In contrast, the structural frame in Old and Decker Mill needed extensive work. In these buildings, 61 of the 133 original timber main floor beams survived. These were single timbers of modest section (average 150 x 320 mm) spanning the entire width of the building, and not capable of carrying the proposed new floor loadings. Strengthening proposals were complicated by the presence of the large faced-fixed cast-iron cantilever brackets installed when the original columns had been replaced in the nineteenth century (*Ch 5, pp 117-9*). The adopted solution was to expose the top face of the beams by carefully removing the floorboards above them. A deep slot was then cut into the beams along their centreline, running from the external wall of the building to the central column position. This slot was cut by a chainsaw held in guide rails to ensure trueness and accuracy. Steel T-section beams were inserted into this slot and fixed to the beams using a polyester resin grout. The result is a composite timber and steel beam, the size of the steel element calculated to make up the shortfall in the load-bearing capacity of the timber element.

Many of the cast-iron columns supporting these beams were also inadequate, largely due to variations in

Plate 149 : Additional columns in Decker Mill

their wall thickness. Columns were surveyed for wall thickness using a small-diameter drill at the top, middle, and bottom of the column, and their capacity was then determined by calculation. Where columns were found to be inadequate, the chosen solution was to add new columns to take up the shortfall in carrying capacity at each position. Various configurations of new column were modelled and assessed, ranging from a single new column, two new columns, and four new columns of decreasing size adjacent to each inadequate original column. The chosen solution was two new columns, offset close to the original column to permit vertical continuity and on the opposite face of the beam to the cast-iron cantilever brackets (Pl 149). Steel gusset plates connect each column to the top face of the inverted steel T-beam embedded in the original timber beams. In this way the original columns continue to carry the original beams, and the new columns carry the load from the embedded T-beams.

In Decker Mill columns installed in the early twentieth century were out of vertical alignment, and the steel beams they supported were also out of line. This resulted in eccentric loading of the columns, and again a shortfall in required carrying capacity. It was therefore necessary to realign these columns and beams.

A survey was undertaken to determine the relative misalignment at each floor level. The existing floors were propped through the building to remove the load on the affected columns and beams, and the ends of misaligned beams were released from the external walls to allow rotation to bring the beams into line with the columns. A sequence of hydraulic jacking of each tier of columns was employed from top down to allow realignment of columns and beams. This exercise proved to be very straightforward, and was achieved in a much shorter timescale than originally envisaged.

Suspended Floors

Many existing floor joists throughout the mill complex were undersized and of poor quality. Here the solution was to provide new supplementary joists alongside existing inadequate joists. Where appropriate, the existing joists were compounded with the new joists to ensure that the new joists carried the shortfall, continuing the effective use of the original components. Replacement of damaged or decayed floorboards was then carried out on a like-for-like basis.

All floorboards were nailed through the baseboards into the new joists to stiffen the floor structures. Resin-anchored bolts were drilled through perimeter joists into the inside face of the external walls at 300 mm centres effectively to connect the floor structures to the external walls, thereby strengthening the overall building form.

Roof Structures

Damage to roof structures was generally localised to truss and rafter ends affected by fungal infestation and decay. The overall roof structure was deformed as a result of these local failures, and also as a result of distortions in the supporting walls below. Following the removal of existing roof coverings, each suspect timber was tested using a small-diameter drill to determine the extent of decayed timber. A vocabulary of repair details was developed according to the timber section, size, and length of decayed timber. These involved the removal of decayed timber and the piecing-in of sound timber. The jointing methods varied from simple half lap joints glued and screwed, to the use of face-fixed steel flitch plates.

Both the New Mill engine house and the northern part of the Murray Street block had lost their original roof structures, but the precise form of these structures was known. In each case new replica king-post roof trusses with tusk-tenoned purlins and rafters were provided (Pl 150). The timber used in the original construction was Baltic pine from ancient forests. In order to meet the necessary structural grade of timber required, Honduras pitch pine from a renewable source was used.

Evidence within the roof voids confirmed that the original slating was of random widths laid in diminishing courses. It was therefore decided to re-roof the buildings using new Welsh slate. The opportunity was taken, however, to provide a much more substantial roof, both in terms of its robustness and of its thermal performance. A new roof covering was provided, comprising 1 in (25 mm) thick redwood sarking boards nailed onto the repaired rafters. These boards follow the contours of the distorted roof, but act as a diaphragm over the roof planes. Onto these boards was laid a vapour barrier and high-performance insulation layer. Counter-battens were then fixed over the rafter positions to provide a ventilated space. Breathable roofing felt was laid over the counter-battens, followed by battens and slates. Clay hip and ridge tiles were then fixed at changes of roof plane.

Plate 150: Installing a new roof on New Mill engine house

Original parapet gutters were of lead, but of a narrow cross-section and inadequate fall, typical of early nineteenth-century construction practices. New timber gutter formations were therefore constructed to best modern practice to support new lead gutters and flashings. The gutters discharge over weirs into new cast-iron hoppers and downpipes, and new or repaired lead hoppers and downpipes where originals survived.

External Walls

Where areas of wall had to be dismantled and rebuilt (primarily the parapet walls and New Mill west gable), this rebuilding was kept to a necessary minimum, reusing the existing bricks. The distorted New Mill west gable was restrained by the introduction of horizontal steel trusses within the floor depth of the bay adjacent to the gable at each floor level. It was apparent that elsewhere a large quantity of bricks would be required, both for the repair of existing elements and the rebuilding of the missing upper storeys of the Murray Street block. In this case it was decided to use new matching bricks, which were made by the York Handmade Brick Company. Where possible, damaged stone elements such as copings and sills were repaired; Hollington mottled sandstone was used where replacement was necessary.

A decision was taken to limit repointing to areas of open-jointed brickwork and areas of cement repointing. Original sound pointing and areas of later sound lime mortar repointing were retained, with the acknowledgement that this would not give a consistent appearance to the finished work.

Windows and Doors

The nine-light timber casements that had replaced the original windows in the nineteenth century were of poor construction, and many were badly decayed. A variety of new window options was investigated, although each was to meet thermal,

Plate 151: New railings along the Jersey Street frontage

acoustic, and operational requirements inherent in the future use of the building. Secondary glazing was rejected, but some form of double-glazing was required to meet performance requirements. There was a strong belief that these Georgian buildings required small pane glazing from an architectural point of view, to reinstate the secondary scale which is an essential quality in buildings of this date. The proposal for the replacement windows was therefore for 36-pane sealed doubled-glazed steel windows with a central pivoting ventilation opening occupying the lower half of the window. The 16-pane vertical sliding sash windows and the surviving bay window, both in the office areas of the Murray Street block, were repaired, and replicas provided for missing sash or bay windows.

Several original wooden doors survived, including an early personnel door on Murray Street. These were repaired. Other doors in the 'polite' areas of the site followed the pattern of these surviving doors.

Gates and Railings

A surviving standard from the original Jersey Street railings was discovered buried below paving, and was used as a model for replacement wrought-iron railings (Pl 151). New wrought-iron gates were also provided for the Great Gate archway (Pl 152), and new wrought-iron balustrades and handrails for the reinstated external stair to the Murray Street block. These are in a simple Regency idiom.

Canal Basin

On completion of the building repairs, the canal basin was excavated down to the original clay base (*Ch 6, p 116*). Repairs were carried out to the brick basin walls and sandstone capping stones, with Hollington mottled sandstone replacements provided where necessary.

Conclusion

The project was concluded in the summer of 2006, having achieved its principal objective of completing the permanent repair of A & G Murray's Mill in order to secure this major group of listed buildings for the future. It is hoped that they will also play a key part of the wider urban regeneration of Ancoats and East Manchester. The repair strategy succeeded in retaining and conserving almost all of the surviving historic fabric, whilst the carefully layered interventions substantially increased the capacity of the buildings to accommodate new uses. The project has led to a full appreciation of the significance and architecture of the mill complex, highlighting its value as an archaeological and historical resource.

It is anticipated that the conversion of the buildings will be carried out by a private-sector developer for a mixture of uses. This will also include the construction of a new building on the footprint of the former Bengal Street block, thereby reinstating the enclosed courtyard form of the 1806 complex.

Plate 152: The new main gate through the Murray Street block (© David Barbour/ BDP)

8

SYNTHESIS

Ian Miller, Robina McNeil, and Chris Wild

Introduction

It is perhaps remarkable that the principal source of wealth in nineteenth-century Britain depended on a plant grown thousands of miles away, and manufactured in the north-west of England into one of the fundamental requirements of mankind (*Appendix 1*). Several primary factors may be identified for Lancashire's rapid ascendance as the global centre of cotton spinning and weaving: a damp climate that helped cotton fibres cling together when being worked; plentiful supplies of coal, which encouraged the introduction of steam power; soft water for bleaching, dyeing, and printing; the progressive development of transport facilities and access to the deep-water port of Liverpool; the availability of cheap land; and the lack of regulation because of the absence of guilds in Manchester, which became the 'Cottonopolis' of the nineteenth century (McNeil 2002, 40-1).

Manchester's position at the heart of Lancashire's cotton industry developed from the town's role as a premier market centre for textile goods in the sixteenth century (Lowe 1972). By the 1780s, the prestigious reputation of this market was attracting foreign merchants to the town, opening up the markets of the world to the cotton trade, and laying the foundations for Manchester's rise as a global centre of the industry (Farnie 1979). The town also boasted a thriving population of hand-loom weavers by the eighteenth century, renowned for producing a wide range of fustian goods and smallwares. The development of an efficient regional transport system that centred on Manchester, based initially on the improved roads and river navigation of the eighteenth century, stimulated the further growth of the town, whilst an increased national demand for cotton goods called for a dramatic expansion of textile manufacturing (*Ch 2, pp 8-13*).

Technological development of textile machinery in Lancashire during this period, especially the carding engine, jenny, water-frame, and mule, was pivotal to the transferral of cotton spinning from the small workshop to the huge multi-storey factory. This transition was pioneered in the English Midlands by Richard Arkwright, who had left Lancashire following the anti-spinning jenny riots of 1768, and established a large water-powered cotton mill and 'factory colony' on the river Derwent at Cromford, Derbyshire, in 1771 (Fitton and Wadsworth 1958). Notwithstanding John Lombe's five-storey silk-throwing mill of 1721, also built on the river Derwent (Pl 153), which may be regarded as the 'realisation of the factory system in England' (Calladine and Fricker 1993, 25), Cromford Mill marked the dawn of a new era characterised by the advance of the powered machine. Arkwright 'created order and system from *ad hoc* developments' (Chapman 1981, 17), and succeeded in designing a total production unit whereby raw cotton was turned into finished yarn. The rapid expansion of the British cotton industry thereafter 'remains one of the most astonishing episodes in history' (Williams with Farnie 1992, 13). By 1780, Arkwright and his partners had erected 20 cotton factories (Guest 1823), although other spinners were building mills that imitated his example and, by 1787, an estimated 208 similar mills had been established in Britain (Chapman 1981, 8).

Plate 153: A nineteenth-century engraving of Lombe's silk-throwing mill of 1721, on the banks of the river Derwent

Arkwright had returned to his native Lancashire in 1777 to build a mill at Birkacre, near Chorley, although strong local opposition to power-driven textile machinery resulted in its destruction by rioters in 1779 (Ingle 1997, 5). Whilst this event generated a reluctance to build any more spinning mills in Lancashire, Arkwright invested in a two-acre site at Shude Hill in 1781, where he established the first cotton-spinning mill in Manchester (Aspin 2003, 72). This was one of the largest of the Arkwright factories, reflecting Manchester's significance as a commercial centre of the cotton trade (Williams with Farnie 1992, 51). The main source of motive power was provided by water, although this was stored in reservoirs rather than being obtained from a river; water flowed to the waterwheel from an upper reservoir to another down slope, from where it was pumped back to the upper reservoir by a steam engine. Crucially, the successful operation of the mill proved that manufacturing by power could be carried out independent of a riverside location, offering an alternative to the rural factory colony (*Ch 4, p 14*). The incorporation of a steam engine also necessitated the inception of the mill chimney, which became a defining feature of manufacturing towns throughout the north of England.

Arkwright's water-frame was only capable of spinning yarn suitable for use as the warp in cotton goods, and therefore operated in tandem with the domestic-based production of weft yarn. Indeed, there is evidence to show that domestic industries were carried out to a much greater extent where there were factories (Marshall 1956, 219). This symbiotic relationship was threatened by the introduction of Crompton's mule in 1779, which was capable of spinning both warp and weft yarn, and emerged as the preferred spinning machine in Lancashire. The lack of patents restricting its use was an important attribute of the mule, and encouraged a growing body of machine-makers in Lancashire to improve on Crompton's design, some of whom were actively engaged in cotton spinning (*Ch 2, p 17*).

Significant advances were achieved in steam-engine technology during this period, as new ways were sought to secure a reliable source of power (*Ch 2, pp 21-2*). Several manufacturers in Manchester experimented with steam-powered pumping engines, following the example of Arkwright's Shude Hill Mill, although it was Peter Drinkwater's Piccadilly Mill of 1789, the first purpose-built steam-powered factory in Manchester (Chaloner 1954), that signalled the viability of the rotary steam engine's application to textile manufacturing. A significant consequence of this achievement was the birth of the 'town mill', and the urbanisation of the factory system (Daniels 1927). This dramatic process was pioneered in Manchester, laying its claim to be the first modern industrial city, a 'symbol of a New Age' (Briggs 1971, ch 3). The application of steam power also secured Britain's position as the world's leading cotton-manufacturing nation; such cotton-spinning machinery was not introduced in France, for instance, until 1812 (Clapham 1936, 65).

The Urbanisation of Ancoats

Manchester expanded rapidly during the final years of the eighteenth century, engulfing rural land, on the fringe of the town. This process of urbanisation, based on the commercial enterprise of landowners and speculative builders, frequently included the laying out of a grid-iron pattern of streets defining plots for development. Green's map of 1794, for instance, clearly depicts numerous intended streets across Ancoats, transcending pre-existing field boundaries (*Ch 3, p 28*). The laying out of streets in advance of development was a key feature of the urban industrial landscape and did not occur, for instance, where industry was dependent on water power. Blocks of workers' housing on Bengal Street and Jersey Street in Ancoats (*Ch 4, p 59*) were built over one such field boundary (Fig 57), which was revealed by excavation to have been a flat-bottomed ditch, some 2.8 m wide. Analysis of the waterlogged plant remains within its fill concluded that the rural landscape of Ancoats had comprised some scrubby vegetation and open waste ground, which supported plants that thrive in a damp environment. These included redshank, rushes, sedges, buttercups, and watercresses, whilst large quantities of wood fragments and thorns in the sample implied that trees and shrubs may also have been growing near to the ditch (OA North 2007a).

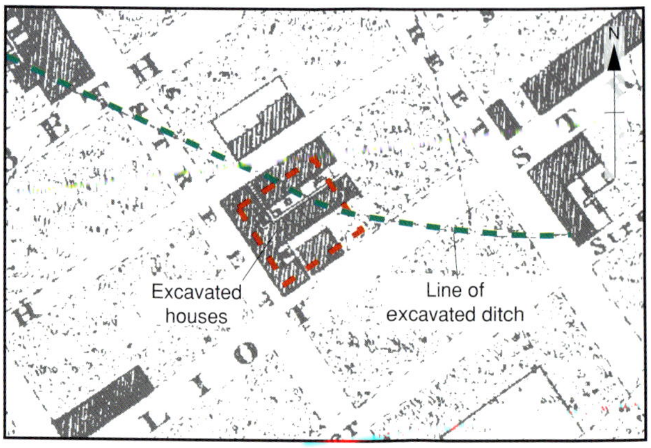

Figure 57: Extract from Green's map of 1794, showing the position of the excavated boundary

The urbanisation of this rural environment occurred with remarkable speed. The underlying clay drift geology is likely to have been an attribute that favoured development, as it provided a readily available raw material for the production of bricks; the cost of importing the building materials in the quantities required would have been prohibitive to the rapid development of Ancoats. Green's map of 1794 marks several 'brickfields' in the area, and advertisements in the *Manchester Mercury* offered for sale excavated clay ready for making bricks (*Ch 5, p 65*).

Figure 58: The distribution of cotton mills in Ancoats, superimposed on Bancks and Co's map (1832), with inset showing a view across Fairbairn's engineering works and adjacent mills in c *1853 (reproduced from Meason 1857)*

The laying out of a grid-iron street pattern had accompanied the sale of the Aytoun and Lever Estates to the west of Ancoats in the 1770s (*Ch 3, p 26*), and the 30-acre development by the Mosley family after 1783 (*Ch 4, p 34*). These estates were mixed developments of elegant residences, artisans' workshop dwellings, shops, and some houses for the poor (Roberts 1993, 15). The rapid growth of Ancoats, however, was characterised by the sub-division of development plots, providing workers' homes that were built alongside the factories. In contrast to earlier developments, moreover, the housing there was intended for occupation solely by the new urban working class. Clauses that regulated nuisances were typically absent in covenants attached to the sale of land in Ancoats, suggesting that this new type of urban industrial landscape may have been anticipated. The intimate mix of factories and housing was a trait of the earliest phase of industrialisation; working-class residential districts in Manchester that developed in the mid-nineteenth century, such as Hulme, display a marked separation between domestic and industrial buildings, a feature of a more mature industrial system (*op cit*, 25).

Within a few decades of initial development, Ancoats contained an incredible density of the new steam-powered mills (Fig 58), forming the greatest concentration of factories in Manchester, and an urban manufacturing area of international repute, with a residential population far larger than entire towns in the surrounding region (*Ch 3, p 32*). A significant factor in the extraordinary rate of industrialism was the canal system. Indeed, without the canals, the construction of these mills and their associated works would not have been possible. The resultant townscape was a precursor for similar towns and cities, and the Manchester model of integrating the dual processes of urbanisation and industrialisation was exported worldwide, representing one of the greatest legacies Manchester has bequeathed to the world (McNeil 2002, 41).

A & G Murray's Mill: The Context for Development

It is against this background that Adam and George Murray established a business in Manchester, and engaged in the town's manufacturing industry. They were part of a group of talented engineers and entrepreneurs who migrated to Manchester from across the British Isles. The most famous names include Ewart, Owen, Roberts, and Fairbairn, although numerous others followed a similar path (Wilson and Reader 1958, 6), bringing experience, skills, ideas, and vigour to the town.

When Adam Murray arrived in Manchester as a time-served textile-machine maker in 1790, several water-powered cotton mills had already been established, including those of Richard Arkwright at Shude Hill (1781), William Edge (1783), David Holt (1785), and James Entwistle (1786) (Aspin 2003). A few mill owners at this time were experimenting with steam power to drive waterwheels, and Peter Drinkwater had just established the first purpose-built steam-powered mill in the town (*Ch 2, pp 21-2*). Drinkwater had ensured that his mill contained 'the most perfect system' of making cotton rovings by using steam power (Hills 1970, 125), but the spinning mules had yet to be adapted for mechanical operation. Indeed, the mechanisation of the mule, in which John Kennedy and Adam Murray played a leading role, proved to be a highly significant stage in the evolution of factory-produced yarn. In particular, John Kennedy is reputed to have first applied steam power to operate a spinning mule in 1793 (*Ch 4, p 36*), which paved the way for Lancashire to supersede the Midlands as the accepted centre of the cotton industry (Mallalieu 1836, 408). These developments inevitably led to the introduction of purpose-built mule-spinning mills, which tended to be of a large scale to maximise the productive capacity and counteract the high capital costs. In retrospect, this progression was not in itself surprising, but the rate at which the factory-based industry developed was both astonishing and unprecedented.

The development of a more efficient transport infrastructure was undoubtedly one of the most widespread features of the Industrial Revolution, and few inventions have had so vast an impact on the landscape as canals and, later, railways. The importance of an integrated transport infrastructure to the urbanisation and industrialisation of Manchester, and especially Ancoats, is exemplified by the Rochdale Canal, completed in 1804 as the first trans-Pennine waterway. In Manchester, it was to have junctions with the Bridgewater Canal, the Ashton Canal, and, via the Manchester and Salford Junction Canal, barges were able to reach the river Irwell (Brumhead and Wyke 2004, 11). The lines of the Rochdale and Aston Canals through Manchester were festooned with branches, serving numerous wharves and individual cotton mills, and other towns.

The close relationship between the canals and the new mills became a hallmark of textile manufacturing in Ancoats: canals not only provided the infrastructure used for the transportation of raw materials and finished goods, but also supplied the water required by the steam plant, obviating the need for dedicated reservoirs. This enabled the construction of closely packed groups of large steam-powered mills, many occupying sites along the banks of the canals, creating one of the most dramatic features of the urban landscape (Fig 58). This unique grouping of mills spans the Industrial Revolution, and epitomises Manchester as a symbol and embodiment of the transformation of society. The regular and constant supply of water demanded by the steam engines for condensing was drawn through pipes that pierced the canal banks (Pl 154), via stop-cocks controlled by the canal companies (Fig 59). The canal companies benefited financially from this arrangement by levying a fee for the use of their water (GMRO B2/10/6). An added benefit was the discharge of warm water from the steam engines, which protected the canals from freezing over in winter months.

Plate 154: Excavation of the Pot Street Arm of the Rochdale Canal in Ancoats, with inset showing the feed pipe that supplied water to Oxley's Mill on Allum Street

Some canal-side mills had private wharfs, such as Beehive Mill on Jersey Street, whilst Brownsfield Mill on Great Ancoats Street had a shipping hole built into the lower storeys to facilitate the trans-shipment of goods, emulating the design of contemporary canal warehouses (Brumhead and Wyke 1997). The ultimate development

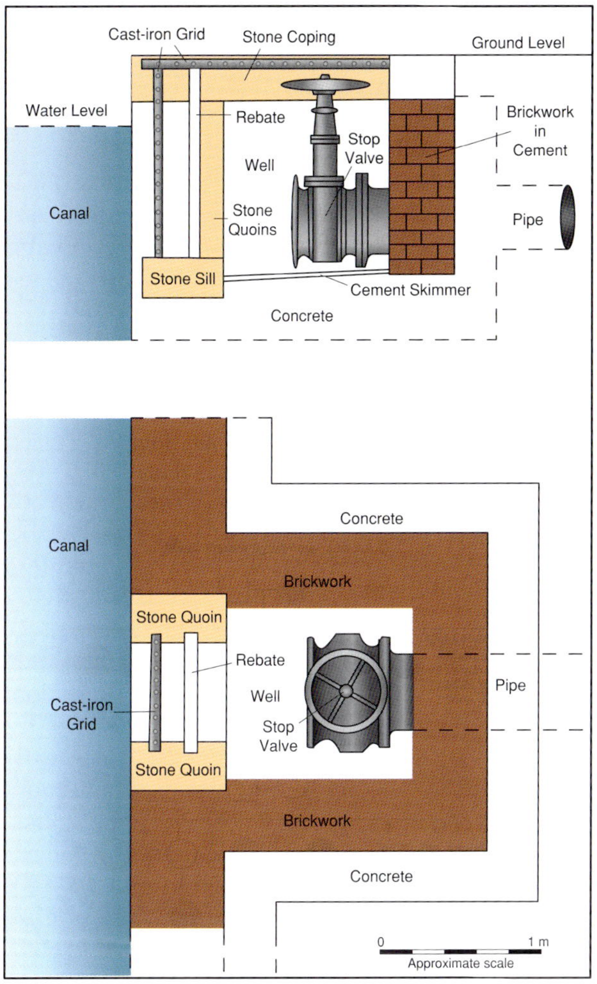

Figure 59: Section and plan of a Rochdale Canal Company water-feed pipe stop-cock

of canal features into mill design, however, is perhaps demonstrated by the private basin within the enclosed central courtyard of A & G Murray's Mill, which allowed raw cotton to be delivered directly to the preparatory rooms, and coal to the boiler houses; excavation of the late nineteenth-century boiler house demonstrated that coal from the boats could be unloaded directly onto the firing floor (*Ch 6, p 130*).

The close association between textile mills and canals was followed subsequently elsewhere in Lancashire, such as by the groups of urban factories built along the Leeds and Liverpool Canal in Blackburn and Burnley after 1818. Even at this date, however, the majority of textile mills in Britain were comparatively small, often comprising a single building of three or four storeys and powered by a waterwheel (Ashmore 1969, 44-5). Nevertheless, it was the huge steam-powered mills that came to dominate industrial townscapes across the north of England, representing the physical manifestation of British cotton manufacturing as the first true global industry, and the most potent symbol of the Industrial Revolution.

Significance of A & G Murray's Mill

A & G Murray's Old Mill of 1798 was amongst the first cotton-spinning factories in the world to have been designed to house steam-powered spinning mules, and represented the culmination of a series of initial developments that produced structures capable of serving the cotton-spinning industry for over 150 years; the mill represents the largest and most technically advanced industrial building in an urban landscape from the pioneer phase of the urban Industrial Revolution. The site is of immense significance in numerous respects (BDP and OA North 2007), and retains considerable elements of the original fabric and fittings, including *in situ* elements of the early power-transmission system, and very rare Boulton and Watt fire-fighting equipment. Perhaps its most remarkable attribute, however, is that it survives largely intact; it is the only remaining example from Manchester's late eighteenth-century boom in factory-building, and forms a key component of a significant grouping of early mills in Ancoats, including McConnel & Kennedy's Mill, Brownsfield Mill, and Beehive Mill. These buildings collectively played a fundamental role in the development of the industrialisation of Manchester, creating an urban landscape that in the early nineteenth century was unique to Manchester. These mills have withstood a period of neglect and decay that resulted in the loss of numerous mills in Ancoats since the collapse of the textile industry in the 1950s. Indeed, the mill chimney of A & G Murray's Mill is one of a very small group that still grace the skyline of Ancoats.

Size, and Construction Techniques

The Murrays' Old Mill was a 'state of the art' textile factory when constructed, reflecting the limits of technical expertise attained by millwrights of the period. This can be demonstrated by comparing its physical attributes with earlier factories, including the Arkwright-type mills, particularly those in Derbyshire, which 'were for a few decades the structurally most advanced buildings in the world' (Pevsner 1976, 275). Arkwright's first cotton mills, and the slightly earlier silk-throwing mills, were of essentially traditional construction, comprising brick or stone load-bearing walls with timber beams and floors. It seems likely that elements of their design were drawn from contemporary corn mills, although the primary requirement of a cotton mill was to house rows of powered machinery, resulting in a huge open-plan structure that was long and thin in plan, thereby creating a new form of building type of 'forthright functional design' (Richards 1958, 7). Arkwright's mills were typically 9 m wide and up to 50 m long, rising to a height of four or five storeys. The Murrays' Old

Mill, measuring 32 m long, was shorter than the largest Arkwright-type mills, but incorporated the same methods of structural engineering: the floors were laid on traditional timber beams, which were supported at one-third span lengths by two rows of cruciform-section cast-iron columns, similar to those introduced by William Strutt in Derby in 1792-3 (Menuge 2001, 43). This method of mill construction was typical of the late eighteenth century, and remained the most widespread, and cheapest, technique until the late nineteenth century (Freeman 1891, 177). Old Mill did, however, attain a height greater than any earlier textile mill by incorporating eight storeys, providing a model emulated in the design of subsequent steam-powered mills, such as Jonathan Pollard's factory on Great Ancoats Street (*Ch 2, p 19*), and McConnel & Kennedy's Sedgwick Mill (*Ch 4, p 52*), which were both also of eight storeys.

Old Mill was also wider than mills of typical Arkwright-type proportions, having a width to length ratio of only 1:2.4, compared to the standard 1:3, perhaps reflecting an intention to house the largest spinning mules then available. The net result was a factory with a productive capacity considerably greater than the Arkwright-type mills. David Dale's five-storey New Lanark Mill of 1789 on the river Clyde, for instance, contained 6556 spindles (Donnachie and Hewitt 1993), which was slightly more than half of the capacity of the Murrays' Old Mill.

In addition to its production capacity, a tall structure would also lend itself more easily for letting as 'room-and-power' space to small-scale firms (*Ch 2, p 19*), as more rooms of a suitable size would thereby be created. Small-scale firms were a characteristic feature of Manchester's early cotton industry, and 'room-and-power' mills accommodated the majority of Manchester's cotton manufacturers before the 1820s (Lloyd-Jones and Lewis 1988, 33). Unlike many of their contemporaries, however, including McConnel & Kennedy (*Ch 4, pp 50-1*), there is a conspicuous absence of evidence for the Murrays ever having rented out space in their Old Mill. Indeed, the Murrays' ability to finance the initial high capital cost of erecting their mill without relying on an income obtained from renting factory space is as remarkable as the scale of their mill.

The other multi-storey factories that had been added to the Murrays' complex by 1806 were of similar construction to Old Mill, although a few subtle differences do exist. Decker Mill, for instance, was nearly 4 ft (1.22 m) wider than Old Mill, which may have reflected the availability of larger spinning mules, and the improvements in steam power to drive them. The addition of New Mill effectively doubled the size and capacity of the Murrays' complex, and this was probably the largest single mill building in Manchester at that time. Notwithstanding its vastly increased size, however, the structural engineering employed in the construction of New Mill was similar to that in Old and Decker Mill; whilst the incorporation of a stepped foundation at the base of each wall in New Mill contrasted with the earlier structures (*Ch 6, p 109*), there is little physical evidence to testify any great advance in construction technique. A notable modification to the design of New Mill was the use of a circular stair tower, in contrast to the rectangular stair tower that afforded access to Old and Decker Mill. The circular plan provided a more stable and load-bearing structure, with a larger internal space than its rectangular equivalent.

The option to increase the spinning capacity greatly was an important attribute of steam-power; excluding the large Arkwright-type factories such as Cromford and New Lanark that were built on powerful rivers, many early water-powered mills used the full potential of the watercourse they were sited on, and could therefore not be expanded easily due to the limitations of available power (Ingle 1997, 7). Conversely, the steam-powered New Islington Mill was greatly expanded in 1800 with the addition of a contiguous range, and the size of Salvins' Factory was doubled in 1819 (*Ch 4, p 39*). Similarly, the Murrays were able to double the size of their Old Mill in 1801 with the erection of Decker Mill, and quadruple their original capacity with the completion of New Mill by 1806 (*Ch 5, pp 69-71*).

The rapid expansion of the Murrays' complex resulted in a mill of an unprecedented size. Indeed, the scale of the mill was still considered remarkable in 1826 when, together with the adjacent complex of McConnel & Kennedy, they were noted by the Prussian court architect, Karl Friedrich Schinkel (*Ch 5, pp 79-80*). Schinkel described the steam-powered urban mills in Manchester as 'monstrous shapeless buildings put up only by foremen without architecture, only the least that was necessary and out of red brick' (Bindman and Riemann 1993, 175). The plain and utilitarian design was especially the case for mills erected during the first decade of the nineteenth century, as the Napoleonic Wars (1793-1815) led to a dramatic rise in the price of building materials, and resulted in even less opportunity for the application of architectural adornment (Pragnell 2000, 92). Nevertheless, the surviving mills from this period are collectively the finest expression of the application of steam power to the textile industry, and created the characteristic style of cotton mills until the 1870s. It was not until the final years of the nineteenth century that new techniques of building construction were applied to the giant spinning mills, which were designed to contain considerably more machinery than their predecessors (Ashmore 1969, 49-50).

Layout

The site chosen by the Murrays for their New Mill, fronting onto Jersey Street and parallel to Old and Decker Mill, betrays their intention to create an enclosed courtyard layout by constructing the Murray Street and Bengal Street blocks. Although unusual for its date, the enclosed courtyard arrangement had been adopted previously, notably by Samuel Oldknow for his textile mill at Stockport in 1791 (OA North 2007b), providing strict control over the access of goods and people. Security was seemingly an important consideration in the design of the early mills, and access was frequently via an enclosed private yard, as at New Islington Mill and Waller's Mill (*Ch 4*). The enclosed courtyard plan was adopted in the design of later mills in the area, a notable example being Brunswick Mill in *c* 1840 (Pl 155), although the incorporation of a private canal basin in the courtyard of the Murray's complex remained a unique innovation.

Plate 155: Engraving of Brunswick Mill (reproduced from Henry Bannerman & Sons Ltd 1893)

A & G Murray and McConnel & Kennedy were probably the first cotton-spinning firms in the world to build mills in which both mules and preparation machinery were powered by steam, thereby achieving the complete mechanisation of yarn production. This was coupled with consideration of the internal organisation of the machinery, culminating in 'the most efficient productive organism devised by human intellect' (Murphy 1911, 150). The firm of McConnel & Kennedy installed preparation machinery in the lower floors of its mill and placed spinning mules transversely across the floors of the upper storeys (McConnel 1913, 38-9), and there is some evidence to show that A & G Murray adopted a similar layout of machinery in their mill (*Ch 6, p 99*). Whilst other early nineteenth-century cotton spinners suggested that the card rooms were best placed on the upper storeys of a mill (*eg* Montgomery 1833, 19; Ure 1836, 253), the layout advocated by McConnel & Kennedy eventually became widely adopted, and significantly influenced the form of the Lancashire spinning mill by the late nineteenth century (Williams with Farnie 1992, 66).

Fire Protection

An important strand in the technological advances in mill building during the early nineteenth century was a focus on increased fire-resistance. The definitive moment in the realisation of the need for fireproofing in textile mills was probably the destruction of the Albion Corn Mill in London in 1791 (Falconer 2001, 11), and fire-resistance became a major and ongoing ambition thereafter. This was achieved during the late eighteenth century by the replacement of timber with cast-iron columns and beams, and brick-arched ceilings, as at William Strutt's Belper Mill of 1793-5 (Pragnell 2000, 84-7). The first application of fireproof construction in the Manchester area was at Philips & Lee's Salford Twist Mill of 1799, although the techniques do not appear to have been adopted widely in Manchester's early nineteenth-century mills. Whilst most of the surviving mills from this period in Manchester are of fireproof construction, this is probably a consequence of the more common type having been destroyed by fires (Williams with Farnie 1992, 58).

With the exception of the stair towers, the blowing room of the late 1820s (*Ch 6, p 121*), and Fireproof Mill of the 1840s, A & G Murray did not utilise fireproof construction in their buildings, which today provide rare intact examples of large mills without this technology. The firm did take some measures to reduce the impact of fires, however, including the installation of fire-fighting equipment in the stair towers. This was supplied by Boulton and Watt, and appears to have been relied upon until an automatic sprinkler system was eventually installed in 1902 (*Ch 6, p 134*); the original Boulton and Watt system was largely retained *in situ*, and today represents the very rare survival of such equipment. The water for the system was pumped by the mill's engine into a tank atop the stair tower, which fed a central stand pipe by gravity within the newel of the tower. The newel also housed cisterns and valves on each floor, to which hoses could be attached. Another early measure taken to protect against fire appears to have been the plastering of the timber ceilings, as noted in New Mill (*Ch 6, p 110*); this was augmented later by thin-section metal sheeting.

A significant fire risk in the earliest cotton mills was presented by oil lamps or candles, which were the only available options for artificial lighting. McConnel & Kennedy was using about 1500 candles to light its mill during the early nineteenth century, burning 125 lbs (56.7 kg) of tallow every day, with an annual cost in excess of £680 (Tann 1970, 123). It is most likely that A & G Murray similarly relied on candles until better technology was available, which was provided by gas lighting. The first large cotton mill in the country reputed to have been fitted with gas lighting was Philips & Lee's Salford Twist Mill in 1805-7 (Hughes 1853, 11), and McConnel & Kennedy installed a similar system manufactured by Boulton and Watt in 1809 (BWA 3147/3/478/19; BWA 3147/3/478/21). It is uncertain precisely when A & G Murray adopted gas lighting, although it may have been in place by 1819, and was supplied from the gas-making plant within Little Mill (*Ch 5, p 79*).

Power Systems

When the Murrays constructed Old Mill in 1798, the vast majority of other textile factories in the country were dependent upon water power. The application of steam power for the mechanisation of the textile industry was progressing rapidly, however, and particularly in Manchester, where considerable numbers of simple steam-driven pumping engines were in use to power waterwheels, and local engineering talent was producing effective rotary motion from atmospheric beam engines (*Ch 2, pp 21-2*).

Although relatively few in number, steam-powered mills of this period were generally fitted with internal engine and boiler houses, together with a chimney; detached engine and boiler houses did not become standard in Lancashire until after 1830 (Williams with Farnie 1992, 54), and even later in Yorkshire (Giles and Goodall 1992, 142). This was certainly the case for McConnel & Kennedy's Mill, where the steam-power plant was placed internally, with the added intention of maintaining high temperatures in the spinning rooms overhead (McConnel 1913, 39). A & G Murray, however, broke with this practice at an early date, and the series of steam engines employed on the site by 1806 were all placed in detached buildings. Conversely, the design of their Doubling Mill in the early 1840s allowed for internal engine and boiler rooms, presumably in response to the limited space available externally (*Ch 5, p 81*).

The Murrays' initial choice of a 12 hp engine is unlikely to have powered machinery throughout the mill, suggesting that either a proportion of the machinery was not driven by steam power, or that they had under-estimated the power required; numerous entrepreneurs of this period invested in steam engines that were of insufficient power for their requirements (Tann 1970, 83), reflecting the ground-breaking nature of their schemes. It is perhaps more likely, however, that Old Mill was not filled to capacity with machinery, as the procurement of machinery would have been a lengthy undertaking. In correspondence with Boulton and Watt on 3 June 1789, for instance, Peter Drinkwater commented that 'the factory at Shude Hill has been more than seven years filling with machinery and I am doubtful whether with convenience it could have been filled much sooner' (BWA 3147/5/44). These hypotheses are reinforced by the Murrays' purchase of a 40 hp engine when Decker Mill was completed in 1801 (*Ch 5, p 69*); whilst the physical size of the mill had been doubled, there was seemingly a requirement almost to quadruple the supply of power.

The power from the steam engines in the early textile mills was usually delivered to the machinery via an upright shaft, which normally rose the full height of the building, and was connected to horizontal line shafting on each floor by bevel gears. Whilst there is no known surviving example of an upright shaft from this period, its former position in A & G Murray's Mill is marked by rare physical evidence, including footstep bearings and a complete transmission bearing in New Mill (*Ch 6, p 117*). However, in contrast to Old and Decker Mill, each of which was fitted with a single vertical shaft, surviving housings in the ceiling of the fourth floor of New Mill represent the position of six vertical shafts. These may have been powered by an horizontal shaft in the mill basement, thereby rising to the full height of the building, although the only remaining evidence for this system on the lower storeys is a bevel-gear scar on the third floor (*Ch 6, p 113*). Alternatively, a single line shaft in the fourth floor may have powered the vertical shafts, driving the mules on that floor and in the storey below, a configuration used in Orrell's Mill in Stockport in 1834 (Ure 1836). It is clear, however, that this transmission system in New Mill was short-lived, and was replaced with a single vertical shaft in the central bay at an early date (*Ch 6, p 117*).

Archaeological recording at McConnel & Kennedy's Sedgwick Mill of 1818 also provided evidence for the use of multiple vertical shafts. There, the main horizontal shaft from the engine occupied the full length of the mill basement and drove a series of upright shafts that passed through the floors in alternate bays (*Ch 4, p 52*). It seems possible that spinning mules would have been powered from a belt drum attached to the upright shafts situated next to the machine, as shown in an illustration of an early mule manufactured by McConnel & Kennedy (*Ch 2, p 14*).

The original shafting almost certainly comprised heavy cast-iron or large wooden shafts with poorly designed couplings. An important advance in mill design was the application of light wrought-iron shafts that were designed to work at higher speeds, thus reducing power losses due to friction. This improved system was reputedly first introduced to the textile mill by Fairbairn and Lillie's improvements to the line shafting within A & G Murray's Mill (*Ch 5, pp 77-8*): elements of Fairbairn and Lillie's work survive in Old and Decker Mill and New Mill.

Spinning Technology

Once mechanisation was introduced to spinning in the late eighteenth century, an intrinsic link between machine size and a sufficient power source was formed. After the introduction of the mule, and its successful combination with rotative power, large-scale production was possible, and advances in engine technology were linked closely to further development. At the time the Murrays had constructed their Old Mill, this relationship was still in its infancy, and this perhaps explains the small size of the first engine, and an apparent unwillingness to operate the mules in pairs (*Ch 6, p 99*). It has been estimated that 1 hp would be required to power 750 spindles (Catling 1986, 53-4), but the ratios between spindles and power throughout the early years of the Murrays' complex suggest a higher value; A & G Murray operated 84,300 spindles in 1811 (Daniels 1930, 108), using two engines with a combined power output of 85 hp.

The Social Revolution

The factory-based system resulted in rapid urban growth across Britain, and created a new social dimension in production. The resultant dramatic shift in working practices and the social structure of a large proportion of the populace were amongst the greatest changes wrought by the Industrial Revolution. The factory system of production, epitomised by the textile mill, was a symbol of the increasing separation of the place of production from the domestic setting, reflecting fundamental changes to the organisation of work and working practices (Mellor 2005, 49). Not least amongst the changes was the strict specification of working hours, which were no longer to be dictated by natural considerations such as daylight, but by the incessant motion and the exhaustless power of the machine (Kay 1832): the comparative independence of the domestic-based cotton spinner was lost to the 'factory bell'.

Plate 156: Styal Mill, showing the cupola tower

Bells were used to signal the starting and ending of working shifts, and were normally housed in cupola towers projecting from either the ridge of a mill, or above a central pediment. These formed an important feature of early 'factory colonies' (Pl 156), although the extent to which bells were used in the steam-powered urban factories is poorly understood. In 1807, the celebrated poet and historian, Robert Southey, noted in Manchester that 'when the bell rings it is to call wretches to their work instead of their prayers' (Southey 1951, 213), and several early mills in Ancoats, including McConnel & Kennedy's Old Mill (*Ch 4, p 50*) and the Ancoats Cotton Twist Company Mill, are depicted with cupolas on contemporary engravings (Pl 157), but these were perhaps exceptions.

Plate 157: Ancoats Cotton Twist Company Mill in 1850 (reproduced courtesy of Manchester Archives and Local Studies)

One study of the development of the textile mill concluded that the spatial, authoritarian, form of a mill represented a powerful way of controlling movement of the people housed within it (Markus 1993). It has been suggested that this helped to establish the new working practices demanded by the factory-based system, both physically and psychologically, and emphasised the increasing separation of the home from the workplace (Mokyr 2001, 8). In broad terms, moreover, the repetitive operation of machinery in the textile mills devalued workers' talents; whilst the mule spinner was required initially to command considerable skills, these were reduced progressively with increased mechanisation.

Social control was imposed at the main entrance, exemplified by the Murrays' imposing great gate through the Murray Street block, which was also overlooked by the principal offices. Social control may be seen to have extended to the spinning blocks, where the spatial structure was based on the stair tower. Those connected to Old and Decker Mill, and New Mill, and subsequently the Bengal Street block, all had a single point of entry from the courtyard, and these provided direct access to all the working floors. Movement around the two main blocks was thus focused on the stair towers, which proved to be an effective way of getting workers around the mill and concentrated attention upon the production process. Workers wishing to move about the building, or from one block to another, had to do so by coming into the view of those responsible for supervision. This layout also segregated the workforce into numerous small groups, each allocated a specific machine or part of the mill, facilitating effective supervision and further restricting social interaction between workers (Mellor 2005, 53). Indeed, it is notable that, until the addition of a canteen in the twentieth century, there were no communal spaces at A & G Murray's Mill for the workforce other than the central courtyard, which was itself dominated by the canal basin.

Conversely, the offices within the Murray Street block were spatially distinct from the rest of the mill complex, placed closest to the main gate and accessed via their own entrance. Interestingly, the office block also incorporated the most ornate architectural embellishment, reflecting their use for business and public relations, separated from the production processes. The engine houses similarly attracted architectural embellishment beyond the utilitarian and austere architecture applied to much of the mill complex. The use of tall, round-headed windows, for instance, was a distinctive characteristic, and these buildings were often seen as a measure of the success of the firm. The late nineteenth-century engine house that served Old and Decker Mill was also adorned with decorative yellow brick and denticulate brickwork below the closed eaves (*Ch 6, p 128*).

A New Civic Elite

The huge profits that could be accrued from the new breed of steam-powered mills led to the creation of a group of wealthy manufacturers, an urban aristocracy, who played an important part in the business affairs of the town (Briggs 1971, 94). Many of these men were connected through informal relationships, and it is notable that the largest fine-spinning firms in Manchester were related by marriage: the McConnels, Houldsworths, Kennedys, Murrays, Birleys, and Gregs (M Watson *pers comm*). This new civic elite accepted some social responsibility and, during the first half of the nineteenth century, factory masters patronised an array of educational and recreational institutions designed to cater for workers who had limited access to formal education (Howe 1984, 283). In 1826, for instance, James McConnel contributed £600 for the establishment of a Mechanics Institute (Lee 1972, 152), and George Murray was the President of the Ardwick and Ancoats Dispensary. Founded in 1828, and funded by subscription to which many of the mill owners contributed, the dispensary was one of the very few public institutions in Ancoats (*Ch 3, p 32*). Indeed, the paucity of public buildings in Ancoats during the first half of the nineteenth century is astounding, particularly as the area housed nearly one fifth of Manchester's population by 1851 (MLSU 107/2225). Similarly, Ancoats had no recognition in local government, emphasising that its development was entirely by the private enterprise of the new manufacturing classes. This control of the building process by a new collection of property interests undermined the established order to some degree, and augmented the power of the emerging manufacturing classes (Springett 1968, 53).

The Murrays, James McConnel, and John Kennedy all accumulated considerable personal wealth and a high social standing that was in sharp contrast to their humble origins. A significant factor in their ascendancy was a thorough knowledge of the cotton-spinning process and the machinery involved, as intimated in Adam Murray's obituary in the *Manchester Mercury*: 'at a very early period of life he formed accurate and enlarged views of the different manufactures carried on in this town, and for nearly 30 years prosecuted one of its principal branches with skill and success' (*Manchester Mercury*, 7 July 1818). It is notable that during the early nineteenth century they all lived in close proximity to their mills, and maintained a very active involvement in the day-to-day running of the business. This close relationship between 'master and mill' appears to have weakened with the later generations of Murrays, who managed the family firm after the death of George Murray in 1855; James Murray moved to London in the 1860s, and Benjamin Murray returned to Scotland in the late 1870s, leaving his two sons in charge of the mill (Burnett 1899, 135). By 1881, the mill was run by a managing director, and the Murray family does not appear to have had any direct involvement thereafter (*Ch 5, p 86*).

This change reflected a widespread maturing of industrial structure and practice, with an increasing tendency for the day-to-day regulation of business to be controlled by managerial personnel (Griffiths 2001). One consequence of this change was a diminished civic role played by the factory owners; in broad terms, employers' social responsibilities during the later nineteenth century were largely restricted to their patronage of working men's clubs, which provided simpler forms of recreation, games, music, and papers (Howe 1984, 285).

Conclusion

Towns and cities can be seen as the greatest works of humanity, the products of interaction between people, which have produced a resource of great variety and density, where buildings, monuments, topography, landscape character, street pattern, and open spaces work together to produce a distinct entity. In Manchester, from the late eighteenth century onwards, a combination of technology, communications, and social and economic developments enabled industrialisation to take place in an urban environment for the first time. The net result was a remarkable ensemble of buildings and structures in an urban environment of outstanding universal significance for human history, which is reflected in Manchester's nomination for inscription as a World Heritage Site. The nomination comprises a series of linked areas, including the underground mines of Worsley Delph and the Bridgewater Canal, Castlefield, the Rochdale and Ashton Canals, the Manchester warehouse district, and the south-western part of the Ancoats Conservation Area, which incorporates the steam-powered mills of A & G Murray and McConnel & Co (Kidd *et al* 2005). These areas exemplify the integration of the key elements that defined and ensured the sustainability of the Industrial Revolution: transport innovation; the application of power; the factory system; and commercial and urban development.

The integration of urbanisation and industrialisation is seen in spectacular fashion in Ancoats, where elements of the streetscape form a coherent whole representative of the urban environment of the Industrial Revolution. The recognition of Ancoats as an urban landscape of international significance follows on from a period of post-industrial neglect and decay. Many of the mills in Ancoats had actually outlived their intended purpose by the end of the nineteenth century (Rowley 1899), and either remained empty or were adapted for new uses; the conversion of the Jersey Street Mill into a tenement block of some 141 dwellings in 1892 (Pl 158) provides an interesting example (Roberts 1993, 24). The demise of the area's manufacturing base in the mid-twentieth century, however, caused depopulation and the collapse of the local commercial and social infrastructure (*Ch 1, p 3*). Large parts of Ancoats were progressively cleared of houses and industrial premises as initiatives aimed at improving local conditions were implemented, whilst other buildings were lost through neglect and vandalism; the Murrays' Bengal Street block was destroyed in this way during the 1990s, and other buildings in the area have experienced a similar fate in the early twenty-first century (Pl 159).

Plate 158: Jersey Street Mill after conversion to dwellings (reproduced courtesy of Manchester Archives and Local Studies)

Plate 159: Bengal Street block of Beehive Mill on fire in 2005

It is against this background that the largely intact survival of A & G Murray's Mill can be seen as remarkable. By the late 1990s, however, the component buildings were only partially occupied, and were in a perilously dilapidated condition that rendered them vulnerable to structural failure. The timely intervention of their repair has undoubtedly averted the loss, and secured the long-term preservation, of an iconic site from the urban industrial revolution.

By 1806, Adam and George Murray had created in their factory complex the epitome of technological and economic progress, a marvel of the Industrial Age. These huge buildings towered above the mills and works that occupied the shallow valley of Shooters Brook, and the domestic workshops that lined Great Ancoats Street and Newton Lane, representing a new and powerful dimension to both manufacturing and the urban development of Ancoats. These same buildings fulfil a similarly inspirational role some 200 years later. The structural repair of the mill, enabling its conversion for sustainable new uses, has acted as a beacon for the renaissance of Ancoats as a reinvigorated and vibrant area, and represents a key component of the wider regeneration of East Manchester.

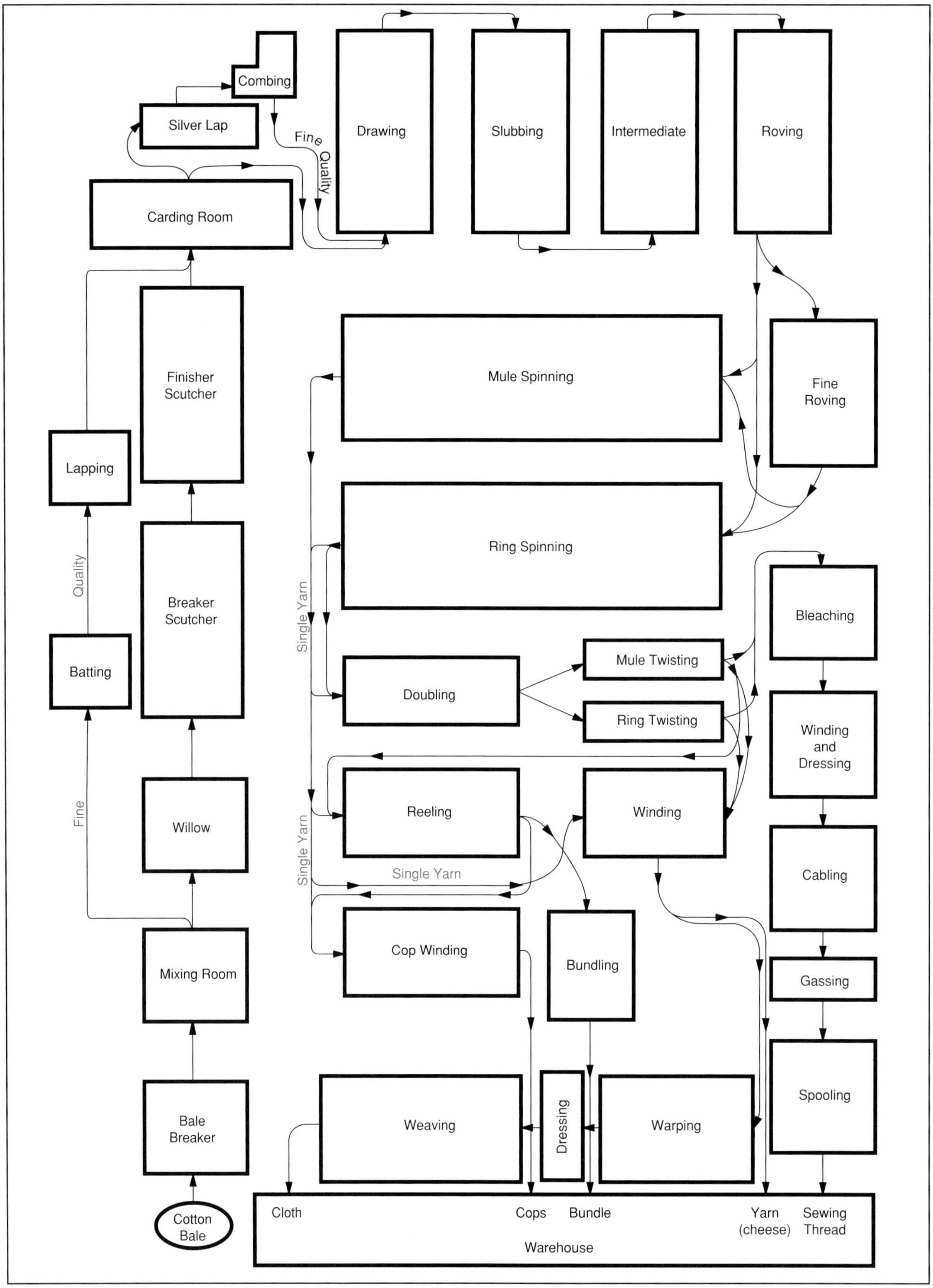

Figure 60: Flow diagram summarising the cotton-manufacturing processes (after Murphy 1911)

APPENDIX 1

THE PROCESSES CARRIED OUT IN A COTTON-SPINNING MILL

Ian Miller

Cotton is a vegetable down of a genus of plants called *Gossypium*, which grows in tropical and sub-tropical climates, and is indigenous in India and America (Chapman 1905, 1). The finest of cotton fibres, known as 'Sea Island', are derived from *Gossypium barbadense*, and is selected by the manufacturers of the highest-quality yarn as it is strong, regular, and much longer in the fibre than any other type (Baines 1835, 297).

The most important characteristic of cotton yarn is its fineness, which is measured as the 'count'. The classification is determined on the amount of yarn spun from a pound of raw cotton, and the highest counts equate to the finest yarn. In broad terms, the yarn produced in Britain could be divided into three main categories: coarse; medium; and fine counts. Throughout the nineteenth century, Manchester and the immediate neighbourhood was a centre for the production of the finest counts, which sold for the highest prices. McConnel & Kennedy had the distinction of producing the finest yarn in the world during the early nineteenth century, having raised their maximum counts from the 170s in 1795 to 250s in 1812, although A & G Murray and T & J Houldsworth were producing counts up to 300+ by 1828 (Williams with Farnie 1992, 20). Mills in other parts of south-east Lancashire specialised in medium counts, with Bolton acting as a centre for the spinning of medium fine yarn (counts in the 60s), whilst Oldham, Rochdale, and Todmorden dominated the production of coarse yarn (typically counts of 32), which was used largely for mass-produced clothing (Marsden 1884, 58).

Initial Preparation

After picking and initial drying, the cotton has to be detached from the seeds which it envelopes. This was achieved traditionally in Asian countries using a crude 'roller gin', but cotton planters in North America were compelled to remove the seeds by hand until the invention of the 'saw gin' by Eli Whitney in 1793 (Murphy 1911, 90). This machine acted as a catalyst for a dramatic expansion of raw cotton exported from plantations in North America, which rapidly displaced the Mediterranean, the Levant, and the West Indies to become the primary source of the cotton consumed by the Lancashire textile industry. However, the importance of having access to alternative sources, such as from Egypt, India, and Polynesia, was made very apparent to the Lancashire manufacturers during the 1860s, when the American Civil War caused severe disruption to the trans-Atlantic trade.

Cotton was imported as compressed bales, and it was in this form that it was delivered to the mills. The size of each bale was not standardised, although those from North America had an average weight of 500 lbs (226 kg). The bales were opened upon arrival and, after careful sampling, were mixed thoroughly in predetermined proportions to obtain the required quality. Very high counts of yarn, for instance, could be obtained by mixing Sea Island with long-stapled Egyptian cotton, the latter possessing greater strength. The cotton from different bales was weighed accurately, laid in layers to form a stack, and then raked down vertically (Murphy 1911, 160-2).

Willowing and Batting

Once it had been mixed, the raw cotton was subject to initial cleaning, which loosened the fibres and released impurities such as sand, dirt, and seeds. For

Plate 160: A scutcher (reproduced from Barfoot 1840)

coarser counts, this process was carried out initially by a machine known as a 'willow', which comprised a drum studded with iron spikes that revolved rapidly within a cage, flaying the cotton and breaking up any matted lumps. This process was continued in a 'scutcher' or blowing machine, which similarly contained a spiked drum that rotated at high speeds, in conjunction with a powerful fan to separate the remaining impurities and mix the cotton fibres (Pl 160).

The scutcher was invented in *c* 1800, although it was only used initially in the production of coarser counts (Tomlinson 1861), and was not adopted by the fine spinners until the mid-nineteenth century; fine cotton continued to be cleansed manually to ensure that there was no damage to the fibres. The raw cotton was spread out on a raised mesh of cords and beaten violently with sticks of hazel or holly, a process known as 'batting' (*Pl 63, p 66*); it was usual to tie four or five thin sticks together, forming a fan-shaped beater. This opened the tangled locks of the cotton, and allowed the loose impurities to fall out through the openings between the cords.

The initial cleaning operation produced considerable amounts of dust, particularly when batted manually, presenting a serious fire hazard. It was therefore frequently carried out in a separate building that was detached from the main factory, such as the 'batting shops' at Salvins' Factory and New Islington Mill (*Ch 4*). The process was carried out at A & G Murray's Mill from the mid-nineteenth century in a segregated fireproof room inside the mill, known as the 'blowing room' (*Ch 6, p 121*), which became standard practice in cotton factories. These rooms were usually fitted with a ventilation system to extract the cotton dust.

Cotton that had been batted by hand was passed to a lapping machine, where it was lightly compressed and rolled upon an iron cylinder (Pl 161); scutchers were fitted with a series of rollers at the back of the machine, which performed the same function. The end product from the initial cleaning processes was a thick sheet of fibres known as a 'lap'.

Plate 161: A lapping machine (reproduced from Redding 1842)

Producing a Sliver

Carding

The next stage in the process was 'carding', which separated the cotton fibres and made them parallel by combing, and also removed the short and broken fibres. This was traditionally carried out using a pair of 'hand-cards', which comprised flat pieces of wood studded with short spikes and fitted with a handle. The mechanisation of this process, principally by Richard Arkwright who introduced his improved carding engine in the early 1770s, was one of the most significant stages in the development of the cotton factory (Williams with Farnie 1992, 6). The carding engine consisted of a wide drum with a surface of wire spikes rotating within a close-fitting casing, which was also lined with spikes (*Pl 64, p 67*). The combing action of the spikes laid the cotton fibres parallel, and converted the lap into a soft, thick rope known as a 'sliver'.

Plate 162: A revolving flat carding engine (reproduced from Murphy 1911)

Until the late nineteenth century, the cotton in fine spinning mills passed through two carding engines, known as the 'breaker card' and the 'finishing card', the latter having finer teeth and a quicker motion. These were superseded in the twentieth century by the revolving flat carding engine, which produced the finest slivers (Pl 162). For the manufacture of the finest yarn, the sliver could at this stage be doubled in a 'sliver lap machine'. Introduced during the late nineteenth century, this machine was designed to produce the greatest possible degree of parallelism of the cotton fibres in preparation for combing (Murphy 1911, 112).

Combing

The production of a perfectly even yarn demanded uniformity in length of the component fibres. This was achieved via the combing process, which aimed to remove all split, broken, and wiry fibres to produce a smooth and uniform sliver. The first successful mechanical comber was patented by Platt and Collier in 1827, and was taken up by woollen manufacturers (Murphy 1911, 103). Its application to the cotton industry, however, awaited the introduction of a combing machine by Josué Heilmann in 1849, although it was only used in the production of the finest counts. In 1851, the patent rights to this machine were acquired by McConnel & Co, in conjunction with four other firms of fine spinners, which probably included A & G Murray and W H Houldsworth. The use of Heilmann's combing machine was recognised immediately by these firms as being 'indispensable in the spinning of fine yarns', and allowed them to maintain their reputation as the manufacturers of the best quality yarn available (McConnel 1913, 12); in 1851, Houldsworth's raised their maximum counts to an incredible 600 (Williams with Farnie 1992, 20).

Producing a Roving

Drawing, Slubbing, and Roving

After carding, the sliver was passed to a drawing frame (*Pl 65, p 67*), which was designed to elongate and attenuate the spongy slivers to straighten the filaments and lay them as parallel as possible. This machine usually comprised three pairs of rollers, which rotated at different speeds. Slivers from several different carding engines were stretched by draughting rollers and combined, or 'doubled', into a single sliver to eliminate any irregularities in thickness (Pl 163); this process was often repeated depending upon the requirements of the spinner. The resultant material was a loose porous cord of cotton, with the fibres arranged in parallel lines.

The cotton sliver then had to be condensed and strengthened in order for it to be suitable for spinning, which was achieved by imparting a slight twist to the cotton to produce a thin rope of lightly twisted fibres, known as a 'roving', which was approximately the thickness of a candlewick (Redding 1842, 17). This was carried out initially on a 'slubbing frame', which imparted the first light touch of twist, and then completed on a 'roving frame'. The latter machine represented the final stage in the preparation for the spinning of all yarn except for the finest counts, which required the use of a 'stretching frame' or, latterly, a 'bobbin-and-fly frame'. These machines had to perform two essential operations: to twist the sliver into a fine roving; and wind the roving in a regular and equable manner upon the bobbin, which was then passed to the spinning room (English 1969, 173).

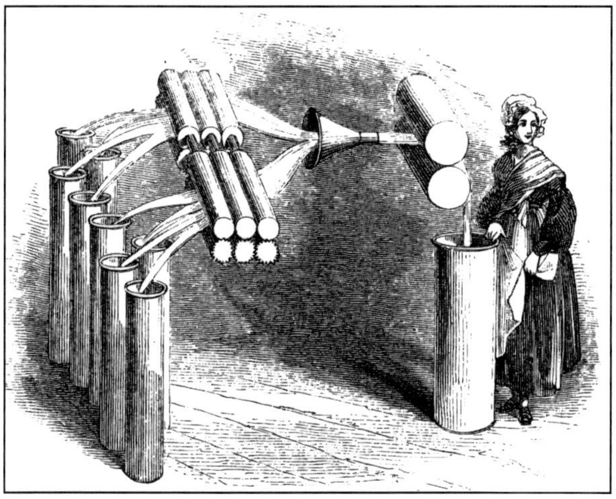

Plate 163: A drawing frame (reproduced from Redding 1842)

Spinning the Yarn

The final stage in the manufacture of cotton yarn was spinning, whereby the roving was stretched and twisted. Several variations of spinning machines were used to achieve this, although all followed one of two basic methods. The first type of spinning machine used in the factory-based cotton industry was the water-frame, patented by Richard Arkwright in 1769 (*Ch 2, p 13*), in which the roving was stretched by draughting rollers and twisted by the action of winding it on to the spindle. The frame was fixed in place, and spinning was a continuous process. The throstle-frame, designed to be driven by steam power, was introduced during the early nineteenth century. Whilst representing an improvement to the water-frame, the throstle adhered to the same principle of continuous operation. A more important advance for the continuous method was the ring-frame, which dominated the world production of yarn by the twentieth century. It was developed originally in the United States of America in 1829, and whilst its design was improved upon by British machine-makers, who became the largest producers of ring-frames in the world, the technology was not adopted in England until the mid-1870s (*Ch 5, pp 90-1*).

In contrast, Crompton's spinning mule embodied the principle of intermittent spinning, which had characterised Hargreaves' spinning jenny; the bobbins containing the roving were installed at the rear of the machine, and the spindles rested on a carriage. The mule carriage could be moved some 1.5 m away from the bobbins, pulling out the rovings, which were simultaneously twisted into yarn. As the carriage moved back in, the spun yarn was wound onto the spindles, during which time no yarn was spun. The mule was a versatile machine that produced yarn fine enough for lighter cloths and, unlike the yarn spun on water-frames, was suitable for both warp and weft. It was much more widely used than the water-frame, and was considerably more important to the Lancashire cotton industry, dominating production into the twentieth century (*Ch 2, p 14*).

During the early nineteenth century, mechanical power was only applied to the outward movement of the mule; the inward run, known as 'putting up', was controlled by the manual exertion of the spinner. 'Putting up' was a delicate operation that demanded accurate calculations and fine adjustments of machinery if the required count of yarn was to be achieved consistently, and this was reflected in the comparatively high wages paid to the mule spinners, the so-called 'barefoot aristocrats' (Mason 1987). This arrangement, however, restricted increased productivity as the extra physical burden of 'putting up' made large mules scarcely worthwhile (Catling 1986, 49). Attempts to address this problem, combined with a growing desire of mill owners to remove the reliance on the skilled spinners, led to the introduction of the 'mule jenny' in the 1820s, which mechanised the 'putting up' motion, although it fell short of a fully automated machine. This latter aspiration was achieved by Richard Roberts in *c* 1830, who introduced the 'self-acting mule'. This significant innovation wound the spun yarn directly onto the spindles rather than the spinner doing this manually, allowing much larger mules to be constructed; the number of spindles, and hence the size of each machine, was increased from about 200 in 1790 to over 1300 in 1890 (Pl 164). The application of self-acting mules, however, was restricted initially to the spinning of coarse yarn, and the machinery was not developed sufficiently to spin the finest counts until the end of the nineteenth century (Spencer 1880).

Plate 164: Self-acting spinning mules, c *1900*

The persistence of the mule has been viewed as an example of the technological inertia and conservatism inherent in the Lancashire textile industry of the late Victorian and Edwardian periods. A recent study argued forcefully that the continued use of the mule in a global industry dominated by ring-frames was a conscious decision, which fulfilled a niche market for finely spun cotton (Saxonhouse and Wright 1984). A & G Murray certainly appear to have employed spinning mules right up to the closure of their mill in the 1940s, although they did use some ring-spinning frames in the twentieth century (*Ch 5, p 91*).

Subsequent Processes

Some spinning mills included yarn-winding machines for transferring the yarn from spindles onto bobbins, which were then taken to the warehouse to await despatch. It is possible that A & G Murray carried out yarn winding in the Bengal Street block which, together with the Murray Street block, may also have been used for warehousing (*Ch 5, p 74*).

During the 1840s, mills were built to specialise in yarn doubling, which involved combining two or more yarns to form a stronger thread (Pl 165). Doubled yarn was used for lace-making or for sewing cotton, and provided a lucrative new market for Manchester's fine spinners. Indeed, James McConnel commented that all the large firms in the town 'doubled more or less' (Lee 1972, 86), and it is likely that A & G Murray built their Doubling Mill specifically for this purpose (*Ch 5, p 81*).

Plate 165: A doubling frame (reproduced from Rees 1819)

Textile finishing processes, such as dyeing, were usually carried out at a separate works. Weaving was similarly carried out in a separate mill during the early nineteenth century, although 'integrated' mills with both spinning and weaving became common in the mid-nineteenth century, as manufacturers attempted to avoid bankruptcy during depressions in the cotton-spinning trade (Ure 1836, 430).

APPENDIX 2

OVERVIEW OF THE FINDS

Ian Miller

The archaeological excavation and survey of A & G Murray's Mill produced only a small assemblage of artefacts pertaining to the use of the site for cotton spinning. Most of the artefacts, moreover, were derived from secondary and tertiary contexts, and dated from the late nineteenth or twentieth century. Nevertheless, several groups of finds proved to be of value in the interpretation of aspects of the site. In particular, a collection of spindles and bobbins can be identified with specific types of textile machinery that had been housed in the mill, whilst a range of stoneware and glass bottles presented some evidence for the patterns of production and consumption of soft drinks in Ancoats. In addition, a few objects, comprising shoes and coins, may represent folklore (Merrifield 1989).

Shoes

Two leather shoes were discovered during the archaeological survey (*Fig 37, p 100*). One of these, a woman's shoe or slipper, was concealed in the roof of Old Mill. Whilst of plain design with no evidence of decoration, it is clearly more than a workaday shoe, having a low front and slightly pointed toe. It is heavily worn and all trace of the outer sole is missing, although the configuration of the remaining insoles and stitching suggests that the shoe did not originally have a heel. Another worn shoe was found in the Murray Street block, where it had seemingly been placed during the construction of the building in *c* 1806 (*Ch 6, p 114*). This was somewhat smaller and had probably belonged to a child, and again was more than a simple workaday shoe.

Both shoes may be dated stylistically to the late eighteenth or early nineteenth century, and both appear to have been deliberately secreted, perhaps reflecting a long-established tradition of superstition that was well known by the seventeenth century (Merrifield 1989). It is of note that the shoe in Old Mill had evidently been replaced when the roof was rebuilt during a reduction in the height of the building (*Ch 6, p 134*), suggesting a continuation of this tradition into the twentieth century.

Coins

Two coins of George III, both halfpennies (third issue) dated 1799 (Pl 166), were recovered from areas of ceiling collapse on the fourth floor of Decker Mill.

Plate 166: A coin of George III, from Decker Mill

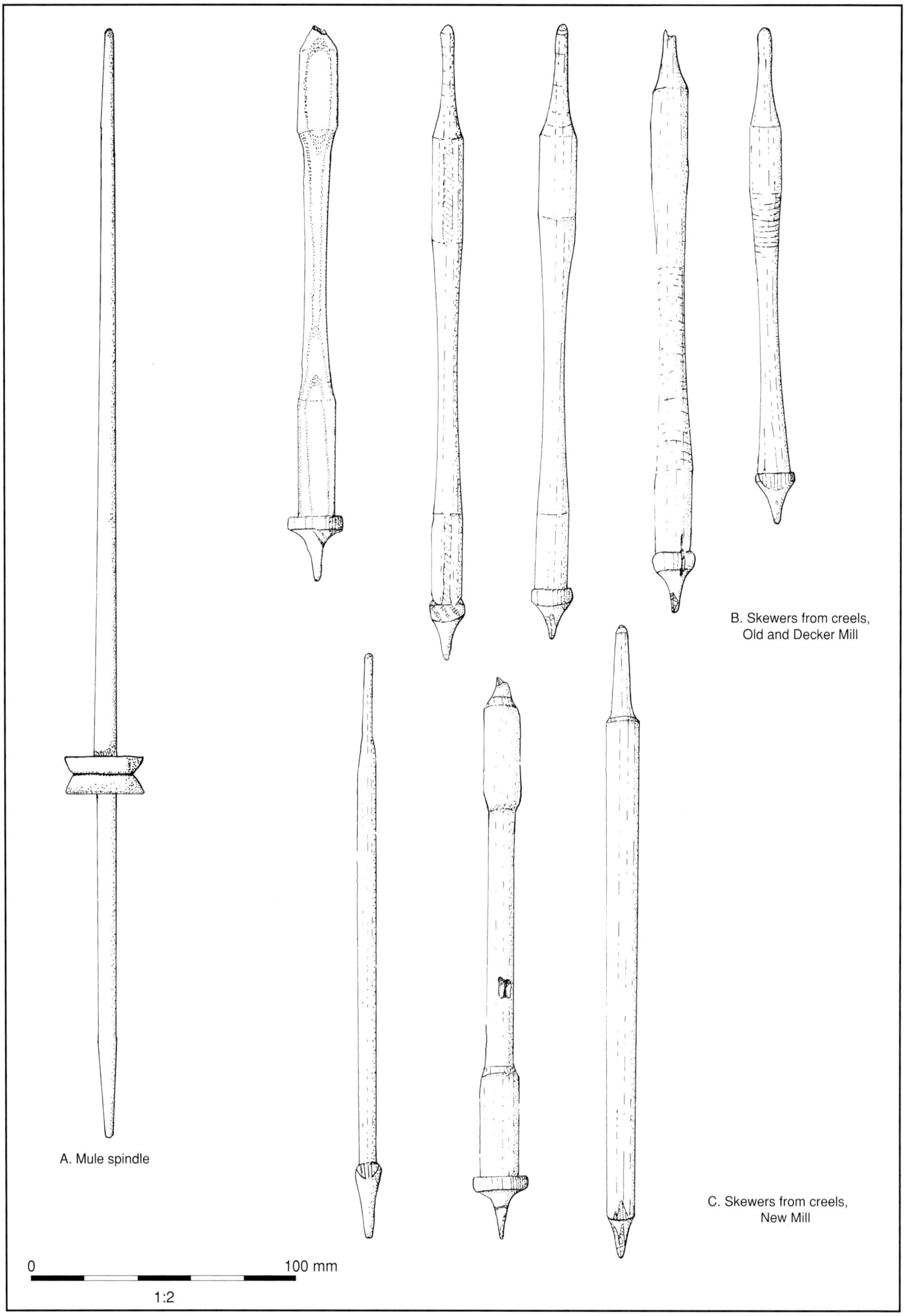

Figure 61: Mule spindle (A) and skewers from creels from Old and Decker Mill (B) and New Mill (C)

They displayed little wear, and had almost certainly been deposited within ten years of minting. Whilst accidental loss cannot be discounted, it perhaps seems more likely that the coins were also concealed deliberately during the original construction of the mill in 1801.

Metalwork

Excavation of the area at the rear of the Old and Decker Mill boiler house revealed eight large damper plates, which had regulated the flow of gases between the boilers and the chimney (*Ch 6, p 130*). Each of these movable cast-iron plates measured 4 ft (1.22 m) high and 1 ft (0.3 m) wide, and all were operated manually from the paved walkway by Decker Mill. The damper plates were not retained, although a single example was taken for long-term storage by the Museum of Science and Industry in Manchester.

Plate 167: Boiler-maintenance warning sign, recovered from backfilled rubble in the flue

Two metal objects of interest were recovered from the backfilled material within the section of the flue that had housed the economiser. One was a fragment of a mechanical scraper, which had been fitted closely around one of the water pipes within the economiser to prevent the accretion of sooting by its continual slow movement up and down the pipe.

The second metal object was an enamelled warning sign, which had evidently been used during periods of boiler maintenance (Pl 167). The sign incorporated the text *F.C.S. & D.A. L*^{d}, demonstrating that the boilers remained in operation during Phase 6 (1898-*c* 1947).

Textile-Machinery Components

The group of textile-machinery components was dominated by spindles, skewers, and bobbins, all of which were wooden, and had seemingly been made from sycamore (*acer pseudoplatanus*). Most of these were found beneath the floors of the spinning blocks, presumably representing accidental loss, although a cache of bobbins had been stacked carefully in a heating tower vent on the second floor (Bay **19**) of Decker Mill (Pl 168). These bobbins all had metal driving pegs attached to their lower flange and contained fine cotton rovings, suggesting that they had derived from a bobbin-and-fly frame (*Appendix 1*).

Plate 168: A cache of bobbins in Decker Mill

A few mule spindles were found, with the characteristic driving wharve fixed on the lower half of the spindle (Fig 61). Most of the objects, however, were skewers derived from the mule creels, where they had supported flanged bobbins containing

Plate 169: Flanged bobbins and skewers derived from mule creels on the top floor of Decker Mill

the cotton rovings. Most of these skewers were 9 in (229 mm) long, although some were 7 in (178 mm) long (Fig 61), perhaps reflecting the increasing size of mules during the nineteenth century. The associated flanged bobbins were typically of 1 in (25 mm) diameter and 170 mm long, with 43 mm diameter flanges at each end (Pl 169). Most had a small metal peg protruding from the lower flange, which would have connected with the driving mechanism.

Several bobbins, which may have derived from doubling frames, were also recovered from New Mill, implying that the doubling of yarn was perhaps carried out in the building at some stage. These were uniformly 5 in (127 mm) long and ¾ in (19 mm) in diameter, with a flange at each end (Pl 170). A slot across the underside of the lower flange on each spindle formed a housing for the driving mechanism. The lower flange on one of the spindles retained a thin steel casting, suggesting that it was of a twentieth-century date (Murphy 1911).

Plate 170: Possible doubling bobbins from New Mill

Evidence for the use of ring-spinning frames was provided by a small group of spindles found on the ground floor of New Mill (Pl 171). These all had a diameter of 26 mm, but varied in length between 7 in (178 mm) and 8 in (203 mm). A few of the spindles contained short lengths of spun yarn, which offered some potential for analysis, albeit from a very limited sample. Accurate weighing and measurement of this yarn (courtesy of Ian Gibson of Lancashire Museum Service) indicated that it had a count of approximately 15, and was thus somewhat coarser than the fine yarn usually associated with A & G Murray.

Plate 171: Spindles possible derived from ring-spinning frames

Plate 172: Bobbins derived from yarn-winding machines, and resembling those used on an early water-frame

Plate 173: Wooden drafting rollers with traces of cotton roving and fabric coating

A group of four bobbins, recovered from various locations in the mill complex, is likely to have derived from bobbin-winding machinery, intended to fit onto the creel of a beaming machine (J R Hornsby *pers comm*). The bobbins are all 78 mm long, with a central diameter of 19 mm, and have a distinctive groove incised around the bottom flange (Pl 172). Interestingly, the size and form of these bobbins closely resemble those used on one of Arkwright's original water-frames. Analysis of a small sample of spun yarn on one of these spindles concluded that it had a count of approximately 47. This contrasted with the results obtained from the measurement of spun yarn discovered in Decker Mill, which had an average count of 90.

Two probable wooden drafting rollers were also recovered from the spinning blocks (Pl 173). These both had short lengths of cotton roving attached to the roller elements, suggesting that they had derived from a drawing frame; the roving had a count in the region of 13, which corresponds to an appropriate feedstock for fine yarn (I Gibson *pers comm*). One of the drafting rollers, seemingly made of elm, had a length of 110 mm, and the diameter of the rollers was 30 mm. The second, composed of pine, was slightly shorter (104 mm) but had a larger diameter (33 mm). This retained the degraded traces of a fabric coating on the roller element.

Plate 174: Stoneware 'botanic beer' bottle, bearing the trademark of R Nuttall

Plate 175: Mineral water bottle, bearing the distinctive trademark of J Pratt & Son

Firm	Address	Product	Years Listed in Trade Directories (Slater)
Richard Bowes	Pearson Street, and (after 1890) Mangall Street, Ancoats	Ginger beer and mineral water	1884-*c* 1895
Patrick Dowd	Initially New Butler Street, then Beswick Street Ancoats, latterly Hillkirk Street, Ashton New Road	Mineral and aerated water	1879-post-1920
William Dales	Mitchell Street, Pollard Street, Ancoats, and (after 1897) Philips Park Road, Beswick	'Botanic beer'	1892-1900
Dales and Son	Philips Park Road, Beswick	'Botanic beer'	1900-9
Richard Nichols	Irlam Street, Newton Heath	'Botanic beer'	*c* 1901-11
R Nuttall	Sutton Street and latterly Marsh Street, Ancoats	Mineral water	1895-1905
J Pratt & Son	Leigh Street, Ancoats	Ginger beer and mineral water	1879-1909
Slack and Cox	Pot Street, Ancoats, and latterly Hyde Road	Mineral water	1895-1914
R White	Heath Street, Newton Heath	Ginger beer and mineral water	1903-10

Table 3: Popular manufacturers of mineral water and ginger beer, from bottles excavated at A & G Murray's Mill

Workers' Drinks

Evidence for workers' drinks was provided by stoneware and glass bottles, including numerous complete vessels, which had contained either mineral water or ginger beer. Most of these were recovered during the excavation of the canal basin, although a small group of nine stoneware bottles was also discovered at the base of the demolished Bengal Street block stair tower.

Most of the stoneware bottles were stamped with trademarks, allowing the identification of the firms manufacturing the drinks. In particular, 'mineral water' and 'botanic beer' manufacturers, 'R Nichols', 'J Pratt & Son', 'R Nuttall', 'W Dales' and 'Dales & Son', were well represented. The archaeological excavations of New Islington Mill and Waller's Mill (*Ch 4*) produced similar collections of stoneware bottles, many also bearing the names 'Richard Nichols', 'J Pratt & Son', 'W Dales ', or 'R Nuttall' (Pl 174).

The assemblage of glass artefacts was dominated by mineral water bottles, the majority of which (47 bottles) were again recovered from the infilled canal basin. Of these, most were dated to the late nineteenth or early twentieth century. Many of the glass bottles similarly had manufacturers' names, the most prevalent being 'J Pratt & Son' (Pl 175), although 'P Dowd' and 'R White' were also well represented.

Most of these firms were based in Ancoats, or the adjacent township of Newton Heath, and are listed in trade directories for the 1890s (*eg* Slater 1895). Trade directories for the mid-nineteenth century do not contain any entries for mineral water manufacturers, with very few producers of ginger beer in Ancoats (*eg* Slater 1863), and the oldest firms, Patrick Dowd and J Pratt & Son, were established in the late 1870s (Table 3). This suggests that consumption of these soft drinks was a late-Victorian trend. The number of soft drinks' manufacturers in Ancoats reached a peak in the 1890s and early 1900s, but declined thereafter; Slater's trade directory for 1914, for instance, only lists three such manufacturers. It is perhaps notable that the drinks had been produced and consumed in Ancoats, with little evidence from the excavated assemblages for drinks' manufacturers from outside the area, reflecting a dominance of the local economy.

Glossary

Building Terms

Bay	The portion of a structure between principal supporting beams, also used as a relative length of measurement.
Birdsmouth	A notch cut from the end of an inclined timber as it bears on an horizontal timber such as a wall plate.
Bow window	A rounded bay window which projects from a wall, normally with an arc-shaped top and base.
Coping	Protective course of masonry or brickwork capping a wall.
Cornice	A flat-topped ledge with moulded underside projecting along the top of a building, or the decorative moulding in the angle between wall and ceiling.
Cotter	Tapering, wedge-shaped key used together with a **gib** to make a tight strapped joint.
Dragon-beam	A beam running diagonally across the corner of a wall to support a hip rafter.
English Garden Wall bond	A pattern of bonding bricks that uses more than one course of **stretchers** between two courses of **headers**. The ratio is usually three or five courses of stretchers, but other combinations exist. It is one of the most popular of all brickwork bonds, particularly in the north of England.
Flemish Bond	A pattern of bonding bricks whereby **headers** and **stretchers** are used alternately in each course.
Garret	An attic workshop.
Gib	U-shaped pieces of wrought iron used in conjunction with a **cotter** to make a tight joint at a strap.
Half-truss	One half of a full truss, set longitudinally to support a **hipped roof**.
Header	A brick laid across the wall thickness to expose an end face.
Hipped Roof	A ridged roof with sloping faces to each end, as opposed to vertical gables.
Newel	A post in a flight of stairs.
Queen post	Transverse frame supporting the roof at each bay division, formed of pairs of vertical struts between tie beam and collar, supporting only the principal rafters, not longitudinal timbers.
Quoin	Shaped stone used to form the corners of walls or door and window openings.
Pilaster	A flat representation of a classical column in shallow relief.
Purlin	A longitudinal member supporting the common rafters of a roof.
Ridge board	A light plank used to support the upper ends of common rafters at the apex of a roof. Often clasped by a truss.

Scantling — A measured or prescribed size, dimensions, or calibre. Generally used to describe the cross-section of a timber.

Soffit — A term usually applied to the under horizontal face of an architrave or horizontal cornice, but also used to describe the under surface of a beam, lintel, vault, or arch.

Sole plate — A structural timber, laid horizontally, forming the base, or housing, for an associated mounting or masonry block.

Stretcher — A brick laid longitudinally within a wall, exposing one long face.

Voussoir — A wedge-shaped stone block or brick which forms part of an arch.

Textile Terms

Backing–off — Part of the operating cycle of the spinning mule, as the spindles are reversed to unwind coils of yarn.

Batting — Beating cotton fibres over a frame across which were stretched cords. This process, usually undertaken by women, cleaned the cotton and allowed for the removal of seeds, which were picked out by hand.

Bleaching — Any process of whitening fabrics.

Bobbin — A round spool for holding yarn, frequently flanged at both ends.

Calender — A series of rolls in a stack, which smooth out paper or cloth to enable it to be printed.

Calico — White cotton cloth with patterns printed in one or more colours.

Card — A fine but stiff wire brush by means of which fibrous materials may be disentangled preparatory to spinning. The term is also used to mean a carding engine, which combed the fibres mechanically into lengths and laid them parallel to form a **sliver**.

Cloth — Any woven or felted fabric.

Count — The number of **hanks** of finished yarn, each 840 yards long, that can be made from one pound of cotton. The higher the count, the finer the thread.

Creel — The bar or stand upon which the bobbins giving off yarn are placed on the spinning frames.

Damask — A richly and highly patterned fabric woven of coloured warp and weft.

Dimity — A stout white cotton fabric, plain or twisted, with a raised pattern on one side.

Doubled yarn — Thread doubled and retwisted for lace thread on doubling frame.

Drawing — Cotton drawn-out and doubled in a drawing frame to straighten the fibres and even out the grist.

Fancys — Cloths woven or coloured in patterns not common to the trade.

Felt	Fabric made by beating and rolling wool fibres under moist heat.
Finishing	After cloth has been woven, it goes through a series of finishing processes, which can include bleaching, dyeing and printing.
Fulling	Pounding newly woven woollen cloth in an alkaline liquor to absorb natural greases and oils that were added during the weaving, and to thicken up the fabric to give a stronger and denser material.
Fustian	Strong twilled cloth, with a linen warp and a cotton weft, whose production increased steadily in the Manchester area during the early seventeenth century.
Gassing	Singeing fine hairs and flying filaments from the surface of yarns and fabrics.
Granderelles	Fancy yarn produced by twisting two or more single threads of different colours or fibres together.
Grey	Unbleached cotton or linen cloth.
Grist	The thickness of yarn.
Hank	Unit of length. In reference to cotton yarn, one hank equates to 840 yards.
Hosiery	Knitted goods.
Lap	Thick sheet of fibres produced from the initial cleaning of raw cotton, and processed further in a carding engine.
Linen	Cloth made of flax yarn.
Minder	Operative who attended the machines, especially the self-acting mules, who were less skilled than the mule spinners of the early nineteenth century.
Mule	Cotton-spinning machine derived from an invention by Samuel Crompton, and so-named because it combined the roller-drawing principle of Arkwright's water-frame and the carriage-drawing of Hargreaves' spinning jenny.
Mule carriage	The front part of the mule frame, which moves in and out, bearing the spindles.
Mule headstock	The major assembly of mechanical components by means of which the working elements of a mule are controlled.
Muslin	A class of goods, the sole distinguishing feature of which is lightness and openness of texture.
Piecer	Operative employed by a mule spinner to tie together strands of cotton which broke whilst spinning. This job was usually undertaken by children.
Putting-up	The inward cycle of the **mule**. The carriage is driven, winding the yarn on the cops.
Ring frame	A continuous spinning machine which largely displaced mules during the twentieth century.
Roving	A thin rope of lightly twisted, substantially parallel fibres from which yarn is spun.
Scavenger	A person, usually a child, employed to clean the machinery.

Scutcher	A machine for opening and cleaning raw cotton, reputedly introduced to Manchester by John Kennedy in 1808-9.
Self-acting mule	A mule spinning frame which automatically performed drawing, twisting, winding-on, and copping motions. The machine was perfected by Richard Roberts in 1830, but was not applied to fine spinning until the 1860s.
Sliver	A thick, soft, untwisted rope of fibre, produced from a carding engine.
Slubbing	A lightly twisted rope of fibre roughly intermediate between a **sliver** and a **roving**.
Smallwares	A cloth that usually comprised a linen **warp** and a **worsted** weft.
Spindle	The centre of the spinning action, commonly a tapering pin of wood or metal.
Staple	Average length of a fibre.
Twist	Yarn intended for use as **warp**.
Warp	Yarn which lies lengthwise in the cloth.
Weaving	Method of making fabric by interlacing threads. Plain weave is a simple, over-under construction giving a flat, even texture, while patterned weaves such as twill and herringbone are obtained by differential raising of warp threads on the loom.

Bibliography

Cartographic Sources

Adshead, J, 1851 *Illustrated Plans of the Townships of Manchester*

Anon, *c* 1822 *Plans of All the Cotton-Spinning Mills Within the Township of Manchester*

Bancks, G, and Co, 1832 *A Map of Manchester and Salford*

Bancks, G, and Thornton, R, 1800 *A Plan of Manchester and Salford*

Casson, R, and Berry, J, 1741 *Plan of Manchester and Salford*, (rev *c* 1745, 1746, and 1755)

Green, W, 1794 *Map of Manchester and Salford*

Laurent, C, 1793 *Map of Manchester and Salford*

Ordnance Survey, 1850 60": 1 mile map, Manchester sheet 24

Ordnance Survey, 1891 10': 1 mile First Edition map, Lancashire sheets CIV.7 and CIV.22

Ordnance Survey, 1893 1:2500 First Edition map, Lancashire sheets CIV.7 and CIV.11

Ordnance Survey, 1933 1:2500 map, Lancashire sheets CIV.7 and CIV.11, Rev edn

Ordnance Survey, 1969 1:2500 map, Lancashire sheets CIV.7 and CIV.11, Rev edn

Ordnance Survey, 1970 Geological Survey, 1:63,360 map, Sheet 85, Drift

Pigot, J, 1819 *New Plan of Manchester and Salford*

Thornton, R, 1824 *Map of Manchester and its Environs*

Yates, W, 1786 *Survey of the County Palatine of Lancaster*

Primary Sources

British Parliamentary Papers (BPP)

PP(HC) 1816 III Select Committee on State of Children Employed in Manufactories

PP(HC) 1833 [450] XX, D1, Factory Inquiry Commission, First Report, Employment of Children in Factories

PP(HC) 1834 [167] XX, A1, Factories Inquiry Commission, Supplementary Report, Part II: Lancashire District

Lancashire Record Office (LRO)

National Probate Calendars 1878 22/59 Jane Murray

WCW 1818 Adam Murray

WCW 1821 James Murray

WCW 1855 George Murray

Guildhall Library, London

Royal Exchange Assurance Company

7253/15/108378 Fire policy register

7253/32A/157421 Fire policy register

7253/158128 Fire policy register

7253/158142 Fire policy register

7253/159180 Fire policy register

7253/164597 Fire policy register

7253/169411 Fire policy register

7253/169894 Fire policy register

7253/170024 Fire policy register

7253/180501 Fire policy register

Sun Insurance Office

MS 945442/11937 Fire Policy

Boulton and Watt Archive, Birmingham Central Library (BWA)

3147/2/10/35 Agreement for Erecting a Steam Engine at Manchester, Endorsed by Adam and George Murray, 1 August 1798

3147/3/41/28 Letter, M R Boulton to James Watt Jnr, 31 October 1803

3147/3/416/74 Letter, Adam and George Murray to Boulton and Watt, Manchester, 26 September 1798

3147/3/42/23 Letter, M R Boulton to James Watt Jnr, 17 March 1806

3147/3/478/19 Sketches, Cross-Sections and Floor Plans of Storeys I-IV of the Old and New Mills, McConnel & Kennedy, February 1806

3147/3/478/21 Memorandum, Sketches and Particulars for Lighting Apparatus for Messrs McConnel and Kennedy's Old Mill, Manchester, 25 March 1809

3147/3/485 Letter, J Mabbot to Boulton and Watt, 17 March 1798

3147/3/51/13 Letter, James Watt Jnr to M R Boulton, 23 June 1802

3147/3/52/18 Letter, James Watt Jnr to M R Boulton, 27 June 1803

3147/3/52/19 Letter, James Watt Jnr to M R Boulton, 30 June 1803

3147/3/52/32 Letter, James Watt Jnr to M R Boulton, 2nd August 1803

3147/5/44 Various drawings and correspondance from Boulton and Watt relating to two engines for Peter Drinkwater, 1789-9

3147/5/167 Engine Drawings for A & G Murray, 1798

3147/5/182 Engine Drawings for J Lees, April 1799

3147/5/295 Engine Drawings for A & G Murray, 1801-2

3147/5/364 Engine Drawings for A & G Murray, 1805

3147/5/465 Engine Drawings for McConnel & Kennedy

3147/5/524 Engine Drawings for A & G Murray, 1840

Bolton Archives (BA)

ZHH/6 Hick, Hargreaves & Co Ltd, Engine Book, nd

Greater Manchester Record Office (GMRO)

B/CTLD/1/48 Memoranda from A & G Murray Ltd, Newcastle, of Courtaulds Northern Textiles, 1 April 1955 and 5 October 1965

B2/10/5 Rochdale Canal Company: Plan of the Rochdale Canal in Manchester from Deansgate to Murray Street, February 1820

B2/10/6 Rochdale Canal Company: List of factories in Manchester which use the water of the Rochdale Canal, February 1820

B2/12/3 Rochdale Canal Company: Water supply to mill owners, nd

Rochdale Local Studies Unit (RLSU)

C/RCC/1/3 Rochdale Canal Company Ltd, list of water users, *c* 1950

John Rylands Library, University of Manchester (JRL)

McConnel & Kennedy Archive

MCK/2/2/23 Letter from McConnel & Co to A H Stott, 12 February 1868

Manchester Archives, Manchester Local Studies Unit (MLSU)

25671 Plans of the Mosley Family Estate, 1805-08

M9/40/2/67 Township of Manchester Rate Books (Poor Rate Assessment), Vol 1, District 1, Ancoats, 1806

M9/40/2/79 Township of Manchester Rate Books (Poor Rate Assessment), Vol 1, District 1, Ancoats, 1815

M9/40/2/100 Township of Manchester Rate Books (Poor Rate Assessment), Vol 1, District 1, Ancoats, 1829

M9/40/2/106 Township of Manchester Rate Books (Poor Rate Assessment), Vol 1, District 1, Ancoats, 1832

107/2225 Folio 390-402 Census returns 1851

MC 3834M 892 Fire services' plan 1902

Newspapers and Journals

The British Architect, 27 January 1893

The Builder, 1 October 1853, **11**

The Builder, 29 November 1862, **20**

Colliery Guardian, 24 November 1939

The Cotton Factory Times, 31 January 1908

Illustrated London News, 29 November 1862

Illustrated London News, July 1909

Manchester Chronicle, 21 December 1849, The Cotton Metropolis, Manchester in 1849

Manchester Guardian, 29 January 1908, A Mill Fire

Manchester Mercury, 13 March 1781

Manchester Mercury, 1 January 1782

Manchester Mercury, 24 July 1784

Manchester Mercury, 8 February 1785

Manchester Mercury, 1 September 1785

Manchester Mercury, 21 March 1786

Manchester Mercury, 1 August 1786

Manchester Mercury, 29 January 1788

Manchester Mercury, 6 July 1790

Manchester Mercury, 27 August 1790

Manchester Mercury, 1 November 1791

Manchester Mercury, 11 September 1792

Manchester Mercury, 4 December 1792

Manchester Mercury, 10 February 1793

Manchester Mercury, 14 January 1794

Manchester Mercury, 10 June 1794

Manchester Mercury, 7 April 1795

Manchester Mercury, 17 December 1799

Manchester Mercury, 31 October 1813

Manchester Mercury, 7 July 1818

Manchester Mercury, 22 May 1827

News Chronicle, 10 February 1959

Pottery Gazette and Glass Trade Review, 1 January 1903

The Times, 24 August 1819

Unpublished Insurance Plans

Goad, Insurance Plan, Manchester, Vol II, Sheet 235, 1927 rev

Goad, Insurance Plan, Manchester, Vol II, Sheet 218, 1943 rev

Goad, Insurance Plan, Manchester, Vol II, Sheet 235, 1966 rev

Manchester City Council, Building Control Department

Building Control Plan 3331 Proposed cage hoist for New Mill, April 1909

Building Control Plan 4454 Proposed building of Paragon and Royal Mills, 1911

Building Control Plan 16604 Alterations to Blowing House, 1924

Building Control Plan 17927 Proposed First-Aid Room in Bobbin Store, August 1926

Building Control Plan 19038 Proposed Rebuilding of Little Mill, June 1908

Building Control Plan 20244 Alterations to Old Beam Engine House, 1930

Building Control Plan 20366 Proposed New Entrances, 1930

Building Control Plan 20558 Alterations to Bengal Street block, August 1930

Building Control Plan 28486 Addition of Lift Shaft and Loading Bay, 1948

Building Control Plan 30000 Various Alterations, 1950

Building Control Plan 30059 Conversion of Air Raid Shelter, 1950

Building Control Plan 45761 Strengthening Proposals, 1959

Building Control Plan 53792 Sanitary Improvements, 1961

Selected Trade Directories

Anon, 1828 *Machester and Salford Director and Memorandum Book*, Manchester

Bancks, G, 1800 *Manchester and Salford Directory*, Manchester

Bancks, G, 1802 *Manchester and Salford Directory*, Manchester

Dean, R, and Dean, W, 1809 *Manchester and Salford Directory*, Manchester

Dean, R, and Dean, W, 1811 *Manchester and Salford Directory*, Manchester

Holme, E, 1788 *A Directory for the Towns of Manchester and Salford*, Manchester

Hosking, A W, 1877 *Hosking's Guide to Manchester Trade*, Manchester

Kelly, 1858 *Post Office Directory of Manchester*, London

Kelly, 1937 *Manchester, Salford and Stretford Directory*, **1**, Kingston-upon-Thames

Kelly, 1942 *Manchester, Salford and Stretford Directory*, **1**, Kingston-upon-Thames

Kelly, 1954 *Manchester, Salford and Stretford Directory*, **1**, Kingston-upon-Thames

Kelly, 1959 *Manchester, Salford and Stretford Directory*, **1**, Kingston-upon-Thames

Kelly, 1965 *Manchester, Salford and Stretford Directory*, **1**, Kingston-upon-Thames

Pigot, J, 1813 *Manchester and Salford Directory for 1813*, Manchester

Pigot, J, and Dean, R, 1815 *Manchester and Salford Directory*, Manchester

Pigot, J, and Dean, R, 1817 *Manchester and Salford Directory*, Manchester

Pigot, J, and Dean, R, 1821 *New Directory of Manchester and Salford for 1821-22*, Manchester

Pigot, J, and Dean, R, 1825 *Manchester and Salford Directory*, Manchester

Pigot, J, and Slater, I, 1841 *General Directory of Manchester and Salford*, Manchester

Pigot, J, and Son, 1836 *Manchester and Salford Directory*, Manchester

Raffald, E, 1781 *A Directory for the Town of Manchester and Salford*, Manchester

Raffald, E, 1788 *A Directory for the Town of Manchester and Salford*, Manchester

Scholes, J, 1794 *Manchester and Salford Directory*, Manchester

Scholes, J, 1797 *Manchester and Salford Directory*, Manchester

Skinner, T, 1930 *Skinner's Cotton Trade Directory of the World*, London

Slater, I, 1852 *General and Classified Directory and Street Register of Manchester and Salford*, Manchester

Slater, I, 1863 *General and Classified Directory and Street Register of Manchester and Salford*, Manchester

Slater, I, 1872 *General and Classified Directory and Street Register of Manchester and Salford*, Manchester

Slater, I, 1874 *General and Classified Directory and Street Register of Manchester and Salford*, Manchester

Slater, I, 1883 *General and Classified Directory and Street Register of Manchester and Salford*, Manchester

Slater, I, 1914 *General and Classified Directory and Street Register of Manchester and Salford*, Manchester

Wardle, M, and Bentham, 1815 *The Commercial Directory for 1814-15*, Manchester

Worrall, J, 1891 *The Cotton Spinners and Manufacturers' Directory for Lancashire*, Oldham

Worrall, J, 1910 *The Cotton Spinners and Manufacturers' Directory for Lancashire*, Oldham

Secondary Sources

Aikin, J, 1795 *A Description of the County from Thirty to Forty Miles Round Manchester*, London

Allen, Z, 1832 *The Practical Tourist*, **1**, New York

Ashmore, O, 1969 *Industrial Archaeology of Lancashire*, Newton Abbot

Ashworth, G, 1987 *The Lost Rivers of Manchester*, Altrincham

Aspin, C, 1995 *The First Industrial Society: Lancashire, 1750–1850*, Preston

Aspin, C, 2003 *The Water-Spinners*, Helmshore

Aston, J, 1816 *A Picture of Manchester*, Manchester

Baines, E, 1835 *History of Cotton Manufacture in Great Britain*, London

Barfoot, J R, 1840 *The Progress of Cotton*, London

BDP and OA North, 2007 *Murrays' Mills, Ancoats: Conservation Plan Review*, unpubl rep

Berg, M (ed), 1979 *Technology and Toil in Nineteenth Century Britain*, London

Bindman, D, and Riemann, G (eds), 1993 *The English Journeys. Journal Of A Visit To France And Britain In 1826*, London

Biographical Publishing Company, 1897 *Men of the Period: Lancashire*, London

British Constructional Steelwork Association, 1984 *Historical Structural Steel Handbook*, London

Bourne, J, 1872 *A Treatise on the Steam Engine*, 10th edn, London

Briggs, A, 1971, *Victorian Cities*, 3rd edn, Harmondsworth

Brown, J, 1832 *A Memoir of Robert Blincoe, An Orphan Boy*, Manchester (1977 facsimile)

Brumhead, D, and Wyke, T, 1997 'The Duke's Agents Have Made a Wharf': Castlefield and its Warehouses, in R McNeil and J S F Walker (eds), *The Heritage Atlas 3: Warehouse Album*, Manchester, 26-9

Brumhead, D, and Wyke, T, 2004 *Moving Manchester: Aspects of the History of Transport in the City and Region since 1700*, Manchester

Brunskill, R W, 1990 *Brick Building in Britain*, London

Brunskill, R W, 1994 *Timber Building in Britain*, 2nd edn, London

Buchanan, R A, and Watkins, G, 1976 *The Industrial Archaeology of the Stationary Steam Engine*, London

Bullen, A, and Fowler, A, 1986 *The Cardroom Workers Union*, Manchester

Burnett, T, 1899 *Manchester and Salford at the Close of the Nineteenth Century: Contemporary Biographies*, Brighton

Butt, J (ed), 1971 *Robert Owen: Prince of Cotton Spinners*, Newton Abbot

Butterworth, J, 1823 *A Complete History of the Cotton Trade*, Manchester

Calladine, A, and Fricker, J, 1993 *East Cheshire Textile Mills*, London

Catling, H, 1986 *The Spinning Mule*, 2nd edn, Lancashire

Chalklin, C W, 1974 *Provincial Towns of Georgian England*, London

Chaloner, W H, 1954 Peter Drinkwater and the Early Factory System in Manchester 1788-1800, *Bull John Rylands Library*, **37**, 78-102

Chaloner, W H, 1962 The Birth of Modern Manchester, in C F Carter (ed), *Manchester and its Region: A Survey Prepared for the British Association*, Manchester, 131-46

Chandler, J, 1993 *John Leland's Itinerary: Travels in Tudor England*, Stroud

Chapman, S D, 1967 *The Early Factory Masters*, Newton Abbot

Chapman, S D, 1970 Fixed Capital Formation in the British Cotton Industry, *Econ Hist Rev*, 2 ser, **23**(2), 238-41

Chapman, S D, 1972 *The Cotton Industry in the Industrial Revolution*, London

Chapman, S D, 1981 The Arkwright Mills - Colquhoun's Census of 1788 and Archaeological Evidence, *Ind Archaeol Rev*, **6** (1), 5-27

Chapman, S J, 1905 *The Cotton Industry and Trade*, London

City of Manchester, 1887 *Copy Proceedings of the Council 1885-86*, Manchester

Clapham, J H, 1915 Some Factory Statistics of 1815-16, *Econ J*, **25**, 475-8

Clapham, J H, 1936 *The Economic Development of France and Germany*, Cambridge

Clark, S, 1978 Chorlton Mills and their Neighbours, *Ind Archaeol Rev*, **2** (3), 207-39

Collier, F, 1964 *The Family Economy of the Working Classes in the Cotton Industry 1784-1833*, Manchester

Collinge, E, 1962 *Historic Places of Manchester*, in N J Frangopulo (ed), *Rich Inheritance: A Guide to the History of Manchester*, Manchester, 168-204

Collinson, R, 1956 *Directory and Guide to the Manchester Royal Exchange Ltd*, Manchester

Cooper, G, 2002 *Illustrated History of Manchester's Suburbs*, Manchester

Cossons, N, 1975 *Industrial Archaeology*, Newton Abbot

Countryside Commission, 1998 *Countryside Character, Volume 2: North West*, Cheltenham

Daniels, G W, 1915a Valuation of Manchester Cotton Factories in the Early Years of the Nineteenth Century, *Econ J*, **25**, 625-6

Daniels, G W, 1915b The Early Records of a Great Manchester Cotton-Spinning Firm, *Econ J*, **25**, 175-88

Daniels, G W, 1927 Industrial Lancashire Prior and Subsequent to the Invention of the Mule, *J Textile Institute*, **8**, 1-16

Daniels, G W, 1930 Samuel Crompton's Census of the Cotton Industry in 1811, *Econ Hist*, **2**, 107-10

Darbyshire, A, 1887 *A Book of Old Manchester and Salford*, Manchester

DCMS, 2001 *The Historic Environment: A Force for Our Future*, London

de Tocqueville, C, 1958 *Journeys to England and Ireland*, London

Dickinson, H W, and Jenkins, R, 1989 *James Watt and the Steam Engine*, 2nd edn, London

Dickinson, T C, 2002 *Cotton Mills of Preston: The Power Behind the Thread*, Lancaster

DoE, 1994 *Planning Policy Guidance Note 15: Planning and the Historic Environment*, London

Donald Insall Associates and Structural Perspectives, 2002 *A Conservation Plan for Murrays' Mills Prepared for Ancoats Buildings Preservation Trust*, unpubl rep

Donnachie, I L, and Hewitt, G, 1993 *Historic New Lanark: The Dale and Owen Industrial Community Since 1785*, Edinburgh

Edwards, M M, 1967 *The Growth of the British Cotton Trade 1780-1815*, Manchester

Engels, F, 1973, *The Condition of the Working Class in England*, Lawrence and Wishart edn, London

English, W, 1969 *The Textile Industry*, London

English Heritage, 2001 *The Shudehill and Northern Quarter Area of Manchester*, **B/066/2001**, unpubl rep

English Heritage, 2005 *Buildings at Risk Register*, London, http://www.english-heritage.org.uk/server/show/nav.1424

Fairburn, W, 1861 A *Brief Memoir of the Late John Kennedy, Esq*, Manchester

Fairbairn, W, 1866 Description of the Removing and Replacing of the Iron Columns in a Cotton Mill, *Proc Inst Mech Eng*, **17**, 181-5

Falconer, K A, 2001 Fireproof Mills – The Widening Perspective, in K A Falconer (ed), *Derwent Valley Textile Mills*, Belper, 11-37

Falconer, K A, 2002 Manchester and Salford - The Proposed World Heritage Site, in R McNeil and D George (eds), *The Heritage Atlas 4: Manchester- Archetype City of the Industrial Revolution*, Manchester, 12-4

Farey, J, 1827 *A Treatise on the Steam Engine*, London

Farnie, D A, 1979 T*he English Cotton Industry and the World Market*, 1815-1896, Oxford

Fine Cotton Spinners' and Doublers' Association Limited, 1909 *Prospectus*, Manchester

Fine Spinners' and Doublers' Ltd, 1948 *Behind the Distaff*, Manchester

Fitton, R S, 1989 *The Arkwrights: Spinners of Fortune*, Manchester

Fitton, R S, and Wadsworth, A P, 1958 *The Strutts and the Arkwrights 1758-1830: A Study of the Early Factory System*, Manchester

Fitzgerald, R S, 1988 The Development of the Cast-Iron Frame in Textile Mills to 1850, *Ind Archaeol Rev*, **10** (2), 127-45

Fowler, A, 2003 *Lancashire Cotton Operatives and Work, 1900-1950*, Aldershot

Frangopulo, N J, 1962 The Growth of Manchester, in N J Frangopulo (ed), *Rich Inheritance: A Guide to the History of Manchester*, Manchester, 1-52

Freeman, J R, 1891 Comparison of English and American Types of Factory Construction, *Textile Manufacturer*, **17**, 175-9

Freeman, M, 1980 Transporting Methods in the British Cotton Industry during the Industrial Revolution, *J Trans Hist*, 3 ser, **1** (1), 59-74

French, G J, 1859 *Life and Times of Samuel Crompton*, London

Galbi, D A, 1997 Child Labour and the Division of Labour in the Early English Cotton Mills, J *Population Economics*, **10**, 357-75

Gausden, T, 1988 Manchester Early Dwellings Research Group, *Manchester Region Hist Rev*, **2** (1), 37-41

George, D, and Brumhead, D, 2002 The Mersey Irwell Navigation - The Old Quay at Manchester, in R McNeil and D George (eds), *The Heritage Atlas 4: Manchester - Archetype City of the Industrial Revolution*, Manchester, 22-4

Giles, C, and Goodall, I H, 1992 *Yorkshire Textile Mills 1770-1930*, London

GMAU, 1990 *Ancoats Mills: Detailed Studies of Three Mill Complexes in the Ancoats Conservation Area*, unpubl rep

Griffiths, T, 2001 *The Lancashire Working Classes c 1880-1930*, Oxford

Guest, R, 1823 *A Compendious History of the Cotton-Manufacture*, Manchester

Hadfield, C, 1994 *British Canals: The Inland Waterways of Britain and Ireland*, 8th edn, Stroud

Hadfield, C, and Biddle, G, 1970 *The Canals of North West England*, **2**, Newton Abbot

Hall, D, Wells, C E, and Huckerby, E, 1995 *The Wetlands of Greater Manchester*, Lancaster Imprints **3**, Lancaster

Harland, J (ed), 1861 *Mamecestre: Chapters from the Early Recorded History of the Barony*, **1**, Chetham Soc, Old ser, **53**, Manchester

Harley, L S, 1974 A Typology of Brick, *J Brit Archaeol Assoc*, 3 ser, **37**, 64-87

Harrison, M, 1993 Art and Social Regeneration: The Ancoats Art Museum, *Manchester Region Hist Rev*, **7**, 63-9

Hartwell, C, 2001 *Manchester*, London

Hartwell, C, Hyde, M, and Pevsner, N, 2004 *The Buildings of England. Lancashire: Manchester and the South-East*, London

Heathcoate, C H, 1876 The Old Halls in the Neighbourhood of Manchester, *Brit Architect*, **5**, 57-8

Henderson, W O, 1968 *Industrial Britain under the Regency: The Diaries of Escher, Bodmer, May and de Gallois 1814-18*, London

Henry Bannerman & Sons Ltd, 1893 *Diary and Buyers Guide*, Manchester

Higham, N J, 2004 *A Frontier Landscape: The North West in the Middle Ages*, Macclesfield

Hills, R L, 1970 *Power in the Industrial Revolution*, Manchester

Hills, R L, 1989 *A History of the Stationary Steam Engine*, Cambridge

Historical Publishing Company, 1888 *Manchester of Today*, London

Hobsbawm, E, 1962 *The Age of Revolution*, London

Holden, R N, 1998 *Stott and Sons, Architects of the Lancashire Cotton Mill*, Lancaster

Holland, A J, 1976 *The Age of Industrial Expansion*, 2nd edn, Sunbury-on-Thames

Hopwood, E, 1969 *A History of the Lancashire Cotton Industry and the Amalgamated Weavers' Association*, Manchester

Howe, A, 1984 *The Cotton Masters 1830-1860*, Oxford

Hughes, S, 1853 *Treatise on Gas Works and the Practice of Manufacturing and Distributing Coal Gas*, London

Ingle, G, 1997 *Yorkshire Cotton: The Yorkshire Cotton Industry, 1780-1835*, Preston

Jewkes, J, 1930 The Localisation of the Cotton Industry, *Econ Hist*, **2**, 91-106

Kay, J P, 1832 *The Moral and Physical Condition of the Working Classes Employed in the Cotton Manufacture in Manchester*, London

Kennedy, J, 1819 Observations on the Rise and Progress of the Cotton Trade in Great Britain, *Mem Manchester Lit Phil Soc*, 2 ser, **3**, 115-37

Kennedy, J, 1831a Brief Memoir of Samuel Crompton, *Mem Manchester Lit Phil Soc*, 2 ser, **5**, 318-53

Kennedy, J 1831b Observations on the Influence of Machinery upon the Working Classes of the Community, *Mem Manchester Lit Phil Soc*, 2 ser, **5**, 25-35

Kennedy, J, 1849 *Miscellaneous Papers on Subjects Connected with the Manufactures of Lancashire*, Manchester

Kidd, A, 1996 *Manchester*, 2nd edn, Keele

Kidd, A, and Wyke, T (eds), 1993 More Than an Example: Ancoats in Historical Perspective, *Manchester Region Hist Rev*, **7**, 3-14

Lee, C H, 1972 *A Cotton Enterprise 1795-1840: A History of M'Connel and Kennedy, Fine Cotton Spinners*, Manchester

Lemire, B, 1991 *Fashion's Favourite: The Cotton Trade and the Consumer in Britain, 1660-1800*, Oxford

Lemire, B, 1997 *Dress, Culture and Commerce: The English Clothing Industry before the Factory, 1660-1800*, London

Little, S, 2002 Ancoats - The First Industrial Suburb, in R McNeil and D George (eds), *The Heritage Atlas 4: Manchester - Archetype City of the Industrial Revolution*, Manchester, 31-3

Little, S, 2005 *The Bridgewater Way: Conservation Management Plan*, unpubl rep

Little, S, 2007 *Report from the Watching Brief during the Refurbishment of the McConnel Mills Complex, 2001-06*, unpubl rep

Liverpool City Council, 2005 *Nomination of Liverpool – Maritime Mercantile City for Inscription on the World Heritage List*, 2nd edn, Liverpool

Lloyd-Jones, R, and Le Roux, A A, 1980 The Size of Firms in the Cotton Industry: Manchester 1815-41, *Econ Hist Rev*, **33**, 72-82

Lloyd-Jones, R, and Lewis, M J, 1988 *Manchester and the Factory Age*, Manchester

Lloyd-Jones, R, and Lewis, M J, 1993 Housing Factory Workers: Ancoats in the Early 19th Century, *Manchester Region Hist Rev*, **7**, 33-6

Lowe, N, 1972 *The Lancashire Textile Industry in the Sixteenth Century*, Manchester

LUAU, 1997 *Rossendale Quarries, Lancashire: Assessment Survey*, unpubl rep

Lunn, J, 1971 *Atherton, Lancashire: A Manorial, Social and Industrial History*, Atherton

Lynch, G, 1994 *Brickwork: History, Technology and Practice*, **1**, London

McConnel, D C, 1861 *Facts and Traditions Collected for a Family Record*, privately publ

McConnel, J W, 1913 *A Century of Fine Cotton Spinning 1790-1906*, 2nd edn, Manchester

McNeil, R, 2002 Manchester - Symbol and Model for the World, in R McNeil and D George (eds), *The Heritage Atlas 4: Manchester-Archetype City of the Industrial Revolution*, Manchester, 39-43

Mallalieu, A, 1836 The Cotton Manufacture, *Blackwood's Edinburgh Magazine*, **39**, 407-24

Markus, T A, 1993 *Buildings of Power: Freedom and Control in the Origin of Modern Building Types*, London

Marrison, A, 1996 Indian Summer, 1870-1914, in M B Rose (ed), *The Lancashire Cotton Industry: A History Since 1700*, Preston, 238-64

Marsden, R, 1884 *Cotton Spinning*, London

Marshall, D, 1956 *English People in the 18th Century*, London

Mason, J, 1987 Cotton Spinning in the Industrial Revolution, in A Fowler and T Wyke (eds), *The Barefoot Aristocrats*, Littleborough, 1-13

Meason, G S, 1857 *The Official Guide to the Great Northern Railway*, London

Mellor, I, 2005 Space, Society and the Textile Mill, *Ind Archaeol Rev*, **27** (1), 49 56

Menuge, A, 2001 The Cotton Mills of the Derbyshire Derwent and its Tributaries; in K A Falconer (ed), *Derwent Valley Textile Mills*, Belper, 11-37

Merrifield, R, 1989 *The Archaeology of Ritual and Magic*, London

Middleton, J, 1920 *The Old Road: A Book of Recollections*, Manchester

Miles, C, 1968 *Lancashire Textiles: A Case Study of Industrial Change*, Cambridge

Miller, I, 2007 Percival, Vickers & Co Ltd, Ancoats: The Archaeology of a Nineteenth-Century Manchester Flint Glassworks, *Ind Archaeol Rev*, **29** (1), 13-29

Mokyr, J, 2001 *Twenty-Five Centuries of Technological Change: An Historical Survey*, London

Montgomery, J, 1833 *The Theory and Practice of Cotton Spinning*, Glasgow

Murphy, W S, 1911 *The Textile Industries*, London

Musson, A E, 1960 An Early Engineering Firm: Peel, Williams & Co of Manchester, *Business Hist*, **3** (1), 8-18

Musson, A E, and Robinson, E, 1959 Early Growth of Steam Power, *Econ Hist Rev*, 2 ser, **11** (3), 418-39

Musson, A E, and Robinson, E, 1960 The Origins of Engineering in Lancashire, *J Econ Hist*, **20**, 209-33

Musson, A E, and Robinson, E, 1969 *Science and Technology in the Industrial Revolution*, Manchester

Muthesius, S, 1982 *The English Terraced House*, London

Nevell, M (ed), 2003 *From Farmer to Factory Owner: Models, Methodology and Industrialisation*, CBA North West, **6**, Manchester

Nevell, M, 2004 The River Irwell and the Archaeology of Manchester's Early Waterfront, *Trans Lancashire Cheshire Antiq Soc*, **100**, 30-50

Nevell, M, and Hradil, I, 2002 *Waulk Mill (Formerly Doubling and Fireproof Mills), Ancoats, Manchester: An Archaeological Building Survey*, UMAU, unpubl rep

Nevell, M, Connelly, P, Hradil, I, and Stockley, S, 2003 The Archaeology of the Texile Finishing Trades in North West England, in Nevell 2003, 91-100

OA North, 2004 *Waller's Mill, Ancoats: Archaeological Evaluation*, unpubl rep

OA North, 2005a *Drinkwater's Mill, Piccadilly, Manchester: Post-Excavation Assessment*, unpubl rep

OA North, 2005b *Salvins' Factory and New Islington Mill, Ancoats, Manchester: Post-Excavation Assessment*, unpubl rep

OA North, 2005c *New Islington Wharf, Ancoats, Manchester: Archaeological Investigation*, unpubl rep

OA North, 2005d *Brunswick Mill, Ancoats: Documentary Account*, unpubl rep

OA North, 2006 *Piccadilly Place, Manchester: Archaeological Excavation*, unpubl rep

OA North, 2007a *Bengal Street Mill: Archaeological Survey and Excavation*, unpubl rep

OA North, 2007b *Hillgate Mill, Stockport: Archaeological Investigation*, unpubl rep

Ogden, J, 1783 *A Description of Manchester*, Manchester

Owen, R, 1857 *The Life of Robert Owen*, London

Pevsner, N, 1976 *A History of Building Types*, London

Pickstone, J, 1985 *Medicine and Industrial Society*, Manchester

Pole, W M (ed), 1877 *The Life of Sir William Fairbairn, Bart, Partly Written by Himself*, Newton Abbot (1970 facsimile)

Pragnell, H, 2000 *Industrial Britain: An Architectural History*, London

Pressnell, L S, 1956 *County Banking in the Industrial Revolution*, Oxford

Pyne, G, 1831 *Lancashire Illustrated in a Series of Views*, London

RCHME, and GMAU, 1989 *The Greater Manchester Textile Mill Survey: Murray's Mills, Manchester*, unpubl rep

Read, D, 1979 *England 1869-1914: The Age of Urban Democracy*, London

Redding, C, 1842 *An Illustrated Itinerary of the County of Lancashire*, London

Rees, A, 1819 *Manufacturing Industry*, **2**, Newton Abbot (1972 facsimile)

Ribeiro, A, 2002 *Dress in Eighteenth-Century Europe*, New Haven

Richards, J M, 1958 *The Functional Tradition in Early Industrial Buildings*, London

Roberts, J, 1993 The Residential Development of Ancoats, *Manchester Region Hist Rev*, **7**, 15-26

Rowley, C, 1899 *Fifty Years of Ancoats, Loss and Gain*, privately publ

Rushton, P, 1977 *Housing Conditions and the Family Economy in the Victorian Slum*, unpubl PhD thesis, Univ Manchester

Rushton, P, 1993 Family Survival Strategies in Mid-Victorian Ancoats, *Manchester Region Hist Rev*, **7**, 37-44

Saxonhouse, G, and Wright, G, 1984 New Evidence on the Stubborn English Mule and the Cotton Industry, 1878-1920, *Econ Hist Rev*, **37**, 507-19

Schoeser, M, 1996 Shewey and Full of Work: Design, in M B Rose (ed), *The Lancashire Cotton Industry: A History Since 1700*, Preston, 187-209

Scola, R, 1992 *Feeding the Victorian City: Food Supply of Manchester 1770-1870*, Manchester

Smiles, S, 1876 *Industrial Biography: Iron Workers and Tool Makers*, London

Smith, E C, 1932 Joshua Field's Diary of a Tour Through the Provinces, 1821, *Trans Newcomen Soc*, **13**, 15-50

Southey, R, 1951 *Letters From England*, 2nd edn, London

Spencer, E, 1880 Improvements in Machinery for Preparing and Spinning Cotton, *Proc Inst Mech Eng*, **31**, 492-528

Springett, J, 1986 Land Development and House Building ni Huddersfield 1770-1911, in M Doughty (ed), *Building the Industrial City*, Leicester, 23-56

Stobart, J, 1998 Textile Industries in North-west England in the Early Eighteenth Century: A Geographical Approach, *Textile Hist*, 29, 3-18

Stratton, M, and Trinder, B, 1997 *Industrial England*, London

Swindells, T, 1906 *Manchester Streets and Manchester Men*, **1**, Manchester

Swindells, T, 1908 *Manchester Streets and Manchester Men*, **5**, Manchester

Tann, J, 1970 *The Development of the Factory*, London

Tann, J, 1974 The Textile Millwright in the Early Industrial Revolution, *Textile Hist*, **5**, 80-9

Thomson, W H, 1966 *History of Manchester to 1852*, Altrincham

Thornley, T, 1907 *Cotton Spinning*, London

Timmins, G, 1996 *Four Centuries of Lancashire Cotton*, Preston

Timmins, G, 2004 Coping with Road Traffic in Expanding Urban Areas: Manchester and its Environs During the Industrial Revolution, *Trans Lancashire Cheshire Antiq Soc*, **100**, 69-90

Tomlinson, C, 1861 *The Useful Arts and Manufactures of Great Britain*, **2**, London

Tracey, W B, 1901 *Port of Manchester*, Manchester

Trinder, B, 1982 *The Making of the Industrial Landscape*, London

Tupling, G H, 1962 Medieval and Early Modern Manchester, in C F Carter (ed), *Manchester and its Region: A Survey Prepared for the British Association*, Manchester, 115-30

UMAU, 2002 *Land Bounded by Great Ancoats Street, Redhill Street, Henry Street and Jersey Street, Ancoats, Manchester: An Archaeological Watching Brief*, unpubl rep

Ure, A, 1836 *The Cotton Manufacture of Great Britain*, London

Vale, D, 2004 Connecting Manchester to the Sea: the Origins and Early Years of the Mersey and Irwell Navigation, *Trans Lancashire Cheshire Antiq Soc*, **100**, 51-68

Vigier, F, 1970 *Change and Apathy: Liverpool and Manchester during the Industrial Revolution*, London

Wadsworth, A P, and Mann, J, 1931 *The Cotton Trade and Industrial Lancashire, 1600-1780*, Manchester

Watkins, G, 1999 *The Textile Mill Engine*, 2nd edn, Ashbourne

Willan, T S, 1980 *Elizabethan Manchester*, Manchester

Williams, M, 1993 The Mills of Ancoats, *Manchester Region Hist Rev*, **7**, 27-32

Williams, M, with Farnie, D A, 1992 *Cotton Mills in Greater Manchester*, Preston

Wilson, C H, and Reader, W, 1958 *Men and Machines: A History of D Napier & Sons, Engineers 1800-1958*, London

Winterbotham, D, 1998 'Sackclothes and Fustyans and Such like Com'odyties'. Early Linen Manufacture in the Manchester Region, in E Roberts (ed), *A History of Linen in the North West*, Lancaster, 22-43

Wood, F, and Wood, K, 1992 *A Lancashire Gentleman: The Letters and Journals of Richard Hodgkinson 1763-1847*, Stroud

Wyke, T, and Rudyard, N, 1997 *Cotton: A Select Biography on Cotton in North West England*, Manchester

INDEX

Page numbers in *italics* denote that the reference is, or includes, an illustration. All street names and locations are in Manchester unless indicated otherwise.